GENDER AND THE UNCANNY
in Films of the Weimar Republic

Contemporary Approaches to Film and Media Series

A complete listing of the books in this series can be found online at wsupress.wayne.edu

GENERAL EDITOR
Barry Keith Grant
Brock University

ADVISORY EDITORS
Robert J. Burgoyne
University of St. Andrews

Caren J. Deming
University of Arizona

Patricia B. Erens
School of the Art Institute of Chicago

Peter X. Feng
University of Delaware

Lucy Fischer
University of Pittsburgh

Frances Gateward
California State University, Northridge

Tom Gunning
University of Chicago

Thomas Leitch
University of Delaware

Walter Metz
Southern Illinois University

GENDER AND THE UNCANNY
in Films of the Weimar Republic

ANJEANA K. HANS

Wayne State University Press
Detroit

© 2014 by Wayne State University Press, Detroit, Michigan 48201.
All rights reserved. No part of this book may be reproduced without formal permission.

18 17 16 15 14   5 4 3 2 1

ISBN 978-0-8143-3894-0 (paperback) / ISBN 978-0-8143-3895-7 (e-book)

Library of Congress Control Number: 2014931742

An earlier version of chapter 4 in this volume first appeared as
"Schatten: Eine nächtliche Halluzination: Staging the Punishment for
Women's Emancipation" in *New German Critique* 40, no. 3 (Durham, NC:
Duke University Press, 2013), 41–64. Copyright 2013 by New German Critique, Inc.
All rights reserved. Reprinted by permission of the publisher (www.dukeupress.edu).

An earlier version of chapter 5 in this volume first appeared in
The Many Faces of Weimar Cinema, ed. Christian Rogowski (Rochester, NY:
Camden House, 2010), 102–15. Reprinted by permission of the publisher.

Designed and typeset by Bryce Schimanski
Composed in Carouge Pro and Dante MT

CONTENTS

Acknowledgments vii

Introduction 1

1. The World Turned Upside Down:
   Changing Society, Changing Gender Roles,
   Changing Medium in Weimar Germany 15

2. *The Eyes of the Mummy* (*Die Augen der Mumie Mâ*,
   Ernst Lubitsch, 1918): From the Monster with the
   "Eyes That Live" to the Passive Object of the Male Gaze 60

3. *Uncanny Tales* (*Unheimliche Geschichten*, Richard Oswald, 1919):
   The Many Guises of the Dangerous Woman 97

4. *Warning Shadows* (*Schatten: Eine nächtliche Halluzination*,
   Artur Robison, 1923): Transgression, Abjection, Projection 147

5. *The Hands of Orlac* (*Orlacs Hände*, Robert Wiene, 1924):
   War Trauma, Injury, and the Return to a Changed World 179

6. *A Daughter of Destiny* (*Alraune*, Henrik Galeen, 1928)
   and *Daughter of Evil* (*Alraune*, Richard Oswald, 1930):
   From Dangerous Hybrid to Self-Sacrificing Woman 216

Conclusion 267
Notes 277
Index 297

ACKNOWLEDGMENTS

I COULD NOT HAVE written this book without the help and support of so many people. I would like to begin by thanking the mentors who shaped me fundamentally as a scholar of German literature, culture, and film, especially Eric Rentschler, Judith Ryan, and Maria Tatar. Their criticism, guidance, and encouragement set me on the path that allowed me to complete this book. As for so many of those who work on German film, Eric Rentschler's guidance was of utmost importance to me: he not only introduced me to the field, but also gave unending support, suggestions, and advice, and listened to, read, and commented on my work. I owe him an enormous debt of gratitude.

This project grew out of questions sparked when I took part in the German Film Institute at Ann Arbor during the summer of 2006. My deepest thanks go to Anton Kaes, Johannes von Moltke, and Eric Rentschler, who organized the institute, and to the participants. The discussions that we had during the week in Ann Arbor shaped the ways in which I have approached the films here as well as my work more generally, and I am deeply grateful for that.

Much of the analysis in this book began as conference presentations or shorter articles. An earlier version of chapter 4 was first printed in the Fall 2013 issue of *New German Critique*, and one of chapter 5 was included in *The Many Faces of Weimar Cinema* (edited by Christian Rogowski). I especially thank those at NGC and Duke University Press and at Camden House for their permission to use the material here. For their feedback on this project, I thank the various colleagues who have listened, read, and commented on my work, as well as those with whom, in conversation and more formal settings, I exchanged ideas and suggestions: Ulrike Brisson, Anke Finger, Patrick Fortmann, Rachel Freudenburg, Barbara Hales, Katharina

Acknowledgments

von Hammerstein, Ritta Joe Horsley, Nancy Lukens, Sabine von Mering, Luise Pusch, Christian Rogowski, Christiane Zehl Romero, Philipp Stiasny, Monika Totten, Margaret Ward, Valerie Weinstein, Joel Westerdale, and the anonymous reviewers whose comments have helped to polish articles and book manuscript. My colleagues at Wellesley have been a great source of support, and I extend a special thanks to Molly Blasing, Alex Diesl, Angela Carpenter, Sun-Hee Lee, Irene Mata, and Tanya McNeill, who shared many hours of early-morning writing.

This project would have been impossible without the support given to me by two institutions in particular, whose faculty research funding enabled me to spend significant time in Berlin: first, Tulane University, which awarded me a grant that supported the preliminary research on the project in summer 2008, and then Wellesley College, which generously helped to fund research during summers since, as well as a year of leave spent doing final research and revisions in Berlin. At the Berlin Kinemathek, I was able to screen so many of the films that are currently unavailable outside of the archives, as well as to collect background sources drawn from their collection of film journals from the Weimar era, and I owe a great debt of gratitude to the staff there, with special thanks to Anke Hahn, who facilitated my many hours of screenings, and to Cordula Döhrer, who helped me to access microfilm sources.

To those at Wayne State University Press, especially to Annie Martin, who supported this project with such enthusiasm from the beginning; Barry Keith Grant, the series editor; Carrie Teefey, the project editor; and Dawn Hall, the copyeditor; as well as to the readers who helped me to sharpen the book's argument, my deepest gratitude for making this process so rewarding and pleasurable.

Finally, I owe an enormous thank you to my family; their love and support has been so important. My parents and sisters never doubted that this would be finished. My husband, Nathan Clarke, has seen me through the entire project, spent months in Berlin while I did research there, never stopped believing in my abilities, has always been willing to listen to my latest idea and help me untangle my thoughts, and has been my unfailing supporter and best friend. And a special thank you to our daughter, Daya, who reminds me every day that there are times at which work needs to be put away.

GENDER AND THE UNCANNY
in Films of the Weimar Republic

INTRODUCTION

IN AN OPULENTLY DECORATED bedroom, a woman tries desperately to escape the intruder who has tracked her from the Egyptian tomb in which he had imprisoned her to this civilized European home. The camera lingers on these two exotic characters, cutting back and forth between close-ups of the man's face, darkened by makeup to crudely approximate a Northern African complexion, kohl-rimmed eyes staring at her as though to hypnotize her, and long shots of the woman, who succumbs to the man's powerful gaze, staggers toward him, and falls to her knees. Taking her in his arms, he draws a dagger, aiming its point at her heart. As he raises the weapon, she collapses dead, victim of a power over her that even her flight to Europe could not break. He drops her body and the camera lingers on a final shot of her, sprawled on the ground like a discarded doll.

Another woman steals silently out of her home, voluntarily going to her death in order to save the man she loves from her own destructive power. She slowly descends a staircase. First bare feet, then immobile face move into the frame, spotlighted in the darkness, revealing no hint of emotion. This image is stylistically vastly different from the previous scene: naturalistic rather than expressionistic, restrained rather than frantic and mobile. Yet it, too, represents a death scene, though here the woman's fatal end is elided in that which is not shown, in the split-second cut between this last glimpse of her dangerous and desired body and the final shot of the film, in which the placid waters of a lake reflect the rising sun.

These very different moments, from Ernst Lubitsch's *The Eyes of the Mummy* (*Die Augen der Mumie Mâ*, 1918) and Richard Oswald's *Daughter of Evil* (*Alraune*, 1930) respectively, mark the beginning and end point of a period in

Introduction

which German film excelled in killing off its female leads, or at least inflicting significant violence on these bodies that represented the feared and desired other. Even among the small percentage of films from the Weimar era that have survived, we find a veritable litany of women killed, injured, or sacrificed. From Ellen in F. W. Murnau's *Nosferatu* (1922), the "pure" woman who sacrifices herself for the community, dying in an oddly lascivious "embrace" with the vampire, to Lil Dagover's heroine in Fritz Lang's *Destiny* (*Der müde Tod*, 1921), who dares to challenge death and demand the return of her lover, only to sacrifice her own life in order to save a child and rejoin the man, to the "evil Maria" in Lang's *Metropolis* (1927), burned like a medieval witch at the stake, to Louise Brooks's Lulu in G. W. Pabst's *Pandora's Box* (*Die Büchse der Pandora*, 1929), whose promiscuity and seductiveness is punished with execution by the ultimate embodiment of sexual violence, Jack the Ripper. Again and again, Weimar film stages the female body first empowered, then overpowered, violated, or eradicated. On one hand, these women are part of a long line of women brutalized in German culture, whose lives end in suicide, murder, or other violent death: from Kriemhild in the *Nibelungenlied* to Lessing's Emilia Galotti, from Goethe's Gretchen to Schiller's Maria Stuart, to the long line of tragic heroines that populated the literature of the nineteenth century. Yet the way in which the brutalized, abject, and dying female body is functionalized in Weimar film takes on new significance. The violence done to these women represents a cultural preoccupation with woman's function in film; not only with the desires and anxieties that she represents so succinctly as the embodiment of the dangerous other, but also with her role as image on the screen and as structuring element within its visual economy. Weimar cinema abounds in such women: victims of aggression, social circumstance, or heredity; victims sacrificed or punished for the good of the hero or of society.

This book traces the ways in which the construction of woman as cinematic object is shaped by and reciprocally shapes the sociocultural construction of subjectivity. Against the backdrop of a culture profoundly changed, even traumatized by the experience of war and social upheaval, the films I examine reveal the ways in which anxieties translated on the screen into these cinematic women whose dangerous potential is ultimately suppressed in such decisive ways. These characters represent a new sociocultural definition of woman: profoundly changed by the experience of war,

Introduction

enjoying some level of emancipation, no longer exclusively the maternal body, but the female body become public, the "New Woman." This representation is both specter and fantasy, less an embodiment of the real status of women in the Weimar Republic than a symbol of the ways in which women's advances were imagined. It is a representation that addresses a double set of anxieties and hopes: that of the men who perceived themselves as "under attack" within the new hierarchies of Weimar society, and that of the women, whose changing positions signaled increased independence and greater possibilities for self-determination, but also new challenges and instabilities.

Beyond raising questions of gender and subjectivity, the films I include in this study need to be considered in terms of genre, for they are all characterized by narratives that foreground the uncanny. While they are not horror films in the sense used today, they nevertheless share certain traits with that genre. The specifics of genre raise the question of why these narratives of transgressive women are so frequently connected to the uncanny, the fantastic, the potentially horrifying; why, in other words, are these women figured either as terrified or terrifying—or simultaneously as both. What is it about these films, which fundamentally aim to frighten and mystify the audience, to evoke in them that frisson that characterizes *das Unheimliche*, that makes them particularly suited to an examination of the ways in which woman-as-image is connected to sociocultural anxieties regarding her changing role? And why is it that these films were so appealing to such a wide audience at the time? I would suggest that in staging these uncanny narratives, these films stage the uncanny emancipated female body, the transgressive femininity that exemplifies the uncanny and becomes itself the image that terrifies. At the same time, these women-as-images become representative of cinema itself, for the quality of the uncanny embodies a characteristic of cinema, with its representation of the semblance of life as an image. And, beyond this, the uncanny nature of emancipated woman and of cinematic medium that emerges in these films appeals specifically to the viewer defined by the historical moment, in which a sort of pervasive "uncanniness" defines the changed social background. Here—in these films that confront the audience with something that evokes the sense of the unnatural, the dangerous, that which is familiar, yet defamiliarized—we see most clearly the way in which cinema took part in constructing the new

Introduction

image of woman, developed the medial structures that positioned woman at the center of its visual economy and spoke to the inhabitants of a world apparently defined by defamiliarization.

Examining these films reveals much, not only about the Germany of that moment and its film industry but also about the ways in which film in general has developed, the part that technical innovation plays in this development, and the interplay between narrative, cultural moment, and representation. Post–World War I Germany can be seen as a sort of test case: isolated from the international film world during the war, how did it develop its own trajectory, confronting technological progress and defining cinema as an artistic medium? What does this development suggest to us about the ways in which national cinemas grow? Indeed, Weimar Germany was arguably the single era in which the hegemony of Hollywood was briefly challenged—what was it about Weimar cinema that made it such a potent art form, a force to be reckoned with?

Beyond the interest that Weimar holds due to its status as a sort of "laboratory for modernity,"[1] we should keep in mind the ways in which it directly and concretely affected the shape of other national cinemas, including that of the United States. When we talk about "classic Hollywood cinema"—especially about the moody film noirs, stylish comedies, and realistic melodramas of the 1930s and 1940s—we are referring to a body of works of which many were directed by German directors, filmed by German crews, and acted by German actors. After 1933, of course, there was a mass exodus of German talent: many of these émigrés were Jewish and were forbidden to continue to work in Germany and so went abroad, where they were a significant influence not only on Hollywood film but also on other national cinemas.[2] Even before 1933, however, the business of film was at its heart an international one, and the influence of German film in particular on Hollywood was almost disproportionately strong.[3] From directors to technicians, from writers to actors—some of the top German talent made the move to (and sometimes back from) Hollywood in the 1920s.[4] Given the general reciprocity between national film traditions in the era and the specific impact of Weimar cinema on Hollywood, we can see that the cinematic traditions that are seen as so fundamentally American—and that underpin and shape the works of the US film industry even today—are in an essential way connected to the works of Weimar Germany. Indeed, it is

Introduction

telling that Laura Mulvey, discussing structures of gender and desire in her seminal essay "Visual Pleasure and Narrative Cinema" (1975), refers to the work of Marlene Dietrich in the films of Josef von Sternberg—two names that immediately draw to mind their initial German collaboration in *The Blue Angel* (*Der blaue Engel*, 1930). A film that we might see as exemplary of some of the anxieties that dominated Weimar Germany and of the technical and narrative concerns that emerged in its cinema thus comes to stand for a distinctly American tradition—testimony to the *international* significance of Weimar film and to the necessity of understanding the forces that shaped its development when considering the Hollywood tradition as well.

Located within the field of German film studies, this book is a part of a current shift wherein scholars have reoriented their focus from a tendency to read Weimar film "backward," through the lens of the Third Reich, to one that works forward from the traumatic experience of the First World War. In the past, many scholars were guided by two seminal works, Siegfried Kracauer's *From Caligari to Hitler* (1947) and Lotte Eisner's *The Haunted Screen* (1952), works that were and continue to be significant, yet that traced such a trajectory at the expense of examining more closely the way in which Weimar films reflected on changes resulting from the experience of the First World War, the radically changed sociocultural and political landscape, and the impact of modernity, and that perhaps thus betrayed certain biases of their authors, both of whom were forced to flee Germany once the Nazis rose to power. For many years, these theoretical orientations dominated the field and necessarily limited alternative explanatory models. Only fairly recently have scholars turned anew to Weimar film, working from the position that the films of the era reflect on and engage with a culture undergoing radical transformation and focusing on the change in the way the subject was constructed and positioned in relation to the state and the other. Works including Richard W. McCormick's *Gender and Sexuality in Weimar Modernity: Film, Literature, and "New Objectivity,"*[5] which rereads some of the seminal cultural output of the era—particularly that classified as belonging to the *Neue Sachlichkeit* (New Objectivity)—as representing gender crises; Anton Kaes's *Shell Shock Cinema*,[6] which focuses on Weimar films as representations of the trauma of World War I; and the collections *Weimar Cinema: An Essential Guide to Classic Films of the Era*[7] and *The Many Faces of Weimar Cinema: Rediscovering Germany's Filmic Legacy*,[8] which

Introduction

bring together a range of scholarly work reexamining canonical and lesser-known films respectively, allow us fresh perspectives on the era, giving us a more nuanced and complete understanding of a filmic tradition that was, above all, incredibly varied, often experimental, and stylistically and generically diverse.

My analysis contributes to a more complete understanding of the sheer range of Weimar films and of the complex ways in which they engaged with cultural anxieties, hopes, and changes. Like McCormick, I see the changing gender roles in post–World War I German culture as perhaps the most influential sociocultural condition; however, what I find most striking is the way in which the anxious responses to these changing conventions and norms find expression in the films of horror, terror, and the uncanny that seem so characteristic of the era. How do these cinematic artifacts reflect this crisis of identity? How do they represent, reflect, and intervene in the changing ways in which gender and social identity were conceptualized? Certainly, the social landscape of the era was fraught. Where hitherto the patriarchal structure of the empire was replicated at the level of the individual, with men always occupying the superior position in their relationship with the other embodied most decisively by women, the end of the war and the birth of the republic turned traditional structures of class, gender, and national identity on their heads. The war dramatically altered traditional social structures: in combat, men found themselves confronted daily with their own mortality and powerlessness, while on the home front women ever more frequently entered the workforce and assumed the support of themselves and their families, thereby seeming to usurp what little power remained to men. The November Revolution in Germany and the subsequent proclamation of the republic were visible markers of a social upheaval that fundamentally shifted the individual's understanding of the self.

Stable notions of subjectivity were thus fundamentally undermined. Masculine subjectivity experienced a sort of "double trauma," first on the front, then in the return to a changed *Heimat*. This trauma emerged in a fear of the other that frequently found expression in a hostility directed at women, whose changing status seemed to express most clearly the loss of masculine power. The position of women was no less complicated. While the Weimar era brought them new opportunities and power that *should* be

Introduction

considered a positive development, these changes nevertheless represented an equally fundamental upheaval and inaugurated the need to redefine the self and its position in the world.

That film should grapple with the anxieties and possibilities emerging from the traumatic experiences of war and modernity should come as no surprise. The filmic medium was itself rapidly developing and exploring new possibilities and structures, and it was doing so from a frequently self-critical stance. This was an era in which function, form, and significance of film were being debated, and in which these debates seeped onto the screen itself. Already fundamentally concerned with the relationship of the individual to the other and to the self—in that the dynamic between viewer and image represented a complex process of identifications and differentiations—many films of the era directly thematized questions of gender and identity. Further, their negotiation of the way in which the human image was represented on screen, always shaped by the anxious perception of a challenge being posed to male subjectivity, contributed to the development of cinematic conventions that have come to define the relationship between viewer and image and the status of women as object of the spectator's gaze.

I focus on a group of films that coalesce around narratives in which women pose a particular danger to the male on-screen hero and, by extension, to the male viewer, and that couch these narratives in terms that draw on uncanny elements. The inclusion of the latter allows these films to be especially self-reflexive; often represented through the use of decidedly filmic techniques, such as superimpositions, these elements point back to the uncanny qualities of watching a film, a process in which the living body is transformed into an image, and one characterized by a sense of the divide between the image and the real. They demonstrate the concerns that emerged in the shaping of a new visual medium, one seen, at the time, as fundamentally at odds with traditional media like the stage, and as posing a very real—and at times dangerous—challenge to existing culture. At the same time, the frequent connection between the central female figures and the uncanny embodies a cinematic representation of the struggle to come to terms with new definitions of gender and identity; with women assuming new roles and gaining some level of social power, they truly have become the uncanny other, both familiar and alarmingly changed. In other

Introduction

words, these films confront both the danger they themselves pose to culture and that posed by the transgressive women at the hearts of their narratives.

I situate my reading in terms of the historical moment, contemporary discussions of film and modern film theory. The dual discussions of sociocultural change and the development of the medium form the crucial backdrop to my readings. My central argument is that in coming together, the anxieties about changing gender roles and the development of cinema and its conventions become inextricably intertwined. At times, the desire to reassert traditional gender hierarchies and codes finds its expression in filmic tendencies that allow a masculine subjectivity embodied in the camera's eye to dominate, by representation and through the process of viewing, the female figure made image. At the same time, many of these films simultaneously undermine that empowerment of the masculine subject, revealing the complexity of the power dynamics that emerge in cinema and opening up a space for female spectatorship that is empowered and runs counter to current dominant models. In terms of the larger field of film theory, I suggest that certain structures assumed to be at work in cinema are not preexisting and universal structures, but rather emerge from specific historical moments and are, in the case of Weimar cinema, far more complex than might initially appear. That is not to suggest that some of the structures of desire and power that we see in these films do not have their seeds in previous eras, nor that they ceased to exist with the end of Weimar. Certainly, the fear of emancipated woman was already in evidence in German culture during the nineteenth century and was an anxiety that cut across Western culture in general; equally so, we can identify such patterns in later cultural traditions, even today. But the specific way in which it was conceived of and dealt with in Weimar Germany—a set of structures that at least partially survived well beyond the end of the era—is connected to the precise historical moment, and the fact that cinema was a medium that aimed to appeal both to men and women lends a dimension of ambiguity and complexity to the problem. Further, in considering the work on the gaze in cinema, we should take into account the fact that the structures identified in modern scholarship are often very different from those that contemporary theorists imagined; in fact, the emphasis in modern scholarship on the process of viewing as dominated by a masculine gaze contrasts sharply with the way in which it was imagined by Weimar theorists, who saw the viewer's as a passive position, "gendered female" rather than male.[9]

Introduction

The way in which anxieties focusing on changing gender roles and power hierarchies shape and are reflected in developing cinematic conventions becomes particularly clear in films in which *das Unheimliche*, "the uncanny," takes a central role. The experience of film itself was originally an uncanny one; we see this in the shock engendered in the audience by early film screenings, in the viewer's ambivalent response to film. Although the audiences of the late 1910s and 1920s were by now relatively accustomed to film, the move away from short and documentary films toward full-length narratives must have presented a new model: with the staging of a narrative, the viewers are presented more clearly with their double on the screen, with the human form defamiliarized and rendered present, yet absent. The primary uncanny object in film is the representation of life on screen, the doubling of the human body, a topos that finds expression again and again, in everything from *Metropolis* to the multiple versions of *The Student of Prague* (*Der Student von Prag*, Rye 1913, Galeen 1926, Robison 1935). Uncanny films masked and thematized this primary object particularly well, evoking a doubly strong reaction through narrative and experience of film. In staging a narrative hinging on uncanny elements that intend to provoke discomfort and shock in the audience, these films effectively stage the viewing process itself. It makes sense that such films might be exceptionally self-aware of the cinematic form and reflective of ideas about the medium.

The female image thus becomes the solution to multiple anxieties; objectifying the female body and "resolving" the narratives in such a way as to allow the audience, identified with the masculine characters on screen, to assert dominance over her becomes a response to the discomfort caused in the audience by the very notion of seeing the human body as object and by the larger, culturally specific anxiety focused on woman's changing social role. Narratively and structurally, these films attempt to reassert power over the threatening woman, subordinating her within the story and the economy of the viewing experience. At the same time, we see, again and again, moments of slippage, of excess, in which the control slips and the "unruly women" demonstrate that they cannot wholly be contained. What these films demonstrate, in other words, is the sheer complexity of the question, the way in which these films that aimed to intervene in the changing ways in which gender and subjectivity were conceptualized are

Introduction

at their heart contradictory, ambivalent, and constantly in tension with themselves.

To begin to understand how Weimar film represented the cultural preoccupation with gender on screen and thereby shaped cinematic conventions that have continued to survive, I examine films that span the era and whose narratives are structured around the uncanny and coalesce around central female figures. My choice of films was motivated by a number of factors. First and foremost, any study of film of the era is necessarily limited by the fact that many works have not survived; I thus began by screening as many available works as possible in order to identify those that would, by virtue of their narrative, qualify for inclusion. Second, I wanted specifically to focus on lesser-known films, moving away from works like *Nosferatu*, *The Cabinet of Dr. Caligari* (Robert Wiene, *Das Cabinet des Dr. Caligari*, 1920), and *Metropolis*, films often seen as embodying the full range of the canon of Weimar film, to pieces that are less well known. In the films I examine, I want to give a broader sense of Weimar cinema, an industry that was by no means made up exclusively of the sorts of "art films" that the aforementioned pieces exemplify, but that included a rich tradition of genre and "popular" pieces as well. Further, by focusing on such films that have hitherto escaped much scholarly analysis, I hope not only to reintegrate them into our understanding of film history but also to anticipate a moment in which they would become, once again, more widely available. The growing availability of works previously available only in archives promises to expand the field of film studies, enabling scholars to access an ever-broader range of films and to integrate them into research and teaching so as to offer a richer and more complete understanding of the medium's development. This book is a part of that potential expansion of the field, grappling with movies that might have long been "lesser known," but that promise to become objects of interests as we gain ever-greater access to "forgotten" works.

I begin with an opening chapter in which I frame my analysis by sketching the historical background: what were the historical and social factors that shaped Weimar cinema? How did anxieties about gender and identity come to determine the cultural moment, and how did cultural discourses attempt to negotiate them? I also lay out key theoretical terms in this opening chapter, discussing the cultural conception of the uncanny, dominated

Introduction

by Freud's views thereof, as well as contemporary and modern theoretical approaches to film, the gaze, and desire. This chapter serves to situate my readings within a larger theoretical and historical framework and to articulate the foundation for my interpretation of the cinematic conventions focused on gender that we see in the films under analysis.

The second chapter focuses on an early film by Ernst Lubitsch, *The Eyes of the Mummy* (*Die Augen der Mumie Mâ*, 1918). One of his first big-budget productions, this film was released at virtually the precise moment of the Weimar Republic's birth and reveals clearly some of the fantasies and anxieties that dominated Germany during the last years of the war and shaped the newly created nation. Stylistically and narratively, it both harks back to the older "cinema of attractions"[10] and points toward the coming developments in cinema. While more precisely a drama, the narrative hinges on the uncanny embodied first in the threatening "mummy" who is revealed to be "only" a living woman, then in her Egyptian kidnapper, who haunts and ultimately kills her once she has been rescued and taken to Germany by the man who falls in love with her. With its emphasis on the danger posed by the doubled "other," the foreign that infiltrates and threatens the safety represented by "home," *Eyes of the Mummy* ultimately reinscribes traditional notions of masculine (European) subjectivity and the power it exclusively wields. Concomitantly, it combats the danger posed by the emancipated woman represented by Mâ, who becomes a public object of desire through her activity as a performer and who threatens to destabilize hierarchies of power, by increasingly fixing her, transforming her from the original "monster" to an ever more passive object of a controlling masculine gaze. And the film raises interesting questions about the staging of the (female) self that will reemerge in a number of the films I examine.

In the third chapter, I move to Richard Oswald's *Uncanny Tales* (*Unheimliche Geschichten*, 1919), an omnibus film that presents a series of stories in which a single actor plays a range of female archetypes, from victim first of a jealous husband, then of the plague, to seductive object of desire that threatens marriages and male friendships. Oswald's film puts changing gender roles at center stage, positioning emancipated woman as the destabilizing element that threatens existent sociocultural structures and confronts masculine subjectivity, and doing so in the context of a work that plays explicitly with the notion of the uncanny and with the structures of film.

Introduction

Ranging from truly uncanny to farcical, the episodes in Oswald's film point to woman as passive object of desire, constructed and imagined by man, and reveal her powerful role within the structures of cinema and narrative. Structurally, *Uncanny Tales* foregrounds its status as film, suggesting an affinity between the processes of watching a film and reading. Particularly when compared to Oswald's second, very different version of *Uncanny Tales* (1932), this film says much about the complex ways in which gender and cinema become intertwined in the era.

In chapter 4 I turn to Artur Robison's *Warning Shadows* (*Schatten: Eine nächtliche Halluzination*, 1923), a film in which the self-reflexive element is foregrounded through narrative and representation. Self-consciously intended, through its reliance on the visual and its eschewal of intertitles, to move toward a more "pure" model of film, *Warning Shadows* coalesces around a narrative in which a woman's transgression of social norms and her subsequent fatal punishment are staged as a visual fantasy not only for the viewer but also for the characters within the story. With its multiple stories-within-the-story, or perhaps more rightly projections-within-the-projection, the film reflects on the very process of cinema, pointing to its inherently uncanny structures and revealing the power structures at work in the relationships between audience and image.

Chapter 5 focuses on Robert Wiene's *The Hands of Orlac* (*Orlacs Hände*, 1924). A "Frankensteinian" tale of a pianist whose injured hands are replaced by those of a purported murderer, *The Hands of Orlac* dramatizes the anxieties resulting from the dual traumatic experiences of war and of loss of masculine power. In the figure of Yvonne, the wife who takes on a newly active role in her relationship and against whom the murderous fantasies of the protagonist, Orlac, are directed, we recognize the New Woman who challenges traditional gender roles and thereby usurps power that was hitherto reserved for men. Cinematically, *The Hands of Orlac* functions as a sort of transitional point between expressionism and New Objectivity; in it, we see not only the stylistic changes that characterize the move from the former to the latter but also the divergent ways in which each represented and conceptualized the relationship between viewer and cinematic fantasy.

The final chapter examines two versions of a single story, Henrik Galeen's *A Daughter of Destiny* (*Alraune*, 1928) and Richard Oswald's 1930 sound version of the same. Based on a 1911 novel by Hanns Heinz Ewers, both

Introduction

films center on a dangerous, "unnatural" woman who was created by a sort of "mad scientist" and who arouses fatal desires in those who encounter her. As such, they act out the dream of male creation and simultaneously reveal the constructed nature of woman as object of desire. Alraune, both erotic object and fatal danger, is no more than the projection of a male fantasy, a male "ideal" of femininity that caters to his desires and challenges his power. Galeen's version locates her power in her own desiring gaze and in her active staging of herself, then works to circumscribe this power by making her progressively more passive, before she is finally "saved" from herself through her (apparent) abdication of her powerful gaze. Cinematically, Alraune is as much an artificial creation as is film itself; thus we see not only the process by which she is shifted ever more into the position of object of the gaze but also some level of reflection on cinema. In Oswald's version, by contrast, the inclusion of sound complicates the networks of power; here, the woman's power is embodied less in her gaze than it is in her voice, in her interpolation of the men around her. We can thus see some of the ways in which the shift from silent to sound films factored into cinematic conventions. At the same time, Oswald's *Alraune* embodies a fundamental generic shift, as well; the story of the transgressive woman is couched not in terms of the uncanny, but rather in those of melodrama. Woman's emancipation is no longer figured as a terrifying and dangerous prospect, but rather as a tragic, misguided, and ultimately fatal impulse.

My aim is to contribute to a broader understanding of Weimar cinema and its impact, and to suggest new ways in which we might approach the historical development of film, of its content, its form, and its conventions. As a medium that has long exemplified modernity itself and that has thus reflected and reciprocally shaped our individual lives and identities, the way in which film works—and its role, here specifically, in contributing to fundamental notions of gender, subjectivity, and representation—is a crucial factor in the development of contemporary culture. I hope to reexamine these films that are too little remembered, if at all, and thus to trace the way in which they demonstrate how quickly the position of women was changing in the Weimar era, how intimately these changes were bound up with the perception of an embattled male subjectivity, and how purposefully the medium set out to address and—often—neutralize the "threat" posed by emancipated woman even as it attempted simultaneously to speak to her

Introduction

desires, fears, and fantasies. And while I hope to offer certain answers to the host of questions these films raise, I want to demonstrate as well the ambiguity of these films, the ways in which they often stubbornly resist a single "explanation" and are able to be simultaneously repressive and revolutionary, to offer at once the fantasy of a return to traditional patriarchal power structures and the potential of female empowerment.

ONE

THE WORLD TURNED UPSIDE DOWN

Changing Society, Changing Gender Roles, Changing Medium in Weimar Germany

THE WEIMAR ERA WAS in many ways immensely messy. Economically, the devastation of war was followed first by destitution, then by a period of stability and prosperity, and finally by collapse—all in a relatively brief fifteen years. Politically, the republic saw twelve different chancellors and twenty-one government cabinets (including that formed by Hitler after his election) and began and ended in brawls and street fights that pitted the disparate ideologies against each other and transformed their theoretical conflicts into the basest violence.[1] Yet perhaps this messiness is what makes Weimar Germany's cultural production particularly interesting; vibrant, contentious, and incredibly varied, it represents the attempt to grapple with the contradictions, anxieties, fears, and hopes that characterized the era. Literature and poetry pushed the boundaries: authors confronted history, society, and ideology with a candor that was hitherto taboo, while poets exploded the limits of form and genre, even of language itself. From Hermann Hesse's *Demian* (1919) to Thomas Mann's *Magic Mountain* (*Der Zauberberg*, 1924) to Alfred Döblin's *Berlin Alexanderplatz* (1929), literature confronted the contradictions and complexities of modernity head on.

CHAPTER ONE

Expressionist poets painted vibrant linguistic images, certain that the individual's emotions and incongruities could be represented through words on the page, while Dada poets questioned and undermined the notion that words could signify anything. Dramatists like Ernst Toller in his *Masses Man* (*Masse-Mensch*, 1921) rejected the staid conventions of the stage and strove to represent the agony of being human, to embody reality in visions, dreams, and nightmares. The contradictions that characterized Weimar culture found their way onto canvases, into Egon Schiele's twisted bodies, Ernst Ludwig Kirchner's inhuman faces, and George Grosz's mutilated women. The contradictions gyrated on stages and sang in cabarets, evidencing themselves in the writhing limbs of dancers like Anita Berber and Valeska Gert. And they unreeled on the screen, presenting eager audiences with visual narratives that reworked reality into hallucination or presented it in all of its mundane details. Weimar Germany, in all its glorious messiness, was all too brief, yet out of it burst cultural production that still offers us a kaleidoscopic view onto this fractured period.

The contradictions that define Weimar seem quite natural, given that the republic was born out of a moment itself profoundly conflicted, one in which relief at the end of the war collided with devastation at defeat, in which the need for stable social structures had perhaps never been greater, but the very fabric of society was being torn apart and reassembled in a fundamentally unfamiliar way. November 1918 marked this radical change in German culture, with military defeat and increasing social and political unrest leading to a descent into temporary chaos. The population had been haunted by the specter of defeat since the battle of Amiens on August 8, 1918, which General Ludendorff had pointed to as representing the "black day of the German army." The monarchy fell quickly, with Max von Baden announcing Kaiser Wilhelm II's abdication around noon of November 9 and Philipp Scheidemann and Karl Liebknecht proclaiming, respectively, the formation of a democratic republic and a free socialist republic a scant two hours later. From across the English Channel, the *Times* documented the crisis, noting already on November 12 that "all reports now arriving run on much the same lines, 'red ruin and the breaking up of laws' being the order of the day all through what was once the German Empire," and stating one correspondent's view that "Germany as we have known it has ceased to exist."[2]

The World Turned Upside Down

How does a nation react when its very identity is suddenly no more, when it has "ceased to exist"? All around the defeated nation, those who had allied themselves against it celebrated, exuberant, hopeful, and certain that the end of the war would mean an end to all troubles. In France, a correspondent reported that "Paris went charmingly off her head.... The din under the windows of *The Times* office is so great that it is almost impossible to dictate this telegram. There is a series of cheering multitudes marching up and down. Students from the Left Bank, Midinettes, business men, and, above all, soldiers, all cheering and singing themselves hoarse."[3] Similarly, in London, "crowds that could not be numbered surged through the streets, oblivious of the rain and muddy roadways."[4] In the allied nations, celebrations expressed not only the respective population's relief at the end of the war but also the sense of national pride emerging from victory over the German Empire.

In Berlin, where the turbulent political climate promised a changed nation and the end of the war represented submission to the Allies, the armistice was greeted very differently. Four years of war had left the population angry, struggling against concrete hardships on the home front and increasingly unhappy with the government. Mary Fulbrook describes the progressively dire domestic conditions, where dwindling provisions had already led to significant strikes in April 1917. Ironically, the instability caused by the populace's dissatisfaction with the war and its effects had played a role in the continuation of hostilities. The military leadership, as Fulbrook notes, "had begun to believe that only a spectacular military victory could now avert the threat of domestic revolution."[5] But there would be no grand military victory with which to appease Germans, no triumph to justify their sacrifices and suffering. By the time Prince Max von Baden introduced a set of democratizing reforms in October 1918 in a last-ditch effort to save the empire, the population had reached a boiling point.[6] However broad those reforms might have been, they came too late. When sailors in Kiel rebelled against the order handed down on October 24, 1918, to undertake one last offensive that was virtually guaranteed to be futile, the lid seemed to blow off the powder keg that was Germany. The populace, seething from its dissatisfaction with a government that had, for four years, used so many young men as *Kanonenfutter*, "cannon fodder," even while its leaders remained safe and protected, had

had enough, and the sailors' rebellion quickly spread to other major cities. Local governments were overthrown or ceded control, and on November 8, Kurt Eisner declared Bavaria a *Räterepublik* (Socialist Republic). Max von Baden, faced with rising chaos and left unable to confer with Kaiser Wilhelm II, who was by then safely outside of Berlin, announced the emperor's abdication and the choice of Friedrich Ebert to lead the new government as a way to try to forestall the worst of the upheaval and to prevent those on the far left from taking over.[7] Yet this was too little, too late. Revolution and the armistice arrived simultaneously, heralding the arrival of a world utterly changed. In Germany, the population seemed, in the end, to have become numb. As a *Times* correspondent reported:

> Taken altogether the people were very orderly, and it was a quiet Revolution. The armistice conditions became known about 3 o'clock. At first they did not make any great impression, the people being too much engrossed by the Revolution. . . . On Monday the people paid more attention to the armistice terms. My impression was that the feeling was more depressed then, as they thought the terms very hard, but every one [sic] realized that Germany had lost the war, and that the only thing to do was to finish it as soon as possible.[8]

This is the backdrop to the films in this study: a society emerging from four years of war into a moment of monumental change. The defeat at the hands of the Allies and the birth of the new republic profoundly affected the development not only of Weimar culture as a whole but also of individuals who had to redefine their own positions in a shifting social hierarchy and in relation to a changing world community. Traditional social structures were thrown into upheaval; as the monarchy gave way to a liberal democracy, constructions of class and gender were fundamentally redefined. Notions of identity—both personal and national—were reshaped by the experience of defeat and the force of a rapidly changing society. And all this in an environment dominated by a sense of loss, one over which, as one article suggested, "hung that appalling gloom which makes the whole country feel like a great funeral."[9] That the Weimar Republic emerged in a moment dominated by such conflicting emotions is emblematic for its development, for it is characterized by profound contradictions, defined both by economic struggle caused by war, inflation, and, later, the Depression, yet also by progressiveness and potential, a golden era of culture and society.

GENDER CHALLENGES

Changing social structures and norms fundamentally impacted the subject in Weimar Germany, especially in terms of gender. Masculine subjectivity, exemplified by the returning soldier, was forced to come to terms at once with defeat and social change. The veteran, already bearing psychological and frequently physical scars that threatened the sense of a unified self, discovered that the idyllic image of "home" as a space of healing no longer existed; the home front, too, was transformed by war. And it was not only a changed social structure with which soldiers were confronted. In addition to facing physical and financial challenges, they had to come to terms with a sense that their own identity was forever changed, that they were no longer the same men who had existed before the war; once become soldiers who were forced to choose between killing or being killed, how to reintegrate into a peacetime society? The physical manifestation of the trauma of war was exemplified by the *Kriegsneurose*, "war neurosis," that emerged in many returning soldiers[10] and that found its expression in a variety of physical and psychological symptoms—from "tremors and paralyses," to nightmares and flashbacks.[11] While there was no consensus on how war neurosis should be viewed, Sigmund Freud's analysis of the disorder is especially interesting. Freud saw the condition as stemming from the conflict between the "old peace-ego" and the "new warlike ego" of the soldier.[12] Freud essentially saw war neurosis as an identity crisis par excellence rooted in the soldiers' return to a changed world as men irrevocably changed by their experiences.

Indeed, simply the act of admitting that the war had been a traumatizing event undermined the individual's sense of his identity, for the sufferers of war neurosis were perceived in Germany not as victims of real trauma but rather as cowardly, unpatriotic, and freeloading. The individual was given the choice between two difficult positions: to deny any trauma and reap the reward of being seen as heroic or to admit to being traumatized and be derided as a coward. War neurosis was conceptualized as a condition rooted in the individual rather than in a real traumatic experience: "The actual source of the illness was thus latent in the soldier himself. His desire not to return to the front, his hope for a war pension, even his 'moral orientation,' his lacking patriotism and an inner rejection of war, were now connected directly to the genesis of the illness."[13] The soldier whose psyche had been so fundamentally shaken by the experience on the battlefield found his suffering questioned and his morality and patriotism doubted; his "illness" was viewed as rooted not in war but rather in a selfish desire to avoid the return to combat and to receive monetary compensation in the form of an (undeserved) pension. To respond emotionally and psychologically to the horrors of combat became a symbol of immorality; even more, it undermined the individual's masculinity: "The tendency ran unmistakably toward pathologizing such states of anxiety as well as stigmatizing the affected soldiers not only as nervously weak but also as morally reprehensible individuals. Courage and masculinity could not be reconciled with such states of anxiety."[14] This gendering of war neurosis and the notion that the condition was incommensurate with masculinity is significant, for it demonstrates yet another way in which male subjectivity was perceived as being under attack during the First World War and the Weimar era. Indeed, the gender trouble embodied in war neurosis and in the debates surrounding the condition did not cease there, for Germany's construction of war neurosis as "feminine" equally suggested that it was a condition that spread—like an "infection"—most steadily not from the front lines, but from the home front: "On the front lines, where camaraderie and a 'healthy and solid constitution' of the men dominated, there was no danger of infection. This danger increased, however, the closer one came to the 'home front,' in other words to the feminine sphere."[15] Women were identified not only with the traits that German psychiatry isolated in soldiers suffering from war neurosis but also with the source of this condition: this was an illness rooted not in the experience of battle, but in the "female sphere of influence" at home. And this gendering of the discourse on war neurosis extended as well to the way defeat was explained, for with both home front and war neurosis feminized, woman became doubly to blame in the postwar discourse, "when *Heimat* and the war hysteric represented similar revolutionary threats in the narrative of the 'legend of the stab in the back.'"[16] Women in the postwar era thus were inextricably bound up with male anxieties, positioned on multiple levels as the internal enemy that, according to that *Dolchstoßlegende*, the "legend of the stab in the back," betrayed the German cause and led to defeat.

Over the course of the war and in the postwar era, masculine subjectivity was thus multiply traumatized. Anton Kaes has pointed to the impact of World War I on the individual, noting the way in which the trauma of the war shaped the cultural output of the era even when it did not do so in an obvious manner: "Unspoken and concealed, implied and latent, repressed and disavowed, the experience of trauma became Weimar's historical unconscious. The double wound of war and defeat festered beneath the glittering surface of its anxious modernity."[17] Kaes's recognition of the "wound" that fragmented even apparently whole bodies and that was masked by Weimar Germany's "anxious modernity" reveals the way in which the massive trauma of war and the experience of defeat were the foundation on which Weimar culture—that "glittering surface of . . . modernity"—was built and which it attempted to both represent and conceal. This was a wound that structured the culture because it was omnipresent, yet never openly addressed: "the classical cinema of Weimar Germany is haunted by the memory of a war whose traumatic outcome was never officially acknowledged, let alone accepted. . . . The shocking conclusion to the war and the silence in its wake had disastrous consequences for the first German democracy and its culture."[18] German masculine subjectivity found itself grappling not only with the return to a radically changed society but also with the awareness of doing so as the defeated; at the same time, the traumatic quality of this return was never acknowledged and could therefore never be directly addressed. If we consider the experience of war and the changed society as the founding trauma of the era, then the very existence of the Weimar cultural production that seems so conflicting, vibrant, and modern becomes the symptom of that trauma.

As men returned to a changed sociopolitical structure within which they had to reposition themselves, women, too, found the norms and expectations that defined them radically changed. The transformation of traditional gender roles was one of the most visible changes in postwar Germany, and, where it proved a challenge to men, it offered to women new possibilities of defining themselves. Undoubtedly, women's emancipation was incomplete; though many perceived women's new socioeconomic position as representing a radical change and as rivaling and threatening that of men, the reality was quite different. Employment patterns show how limited women's advancement in fact was; in spite of the initial effect of the war, during which many more women entered professions traditionally reserved for men, such as industry, most women had minimal prospects in terms of promotion and earning potential.[19] Nevertheless, women's roles were changing. These fundamental shifts in the construction of gender roles impacted men and women respectively in very different ways, of course. To the already embattled male subject, these changes represented a direct challenge, even another trauma, with women's emancipation the symbol of the changes that undermined masculine subjectivity on every level. Soldiers returned from war already carrying the burdens of the horrors they witnessed, only to be confronted by a new society in which their own status had apparently been undermined by the very figures that represented that which was to be protected. In this cultural fantasy, women were doubly guilty, by embodying, in the image of the "New Woman," a threat to traditional models of masculinity and by representing "a covert enemy"; after all, they had "cheered on" the soldiers,[20] sending them off to their deaths, and were thus agents of the betrayal articulated as the "legend of the stab in the back."[21]

Adding insult to injury, women's changed role was a direct result of the war, which had pushed them into the workforce and allowed them to literally take the places of the men who had been deployed. Out of necessity, women—whether temporarily or permanently—became the heads of their households, the providers for their families. In the responses to these changes, we can trace not only the more "obvious" resentments men held toward these newly empowered women but also the equally ambivalent responses of women to their own new roles. Women were suddenly an integral part of the health of the nation; as Luise Zietz noted in 1926: "Had the gaps thus torn into the army of workers not been consistently filled by women, Germany, given the same rate of conscription, would have collapsed economically. Witness that, in the first half of 1915, the number of female industry workers rose by more than half a million."[22] The new constitution of 1919, born out of the revolution at the end of the war, at least legally eliminated the hierarchies previously structured by sex and social position, granting women not only the vote but also more general equality before the law. The fact that these new opportunities and rights were the direct result of the devastating war was acknowledged at the time. The continued employment of women after the war drew explicit attention to the reality that many returned soldiers were incapable of reassuming their previous role as breadwinner: "The women in those families in which the man returned mutilated and unable to contribute much to his pension will have to produce the lacking money through paid employment."[23] A woman's employment thus suggested an inability on the part of the man to work and pointed back to his mutilated body; at the same time, it implied not only new responsibilities but also a potentially profound loneliness for these women whose former partners had thus "returned mutilated." And it was not only on the level of the concrete that women's emancipation was tied to the effects of the war; rather, "modern woman" as a whole was seen as a category emerging directly from the experience. As Elsa Herrmann wrote in *Thus Is the New Woman (So Ist die Neue Frau)*, "It should never be forgotten that today's woman . . . must be seen as the direct product of the war and its aftermath, which pushed her into active life."[24] Modern woman as the "direct product" of the conflict that had killed and maimed so many; little wonder, given the physical and mental wounds carried home by the returning soldier, that emancipated woman should become the focus of the complex of fear, hostility, blame, and desire with which the culture reacted to the war and its aftermath. "Woman" in Weimar became a fundamentally problematic category of identity: the emblem of masculine loss to the men who perceived themselves as under siege; the representation of hopes for empowerment and self-determination that came at the cost of fathers, brothers, husbands, and sons to the women who tried to inhabit that new role.

Gender thus became the site at which anxieties about war, defeat, and change were focused; "emancipated woman" became the symbol of the loss of a previous worldview. As Luise Scheffen-Döring noted in 1931: "We are a gender between the times. Only from afar do the sounds of last century's cultural belief in development reach our ears over the ruined field of the World War which we experienced. . . . Nowhere does it become as evident how deeply the balance is shaken as in the sphere of gender."[25] Scheffen-Döring's statement demonstrates the recognition even at the time of the fundamental role emancipated women played as symbols of a new order that many did not welcome: however positive a development emancipation might represent for women of the time, it figures them as "a gender between the times," and represents a disruption of the "balance" that has hitherto governed categories of identity and the relationships between genders. Emancipated woman became the emblem of a shift in social structures viewed by many as running counter to nature, to religion, to national identity. She became associated directly with a moral decline that critics such as Fanny Imle, who argued for a return to traditional, religiously based norms, sought frantically to combat: "Since [August] Bebel attempted, in his book "Woman,"[26] to irrevocably link woman and revolution, millions of misled fellow citizens have been certain that revolutionary violence will free the female sex, and that that free woman would do away with the last remnants of bourgeois order, legality, morality, and religion."[27] Woman as the force that would sweep away "the last remnants of bourgeois order, legality, morality, and religion": we see the way she was functionalized by a conservative culture that perceived itself as under siege. Imle's comments further make clear what should be a given but is nevertheless often disregarded: that the response to women's emancipation cannot be generalized along gender lines, that is, that the notion of a "New Woman," itself in many ways an imaginary construct, struck fear into the heart not only of men (and not of all men), but also of (some) women. What remains constant, however, is the linkage between emancipated woman and a fundamental change in norms and codes of behavior that points to the critical role that the New Woman and modern women in general played as symbol of the new order.

Little surprise, given the way in which this change affected every level of society, that women became the focus of the anxieties bound up with masculine subjectivity's sense of being under attack amid changing social structures and hierarchies. As McCormick notes in his discussion of film and gender in the Weimar Republic, "anxiety about changing notions of gender roles and sexuality permeated Weimar culture."[28] McCormick emphasizes women's position as "most marginal, most archetypally 'other'"[29] in relation to the traditional understanding of male subjectivity in Germany, and suggests that "male resentment of women in Germany at this time can be connected to a more widespread 'crisis of male subjectivity' in the aftermath of Germany's defeat."[30] The "real" resentment against the women who, in moving out of the private and into the public realm, became visible manifestations of men's loss of power both contributed to and was based in the complexity of the image of "woman," which became an ambiguous symbol, with connotations at once of nostalgia and *Heimat* and of danger. If the home front stood both for protection and that which must be protected, then "woman"—as mother and wife—embodied that home. Because the construction of femininity was linked so intimately to the static image of home before the experience of war, the change in this construction reinforced a sense of loss and alienation. In occupying a new social and economic role, women challenged masculine subjectivity not only because they took on power previously reserved for men, but also because, in doing so, they destroyed the nostalgic image from the past that became that for which soldiers fought. At the same time, they became representative of the enemy within, the body that emerged unscathed from a conflict that had decimated the male body. This certainly connects with the way in which so much of the anxiety about the perceived emancipation of women was couched in terms of the physical; in the context of a culture in which the soldiers' physical experience of war had left visible scars on their bodies, the uninjured bodies of women came to signify beyond their own physical selves. Whatever privations women might have experienced during the war, the cultural construction of woman's body acted as a cruel foil to the wounded body of the soldier, effectively representing a threat of castration not, as Freud would have it, as a symbol of "lack" on her part, but as an embodiment of "wholeness" that drew attention to a lack manifested in the male body. The female body, in other words, pointed not toward a hypothetical and potential lack, but rather toward one that was devastatingly real, one that characterized the masculine body in this time period and required, in a sense, a fundamental reevaluation and reconstruction of notions of masculine identity and subjectivity.

That the female body became the material representation of the threat of emancipation points to the representative function of female sexuality, for, of women's gains, those in the area of sexuality were most visible and potentially shocking.[31] The New Woman, personifying the changed role of women in its most extreme form, flaunted her freedoms through dress and public behavior, wearing less restrictive and more revealing clothing, smoking and drinking, and brazenly pursuing sexual satisfaction and staking out a woman's right to actively desire.[32] Hence the second impetus behind the cultural inscription of emancipation on the female body: as Dorothy Rowe notes, "the way in which many male writers and painters of German modernity sought to control this challenge [to traditional power hierarchies] was by projecting their fears onto paper or canvas in a way which objectified women purely in terms of their sexuality."[33] Expressed another way, the cultural imaginary subsumed the threat of general female emancipation within a discourse of sexuality, reimagining the "complex of anxieties around loss of power, control, and mastery—ultimately issues of social, political, and economic power, not sexuality" in terms of the sexual and drawing on what McCormick terms a "discourse of castration" in which female emancipation threatened masculine power coded specifically as sexual.[34] With sexual emancipation representing all advances women made, Weimar culture concentrated its responses to the anxiety caused by this within the realm of the sexual, as well, representing the masculine assertion of "sexual potency and sexual identity [as] power over women and social power in general."[35]

Thence the barrage of cultural production thematizing the enactment of violent fantasies of domination, in which power over women is regained through the restriction of their sexual liberty or through outright sexual domination.[36] As Rowe notes, the violent sexual imagery in paintings by George Grosz, Otto Dix, and others functioned as a "literal depiction of the punitive consequences for women who step out of rigidly defined bourgeois spheres of the private and into the public realm of the masculinized spaces of urban modernity."[37] The illustrations of female subjugation through sexual dominance and even murder are thus part of a larger cultural project attempting to reassert traditional power hierarchies. And, certainly, films of the era took part in this: as Carol Diethe observes in her reading of *The Cabinet of Dr. Caligari*, *Nosferatu*, and *Metropolis*, "the underlying message [of German expressionist films] usually upholds patriarchal conservative values which undermine woman's position."[38] This tendency to stage fantasies of male dominance and female subjugation and punishment extends beyond such expressionist fare, for cinematic representations of emancipated women—indeed, of any woman who challenges masculine dominance or embodies an active power—follow a familiar pattern in which there are effectively only two possible outcomes: they are either, as in films like Wiene's *The Hands of Orlac*, Galeen's silent version of *Alraune*, or Pabst's *Diary of a Lost Girl* (*Tagebuch einer Verlorenen*, 1929), reassimilated into traditional, phallocentric power hierarchies, or, as in films as diverse as Lubitsch's *The Eyes of the Mummy*, Pabst's *Pandora's Box*, or Oswald's version of *Alraune*, punished with death.

In examining the shifting constructions of women in Weimar, the traumatic experience of war thus functions as a crucial backdrop and influence. At the same time, we can trace changes in the ways in which women were positioned over the course of the Weimar era. The social, economic, and cultural changes that characterized the short-lived republic affected the construction of gender, too; if we compare the image of the New Woman that dominated early Weimar to the maternal body defined by *Kinder, Kirche, Küche*, which formed the basis of femininity in the Nazi era, we can see clearly how the role of "woman" changed over these fourteen years. We can roughly divide the Weimar Republic into three periods: the post–World War I crisis years, fraught by political upheaval and the economic inflation that spiraled out of control in 1923–24; the years of stabilization, inaugurated by the introduction of the *Rentenmark* in 1924 and encompassing that period of relative prosperity we often think of as the "Golden Twenties"; and the end of the republic, precipitated by the Great Depression that plunged the nation back into poverty and certainly facilitated the rise of National Socialism. Over the course of these fourteen years that were so fraught by instability, it is quite natural that the ways in which the self was conceptualized would also change. What makes it particularly interesting to connect the change in the way in which femininity was envisioned to its cinematic depictions is that sociocultural and political transitions ran alongside advances in the cinematic medium. We should consider how these changes affected the concurrent advances in cinema and whether and how they influenced the cinematic conventions developing at the time.

DEVELOPING MEDIUM, CHANGING SOCIETY

The Weimar era is often viewed as the "Golden Age" of German cinema, a time when formal experimentation and technological advances flourished, and new modes of production came into being. The period saw the consolidation of the film industry through various mergers and acquisitions that left UFA, the Universum Film-AG, a force to be reckoned with. Indeed,

CHAPTER ONE

German cinema became international during this time period, particularly after the release of Wiene's *Cabinet of Dr. Caligari* in 1920. A success in Germany as well as abroad, that film proved that German cinema could be successful outside of the national setting and might indeed aspire to rival Hollywood.[39] When German star Emil Jannings received the first Oscar for best actor in 1929, honoring his work in *The Way of All Flesh* (Victor Fleming, 1927) and *The Last Command* (Josef von Sternberg, 1928), it was a resounding affirmation of the international reputation of German cinema.

In many ways, Weimar cinema's ascendancy is an outgrowth of the war; we can regard World War I as a crucial influence on the development of German film even without considering it as a catalyst for anxieties and social changes that influenced cinematic narratives and conventions, for it served as a momentary caesura in the process of German film's development within a larger, international context. That is, the war, in leading to embargoes on the export of German films and the import of international films into Germany, served to isolate the German film industry, forcing—or enabling—it to develop, for a brief but important time, in a unique way. As Kristin Thompson notes, the ban on foreign films, lasting from the spring of 1916 to December 31, 1920, cut Germany off from international cinematic developments at precisely the time in which filmmakers were introducing certain approaches that would define classical film: "German filmmakers had a period of nearly five years in which they were cut off from most influences from abroad. These happened to be the same years in which Hollywood brought most of the norms of classical filmmaking into full play."[40] The ban on foreign films enabled Germany's industry to flourish, given that it had no rivals for its audience, even as it pushed it to develop distinct stylistic conventions. We might thus consider the cinematic conventions arising in Weimar cinema in terms not of a universal set of norms but of the unique circumstances in which they developed.

The development of the medium mirrored the changes wrought by economic and political concerns, with cultural production of the era organizable into three phases that roughly correspond to the socioeconomic phases: expressionism (from 1919 to 1924), *Neue Sachlichkeit* ("New Objectivity," from 1924 to 1929), and the final years of the Weimar Republic, 1929 to 1933, during which technological innovation, particularly the introduction of sound, radically changed the film industry. Much of the scholarly inquiry on the era has focused on expressionist films, exemplified by the aforementioned *Caligari*. Although the term is a problematic one,[41] expressionism in cinema has been used to refer to a distinctive style as well as a specific set of themes. Stylistically, it is characterized by sets that suggest an external representation of the psyche and by odd angles and perspective, the emphasis on the play of light and shadow, and a style of acting in which emotions are strongly externalized. Thematically, expressionist cinema confronts what Sabine Hake calls "a profound crisis of identity in modern mass society"[42] focusing on some of the central anxieties of post–World War I society: generational and gender conflict, urbanization and modernity, and the "darker" elements of the human psyche, such as madness and criminality.[43] Hake, while noting the slipperiness of the term, emphasizes that it defines these films in terms of narrative and thematic content and of a specific aesthetic and draws attention to the self-reflexive tendency of expressionism, which shows "an almost obsessive concern with visual relations, modes of spectatorship, and problems of perception," in other words, with the building blocks of cinema itself.[44]

Just as the chaos and uncertainty of immediate post–World War I Germany gave way to stabilization after 1924, so did expressionism yield at that time to New Objectivity. As social and economic upheaval receded, filmmakers abandoned the "haunted screens" of works like *Caligari* and *Warning Shadows* for a cinema that emphasized realism, replacing expressionism's fear of modernity with a "celebration of technological progress and [a] willing acceptance of the *status quo*."[45] With this shift, we see a turn away from the overtly uncanny or fantastic films of the earlier years; still, New Objectivity by no means abandoned the problematic of gender and emancipation. These themes—and the uncanny itself—are simply thematized differently in the years after expressionism waned.

In his discussion of Weimar cinema, McCormick argues that German films from the era must be viewed in the context of this very specific historical moment: "The sexual politics—and misogyny—in the Weimar cinema were not merely matters of cinematic style in relation to some kind of "timeless" male psyche. Misogyny may be timeless enough, but in Germany during the 1920s social forces were in conflict about issues specific to the new role of women in German society."[46] While this might seem merely a nuance of an argument, it is, in fact, a crucial assumption, and one that underlies my analysis. However useful models of cinema and analyses of the power dynamics involved therein might be to a reading of the films under examination, and however recurrent thematizations of the anxious and oft-violent attempts to assert masculine power are in these works, I, like McCormick, see them as the result not of a monolithic "male psyche" but rather of a construction of male subjectivity specific to the historical moment. Reexamining representative examples of the era's cinematic output serves not only to trace the ways in which these films draw on recurrent structures in their representations of women in film but also serves to identify how these structures served as responses to specific anxieties, how these fears dominating German culture at the time shaped the way in which women were depicted and subordinated through narrative and cinematic means.

THEORETICAL FRAMEWORK

In approaching these films, I am building on scholarly works going back to two seminal texts that long dominated the field and continue to inform it: Siegfried Kracauer's *From Caligari to Hitler* (1947) and Lotte Eisner's *The Haunted Screen* (1952). Kracauer's book is at once a film history and a narrative with a clear trajectory. Written in New York between 1941 and 1946, the work involved a painstaking examination of the collection of Weimar films held by the Museum of Modern Art.[47] As the subtitle indicates—*A Psychological History of the German Film*—Kracauer turns to the cinematic production of the Weimar Republic in order to unearth the collective psychology it reveals and to unravel the social processes it mirrors. He does so with the aim of tracing, as the title suggests, a direct link between "Caligari and Hitler," between early Weimar culture and the rise of fascism. Kracauer attempts to expose, through an examination of what he calls the "motifs pervading films of all levels,"[48] the "deep psychological dispositions predominant in Germany from 1918 to 1933 . . . which influenced the course of events during that time and which will have to be reckoned with in the post-Hitler era."[49] In the "psychological history" he thus constructs, Weimar films point forward to the coming horrors of the Third Reich, functioning not simply as examples of the new medium or representations of certain narratives or cultural moments but rather as embodiments of a uniquely German character that will lead inexorably to war and the Holocaust.

While Eisner focuses more closely on the formal elements that distinguish expressionist film, in certain significant ways her approach nevertheless parallels that of Kracauer. She, too, works from an assumption of a monolithic, unified "German psyche," couching her argument from the outset in terms of "the German mind."[50] Eisner argues that the details of expressionist films reveal their roots in Romanticism and, as such, express something particularly German, some innate national tendency. And, like Kracauer, she sees in this a fundamentally problematic character that suggests an inevitable trajectory toward the Third Reich.

Kracauer and Eisner both make significant contributions to the study of film, essentially founding German film studies. Nevertheless, they have a set of specific biases that inform and limit the scope of their inquiries. Writing from the vantage point of Jewish émigrés during and immediately after World War II, both Kracauer and Eisner begin their analyses with the implicit assumption that the filmic production of the Weimar era points inexorably toward fascism. Contemporary film scholarship long tended to orient itself in accordance with such a reading; however, in recent years, this monolithic view of Weimar cinema has been rightly challenged. In the case of Kracauer's work, scholars have not only pointed to the limitations of *From Caligari to Hitler* but also to the necessity to consider that piece as part of a larger oeuvre, as a (late) entry among the writings Kracauer produced. *From Caligari to Hitler* was, in fact, the culmination of Kracauer's many years of work as a cultural critic and film reviewer, first in the position of an editor at the *Frankfurter Zeitung*, then, having to flee Germany in 1933 and spend eight years in France before arriving in the United States in 1941, as an occasional reviewer and freelancer. Among his early works, there are certain essays, notably "The Mass Ornament"[51] and "The Little Shopgirls Go to the Movies,"[52] which have commanded critical attention, beginning with Miriam Hansen, who in her work on Kracauer sought to "[restore] Kracauer's complexity as an intellectual figure" and "to elucidate the relevance of Kracauer's early writings for current debates."[53] Still, *From Caligari to Hitler* tends to eclipse his other work, undermining his significance as a cultural critic in Weimar Germany and the nuances of his work.

To start a reevaluation of Weimar film with Kracauer makes sense not only because he represents an important origin of German film criticism, but also because, despite all the flaws and the blind spots one might trace in them, his works offer compelling ideas about the cinematic output of Weimar; indeed, at times his reviews are all that remain for us, as so many films of the era have been lost. As Noah Isenberg states in his introduction to *Weimar Cinema: An Essential Guide to Classic Films of the Era*, the aim of much current work on Weimar film is to function as "not so much a replacement for, but a much-needed supplement to, Kracauer's and Eisner's work."[54] Works like Isenberg's volume, in which some of the best-known films of the Weimar canon are revisited from the standpoint of the twenty-first century and through the lens of a variety of theoretical approaches, represent contemporary attempts to expand beyond the works of Kracauer and Eisner and to reconsider Weimar films with an eye to how diverse, contradictory, and often enigmatic they are. Still, Kracauer's work is certainly compelling, for he seeks to trace sociocultural anxieties in cultural output and poses an important question at the onset of his inquiry: "What fears and hopes swept Germany immediately after World War I?"[55] From his post–World War II vantage point as an émigré, Kracauer loses sight of this question over the course of his argument, shifting instead to an exploration of the films as "pre-Hitler," rather than "postwar." Kaes's *Shell Shock Cinema* suggests that an analysis of Weimar film might be well advised in returning to that original question and undertakes just such a reading, suggesting that most filmic production from the post–World War I period might be seen as "war films," even when combat itself nowhere enters into the narrative.[56] His analysis convincingly locates the war as *the* foundational trauma that dictated the shape of Weimar culture. This is a notion that we might productively expand on, attempting to excavate another aspect of the way in which the films emerging out of the moment function if we take questions of gender into greater account. In doing so, we might be able to uncover not only the "male anxieties" articulated but also the "female fears and desires" that are as compelling and as much shaped by the experience of war and social change.

For gender seems at times to be the sticky wicket in Weimar film studies. Too often it is addressed within the limited paradigm suggested by Kracauer. Thus Thomas Elsaesser, in assessing Kracauer's work, notes that Kracauer "got it right in one respect: that of gender. He had rightly recognized how many of the films from the early 1920s dealt with specifically *male* anxieties centered on vision, perception and fear of symbolic castration."[57]

Elsaesser's work on Weimar film is seminal, and his rereading of Kracauer's texts not only points to the flaws of *From Caligari to Hitler* but also productively reevaluates the piece, bringing it into dialogue with his other works.[58] But this emphasis on anxieties gendered male and the concomitant elision of those "gendered *female*" exemplifies a critical gap in much (though by no means all) scholarship focused on the era. This emphasis expresses itself in a tendency that extends beyond the study of Weimar film and that reads films always through the eyes of an imaginary male spectator. This is especially striking given the reality of an audience in which women were well represented, if not overrepresented.[59] Elsaesser recognizes the presence of women in the audience and implies that their gaze at the screen was fundamentally different from that of men: "Women as cinema spectators had the right to a look that previously was denied to them, and films, knowing that they catered for women spectators, seemed ready to accommodate this different look."[60] Yet even as he acknowledges "this different look" of the female spectator and notes that "early cinema admits for its female spectators the right to look on equal terms with men, and thus to appropriate the world in a mode not readily sanctioned socially,"[61] Elsaesser says little about the specifics of this dynamic. He points to an important aspect of film in noting that audiences—and women in particular—found in them models for behavior that transgressed social norms and simultaneously engaged, in their positions as women-as-spectators, in a transgressive activity. Still, Elsaesser does not interrogate the position of female spectator in more detail but rather presupposes a unified and de-individualized male viewer. This tendency is one that Patrice Petro criticizes and uses as the jumping-off point for *Joyless Streets*, her analysis of Weimar melodrama: "It is the existence of a female spectator, and the function of representation for mobilizing her desires and unconscious fantasies, that analyses of the Weimar cinema have repressed or ignored in order to reproduce the same story—the story of male subjectivity in crisis—which is then taken to be the story of German history or culture itself."[62] Petro examines gendered representation in the illustrated press and film and presents a sensitive reading of how melodrama in particular opened up spaces of identification and empowerment for the female viewer. She argues that certain characters in these films—in particular "feminized men"—perform a very specific function for the female viewer, giving her the possibility to identify with a male on-screen double "upon whom feminine desires for freedom from patriarchal authority may be projected."[63] Similarly, in the illustrated press, the flip side of this feminized man, the "masculinized woman," holds very different appeal for men and women respectively:

> Where Weimar films tend to focus on a destabilized male identity, rendering it passive or "feminine," the illustrated magazines of the period focus on a destabilized female identity, rendering it aggressive, "masculine," even threatening. To a certain extent, the representation of the modern woman was a projection of male anxieties and fears—anxieties and fears emanating from various phenomena of modernity that were recast and reconstructed in terms of an uncontrollable and destructive female sexuality. . . . But when we turn to the magazines and films that made their appeal explicitly to women, it is indisputable that the representation of the modern woman did address women's experiences of modernity—their dissatisfactions with traditionally defined gender roles and their desire for a transformation of these roles.[64]

Petro interrogates the images of masculinity and femininity with which Weimar culture confronted the viewer and suggests that these images addressed themselves differently to men and women, attempting (and sometimes managing) to simultaneously embody "male anxieties and fears" and "women's experiences of modernity." The images function not as replications of reality but as expressions of an imaginary bound up with notions of the self: "woman" as image embodies simultaneously men's fear of a "modernity" couched in terms of "female sexuality" and women's "dissatisfactions" with the roles assigned them by their cultural environs.

Petro's sensitivity to the need to examine both sides of the "gender divide," her recognition that "to speak of a viewing subject is to speak of a male as well as a female subject"[65] is important. To Petro, the fact that gender roles were being destabilized in Weimar culture and that thence resulted certain male fears and anxieties does not preclude a dual address by films thematizing these anxieties. She articulates an understanding of what I see as the fundamentally inextricable relationship between male and female identity, between masculine and feminine gender norms: "What did the destabilization of male identity mean for female viewers in Weimar, especially given the perceived crisis in conventionally defined male and female gender roles? If traditional notions about gender were in crisis as a result of social, economic, and cultural change, how did changing representations of sexual difference function for female viewers?"[66] Petro pushes us, in other words, to look below the perhaps more easily identifiable cinematic concerns—those that focused on the "anxious males" and articulated and transformed their fears and desires—to the moments that addressed the women in the audience.

At the same time, the entire notion of the gendered spectator seems to me one that is fundamentally problematic. On one level, it constructs a binary relationship that obscures the way in which "male" and "female" anxieties about changing social structures and norms in this era must necessarily be inextricably entangled with each other. Yes, the majority of men experienced World War I in a very different way than did the majority of women, and yes, certain common experiences can be assigned to men and women respectively. But the trauma of change certainly affected both genders. On another level, to take for granted this notion of the gendered spectator makes it too easy to forget that such positions are imaginary ones and, indeed, presupposes the existence of two "stable" heterosexually based genders. This assumption is deeply problematic, eliding questions of sexual orientation, class, and ethnicity, indeed, any individual experience that would lead a given spectator to relate to a film in a particular way. For the sake of expediency, we may well imagine "the viewer," yet we should do so always with the awareness that this is an idealized and imaginary construct.

SCHOLARS ON THE GAZE

The significance of spectatorial position and the power dynamics implied in the cinematic gaze have been grappled with extensively in feminist film theory since the 1975 publication of Laura Mulvey's seminal essay "Visual Pleasure and Narrative Cinema." In spite of the essay's age, the model of cinematic pleasure and of the positions of viewer and image it outlines is still significant today. Mulvey argues that classic Hollywood film provides the (male) viewer with two types of pleasure: scopophilic, bound up with the gaze onto the female object of desire, and narcissistic, connected to the identification with the male characters on screen.[67] A woman's function is split: she is both erotic object (for male characters and spectators) and symbol of "lack," of the castration anxiety that structures male subjectivity; in both roles, she is a passive figure. A male character, in contrast, works as an idealized representation of the viewer, allowing the man to gain control over the images before him and the lack represented by "woman."[68] The woman thus functions as both object of desire, attracting and appealing to the male gaze, and as its inverse, threatening and repulsing it.[69] Hence her function as a symbol, the contradicting significances of which must be neutralized. Mulvey argues that classical cinema—representing male subjectivity—confronts this symbolic value in two ways:

> The male unconscious has two avenues of escape from this castration anxiety: preoccupation with the re-enactment of the original trauma (investigating the woman, demystifying her mystery), counterbalanced by the devaluation, punishment, or saving of the guilty object (an avenue typified by the concerns of the *film noir*); or else complete disavowal of castration by the substitution of a fetish object or turning the represented figure itself into a fetish so that it becomes reassuring rather than dangerous (hence overvaluation, the cult of the female star).[70]

Mulvey focuses specifically on classic Hollywood films and those traditions that align themselves with them; still, this qualification is oft overlooked when her model is drawn on, and her ideas about the gaze have been widely applied to film in general. Quite understandably, for the paradigm offers a temptingly coherent way to read film, and certainly some of the structures Mulvey identifies are relevant in this study. However, in the context of Weimar culture, the identifications between viewer and characters and the ways in which male and female figures are represented and constructed frequently runs counter to Mulvey's model. Again and again, we see problematic identifications, ones that would align the viewer not with a dominant, superior male counterpart in the film but with one who is flawed or whose identity is fractured, a male identity "feminized," as Petro might have it, ones that draw a sharp division between the male viewer and another outside subjectivity that guides the filmic narrative. The women we encounter are far from passive, instead representing active dangers to the male character and viewer, disrupting the male character's activity through actions of their own, and challenging his power as symbolic representations not of the castrated other, but of a "wholeness" that stands in marked contrast to the disempowered male "hero."

Mulvey's essay has spurred critics to investigate further the place of gender within the cinematic apparatus and in particular in the spectatorial position. Working directly in response to Mulvey's essay, Gaylyn Studlar examines Josef von Sternberg's films starring Marlene Dietrich through the lens of Gilles Deleuze's work on masochism. Studlar shifts the emphasis to "the pre-Oedipal rather than the Oedipal stage" in hopes of discovering how "film may be capable of forming spectatorial pleasures divorced from issues of castration, sexual difference, and feminine lack."[71] She takes issue with Freud's suggestion that the castration complex forms masochism's basis and instead aligns herself with theorists who locate its genesis in the relationship with the mother, suggesting that it is a complex "rooted in the child's fear of abandonment and ambivalent wish for symbiosis" in which "the female is mystically idealized as the loving inflictor of punishment. The masochist's desire for pain reflects the attempt to negate the father and disavow his likeness—the phallic inheritance—in the son."[72] Studlar allows for an entirely different model of spectatorship from that Mulvey articulated, tracing the structures that engender masochistic pleasure through the relationship with the maternal in von Sternberg's films and suggesting that it, "through the mobility of multiple, fluid identifications ... allows the spectator to experience the pleasure of satisfying 'the drive to be both sexes.'"[73] Studlar points particularly to the number of male figures in von Sternberg's films who are humiliated at the hands of the desired women as indicative of a very different dynamic of desire, possession, and spectatorship from that articulated elsewhere. Here, the male viewer of these films necessarily occupies a "feminized" space: "If the male spectator identifies with the masochistic male character, he is aligned with a position usually assigned to the female. If he rejects identification with this position, one alternative is to identify with the position of power: the female who inflicts pain. In either case, the male spectator assumes a position associated with the female."[74] Studlar sees the roles assigned to Dietrich as powerful ones, where she "is the object of male desire, but she is not the passive object of a controlling look. Dietrich looks back. She seems to question her objectification. . . . Possession of the performer through the gaze is really nonpossession."[75] Studlar's notion of the powerful gaze thus turns Mulvey's theory on its head, for it is explicitly female: "The *femme fatale* does not steal her 'controlling gaze' from the male, but exercises the authority of the pre-Oedipal mother whose gaze forms the child's first experience of love and power. . . . The masochistic gaze leads to the male's subjugation to the female, not his control of her."[76] Studlar's reading of these films points to the type of complex power dynamics that we see at work in many of the films in this book, where women are both desired and desiring, where they are both the object of a desiring gaze and the bearers of a look that is sought after by the men around them. Her notion of powerful women is particularly interesting when we examine the dynamics of the gaze in a film like Galeen's *Alraune*, or the way in which women act as performers in *Eyes of the Mummy* or in some of the episodes in *Uncanny Tales*.

Other scholars have similarly proposed ways to avoid the problematic position of the (nonexistent) female spectator in Mulvey's original essay. Mulvey herself reevaluated her original premise six years after the publication of "Visual Pleasure," suggesting, in reference to melodrama, that the female lead's "oscillation, her inability to achieve stable sexual identity, is echoed by the woman spectator's masculine 'point of view.' Both create a sense of the difficulty of sexual difference in cinema that is missing in the undifferentiated spectator of 'Visual Pleasure.'"[77] Mulvey, much like Elsaesser,[78] suggests that female spectatorship functions by taking on a masculine position, even within the context of the "woman's genre" of melodrama. Mary Ann Doane also focuses on a genre aimed primarily at women as a way to trace the female viewer's position. She suggests, in her examination of the "woman's film," that the woman in the audience finds herself shifting between "feminine and masculine positions." Indeed, certain films, in particular those focusing on "the medical discourse," actively push women to identify with the masculine gaze: "If female spectatorship is constituted as an oscillation between a feminine and a masculine position, the films of the medical discourse encourage the female spectator to repudiate the feminine pole and to ally herself with the one who diagnoses, with a medical gaze."[79] Doane sees in the woman's film an "obsessive attempt to circumscribe a place for the female spectator,"[80] yet her analysis demonstrates how, again and again, the female spectator is pushed to identify with the masculine gaze at the female body and to repudiate her own gender. These "medical discourse films" refigure the woman's body as object not of desire but of scientific inquiry and connect female illness to this shift in woman's status as image: illness is represented as female undesirability, while "the doctor's work is the transformation of the woman into a specular object. . . . The narratives thus trace a movement from the medical gaze to the erotic gaze in relation to the central female figure, activating a process of despecularization/respecularization."[81] Doane's analysis suggests that the genre is ultimately a conservative one, in which "femininity is *stylized*" and "the familiar scenarios of waiting, giving, sacrificing, and mourning [are] ennobled and made acceptable," even while the genre offers a potential critical dimension in revealing the constructed nature of that which it represents: "The credibility of these representations is sometimes undermined, in isolated images or scenes. . . . In the woman's film, the process of remirroring reduces the mirror effect of the cinema, it demonstrates that these are poses, postures, tropes—in short, that we are being subjected to a discourse on femininity."[82] The potential of the woman's film lies not in its offering to the female spectator a newly liberated, specifically feminine, and yet independent gaze, but in its glimpses of itself as a construction, as a "stylization" of woman's identity. This is, of course, an extremely limited liberating potential that Doane posits, a fact that might, as Kathleen Rowe points out, actually have to do with Doane's emphasis on melodrama. Rowe suggests that Doane and other scholars who focus on melodrama and similar "women's genres," in other words on what she sees as "artistic forms centered on their victimization and tears rather than on their resistance and laughter," are fundamentally overlooking the potential in other genres to challenge and undermine the status quo.[83] Drawing on notions of excess and the carnivalesque, Rowe suggests that feminist critics need to look at texts that "position women as subjects of a laughter that expresses anger, resistance, solidarity, and joy—or those which show women using in disruptive, challenging ways the spectacle already invested in them as objects of a masculine gaze."[84] While Rowe's focus on modern American culture and comedy specifically makes many of the details of her analysis less relevant here, this notion that we might examine how women draw on "the spectacle" that they always already represent in "disruptive, challenging ways" connects to certain moments that we will find in the films examined.

More generally focused on spectatorship, Judith Mayne's *Cinema and Spectatorship* interrogates the ways spectatorship has been constructed and theorized in film theory. Mayne outlines cogently each phase and direction in film theory; in doing so, she reveals the ways in which each has effectively developed in reaction to those that came before and problematizes some of the "large dichotomies . . . and sweeping generalizations"[85] that characterize 1970s film theory and often seem to persist in contemporary work. Of particular interest here is the way in which Mayne questions the notion that the central structures underlying (classical) cinema are oedipal ones, and she asks whether this is applicable to a narrowly defined type of film, or more broadly:

> Does the analysis of the cinematic institution as a staging and restaging of the crises of male oedipal desire, as a regressive plenitude, apply only to a specific historical mode of the cinema—i.e., the classical, narrative Hollywood film? Or, rather, given that the emergence of the cinema is so closely linked to the fictions of Western patriarchal culture, is the cinematic apparatus as theorized in film theory bound to be the condition of *all* cinematic representation?[86]

Mayne's analysis articulates a central problem in applying these theoretical structures more broadly: are these to be understood as valid in terms only of "a specific historical mode of the cinema," or are they universal? This book emerges partly in connection with this question, for I want to suggest that certain affinities between the films examined and those of classical Hollywood cinema point not necessarily to universal psychic imperatives, nor to the universal applicability of "the cinematic apparatus as theorized in film theory," but at least partially to the effects of specific sociocultural circumstance on the ways in which these films represent their content and appeal to their audiences. Further, Mayne articulates one way to avoid "that tension between 'woman' and 'women,' where it is not always clear just where the image of woman as contained by patriarchal ideology leaves off and where the woman as historical subject begins"[87] that feminist film theory often runs up against, pointing to the work of historian Linda Gordon as a potential model. Mayne notes that Gordon confronts the tendency in women's history to either "[seek] to uncover the truth of women's lives that have been obscured by the falsehoods of previous generations of historians [or define] history as myth-making and storytelling"[88] by looking for a "method in between."[89] She suggests that precisely such an approach should be taken to cinema and spectatorship, pointing to "Gordon's emphasis on tension, and her refusal of easy 'synthesis'" as a way to negotiate "between the competing claims of homogeneity and heterogeneity, domination and resistance."[90] In other words, film theory might work in a mode that acknowledges and, indeed, builds on the "tension" that characterizes the position of the feminist critic and points to the need for "a recognition that the cinema functions in contradictory ways."[91] This ambiguity is a characteristic that we will find again and again in the films here examined. In their contradictions, their inconsistencies, their moments of excess, we can trace the way that they are at once tools that work with dominant ideology, acting out the anxieties and fantasies of a patriarchal social structure that perceived changing gender norms as an attack and answering these fears with the swift punishment of the transgressive women who embodied that attack, and the site at which such transgression might be acted out, tested, "tried on." They are, in other words, never entirely coherent, but rather characterized by an at times uncomfortable undecidability.

I focus in this study on uncanny films, on those that relate most closely, among genres of the era, to modern horror. It is by no means unheard of to examine such a genre that seems to appeal more clearly to men. Linda Williams, in her influential essay "When the Woman Looks," examines the relationship between woman-as-image and the on-screen monsters who confront her and the audience. Emphasizing the way in which these films thematize a dangerous female gaze, Williams suggests that such a gaze is inevitably punished.[92] She posits a structural similarity between on-screen monsters and woman, in that both represent "the power to mutilate and transform the vulnerable male."[93] Williams allows both woman-as-image and woman-as-viewer a potent power, suggesting that both female gaze and image confront and challenge the male viewer: "The woman's look at the monster is more than simply a punishment for looking or a narcissistic fascination with the distortion of her own image in the mirror that patriarchy holds up to her; it is also a recognition of their similar status as potent threats to a vulnerable male power."[94] While her analysis demonstrates how limited the female viewer's empowerment is and draws attention to the genre's conservative moral orientation, by which woman's power is tied to her "absence of sexual desire" and she must ultimately be punished for her dangerous gaze, Williams's work reveals how films carry the potential to "[lay] bare the voyeuristic structure of cinema and that structure's dependence on the woman's acceptance of her role as narcissist [and to expose] the perverse structures of seeing that operate in the [horror] genre."[95] Williams's analysis draws attention to the ways in which a genre that ultimately offers a conservative resolution to "dangerous" female empowerment nevertheless is able to unmask that very conservativeness, to draw attention to its own structures of control. To varying degrees and effectiveness, the films on which I focus do precisely this; even while developing patterns of seeing that objectify the image of woman and thereby neutralize the active and dangerous challenge she represents, these films draw attention to the structures they use, referencing and commenting on the power relationships at work. We will see this most clearly in a film like *Warning Shadows*, where the punitive fantasy that plays out for the spectator simultaneously reveals itself as fantasy and uncovers the complex and shifting power relationships between the transgressive woman and her admirers, between image and viewer. And, as Williams suggests, the challenge that women pose to the male viewer is often embodied in her gaze. Where these films differ from those Williams examines is that, here, the woman on the screen is not merely congruent to a monster that appears alongside her; rather, she takes on the role of monster, herself becoming that which confronts and endangers male power. Her gaze, when thematized, is more often than not a gaze at the masculine body, rather than at an "other" that both threatens and represents her.

Like Williams, Carol Clover focuses on the horror genre. In her essay "Her Body, Himself: Gender in the Slasher Film," Clover examines the complex gender roles in the modern slasher film, suggesting that they deploy a network of identification that invites a predominantly male audience to identify with the heroic "Final Girl," and that this identification allows a vicarious experience of the violence acted out on the female body.[96] The slasher film upsets gender dynamics not only on the narrative level and through cross-gender identification but also on the level of the cinematic apparatus, as, here, it is the *female* hero who drives forward the narrative rather than functioning to interrupt and divert it.[97] This notion of the female character not just as image but also as catalyst for the narrative action is important because we find a similar dynamic in many of the films in this book. For example, *The Hands of Orlac* coalesces around precisely such a situation in which a woman takes narrative control; it is this shift in her role that embodies most clearly the danger she poses to masculine subjectivity. In "The Eye of Horror," Clover shifts focus to the gaze in particular and poses an important question: "The chief complaint has to do with the place (no place) of the female spectator in the model, but the question I would like to raise here is a rather different one—namely, whether cinematic looking always and inevitably implies mastery over its object, even when the looker is male and his object female."[98] Clover draws attention to an assumption accepted perhaps too unquestioningly: that there exists a fundamentally powerful gaze that is necessarily male. While Clover counters this by examining the way in which horror repeatedly displays and enacts a "failed male gaze,"[99] part of what I want to suggest is that such a "powerful male gaze" is effectively an imaginary construct, a way of structuring film in such a way as to counter the anxieties arising out of that projected onto the screen. Indeed, as we will see in films like *Warning Shadows* and *The Hands of Orlac*, we often find male figures whose gaze is compromised, flawed, or disempowered; in other words, we see such a "failed male gaze" as Clover stipulates, but as a part of a larger notion of male identity as imperfect, fragmented, mutilated.

Like Williams and Clover, Rhona J. Berenstein concentrates on horror film, but seeks to problematize the notion of spectatorship and identification through "the detailed investigation of the third category of spectatorship, which conceives of multiple viewing positions . . . with a view to dislodging the field's favorite dualities: male/female and heterosexual/homosexual" and by considering "historical and generic specificity."[100] Berenstein's emphasis points to some of the limitations of the work that has hitherto been done; even those scholars attempting to move beyond a conceptualization of film as structured around a single, monolithic male gaze risk essentializing by retaining a notion of a single *female* gaze. Berenstein's analysis at least partially avoids this problem by focusing on cross-identifications, posing the question of how "sexual and social identities of viewers determine the identifications and desires deployed in viewing,"[101] and suggesting that we move beyond notions of "viewing pleasures via similarities . . . and sexual drives"[102] to theories that take into account "the dissolution of a one-to-one viewer-character relationship."[103] Her ultimate suggestion is that in horror film, the audience engages in a range of pleasurable cross-identifications, what she terms a sort of "spectatorship-as-drag," yet that these identifications remain in service of conventional gender norms: "As a framework for spectatorship, drag suggests both that transgressive identifications and desires lurk beneath or on the surface of gender displays and that the lure of conventional roles does not counteract social expectations. That is, classic horror's transgressive spectatorial pleasures are intimately connected to the genre's simultaneous support of conventional desires."[104] Berenstein is quite correct in drawing attention to the flexibility of audience identification; as she notes, echoing Studlar, one of the pleasures of cinema lies in its ability to allow the fantasy of "being other" than one's self. And this notion of flexibility in terms of identification is one way out of the quandary models focused on gender and identification present. Anne Friedberg points to this as precisely that which allows for pleasure-in-viewing and that characterizes a *feminine* gaze. Friedberg locates the root of a feminine gaze in the figure of a female flaneur connected to shopping as a leisure activity.[105] The woman as film spectator is, for Friedberg, linked to this origin and thereby to a gaze that aims to possess: "New desires were created for her [the female flaneur] by advertising and consumer culture; desires elaborated in a system of selling and consumption that depended on the relation between looking and buying and on the indirect desire to possess and incorporate through the eye."[106] Here, Friedberg offers a tangible origin for a female gaze associated with "power" in the sense of "taking possession of" its object. Friedberg's analysis is an interesting one in that she figures the female viewer as fundamentally interested in the multiplicity of "identities" available to her in film:

> The newly conjoined *mobilized and virtual* gaze of the cinema answered the desire not only for temporal and spatial mobility

but for gender mobility as well. The spectator-shopper—trying on identities—engages in the pleasures of a temporally and spatially fluid subjectivity. Theories of spectatorship that imply a one-to-one correspondence between the spectator position and gender, race, or sexual identity—as if identity were a constant, consistent continuum unchallenged by the borrowed subjectivity of spectatorship—do not consider the pleasures of escaping that physically bound subjectivity. Isn't cinema spectatorship pleasurable precisely because new identities can be "worn" and then discarded?[107]

Friedberg suggests that cinema has an emancipatory function because it allows an escape from not only time and place but also individual identity: the viewer experiences a "gender mobility" that allows her the pleasure of "escaping that physically bound subjectivity." Her argument is important because it notes the ambiguity and oscillation inherent to any spectatorial position even as it furnishes the historical precedent of a powerful and desiring female gaze.

What this survey of some of the major voices in the field makes clear is the complexity of issues of gender, power, and spectatorship in film. These scholars articulate some of the central questions the films in this study raise: how exactly does gender relate to spectatorial position? Is the gaze always gendered male, or does there exist a female gaze, or is the gaze entirely ungendered to begin with? What are the universal psychic structures that underlie film, or is it determined not by something universal but by the local, the cultural, the historically specific? And how, if at all, does genre play into these dynamics? My own approach to the uncanny films of the Weimar era builds on these scholars and their work and draws on their findings. I take as the basis of my analysis several central assumptions. Firstly and perhaps most importantly, I want to move away from suggesting a universal and ahistorical tendency in these films; if they do build on certain psychic tendencies, then I would argue that these are nevertheless historically specific and culturally contingent tendencies. Secondly, I want to address the ways in which these films might signify ambiguously, even conflictingly, the ways in which they speak to a heterogeneous audience, address both "the" male and "the" female viewer. And thirdly, I want to consider explicitly the self-referential dimension of these films, the ways in which they work as individual narratives and as reflections on the medium itself.

THE GAZE IN WEIMAR FILM THEORY

The work of modern feminist scholars forms an important background to this book, but I want also to consider how issues of spectatorship, power, and gender in film were discussed at the time. Sabine Hake's study of film criticism and theory in early twentieth-century Germany, *The Cinema's Third Machine: Writing on Film in Germany, 1907–1933*, provides an important source for the way Weimar culture conceptualized the complex gendering of film and the process of watching a film. On one hand, woman's symbolic value as an embodiment of a dangerous modernity was not a new development: "Since the late nineteenth century, images of the feminine—in literature as well as in the visual arts—had been put into circulation to represent the liberating and threatening aspects of modern society."[108] This tendency seems ever more powerful in Germany after World War I, where woman becomes the embodiment of the perceived challenge to masculine power and subjectivity, her body a doubled signifier that points to that body's new freedoms and to sociocultural changes that challenge traditional notions of identity and power. The female body thus is symbol of the danger it poses itself. Beyond her symbolic function, woman in film referred back to the real presence of woman as spectator. The female audience was both significant and anxiously debated: on the one hand, film audiences were increasingly female, a fact that necessarily would influence filmmaking; on the other, the visibility of a female audience and the notion of a woman being an active spectator came to represent larger trends of emancipation:

> The presence of "unchaperoned" women in a predominantly male audience became an important topic in reformist writings. . . . Their presence confirmed widespread anxieties about the changing social and economic status of women; the early women's movements and their fight for equal rights only reinforced such anxieties. The image of women seeing, rather than being seen, contributed to the impression that the cinema had a liberating effect on women.[109]

Women's presence in the audience was symbolic of their movement outside of the domestic sphere, of their new visibility in the public sphere and their new rights and powers. The intimacy implied by cinema-going—with viewers seated closely together in a darkened room, experiencing communally the emotions and reactions elicited by the images on screen—pushed the experience as a symbol of emancipation into a decidedly sensuous realm. In other words, the experience of watching a film functioned to break down the boundaries between the individual viewers and to imply shared emotions that further threatened conservative gender ideals. And the notion that the women in the audience challenged traditional power structures by becoming, in Hake's terms, "the image of women seeing, rather than being seen" interestingly doubles the way that women in so many Weimar films challenge the male viewer. As the bearers of a dangerous and destabilizing gaze, these women come to embody their doubles in the audience, whose positions as active spectators undermine traditional gender norms.

The notion that the relationship between spectator and filmic image is a gendered one is further complicated because critics at the time conceived of this in a very different way than do modern theorists. Of particular interest in this regard is the work of cinema reformers, who, as Hake notes, linked the respective dangers women's emancipation and cinema posed, ultimately suggesting a "gendering" of cinema:

> Most reformers were more concerned with rhetorical effects than sociological accuracy; their goal was to reverse the process of women's emancipation, not to explain it. The result was a conflation of the spectacle of women at the cinema and the spectacle of cinema. By associating the cinema with the feminine, the reformist authors responded to something real—the dramatic changes in the definition of gender roles—but used that reality to construct an idea, both of cinema and of women. The problem of female spectatorship was translated into various scenarios of seduction, and the experience of real women was suppressed in the process. At times, the cinema was depicted as a cruel seductress who exercised her powers over a weak, emasculated audience. The aggressive assault on the senses inspired comparisons to castration. At other times, the audience was cast in the feminine role, either as the cinema's

helpless victim or its unwilling accomplice. Here, spectators came to represent the nation that had fallen prey, been raped and sucked dry by a vampirelike creature, the cinema.[110]

We again see the way in which the image of woman was functionalized, "used . . . to construct an idea, both of cinema and of women." Cinema was as much a social problem as was woman's emancipation; they became identified with each other, symbols of social decay. To these critics of the cinema, the precise role of the audience might well fluctuate, but it remained always "victim," whether explicitly "feminine" or "weak [and] emasculated." In other words, the on-screen image of the femme fatale, of the dangerously emancipated woman—indeed, of "woman" in general, on the screen and in the audience—all these came to stand for themselves and for the medium. The act of asserting power over these images of woman, through the narrative and through cinematic conventions, represented the taking control of the woman who, through her new social roles and powers, undermined male subjectivity and the medium for which she stood.

The idea that cinema could be either the "cruel seductress" or the "vampirelike creature" that "rapes" the passive audience demonstrates the slippage that occurred in the way in which critics constructed the experience of watching a film as a gendered one. The gaze as conceptualized at the time was distinctly *not* masculine, and was anything but powerful:

> Visual pleasure was most often perceived as becoming feminine in the act of looking; in that association with the feminine, the cinema further revealed its foundation on sexuality, or rather, on the existing discourses of sexuality. The majority of male writers described the cinematic experience as threatening and victimizing, in other words: as feminizing . . . looking was still perceived as a passive activity.[111]

Here we see one of the central tensions at work in cinema. Much current film analysis is based on the implicit assumption that, as Mulvey suggests, "pleasure in looking has been split into active/male and passive/female," with man as the bearer of a powerful gaze and woman as object.[112] In contrast, the understanding of spectatorship that these Weimar critics had suggests that the gaze is far from empowering, and the process of looking represents not an active process of taking control of the image but rather a passive state in which the viewers are themselves "victimized" and controlled through the images displayed. This construction of spectatorship reveals the equation of "the act of looking" and the feminine. Indeed, it sets the stage not for a representation of an innately powerful and controlling male gaze, but rather for an attempt to construct such a gaze, to inaugurate a way of watching that enables the transgressive and threatening woman on screen—and the medium for which she stands—to be mastered and neutralized.

What critics' voices from the era make clear is that there was an element of discomfort in the relationship between viewer and film, an awareness of the process as one in which the audience subjected itself to another guiding consciousness and effectively abdicated control. The escapist quality of cinema, in other words, was based on a curious mixture of pleasure and anxiety, bound up with a loss of control both satisfying and destabilizing. Following Mulvey, we might suggest that one way to deal with such ambiguity is through the inclusion of an aggressively active on-screen double, allowing what is a doubly dangerous structure—the passive male viewer gazing at the image of the man on screen—to be reconfigured as an apparent projection of an *active* male viewer's gaze through his on-screen double onto woman as image.[113] Yet what we will see in the films examined here is that this structure repeatedly reveals its own inconsistencies, representing the limitations of the viewer's power through male protagonists who are challenged and are never entirely able to reassert themselves. In this, these films come closer to the model presented by Clover, who suggests that horror films stage an *apparently* powerful male gaze assigned to the "monster" and connected to the camera, only to punish it in the cinematic resolution: "What is striking about this male gaze . . . is how often it remains at the level of wish or threat—how seldom it carries through with its depredations and, even when it does succeed, how emphatically it is then brought to ruin."[114] Like that of Clover's on-screen monsters and killers, the male gaze in the films examined here is often proven unsuccessful. This is not due to its being attributed to those figures in the film who must be destroyed, but rather is connected to a construction of masculinity as fragmented and (temporarily) disempowered. Elsaesser suggests that "power relations are equated with a voyeuristic structure, via a hierarchy of gazes and views. But the gaze and power also encompass another pole, the pleasure of constituting oneself as the object of someone's look."[115] While this notion seems to me problematic in that it draws on that same binary ascribing the gaze to man and implicitly relegating woman to the position of object and thus replicates a tendency to deny even the existence of a gaze gendered female, it nevertheless points to the complexity of the film/spectator relationship in the Weimar era, for Elsaesser is clearly grappling with a sense of the *mitigated* power of the masculine gaze. And certainly, this notion of *some* element of power associated with the construction of the self as image is one that I will discuss in relation to the films here examined.

Existing theoretical models thus raise significant questions as to the way in which gender might be connected to the structures of Weimar film and power might be implicated in the dynamics of spectator and image therein. However, the models seem insufficient, given how complexly the construction of spectatorship and of cinema itself was gendered. Above all, these films point to historical specificity; rather than representing a universal and innate cinematic structure, the interplay of viewer and film, gaze and image in the films examined deploy narrative and cinematic strategies that respond to specific cultural anxieties in order to neutralize the danger posed to viewer and male protagonist. Further, the rhetoric employed by the critics of the time not only suggests that when examining Weimar cinema we might move beyond contemporary models in which the default viewer position is that of the powerful, active male spectator, but also that gender—already signifying sociocultural change on multiple levels—becomes as well a representation of cinema itself. In other words, in the films I examine in this study, where vision and power take center stage and seduction and emasculation are crucial terms, we can seek out meaning in terms not only of the real anxieties centered on changing gender norms at the time, but also of the role and structure of the developing medium.

UNCANNY FILMS, GENDER, AND THE DEVELOPING MEDIUM

In the choice of the films I examine, I focus very deliberately on films in which uncanny elements take center stage. These are not horror films as we define them today, for they engender more a *frisson* than the repulsion or fear that Noël Carroll points to as the audience's primary response to that genre;[116] nor are they all "tales of terror" as S. S. Prawer might deem at least some of them.[117] Perhaps the closest genre might be "fantastic films," but this, too, seems to counter the ways in which some of these films function. Nevertheless, the work that scholars have done on the horror film and related genres carries certain important points of contact with this study, particularly in the various ways in which they have pointed to the cultural specificity of the "monsters" that populate the genre and the potential for these to be read symbolically and in their theorizations of the relationship, if any, between horror and the uncanny. On one end, we see critics like Carroll, who, in *The Philosophy of Horror*, stipulates that it is the presence of "monsters" who are defined as "impure" that characterizes horror;[118] on the other, we see those like David J. Russell, who criticizes Carroll as well as the similarly symbolic work of Robin Wood as being guilty of oversimplification, the former because of his emphasis on the "fantastic biology" of the monster and concomitant exclusion of the "psycho-killer" that populates slasher films,[119] the latter because his process of "conflating the related but certainly not identical themes of (cultural) monsters and (social) Others and boiling them down into a single condensed and overarching theme of politicized and homogenized sexual Otherness" is "reductive" and "too literal."[120] While the work of Carroll and Wood is limited in its applicability here, it nevertheless offers some parallel to mine, in that I read the uncanny elements of these films as symbols of fears based concretely in social change. Still, the films on which I focus are decidedly not horror films, and thus fall into a group that Carroll, Wood, and Russell specifically exclude from their analyses. Other scholars have recognized the significance of the uncanny to the horror genre. Steven Schneider views horror as fundamentally related to the Freudian uncanny by "reconfirming for audiences infantile beliefs that were abandoned long ago" and deploying monsters that are "metaphorical embodiments" of these beliefs while being "historically and culturally contingent."[121] Schneider suggests that horror is founded not on castration anxiety but on "previously surmounted beliefs."[122] In this emphasis, Schneider's analysis parallels my reading of the transgressive woman as a "monstrous" figure that stands in for cultural anxieties associated with changing gender norms that render woman (and man) uncanny. Similarly, in his *Caligari's Children: The Film as Tale of Terror*, S. S. Prawer notes the significance of the uncanny in films that aimed to frighten. Prawer suggests that the films he examines—which include *Caligari* and others of the Weimar era—should be termed "terror film" and notes the specifically German roots of the genre:

> It was, in fact, the Germans, in the years just following the First World War, who most forcibly showed the world—with films like *Caligari, Dr. Mabuse the Gambler* (1922), *Waxworks* (1924), and *(Warning) Shadows* (1924)—the powerful attraction tales of terror could exert in the cinema even on the sophisticated. The early German film-makers were able to do this not only because the mood of the time favoured the evocation of uncanny fears . . . but also because they had a rich heritage of demonic folklore, Gothic fiction, and black Romanticism on which to draw for their themes, and because the artistic and literary movements subsumed under the general heading of "Expressionism" had furnished a style of acting and scene-design that proved admirably suited to the translation of these Romantic themes into terms of the silent film.[123]

While Prawer's analysis perhaps does not go far enough in explaining *why* "the mood of the time favoured the evocation of uncanny fears" and allowed for the predominance of the "rich heritage" of uncanny imagery—much like, as Kaes points out, Eisner's *Haunted Screen* did not "account for the reemergence of [romantic] motifs in the Weimar Republic"[124]—it is nevertheless important because it offers a generic framework specific to the uncanny films of the Weimar era. He notes a fundamentally uncanny quality to film itself that might stem from the fact that "the image we see on the screen is a kind of spectral double, the simulacrum of landscapes and townscapes filled with human beings that seem to live, to breathe, to talk, and are yet present only through their absence. Their originals, indeed, may already be dead."[125] That cinema is built on this sort of "spectral double," its images already inherently "frightening" and uncanny, is evident in the films I analyze here and contributes to the way in which these uncanny films are particularly self-reflexive. Further, Prawer points to the social function of the films he analyzes: "The fantastic terror-film responds to a need one can also observe in any fairground: the need to be safely frightened, the need to test and objectify and come to grips with one's terrors in a setting of ultimate security."[126] Prawer thus identifies a central quality of these films that stage the fears and hopes bound up with changing gender norms, allowing the audience to "come to grips with [its] terrors" even as it revels in their flip side as fantasies and embodiments of women's hopes. Indeed, this concept of film as symbolic "fairground" suggests that it might function in Mikhail Bakhtin's sense of the carnivalesque, as a space of multiplicity, with the potential to signify on different levels and in different ways.[127]

While the critical engagement with horror films and related genres is not applicable wholesale to this analysis, it nevertheless presents certain significant ideas. In particular, these critics point to the idiosyncratic ways in which the genre enacts sociocultural anxieties, whether specific to a historical context or, as psychoanalytical readings would have it, applicable across cultures and moments. They offer a critical framework in terms of and against which I define my own. I see the uncanny films of the Weimar era as engaging with specific cultural anxieties, ones that are perhaps rooted in certain "primeval" fears that have been frequently expressed in terms of notions such as castration anxiety but that are nevertheless historically and contextually specific. While I do not want to undertake strictly psychoanalytical reading of these films, certain *terms* that Freudian psychoanalysis offers are important to my analysis—foremost, of course, his notion of the uncanny—not only because they offer a paradigm for the way in which we might read these films, but also because they were very much a part of cultural discourse in Weimar Germany and factored into the ways in which uncanny films were conceived of and structured.

In his essay "The Uncanny," Freud defined the term as "that class of the frightening which leads back to what is known of old and long familiar."[128] Citing Ernst Jentsch, Freud agrees, to a point, that one example of an uncanny representation is when, as in E. T. A. Hoffmann's "The Sandman," the reader is left in doubt as to whether a figure is alive or is an automaton.[129] In other words, the confusion between life and the semblance thereof evokes a response in the reader (or viewer). Another potentially uncanny construct is that embodied in the doppelgänger, where the individual "identifies himself with someone else, so that he is in doubt as to which his self is, or substitutes the extraneous self for his own. In other words, there is a doubling, dividing and interchanging of the self."[130] These concepts are especially applicable to early film, where we can see them as pointing toward the way in which the viewing experience might itself be uncanny; not only do the viewers experience the slippage between life and its appearance, seeing the characters moving on screen and yet knowing that this is an illusory reality, but they also, through the web of identifications and disavowals involved in the role of spectator, suffer the "doubling, splitting, and confusion of the self" that, at least momentarily, suggest a fracturing of subjectivity. Freud expands on his discussion, arguing that these examples are secondary and concluding that the uncanny is based in the return of the repressed: "If psycho-analytic theory is correct in maintaining that every affect belonging to an emotional impulse, whatever its kind, is transformed, if it is repressed, into anxiety, then among instances of frightening things there must be one class in which the frightening element can be shown to be something repressed which *recurs*."[131] Differentiating between the uncanny experience and the uncanny in art and literature, he notes: "An uncanny experience occurs either when infantile complexes which have been repressed are once more revived by some impression, or when primitive beliefs which have been surmounted seem once more to be confirmed."[132] In other words, the confrontation with that which has been overcome through development or maturation leads, according to Freud, to that experience of the uncanny.

The notion that the films I examine are uncanny in the sense in which Freud defines the term has important repercussions for the way we might read them; at the same time, I do not want to suggest that their significance can be exhausted by pointing to them as embodying a castration complex divorced from specific sociocultural context and historical moment, let alone from the medium of cinema. One potential model for such a use of the Freudian concept is Cynthia Freeland's reading of *The Double Life of Véronique* (*La double vie de Véronique*, Krzysztof Kieslowski, 1991), in which she attempts to reexamine the uncanny in its relationship to film, but focuses on its aesthetic implications and identifies thereby its relationship to the sublime and its inherent reflexivity. To Freeland, Freud effectively ignored the aesthetic implications of the uncanny[133] and elided an important characteristic: "The uncanny as Freud analyzes it seems wholly one-sided; pleasure in particular is missing."[134] This aesthetic and pleasurable dimension to the uncanny is crucial to Freeland, as is what she sees as its fundamentally self-reflexive quality: "The sublime is what a narrative shows without expressing, or what it indicates without spelling out—what is in the margins. Various literary theorists have discussed a similar function of "excess" in works by authors of the uncanny. . . . Reflexivity is crucial to both the sublime and the uncanny to explain their combined effects of pleasure and pain."[135] Freeland's analysis opens up possibilities for approaching uncanny films of the Weimar era. First, her notion that we need to recuperate the "pleasurable" aspect of the uncanny suggests the possibility that a single filmic moment might be read in multiple ways, might oscillate between anxiety and desire, fear and hope. In other words, pushing her reading further, this ambivalent quality of the uncanny suggests a special mode of appealing simultaneously to a diverse audience. If we seek out this "excess," that which is "in the margins," we can perhaps identify how these films attempted to speak to the complexity of the fears and desires they articulated, to respond to changing gender norms in terms of the masculine subject that might have feared loss of power and the feminine subject that might have hoped for positive emancipation. Further, Freeland's emphasis on the essential quality of "reflexivity" connects with my suggestions that in the uncanny films of the era, the intersection between the construction of woman-as-other and the development of cinematic tropes becomes most clear. On one level, uncanny elements in these films point to their parallels in the cinematic experience itself; the existence of moving images on screen, the semblance of life where there is none, exemplifies the uncanny. On another, these films draw on uncanny moments and elements in order to mask that which—culturally—embodies the quality: the notion of emancipated woman, woman reimagined in terms of a public role and new rights.

Taking this notion of oscillation and ambiguity into account, we can see that the films under discussion embody the uncanny in multiple ways. Perhaps most basically, the notion of woman as the threatening other draws on her position as "that which is long known and familiar"; she becomes the ultimate uncanny figure because of her primeval status as maternal body. By shifting her role, by destabilizing her identity and presenting her not in her guise as mother, but as challenger, as transgressor of boundaries and norms, she directly threatens the viewer. She embodies the uncanny that "proceeds from repressed infantile complexes, from the castration complex, womb-phantasies, etc."[136] In the woman who confronts the viewer in these films, the woman who contests masculine power and reveals the fault lines in the power structures assumed as stable and "natural," we see the return of these repressed fears: the physical embodiment of the castration complex and of the fantasies of the dangerous maternal body.

Beyond its function as a representation of what Weimar culture had effectively assimilated as an embodiment of masculine fears, the female body as the uncanny simultaneously masks and is masked by the uncanny that emerges from the experience of cinema. In this conflation between narrative, content, and form, we see both metafilmic reflection and embodiment of the cultural moment; this narrative constellation in which woman represents existential threat is uniquely suited to reflect on the form and structure of film, just as film is uniquely suited to dramatizing the way in which woman functions as such a threat. The uncanny in these films thus takes on a double function, arising out of the experience of watching a film and through the narratives and cinematic devices themselves. And indeed, contemporary discussions of the fantastic in film point toward an understanding of some fundamentally uncanny component to the medium. In 1919, one critic noted in *Film-Kurier* how any film evoked in him a sort of uncanny response:

> Even a bad film, which I fully realize to be kitschy and which annoys me with its tastelessness, acts like magic on my mood and feelings. Even if the piece plays in our usual reality, it is as though I were taking a trip to a different country, as though I were coming into a strange city in which I see people rush around and work without having anything to do with their actions, since I experience everything purely as a spectator. When I step back onto the street after the film, ordinary life, too, seems transformed and unreal. I think that the fascinating appeal of the cinema and its incredible attraction is based on this sense of being torn out of the usual, on this sudden transition from one reality into another.[137]

Two things are particularly interesting: first, the sense of the viewer as passive, experiencing the film "purely as a spectator"; second, the fact that film embodies a process of being "torn out of the usual," in which one moves suddenly "from one reality to another," and after which one finds even "real life" "transformed and unreal." And because the experience of cinema is based in this uncanny experience, this critic suggests that such narratives are particularly suited to the medium: "It is clear that the main desire of the movie-goer, this sensation of being distanced, is much more fully satisfied when the subject-matter, too, is fantastic and illusionary."[138] Three years later, another critic expounded on the need to develop a new sort of "fantastic film." To him, previous attempts to do so—including such highly esteemed works as *Caligari* and *The Golem* (*Der Golem, wie er in die Welt kam*, Wegener and Boese, 1920)—had been unsuccessful because they drew on literary models: "We have a fantastic in film, but one borrowed from literature. We reproduce the fantastic of E. T. A. Hoffmann, of Eichendorff, of Chamisso, of Meyrinck: an overly conscious, overly aware fantastic, in a naive, sub-conscious artistic sphere, namely in the sphere of film. That is the secret of the failure."[139] The suggestion that film functions on the level of the un- or subconscious is significant; in a sense, to watch a film means taking part in a "naive" process that represents a sort of return of a stage previously repressed or overcome and represents an innately uncanny experience.

Although audiences of the late 1910s and 1920s were certainly familiar with movies, the rapid changes in the medium during the time necessitated ever-new models for how to deal with the experience of watching a film. For one, the move from short and documentary movies to full-length narrative confronts the viewer more directly with his on-screen double, requiring identifications that would not be so central in nonnarrative films. In the late 1920s, the shift from silent to sound films represented yet another step toward creating a more faithful appearance of life on the screen. Robert Spadoni has noted the way in which the experience of the viewer in the early years of film paralleled, in certain fundamental ways, that of the viewer of early sound film. Drawing on Yuri Tsivian's notion of the "medium-sensitive viewer," Spadoni suggests that the coming of the sound film increased the audience's awareness of film as a production to a level similar to that in the spectators of early film:

> The addition of synchronized sound triggered perceptions of ghostly figures in a shadowy world, just as the addition of movement had when, at the first Lumière screenings, the projected still photograph that opened the show was cranked suddenly to life. At

both times, the discursive element that was new raised awareness of the remaining silences and blank spots in the total sensory package, and the perceptions that could result had the power to infiltrate and counteract viewers' sense of the general advancement of the medium towards greater realism.[140]

Spadoni's analysis supports my suggestion that the moviegoer in Weimar Germany was quite aware of the technical elements that make up film. Cinema might well have represented an approximation of the real, but it was never perceived as identical. Spadoni locates the primary effect of cinema at the two historical points he compares in the uncanny, suggesting that in spite of the many differences between the respective receptions of early silent and early sound film,

at both times, conflicting perceptual cues clashed in the minds of viewers, who were trying to make sense of a new representational technology. At both times, a possible outcome of their effort was to find the filmic world altered in a way that made it appear uncanny. And at the dawn of the sound era, both the immediate and the ingrained centrality of the human figure within the viewing experience guaranteed that the foremost manifestation within the freshly resurrected ghost world of the cinema would be an uncanny body.[141]

His contention that film of the era produced an inherently uncanny experience connects to and supports much of my analysis. The very process of attempting to replicate "life" on the screen becomes an uncanny project. And if the primary uncanny element in film is the representation of life where there is none, the illusion of the human body on the screen, then the films I examine both mask and thematize this in a particularly interesting way, evoking a doubly strong reaction through narrative and experience of film. In staging narratives that hinge on elements intended to provoke discomfort and shock in the audience, these films stage the process of spectatorship itself, even while displacing that uncanny moment into their narratives. In other words, we might regard these films as exceptionally self-referential in that the very response they aim to evoke through their narrative is that which their form inherently evokes.

What we find is effectively a mise en abyme in which narrative, mise-en-scène, central image of the emancipated woman, and experience as spectator all evoke the uncanny and refer back to one another. Thus the resolutions of these films—the overcoming on the visual and narrative levels of the threat implied by all of these elements—represent a restabilization of spectatorial control and an assimilation of these uncanny elements. And the particular form that these resolutions so often take—the repositioning of woman as absolute object-to-be-looked-at, as passive image displayed for the enjoyment and consumption of the viewer—represents not only the reimposition of conservative gender norms but also the affirmation of a visual economy in which the audience retains control over the images on the screen. In other words, I want to suggest that the films I examine here, because of their uncanny content, serve to address not only questions of gender and subjectivity but also of the cinematic medium; we see strongly metafilmic elements in each of the films I examine. I go to these films in hopes less of discovering a single, coherent "explanation," a way of reading their engagement with gender as either revolutionary or reactionary, and more in order to begin to answer certain questions that will inevitably open up more. Why do these films grapple as they do with questions of gender identity? What role does the audience play? How is its relationship with the image on the screen imagined and how does it actually play out? How do men and women respond to the new sociocultural order? And why are these questions of gender and social roles, of relationships between individuals, of subjectivity itself so bound up with the way in which film develops? Why do they reappear in narratives that are couched so consistently in uncanny terms? Can we see these connections—between gender, subjectivity, the uncanny, and cinema—as furthering our understanding of the way in which modernity constructs identity, in which the very existence of cinema changed the way in which identity and the self were conceptualized? I will begin by turning to a film that stands simultaneously at the end of Wilhelmine film and the beginning of Weimar cinema, Ernst Lubitsch's *The Eyes of the Mummy* (*Die Augen der Mumie Mâ*, 1918).

TWO

THE EYES OF THE MUMMY (DIE AUGEN DER MUMIE MÂ, ERNST LUBITSCH, 1918)

From the Monster with the "Eyes That Live" to the Passive Object of the Male Gaze

> The Unionpalast is showing The Eyes of the Mummy (Union), an exotic, mystical film which evokes strong and justified interest in its audience.... The film, directed by Ernst Lubitsch with remarkable aptitude for the cinematic, unrolls in a believably connected sequence of well-constructed, lively, and exciting images. Pola Negri plays the title role: her first work under her new contract with Union. Without a doubt she found in the felicitous direction the support that was able to lead her excellent acting abilities to their most effective. Emil Jannings and Harry Liedtke were no less good.[1]

IT MIGHT SEEM LIKE faint praise to extol the "believably connected sequence of well-constructed, lively, and exciting images" that makes up Ernst Lubitsch's first major dramatic movie, *The Eyes of the Mummy*, which premiered in Berlin on October 3, 1918. Still, this review, published in *Der Film*, one of the leading German cinema journals, gives us a sense of the popularity of a film that strikes the modern viewer as artistically and cinematically far less sophisticated than the better-remembered ones of the era. It also foregrounds Pola Negri's role in a way that makes clear the privileged position that woman—constructed as exotic other—occupies in the film, both as visual object and as actor. Indeed, *Eyes of the Mummy* exemplifies the point at which German cinema was located at the time of the film's release, for it represents an attempt to realize a full-length narrative film while drawing on new cinematic techniques and demonstrates the ways in which women were dealt with both as participants in the project and as constructions on the screen. *Eyes of the Mummy* is equally of stylistic interest because it draws on elements that characterized what Tom Gunning has termed the "cinema of attractions," the early film that is so fundamentally different from the narrative film that came to dominate cinema. That remnants of this film should surface in *Eyes of the Mummy* is not terribly unusual, as Gunning notes:

> The scenography of the cinema of attractions is an exhibitionist one, opposed to the cinema of the unacknowledged voyeur that later narrative cinema ushers in. This display of unique views belongs most obviously to the period before the dominance of editing, when films consisting of a single shot—both actualities and fictions—made up the bulk of film production. However, even with the introduction of editing and more complex narratives, the aesthetic of attraction can still be sensed in periodic doses of non-narrative spectacle given to audiences (musicals and slapstick comedy provide clear examples). The cinema of attractions persists in later cinema, even if it rarely dominates the form of a feature film as a whole.[2]

We find, in *Eyes of the Mummy*, a curious amalgamation of the qualities that Gunning sees as defining these two cinemas. In particular, the narrative itself is repeatedly interrupted by the title character's dance performances—which act as "periodic doses of non-narrative spectacle"—and the position of the viewer thus seems to oscillate between taking in an openly "exhibitionist" performance and acting as an "unacknowledged voyeur" to the scenes on screen. At the same time, these essentially nonnarrative moments are subsumed in the story and ostensibly narratively justified; the exhibitionism of these moments, in other words, is at least partially masked. The film's peculiar positioning, its status as a sort of (late) transitional piece, is important, for it demonstrates the way in which this early cinema attempted to come to terms with woman's position within the medium.

We need also to consider the impact of World War I on the film and on the burgeoning industry as a whole. The isolation the war imposed on the country forced—or allowed—the medium to develop its own conventions, techniques, and aesthetics, fully rejoining the international film world only after 1921, when the ban on imported films was lifted.[3] To some extent, the German film industry was left to its own devices in terms of constructing its visual language. With regard to women, this language was certainly informed by the ways in which they were figured in earlier art forms, but the unique circumstances of post–World War I Germany irrevocably shaped the way in which the new medium dealt with them. At the same time, in spite of the industry's relative isolation, Negri's top billing demonstrates that there was some level of internationalism in the German industry. Born in and having started her film career in Poland after an injury prevented her from continuing her training as a dancer,[4] Negri would become a star in Germany, one of Lubitsch's favored actors and the embodiment the exotic, alluring, and oft-dangerous woman. Her role in the film speaks to the peculiar position she occupied for a German audience, representing both an appealingly foreign and mysterious object of desire and the threat of someone *too* foreign, *too* fundamentally "other."

Might we not see *Eyes of the Mummy* as exemplifying a specifically German type of film, marking one of the end points of an era in which the industry was moving in its own direction, little affected by international—and, especially, Hollywood—conventions? In this sense, *Eyes of the Mummy* becomes an especially interesting object with which to begin this analysis. It represents a number of both "firsts" and "lasts": Lubitsch's first big-budget film, Negri's first film with the Union studio, one of the last films produced and released before the war had officially ended, one of the last films produced in an era in which Germany's film industry was still isolated from the rest of the world. For all its failings, *Eyes of the Mummy* is a fascinating object of study by virtue of its status as a sort of transitional object between two eras, two styles of filmmaking, and two phases of the careers of its director and stars.

Lubitsch's path to directing began with an acting career, first briefly on stage, as one of Max Reinhardt's actors at the *Deutsches Theater* in Berlin,[5] then as a character actor in short films, playing everything from "old-men roles" to "pubescent boys and eternal juveniles."[6] Although successful as an actor, Lubitsch was "increasingly frustrated" in that role and soon turned to directing as a way to increase his control over his career, beginning by writing, directing, and starring in comedies such as his first piece, *Miss Soapsuds* (*Fräulein Seifenschaum*, 1915).[7] His career as a director took off quickly, and he was soon churning out "an average of five to eight one- and two-reelers per year."[8] Lubitsch assembled a team made up of "the artistic and technical elite of the German cinema": Hanns Kräly, who collaborated with him on the screenplays for everything from *The Merry Jail* (*Das fidele Gefängnis*, 1917) to *Eyes of the Mummy* and *Passion* (*Madame Dubarry*, 1919); Theodor Sparkuhl, who did the camera work for the same films and many others; and a range of set designers, including Kurt Richter (*Eyes of the Mummy*, *Carmen* (1918), *Madame Dubarry*) and Paul Leni.[9] He did the same with his actors, repeatedly casting a small group of stars that included, beyond Negri, Ossi Oswalda, Harry Liedtke, and Emil Jannings.

The Eyes of the Mummy was intended to inaugurate Lubitsch's career as a dramatic director of "Sensationsdramen," big-budget films with star casts, expansive sets, and epic narratives. Yet in spite of the success of films like *Eyes of the Mummy* and *Sumurun* (1920), which again starred Pola Negri and Harry Liedtke, they were, in retrospect, not as determinative of his career as they might have been. When one thinks now of Ernst Lubitsch, these films are certainly not the first to spring to mind, nor, perhaps, are his successful early historical dramas, such as *Carmen* and *Passion*. Rather, Lubitsch's name is more likely to evoke his witty early comedies, like *My Lady Margarine* (*Die Austernprinzessin*, 1919) or *The Wildcat* (*Die Bergkatze*, 1921), or his later Hollywood productions, including *The Marriage Circle* (1924) and *To Be or Not to Be* (1942).

One reason why *Eyes of the Mummy* is so often overlooked when considering Lubitsch's body of work might be that it has not aged as well as have many of the other films: title and narrative seem to have little to do with each other, the filmmaking does not evoke the expressionist films most often associated with Weimar Germany, even Pola Negri's "exoticized" dance numbers strike the modern viewer as more amusing than erotic. In many ways, *Eyes of the Mummy*, to put it subjectively, just does not seem like a very good film. Even a relatively short fifteen years after its release, a reviewer, in response to a retrospective including it and *Erotikon* (Stiller, 1920), notes the amused response of the audience to the drama: "Naturally, nowadays we laugh at the fidgetiness of the exaggerated gestures and the state of the 'decor.' . . . The audience of the 'Kamera,' unencumbered by historical reminiscences, received the whole thing as a delicious joke."[10] By 1933, *Eyes of the Mummy* appeared dated, "primitive" by virtue of both its style and the locations and sets intended to evoke first Egypt, then Germany, as well as by its "pantomime acting," a style that, as Kristin Thompson has noted,[11] characterized German film well into the 1920s, but would certainly strike the audience of 1933, acclimatized to a model of cinematography more focused on facial expressions, as "fidgetiness."

Another factor in the limited modern estimation of the film might be its release at such a precarious moment in German history. It premiered on October 3, the day before Max von Baden sought an armistice with the American forces, taking the first political step toward the radical changes that would sweep the nation in November. *Eyes of the Mummy*, a film that stages a narrative of masculine domination and reaffirms traditional power structures involving nationality, gender, and ethnicity, was thus released at the precise moment in which the sense of national identity was dealt a crucial blow. Its narrative fundamentally involves a process of questioning Western masculine power: through the intrusion of the "Eastern man" and the dangerous, exotic woman into "civilized" European culture, the stability of masculine identity is attacked. However conservatively it might be resolved, the film, given the historical context, reinforces the prevalent anxieties of the historical moment and presents in its resolution a jarring contrast to the realities of social and cultural change with which the German population was faced. It might well have functioned as an escapist fantasy,[12] but the sheer incongruence between fantasy and reality certainly would draw attention to the traumatic present in a troubling way.

The Eyes of the Mummy articulates certain anxieties that predate the end of the war and casts a new light on those dominating the moment of its release. It is a piece that allows us to trace the origins of these anxieties—in particular of those fears bound up with shifting gender roles—and to pinpoint certain developments in these fears and the manner in which they were dealt with in postwar films. In the construction of the female lead, *Eyes of the Mummy* points back to early cinematic conventions, demonstrating how they changed over the course of the Weimar Republic. Hake suggests this connection between the female leads in many of Lubitsch's early films and early filmic traditions: "The association between woman and spectacle, as well as the close links between the camera, the object, and the look, are residues of an earlier 'cinema of attractions.'"[13]

In terms of its genre, *Eyes of the Mummy*, though no real horror film even in the sense of films like *Caligari* and *Nosferatu*, evokes a framework of the uncanny through its title and initial premise. It addresses anxieties bound up with shifting understandings of the self in terms of gender and national identity by thematizing and playing with structures of the gaze. It derives its tension not from that original danger embodied in the mummy's gaze but rather from the depiction of the process by which that danger is neutralized, the "monster" subjugated and, unavoidably, destroyed through being repositioned as the object of the gaze. The eponymous heroine may well start out capable of exerting dangerous power over the men at whom she gazes, but she ends "tamed," the passive object of the spectators and the victim of the hypnotic gaze of her nemesis, the obsessively jealous Radu (Emil Jannings). In staging this transition, the film not only engages with cultural anxieties revolving around gender, national identity, and social change, but also takes part in and shapes cinematic conventions, in that it thematizes and stages the "classic" convention of woman as object of the (voyeuristic) gaze of both male characters and audience, even while suggesting the fatal consequence of such a position.

That this fatal gaze is embodied in the hypnotic relationship between Radu and Mâ puts *The Eyes of the Mummy* into a group of films that includes such canonical works as *The Cabinet of Dr. Caligari* and *Dr. Mabuse, the Gambler* (*Dr. Mabuse, der Spieler*, 1922) and connects to a very real sociocultural concern. As Paul Lerner notes, hypnosis was originally seen as a useful tool in combating war neurosis, but then quickly became a source of both entertainment and anxiety as it moved from medical practice and became "a popular street-level phenomenon" in which performers showcased their abilities by hypnotizing audience volunteers, generally women.[14] Lerner sees hypnosis and the governmental classification of it as a sort of social scourge as indicative of larger trends in German culture at the time:

> A practice with the potential to destabilize the relationship between mind and body, hypnosis highlighted issues of individual will, medical power and social order in a period of terrifying transition. The campaign against hypnosis performances, I will argue, reflected a deep concern with re-establishing the professional and scientific status of psychiatry after the war and with asserting medical control and agendas over a populace deemed pathologically vulnerable to nervous illness, criminal behaviour and sexual depravity.[15]

Lerner's suggestion carries interesting implications for *The Eyes of the Mummy* and for cinema as a whole. The eponymous Mâ, controlled by Radu's hypnotic gaze, comes to stand in for a population "deemed pathologically vulnerable" to immorality. At the same time, what characterized the victim of hypnosis was, Lerner notes, a set of symptoms that are essentially the same as those of war neurosis: "blindness, states of semi-consciousness, acceleration of the outbreak of mental illnesses, states of panic, all kinds of psychogenic nervous disorders . . . states of agitation which necessitate admission to an asylum, and hypnosis-addiction."[16] Over the course of the film, Mâ suffers from precisely such symptoms as she endures and eventually succumbs to Radu's power. She becomes symbolic of both the larger, morally vulnerable German population and the specifically male victim of war neurosis, a notion that complicates the gender dynamics of this apparently straightforward film.

Lerner's examination of hypnosis focuses on its simultaneous status as medical treatment and dangerous entertainment form, but hypnosis is equally associated with cinema itself. As Kaes notes in connection with his examination of *The Cabinet of Dr. Caligari*, "the filmmaker as hypnotist, sideshow entrepreneur, and psychiatrist: Caligari lays out a panorama of the conflicting roles film artists assumed in the early years of cinema. His hypnotizing gaze controls his medium and his audience, recreating the trance state of film viewing itself, and situating cinema at the juncture of science, magic, and trickery."[17] *Eyes of the Mummy*, however straightforward it might appear, thus participates in a cinematic discourse that is necessarily self-reflexive and that recurs frequently in Weimar film; indeed, it is evident in different form in *Warning Shadows*. Even more than *Caligari*, Lubitsch's piece figures the potential danger of cinema by associating the power of the

The Eyes of the Mummy

gaze and thus of film with the unrelentingly "evil" character of Radu. Yet Radu is both evil and comic, by virtue of the exaggerated gestures and the "broadness" of Janning's acting. Given Lubitsch's background in comedy, it is difficult not to see these elements of Radu's character as intentional, and perhaps as the result of a certain self-deprecation; if Radu is the stand-in for the director, he wields a powerful, potentially fatal gaze but equally becomes a target of ridicule. Here in a nutshell the predicament of film in the era: simultaneously the source of great anxiety—when viewed as a potential corruptor of the populace—and of derision—when situated as the ultimate embodiment of "low" popular culture.

Eyes of the Mummy should thus be considered in view of its historical moment, its potential metafilmic significance, and its surprisingly complex gender relationships. How did this film appeal to its audience? How did it speak—perhaps very differently—to the men whose familiarity with war neurosis might lead them to identify with the stricken Mâ even as their anxiety about their own changing roles might cause them to revel in her abjection as well as to the women whose awareness of their own precarious situation might push an identification with the tragic title character? The film aims to appeal to a wide audience; it focuses on a young painter, Wendland (Harry Liedtke), who, while visiting Egypt, seeks out a burial chamber purportedly haunted by the mummy "Mâ," in spite of being warned that such a visit has proven "verhängnisvoll" to all others. Shown the mummy (Negri) by a ragged attendant, Radu (Jannings), Wendland discovers that these "dangerous eyes" in fact belong to a young woman who was abducted and held by Radu. He frees her and takes her to Germany, where she becomes a celebrated *Varieté* (vaudeville) dancer. Radu, obsessed with reasserting his power over her, insinuates himself into the services of Prince Hohenfels (Max Laurence), with whom the painter is acquainted, and pursues Mâ, who suffers under the mysterious control he continues to exert over her. After seeing Mâ at one of her performances and subsequently mutilating the portrait of her, painted by Wendland, that Hohenfels purchased, Radu seeks her out and—through little more than his "hypnotic" stare—kills her. Suddenly distraught, he then commits suicide, just as Wendland and the prince burst in to try to save Mâ.

The Eyes of the Mummy received enthusiastic reviews; as Kristin Thompson notes, it was "a hit."[18] *Paimann's Filmlisten* described Lubitsch's work as a "Sensationsdrama," summarizing the action by noting that Wendland "visited the tomb of Queen Mah in Egypt, overpowered the guard, Radu, and abducted the Indian woman Mah [sic] whom Radu held captive, later marrying her in Europe," only to see Radu recognize "his escaped Mah [sic]" and kill her.[19] Another reviewer called it "an exotic cinematic play, carried by its mystical tension."[20] And a critic in the *Lichtbild-Bühne* praised its "very interesting subject that forms the basis of the film and gave the actors the possibility to develop their advanced artistic abilities" and noted that the audience was "entirely under the spell of the grandiose acting by Pola Negri."[21] What is striking about these contemporary reviews is that they focus on the "exotic" and "mystical" nature of the film while virtually ignoring the bulk of the action dedicated to the fashioning of Mâ as spectacle, a process intimately connected to the very structures of film. The notion that Wendland "abducts" Mâ seems to get closer to the questions of control and agency addressed in the film, while the last critic's mention that the audience was "under the spell" of the heroine echoes Mâ's admission of having been "im Banne," "under the spell" of Radu, and touches implicitly on the dominant theme of the power dynamics in the relationship between viewer and spectacle. Yet the reviews are marked, chiefly, by their inability to coherently summarize the action and theme of the film, speaking in generalities more to the atmosphere and mood it generates than to the desires and anxieties it evokes.

These contemporary reviews make clear that *The Eyes of the Mummy* falls outside of—or straddles—multiple genres; it is titled and begins like a horror film, then shifts to a romance with a bit of costume- and theater-drama thrown in, and ends as a tragedy. We might see this as characteristic of such early films. Berenstein notes the fluidity of genre in early cinema, suggesting that in terms of structure and of reception, early horror film might most productively be viewed "in cross-generic terms."[22] Indeed, as Berenstein suggests, we can see *Eyes of the Mummy* as a film that integrates crucial uncanny elements and "mystical" structures with drama. More importantly, Berenstein draws attention to the relationship between power and the gazes exchanged by the figures in the films she examines. She suggests, in examining what she terms the subgenre of "hypnosis films," that "the looks shared between characters, especially the monster and heroine, are this sub-genre's favorite mode of communication. . . . Seeing is constructed as both powerful and terrifying. When looks are exchanged, vision is equated with possession and acts of seeing and being seen play out flip sides of a monstrous power dynamic."[23] *Eyes of the Mummy*, in terms of narrative and structure, fits neatly into this category. In Radu's gaze at Mâ—and in those of the men around her and the viewer—"vision is equated with possession"; she becomes an eroticized and commoditized image. The reversal of the initially suggested positions—Mâ's systematic objectification and the revelation that she is in fact the doomed object of Radu's gaze—serves to reassert power over the other represented in terms of gender and culture. On the one hand, the film reasserts a conservative, European, masculine power in a setting in which Mâ represents a transgressive femininity that, though erotically appealing, must ultimately be destroyed. On the other hand, the explicit evocation of the power dynamics at play in the network of gazes constructed and the complication of the structures of identification force the viewers to confront and reflect on their relationship to the filmic image.

The title establishes the expectation that Mâ represents a danger: the audience is primed to encounter a mummy, one of the "horrific monsters" that "violate our categories of things" by being both "living and dead at the same time."[24] But the film, from its first image, defies this literal interpretation of the titular monster, instead substituting Mâ, who is positioned as exotic and beautiful, rather than in any overt way "monstrous." Even before the film opens with its first act,[25] we are introduced to the central character; the opening credits close with an intertitle first teasing "Mâ . . ." and then a next announcing "Mâ: Pola Negri," after which the film cuts to a medium profile shot of Negri, wearing a fur coat and hat, turning to look toward the audience, then lowering her eyes.[26] The theme of the gaze the title introduces is referenced in her pointed refusal to look directly into the camera (and "at" the viewer). With Negri arranged against a backdrop that echoes the darkness of her clothing, the lighting spotlights and thus emphasizes her face and eyes. In this brief opening shot, she is already put on display, positioned as a virtually static object of contemplation. The movement of her head and eyes—teasingly suggesting, then denying the viewer eye contact—emphasizes her status as one who is looked at, rather than one who looks, even as the lighting, which draws attention not to her body but rather to her face and eyes, again points to the filmic evocation of her potentially dangerous gaze. Because the shot falls outside of the narrative, pointing forward to Mâ's eventual "integration" into Western society, it suggests a self-referential element in the film; the shot is one of both Negri and Mâ, drawing attention to the way in which actor and character share a common status, functioning as an eroticized image that attracts (and, as we shall see, simultaneously threatens) the viewer's gaze.

The opening shot also places the emphasis squarely on Negri as the star of the film. In this sense, *Eyes of the Mummy* reflects on the business of cinema itself, for Mâ's arrival in Germany and her fashioning as a star parallels to some degree Negri's own story. The opening image of star-as-character suggests Negri/Mâ's function as both character and actor: she is the central visual of the film, the image that engenders pleasure in the spectators and around which the narrative circulates. The film stages Negri as image within a narrative focused on the staging of Mâ as the same; in its revelation of the fatal result of this staging, it thus profits from the visual appeal of woman-as-object even as it exposes the dangers of this functionalization.

Negri's career in Germany, fundamentally shaped by her status as other, as an exotic import into the dominant, Western European culture, in many ways exemplifies those dangers. Born in Lipno, Poland, as Barbara Apollonia Chalupic, Negri came to Germany during World War I and quickly became a star who drew large audiences. She tended to be cast as "an exotic, threatening woman,"[27] always already identified by her origin, marked as diametrically opposed to the dominant notion of German-ness. This quality of otherness made her a star and also positioned her as a threat: "Those roles that made Negri a star . . . tended to emphasize her guile and her primitivism and to link strongly these attributes and her broad destructive influence to a vaguely ethnic and regional identity."[28] In other words, Negri came to embody the vamp, representing, in her "exotic, almost oriental eroticism," one of these "sexual phantasms" that so dominated the cultural imaginary in Germany of the 1910s and 1920s and that was so potentially disturbing that it need be destroyed; her function as "the ultimate Other . . . explains the numerous aggressive impulses against her."[29] Here, again, the line between actor and character blur; her function as "the ultimate Other" is what defines Negri and what serves as the central danger in *Eyes of the Mummy*.

Even before the narrative proper begins, *Eyes of the Mummy* reflects on the centrality of woman as image and danger and points outside of itself to the real sociocultural structures that are implicated in film. The film continues to develop this theme in its opening intertitle, which explains that "the young painter Albert Wendland is on a study trip in Egypt"[30] and thereby suggests the disruptive quality of Mâ, whose appearance quickly subverts the original aim of the trip, then introduces that same disruption visually in the first narrative sequence, fading in to a long shot of sandy hills, the landscape in Kalkberge-Rüdersdorf that stands in for the Egyptian sand dunes.[31] A figure moves into the frame, descending the hill at the center of the screen, then putting his hands on his hips as he ascends a slight rise toward the camera. We cut to a medium shot: this is Wendland, positioned facing the camera imperiously. The impression of authority that he exudes is emphasized by his markedly European and colonial dress. He wears dark slacks, a light jacket, and light hat, and holds a riding crop horizontally across his body. As he looks toward the camera, he moves slightly, as though he has caught sight of something that catches his interest, and we cut to a close-up of Mâ. She presents a very different image than in the opening shot; here, her clothing, jewelry, and loose hair mark her as "Orientalized," and she faces the camera with an anxious expression on her face as she steadies an amphora on her shoulder. As she draws back, startled, we cut back to a medium shot of Wendland, still standing at center frame, before cutting to a long shot of Mâ, who backs slowly away from the well and runs toward the rear of the frame. The sequence continues to cut back and forth between Wendland pursuing and the woman fleeing his pursuit, until he loses sight of her and the scene fades out.

The insertion of the opening shot of Mâ/Negri mitigates the viewer's expectation: if this is the dangerous "Mummy Mâ," as is suggested by the cut from opening credits to the image of Pola Negri, then the danger she poses is not expressed through any external monstrosity, but must reside in some other qualities. What defines her is her exoticism; Wendland encounters her as unfamiliar, alien, and mysterious, a sort of illusion or hallucination that he pursues through the foreign landscape. At the same time, the emphasis on Mâ's gaze at Wendland—repeated as she pauses to look back at him while fleeing—suggests that he, too, becomes a visual object. And within the setting that evokes the foreign, with its miniature "oasis" nestled among sand dunes, it is actually Wendland who appears incongruous. We might read this initial exchange of glances as the impetus for Wendland's pursuit of Mâ; the sight of her—more specifically, of her looking at him—represents a direct challenge to him. He becomes the object of Mâ's gaze as much as she becomes that of his. Here is the first challenge to his power: in this exchange of gazes, he is positioned as the other; his pursuit of Mâ represents the beginning of the process by which this "uncomfortable" configuration will be realigned.

If the opening scene presents Mâ as an object of fascination through her being positioned as other in terms of gender and culture, even while it already undermines the notion of woman as passive image, the next sequence reminds the viewer of the original expectation of a monstrous figure. The sequence takes place on an elegant hotel terrace, where Wendland overhears the hotel manager advising Fürst Hohenfels that "visiting Queen Mâ has in the past been fatal to all,"[32] indicating a "victim" of the "dead queen" as proof of this. The latter is presented wrapped in heavy blankets, his eyes unfocused and hands shaking as a nurse leans solicitously over him. After the manager and Hohenfels depart, Wendland approaches the invalid, asking him to relate his story. Turning slowly away from Wendland, the man seems initially only half-conscious, then starts up, his eyes wide: "The eyes are alive! The eyes are alive!"[33] He collapses back into his chair, unconscious.

Here we have the suggestion of a true monster: this "queen," whose "victim," significantly, seems to have been struck by her "living eyes" with a sort of blindness himself. Like the Medusa, she has an active gaze—one that challenges and ultimately destroys the power of the men on whom she turns it, thus simultaneously repositioning them as object and asserting her own power. In a sense, the film reveals immediately the very nature of that which is monstrous. Linda Williams, in discussing the significance of the female gaze in horror films, notes Stephen Heath's statement, "If the woman looks, the spectacle provokes, castration is in the air, the Medusa's head is not far off; thus, she must not look, is absorbed herself on the side of the seen."[34] While Williams focuses her analysis on "the woman's look at the monster," her recognition that this look "offers at least a potentially subversive recognition of the power and potency of a nonphallic sexuality" and is therein "threatening to male power" fits neatly with this present analysis.[35]

Monster and woman are temporarily fused, and both are endowed with a potentially destabilizing power of looking. Over the course of the film, the danger that Mâ represents in her act of looking is negated by assimilating her, as Heath suggests is the norm in horror films, "on the side of the seen."

At the same time, the emphasis in this moment on the fact that the eyes "are alive" suggests a second dimension to that which is monstrous about the mythical "Mumie Mâ": the gaze marks the shocking transition from death to life, from apparent inanimate object to living being. That which Mâ appears to be fulfills Carroll's definition of the monstrous; the danger she represents lies in her positioning between living and dead, between two categories that we view as natural and absolute.[36] This prospect of danger attracts Wendland, whose interest in the manager's story was piqued by the notion that seeing her would be "fatal," and whose encounter with her victim seems to infuse him with a decisive purpose. In the next crucial sequence, this emphasis on the danger caused by the line between living and dead, subject and object, will be borne out by the filmic representation of Mâ's "living eyes." Wendland, the proxy for the audience, seeks out Mâ's tomb, unimpressed by the warnings he is given while searching for a guide in a Cairo market. Displaying a nonchalance that contrasts markedly with the superstition of the locals, who are epitomized by a man who refuses at all price to act as Wendland's guide and by the crowd that gathers to watch the simplistic performance of a magician, Wendland finally convinces a young man to supply him with a horse and direct him to the tomb. His visit there marks the beginning of the second act, which opens with a long shot set in front of the ostensible burial chamber. In the sand in front of a narrow door flanked by a statue of a seated pharaoh and various bits of rubble, Radu, dressed in shabby, "Eastern" clothes, is sleeping. He slowly rises, yawning and stretching, then starts and looks into the distance before dropping to press his ear against the ground and listen. A series of shots-countershots shows us Wendland approaching on horseback as Radu prepares for his arrival by summoning Mâ and ordering her to prepare for the visitor. Once Wendland arrives, Radu mimes the "expected" behavior of the social inferior, partially covering his face before lowering his hand and looking up at the European.

On one level, this scene is particularly interesting in that it reveals the crude construction of the other. Jannings draws on a hodgepodge of

CHAPTER TWO

FIGURE 1. "Queen Mâ" with her "eyes that live"

stereotypes in performing the imagined non-European: his face made up to indeterminate darkness, his gestures recalling everything from the stereotype of the impoverished street urchin to that of the Native American who judges the distance of the approaching rider by pressing his ear to the ground. Above all, Radu's depiction serves to contrast with that of Wendland; the latter, shown astride a horse within a large open space, becomes a powerful symbol of the European colonizer, purportedly born to rule over characters like the "abject" Radu.

Beyond demonstrating the fundamentally problematic way in which the cultural other is conceptualized, this moment reveals the real identity of the "mummy" and thereby shifts the source of the narrative tension. The audience is made aware of Radu's deception and of Mâ's involvement even before Wendland is; consequently, the first sight of "Mâ," the mythical dead queen with the living eyes, has little shock value. Almost as soon as Wendland enters the tomb, he discovers Radu's subterfuge and Mâ's true identity. As Radu shows him into the chamber, holding a torch to illuminate the paintings on the walls and what appears to be a narrow sarcophagus set into the rear wall, Wendland moves about, hands on hips, apparently unimpressed. In a medium shot, Radu, half-crouched before the young European, who looks down at him sternly, gestures toward the sarcophagus; we then cut to a close-up of a rough face mask, in which the eyes slowly open, looking into the camera (fig. 1). Cutting back and forth between Wendland, Radu, and the mysterious mask, the sequence emphasizes Radu's cunning—and Wendland's superiority. When Wendland suddenly runs toward the mask, Radu drops the torch in his hand and attacks him, but his plan proves fruitless. After a brief struggle, Wendland pushes Radu to the

FIGURE 2. The real Mâ, fixed by Wendland's rational gaze

ground, takes out a gun, and fires a shot. As Radu remains collapsed on the ground, Wendland again approaches the sarcophagus and peers through one of the now empty eye holes, as the sequence cuts to a matted point-of-view shot of Mâ, cowering against a wall, one hand clutching her throat protectively (fig. 2).

Once again, this sequence emphasizes the hierarchical positioning of the main male characters; though Radu might be crafty, he is no match for Wendland's intellect, courage, and the modernity represented by the gun. We have, thus, an interesting configuration: the two men involved in the triangulated relationship in which Mâ is the third term are by no means represented as equals. As we will see, both deploy powerful gazes, yet they do so in very different ways, a fact that echoes their very different power positions. In relation to Mâ, this scene works on the narrative level and the profilmic level to dispel the danger originally suggested by the story of "Queen Mâ." In terms of the story, it repositions her as the victim of a man's power, asserting masculine subjectivity and undermining the notion of a threatening other. It reveals Mâ to be no more than an object, staged by Radu, performing a simulation of power. The details of camera work and editing affirm and expand on this. Perhaps most significantly, the two key images are presented from the point of view of Wendland. First, when Mâ opens her eyes, the viewer experiences this, as does Wendland, as an uncanny moment in which he is confronted by a gaze where there should be none. When Wendland then looks into the hidden room, he again stands in for the viewer as the sequence reveals the threatening gaze to be as empty as the eye hole of the mask through which the camera looks and affirms Mâ—more specifically, her frightened, yet eroticized body—as object of the gaze. The fact that the matting emphasizes Wendland's position—he looks at her unseen, through a circular opening that mimics the camera's lens—implicitly draws a parallel between his position and that of the audience, suggesting the dominance of his subjectivity and the inherently cinematic nature of the relationship between object and viewer.

The visually striking moment in which Mâ opens her eyes behind the mask is further interesting in that, as S. S. Prawer notes, it foreshadows that moment in Wiene's *The Cabinet of Dr. Caligari* when Cesare is first presented to the carnival spectators.[37] There, the audience sees a close-up of Cesare in his box as he, in response to Caligari's command, struggles to open his eyes, then raises his hands and steps out of his box, blank stare fixed in the camera. To Prawer, who relates Cesare to both zombie and automaton, "Cesare is a tragic figure in a way the robot can never be. He is a human being robbed of an essential part of his humanity: his consciousness and his will. He is a human dreamer forced, by a malevolent agency, to lose himself in his dream."[38] Similarly, Mâ—initially presented as a danger to the men at whom she gazes—ultimately is revealed to be quite the opposite; like Cesare, she has neither "consciousness" nor "will" of her own but rather finds herself under the control of Radu's "malevolent agency." Yet in spite of this parallel, we see a crucial difference in the way that she, as compared to Cesare, is constructed, a difference we might trace to the qualities gender roles prescribe; for Mâ might well be the victim of Radu's machinations, yet she is not positioned as tragic in the manner that Cesare is. She is the victim of Radu's control (and, equally, of her objectification as performer and subject of Wendland's painting), but her status as object of desire is essentially a component of her identity as woman. It is through initially appearing to challenge this passive role—through her apparent power as the "deadly mummy queen," through her status as "other" once in Europe, and through her transgression of norms of Western, conservative gender behavior, embodied in her eroticized dance—that she precipitates her fatal end.

Where Cesare goes on to murder and terrorize, acting out Caligari's anger toward the denizens of Holstenwall, any violence associated with Mâ will be directed inward. She quickly reveals her true identity to Wendland in a moment that reinforces her transformation into the object of a controlling male gaze. After Wendland breaks into the hidden room, Mâ first cowers in a corner, then runs to him, hands folded imploringly as she drops to her knees in front of him. The man reassures her, then leads her toward the bed in the corner of the room, where he sits next to her and grasps her hands as he asks who she is. His question—"Who are you, girl?"[39]—emphasizes her position of powerlessness and asserts his dominance in terms of gender, power, and culture, as he addresses her with the informal "you" and calls her a "girl." Her story is shown in flashback: we see Mâ in a medium, slightly high-angle shot as she stands in knee-deep water, wringing out a cloth. The film cuts to a long shot of the same scene, showing Radu leading a white horse into the shot and toward her. After a brief struggle, Mâ loses consciousness and Radu puts her on his horse. The film cuts to a medium shot of Radu on the animal, holding the unconscious woman in front of him as he rides away.

The representation of Mâ's abduction positions her as object; she loses all agency as Radu claims her. The high-angle shot showing her alone as she washes her clothes and the fact that she faints emphasizes her powerlessness. What is striking is the odd ambiguity of the sequence; the details, in particular Radu's arrival on the white horse, push the moment to read like a twisted restaging of the fantasy of a knight arriving on a white horse. A second flashback makes clear that Mâ has essentially become Radu's possession. We see a long shot of Mâ stretched on the bed, her head on Radu's lap as he caresses her. As she wakes up, she rises slowly, looking confusedly around the room, then, turning toward Radu, draws back in terror. He falls to his knees and kisses her hands, but she struggles away from him. Yet Mâ does not get far; Radu grabs her hand, then pulls her toward him, now looming over her and saying, as she falls to her knees in front of him: "I will do without your love, but from now on you will do as I command!"[40] He raises her up, their gazes locked. Mâ responds as though hypnotized; her body becomes rigid, she drops her hands and sits down on the bed in front of him.

The fantasy of control that is staged in this moment is a peculiar one, at once clearly framed as immoral, as the abduction is orchestrated by a character figured as despicable, and erotic, as Radu's gaze at Mâ stands in for that of the viewer and thus enables him to exert control over her. In the scene in the burial chamber, where first Radu is positioned on his knees in front of Mâ, then she takes this position before him, we see a rapid reversal of power dynamics, a suggestion that on the one hand, Radu is subject to her beauty, while on the other, she becomes subject to him once he has claimed her. That his control over her is the more powerful is evoked by Mâ's statement to Wendland: "Since that day I am under his spell."[41] Radu's control over Mâ, imposed through his gaze, reveals the potentially dangerous power structures implicit in the relationship between the bearer and the object of the gaze. And through implicating the viewer of the film in Radu's look at Mâ as a desired object, the moment points back at the cinematic process, drawing attention to the problematic structures of that relationship and to the viewer's participation therein.

Although superficially Wendland's discovery of Mâ is figured as her rescue, there are key parallels between the depiction of Mâ's abduction by Radu and the couple's flight that suggest that she has simply exchanged one form of subjugation for another, and that imply a certain similarity between Radu and Wendland. After the second flashback fades out, Mâ collapses on her savior's lap, weeping, before he raises her up again, promising never to leave her. We then cut to a long shot of the room as Wendland helps her toward the exit, then to an exterior shot as he gets on his horse and helps her climb up in front of him. There is a clear parallel in the way in which the two events are presented; here, too, Mâ is little more than an object that Wendland takes with him. Mâ's repulsed behavior toward Radu—her falling at his knees and clawing at him as she realizes her imprisonment—is curiously doubled in her response to Wendland when he first enters the tomb to "free" her, and certainly the moment in which they ride away, just as Radu rode away with her, draws a connection between the two events. The similarities between the two scenes underline those between her relationships with the respective men. However willingly Mâ might accompany Wendland, however openly she displays her desire for him, she nevertheless is as much his "creation" as she is that of Radu. Where her first abductor constructed her role as the threatening mummy queen, her savior constructs it as that of the exotic object of desire; in both cases, her true identity is lost behind the image staged by the men who dominate her and put her on display.

Mâ's progressive transformation once rescued shows that she continues to be defined by the ways in which men construct her identity. While Radu, enraged at having lost her, chases the couple into the desert, only to collapse and be found by Hohenfels, who agrees to take him on as a servant, Wendland returns to Europe with Mâ. On the boat, we see him modeling European behavior for her; though she is still dressed in the Eastern clothes in which he first encountered her, Mâ awkwardly mimics his way of drinking tea, then, to his amusement, eats a cube of sugar. Like in the opening scene in which Mâ first encountered Wendland, here we see another instance of Mâ's gaze at Wendland, constructed explicitly as the gaze of an "other" onto the on-screen proxy for the viewer. Her attempt to mimic his behavior in order to assimilate to his culture suggests that culture itself is a sort of stage persona, albeit one that she does not succeed in emulating. Yet if Mâ's observation of Wendland is an attempt on her part to seize control of how she herself is constructed, it fails quickly, as we see in the subsequent scene.

This sequence, the beginning of the third act, opens with an explanatory intertitle stating that "in order to familiarize Mâ with European education, Wendland has her instructed by a teacher."[42] Set in a room dominated by chaises, cushions, and draperies that emphasize a quality of exoticness and sensuality, the sequence presents the fairly unsuccessful—and half-hearted—attempt to educate Mâ once in Europe. Mâ's appearance—still dressed in Eastern clothes, with hair loose and large hoops decorating her ears—contrasts sharply with that of her teacher, who is dressed conservatively and wears her hair tightly pulled back as she lectures Mâ, a book in front of them. Mâ is clearly uninterested in her lesson, playing instead with the kitten she holds, then chasing it across the room. Just as Mâ returns to her lesson, Wendland joins them, approaching the camera, then pausing at the center of the frame. In a medium shot, Mâ rises, raising her arms, and we cut to a long shot of the room as she runs to him, launching herself from the chaise into his arms, then proceeding to embrace and kiss him repeatedly.[43] The lesson apparently concluded, the teacher departs as Wendland sits down on a luxuriously draped chaise with Mâ half on his lap, half kneeling in front of him. We next cut to a medium shot of the two, Wendland still seated, Mâ looking at him adoringly. In a long shot, we see a door open and a servant enter; the servant announces the arrival of a professional dresser. We cut back to Mâ and Wendland, who are joined by a woman with a large trunk that Mâ immediately opens. Pulling out dresses and various lengths of fabric, Mâ caresses them as Wendland looks on, amused. Clearly pleased with this part of her "education," Mâ rises and kisses the man's hands.

Her quality of otherness, her embodiment of "the foreign," is emphasized not only by mise-en-scène, in particular the drapery and chaises that transform the European room into a far more exotic space and the clothing that continues to mark her as other, but also by the presence of the woman, who represents a conservative, Western gaze at Mâ's exoticism. Mâ's behavior—her disinterest in "book learning," her distraction, and her openly erotic behavior toward Wendland—clearly transgresses cultural norms. The emphasis is entirely on Mâ as image; intellectual education is abandoned in favor of fashioning Mâ into the embodiment of the exotic other; books are abandoned in favor of the clothing that will define her appearance. Even once transplanted into the modernized, European setting, Mâ's behavior remains "Eastern"; she acts like the concubine to Wendland's "master," openly expressing sensual desire toward him. The implication is that her "otherness" cannot be assimilated, that it, indeed, defines her role; she draws the gaze of Wendland—and of the viewer—because she contrasts so sharply with the Western setting.

The process of constructing Mâ as the exotic object of a (desiring) gaze continues in a sequence focused on a party Wendland hosts in order to introduce Mâ to his social circle. The scene opens with a long shot showing people dancing and talking while musicians play on a raised mezzanine at the rear of the room. Wendland, having found Mâ in her room and pulled her with him, first moves to the center of the shot in order to arrest the attention of his guests, then moves out of the frame briefly and returns with Mâ. This moment draws attention to the way in which woman-as-image is staged by an external force—embodied in Wendland—even when she is herself hesitant to take (literally) center stage. Yet as the guests begin to dance, Mâ remains on the margins. We see her among the guests as they move around her, jostling and finally concealing her; we then cut between a series of shots of the party and Mâ, first alone on a staircase watching the dancers, then fleeing to her room. Once there, she moves slowly toward the front of the frame, wringing her hands and collapsing on the chaise in tears, then she suddenly revives, running to her dressing screen and picking up a spangled garment that she carries to the chaise and caresses, then puts on.[44] Having noticed her absence, Wendland and a group of his guests go in search of her, and the sequence cuts to a long shot of Mâ, seated at a low table in a luxurious bedroom and looking at her reflection in a hand mirror. Her dress is anything but Western; she wears a small top that leaves arms and stomach visible, tight pants, a spangled shawl, and an "Eastern" headdress. We thus see Mâ staging herself for the gaze of others, a self-positioning that is emphasized through her look at her own image in the mirror. Uncomfortable in a setting that is alien to her, Mâ loses her shyness when she puts on—like a mask—an exaggerated version of her exotic exterior. In one sense, this moment suggests a level of agency in thus staging the self for the audience, emphasizing the constructed nature of her exotic appearance and thereby drawing attention to the spectacle as such. It endows Mâ, in other words, with some type of power and belies an easy interpretation of her appearance and her subsequent performances as catering to a powerful male gaze that essentially possesses her, recalling Studlar's assertion that "possession of the performer through the gaze is really nonpossession."[45] Her repeated glances into the mirror suggest an awareness of the relationship between image and viewer. But Mâ quickly loses control of her image; joined by Wendland and his guests, she reacts uncomfortably, only to be picked up and carried out of the room as though made literal object. Further, she projects not so much her actual identity as a Western fantasy of the exotic. Consider the divergence between her original appearance and that in Wendland's home. Her costume in Egypt, while certainly Eastern, is neither revealing nor eroticized; here, clothed in the garments supplied by a (European) seamstress, she resembles a stereotype of the exotic, a figure that would be at home in a harem or dancing for a sultan.

This notion—of Mâ as a "dancing girl"—is soon acted out, for it is at the party that Mâ moves from exotic image to performer. Having "retrieved" Mâ from her room, Wendland carries her to a low chaise and the crowd of guests surrounds her. Someone requests "fitting" music: "Play something Oriental for Mâ!"[46] The pianist's compliance with this request has a curious effect on Mâ: she gestures at the men surrounding her to be silent, then rises. We cut to a medium low-angle shot of Wendland, who stands at the top of a small staircase and watches, laughing, then back to Mâ, who has risen and is breathing heavily, eyes half-closed. She moves toward the rear of the frame, turns back to the camera, drops her shawl, and begins to dance. As the guests and Wendland watch, she performs an "exotic" dance that fascinates her audience, particularly one man who is identified as the vaudeville agent Bernhardi. When Mâ is finished dancing, Wendland quickly runs to her, followed by the guests, who comment, as she sits back down on her chaise: "That girl has to join the *Varieté* (vaudeville)!"[47] Although Wendland brushes off the idea, Bernhardi approaches Mâ, saying, in response to her question as to what she might do there, "Dance! Dance! Dance!"[48]

On the one hand, Mâ's dance draws attention to its status as a staged performance, emphasizing and reflecting on the relationship between spectator and spectacle. We see her in a long shot, facing the camera, as though at the center of a stage with her audience seated around her. Through the depiction of the audience on screen and the viewer's alignment with that audience, the moment points to the structures of film and thereby distances the viewer from the action. Mâ's dance, the sequence reminds us, is a performance intended to manipulate the viewer's desire. Thus the moment suggests some level of agency, in that Mâ becomes a performer. At the same time, it complicates this notion by representing her dancing as a moment in which she effectively loses agency—note the "hypnotic" effect of the "Oriental" music on her, her half-closed eyes and labored breathing, and her trancelike movements. Mâ's performance is made up of little more than poses—balancing on one foot with her hands clasped over her head, throwing her head back and arms wide, finally on her knees, arching her back into a bridge—strung together with motions so jerky and sudden as to suggest they are involuntary. Even as performer Mâ is, in some sense, passive: she acts as the unconscious medium of a power outside herself. Mâ counters the isolation she experiences in the setting of the party in the only way she knows: by taking on the role of spectacle. Yet this staging of the self is represented as undertaken by a power outside of the self, embodied not only in the music—connecting her, again, to an exotic, mysterious other—but also in the controlling gaze of Wendland, who stands elevated over her and observing the scene he has orchestrated.

Just as Mâ embodied a certain danger when staged as the living mummy queen, so, here, she functions as the object that attracts the viewer's gaze and that threatens him. The dance is presented in a long shot of the room, Mâ at center, the spectators loosely gathered around her. Her movements are crosscut with reaction shots of men in the room, including one who is so entranced by the dancer that he brushes off the attention of a woman he is presumably with;[49] another who takes notes as she moves; Wendland, whose expression shifts from initial enjoyment to a sort of ambivalence exhibited in his faintly shaking his head as he looks on; and, finally, Bernhardi, the vaudeville director, who reacts with an expression mingling lasciviousness and greed. The gaze of the viewers—both on screen and in the film's audience—is constructed as a desiring one, fascinated by the foreignness of Mâ's appearance. The relationship between spectator and spectacle is ambivalent, not exhausted by the structure of active viewer and passive object, possessor and possessed. Even if Mâ's performance is, at some level, unconscious and thereby passive, part of this passivity is transferred to the viewer, so "entranced" by her image as to ignore the "real" world around him—witness the young man brushing aside his date. And yet another dimension is injected into the question of the relationship between viewer and image through Bernhardi's reaction. His exhortation that she must take this performance into the public suggests a recognition of and desire to profit from the monetary value associated with her image, explicitly drawing attention to the business of performance and of film. Wendland's ambivalence—clearly displeased at the thought of Mâ becoming a performer, he is only convinced when she pleads teasingly with him—demonstrates that in taking on the role of performer and entering into the economic relationship suggested by the contract that Bernhardi offers to draw up immediately, Mâ in some crucial way asserts a level of control over her own image and its dissemination.

If her first performance simultaneously suggests and undermines the agency of the performer, the representation of Mâ's act at the *Varieté* shifts the balance toward the latter. After a long shot of the theater filled with an audience seated at small tables in front of a raised stage, we see a series of medium shots, first of Hohenfels, then of Radu, and finally of Wendland, in the two Europeans' private boxes. As the curtain rises, we see a rudimentary stage set dominated by a background representing a star-filled sky and two boxes painted with Egyptian-style murals and topped by large basins. Mâ moves slowly onto the stage, wearing the same costume she did at the party. The scene cuts between Mâ as she begins to dance and members of the audience, including Hohenfels, Radu, and a clearly displeased Wendland, who silences the applause of his enthusiastic friends. The sequence next cuts to a static long shot of the stage with the musicians visible in front of it and Mâ the focal point before crosscutting between close-ups of Radu, staring aggressively at her as he realizes that the dancer is Mâ, and long shots of her on stage, first dancing undisturbed, then, suddenly, seeming to feel Radu's gaze on her. She pauses, turns toward him, eyes wide and hands reaching in his direction, then collapses on the stage.

Even more explicitly than at the party, Mâ is represented as the medium of an external and potentially dangerous power. Where the loss of control associated with dancing was initially presented as somehow pleasurable for Mâ, this time, Radu's presence injects an element of danger. His gaze focused on her—emphasized by Jannings's fixed, "bulging" eyes—represents a force that takes physical possession of her. The fact that she immediately turns toward him before losing consciousness recalls her earlier mention of being "under his spell";[50] in fainting, she succumbs to him again and loses even what little control of her body she maintained during the trancelike performance. The film reveals another aspect of the relationship between viewer and spectacle: if the performer holds the power to fascinate, the viewer nevertheless exerts a certain reciprocal control, taking part in the staging of the spectacle in a manner that implies possession of the image. It is not only Radu but also the audience of the film who is implicated in this structure, for, after introducing Radu, the sequence shows Mâ from a slightly different angle than before, suggesting that we might read these shots as representing Radu's point of view. Here the viewer is subtly aligned with the man, who exerts such a dangerous power through his gaze.

The specific implication of Radu's power is a topic to which I will return after tracing Mâ's progressive transformation into a passive object. This process, in which Mâ's performances represent yet another step, culminates in the creation and eventual destruction of her portrait. The painting is introduced when, after Mâ's dance performance, Hohenfels visits an art exhibit at which it is prominently displayed. The portrait of Mâ—posed in Eastern clothing, balancing a jug on her shoulder, with her eyes half-closed—recalls her initial appearance in the desert, and it immediately arrests Hohenfels's attention. Introduced to Wendland and Mâ, Hohenfels seems to transfer his attraction to the portrait's beauty to the woman, whom he treats solicitously. The equation of the woman with her image is suggested by his similar reactions to each. Mâ becomes identical to her fixed image: she is the exotic object, staged and constructed by Wendland, her own gaze lowered so as to allow the spectator to look at her unchallenged. In fixing her image on the canvas, Wendland reasserts control, overcoming the ambiguous power she held when he initially encountered her in the desert and continues to hold as performer, and conclusively situating her as object of the controlling masculine gaze—a fact that is stressed by Mâ's apparent relinquishment of her status as performer after her traumatic number at the vaudeville. Hohenfels is so entranced by the painting that he purchases it, announcing to Wendland that he has done so in a letter delivered by Radu and precipitating the final crisis in the film. As Mâ reads the letter, she reacts with horror, imploring her husband to get back the painting and impressing on him, when he responds with confusion: "I feel it—my life depends on it!"[51] Although Wendland might not, Mâ recognizes the danger posed by her transformation into image and by the circulation of this image; the fact that the portrait is in the possession of Hohenfels—and, thus, accessible to Radu—carries potentially fatal implications.

This identification between painting and woman is borne out by the following sequence, in which we see the effect on Mâ of Radu's confrontation with the work. Even as Wendland seeks out Hohenfels, Radu, entering the drawing room, catches sight of the portrait, holding pride of place over the mantle. He starts, then we cut rapidly from a medium shot as he stares angrily at the piece to a point-of-view shot of the painting and back to Radu as he pulls out a dagger. Lingering on him for a moment as he stands, visibly angered, the scene then cuts to a long shot as he lunges at the image and stabs his dagger into it. The camera remains steady on him as he stands in front of the "injured" painting, his knife still planted in it, raising his fist at it. He calms only long enough to discover Wendland's signature and departs.

The use of the point-of-view shot aligns the viewer with Radu's aggressive gaze at the painting, motivated by the desire to both possess and destroy. The destruction of the portrait foreshadows the murder of Mâ; we might even say that it constitutes the definitive act of violence in that Mâ is at this point entirely identified with the image that Radu attacks. The film continues to develop this notion that there is power associated with the possession, through the gaze, of a woman's image. The portrait with which Mâ is identified acts as a material good, just as Mâ, in a sense, has come to function as an object of exchange. That the fatal climax of the film is enabled by the sale of the painting implicitly links the commoditization of woman's image with her destruction.

The final sequence merits particularly close examination, for it shows us how Radu locates and reclaims Mâ in a process that ultimately results in her death. Building the suspense as to whether Wendland will return from his meeting with Hohenfels in time to save his wife, the sequence crosscuts between the interior of Hohenfels's home, Mâ's room, where she waits anxiously, and shots of Radu, who moves inexorably from one house to the other. Lubitsch increases the tension in the moment by delaying the discovery of the mutilated painting and interjecting a moment in which the frightened Mâ telephones in vain for her husband, as a sleeping servant awakens only after what will be a fatal delay. All the while, the sequence tracks Radu's progress: running across the grounds of the house, reaching an ivy-covered wall, then beginning the climb to her window. When he reaches the house, we cut to a close-up of Mâ, who is leaning on her vanity but looks up anxiously as though in response to his arrival. The "mystical" link between the two is emphasized by crosscutting between shots of the increasingly terrified Mâ and shots of her pursuer. Once Radu climbs into view outside of the window and enters the room, Mâ panics, seeking vainly to escape him. Her attempted flight is crosscut with close-up shots of Radu's fixed stare at her. His hypnotic gaze has its desired effect. Just before she reaches the door, she pauses, arms still outstretched toward it, then stumbles back, walking jerkily, as though under Radu's "spell." We cut back to a close-up of him, still immobile, still staring at her, then back to Mâ, who turns fully back toward the camera and thus toward Radu. We next cut back and forth between close-ups of Radu as he moves slowly toward Mâ and those of her, immobile, her face blank. The sequence then cuts to a long shot of Mâ as Radu approaches the short flight of steps to the door, at the top of which she stands. As he reaches her, she turns towards him, then falls to her knees in front of him, one hand stretched upward, grasping at his chest. He pulls out a dagger and raises it, at which Mâ recoils, then begins to rise.

Again, Lubitsch delays the main action between Radu and Mâ by inserting a moment in which we see her husband and Hohenfels as they leave the latter's home, having discovered the mutilated painting and hoping to be able to intercept the murderous servant. The scene moves back to Mâ's room. In a medium close-up, we see Radu still holding Mâ, their eyes locked, his dagger in his hand. As he raises the weapon, she looks at him desperately, clutching at her chest, then collapses in his arm, eyes open and staring in death. Radu holds her body briefly at the top of the stairs, then drops her. We cut to a close-up of the man, now shocked, then to a high-angle point-of-view shot of Mâ's body at the bottom of the stairs. Back to a close-up of Radu, then to a long shot as he moves down the stairs and to her side, then picks her up and carries her toward the camera, before turning his back on the camera and arranging her on the pillows scattered at the foot of the stairs. In a medium shot, he first shakes her as though to awaken her, then kisses her before collapsing, weeping, on her chest. He looks up, then slowly reaches for his dagger; the sequence then cuts to a long shot as he rises and moves toward the camera, then raises his dagger toward his chest and closes his eyes. The shot fades out.

Where Mâ's death is shown clearly in the moment in which she collapses in Radu's arms, his is elided in the black screen between his final gesture and the discovery of the tragedy. We fade back in on a long shot of the room, Radu's body visible on the left, that of Mâ still on the right, at the foot of the steps. Wendland runs in, then collapses on his knees next to her. An intertitle laconically states: "Too late."[52] We cut back to the shot as Wendland picks up Mâ and carries her to a chaise at the front of the screen, laying her down so that we see her lifeless body, her face tilted toward us to show us her closed eyes. Wendland keeps his stare fixed on Mâ's body, even as, in the rear of the shot, the prince moves toward Radu. The film fades out here.

In one sense, this sequence impresses the mystical connection between Radu and Mâ; she appears to sense his approach, reacting with fear when he reaches the house and with a sort of awareness of the inevitability of her death once he holds her in his gaze. We see the uncanny link between the man and the woman he, both literally and figuratively, possesses. She cannot escape his power even in his absence, and, as is evidenced by her subjugation to him, her hand reaching both imploringly and caressingly toward him as she falls at his feet, continues to be "under his spell" even once she is "rescued" by Wendland. In a sense, this final moment emphasizes the fundamental similarity between Radu and Mâ: both are the representatives of a foreign culture, of an exotic that confronts the "Western civilization" embodied in Hohenfels and Wendland. When the two Europeans stand over the corpses, the similarities between Radu and Mâ are drawn into sharp relief; not only do both represent a foreign element that challenged—and was ultimately incompatible with—Western culture, but both also were in relationships in which they were subordinated to their European "masters." Their respective positions as "other" are, of course, inextricably linked to and shaped by gender roles. Where Mâ functions as an eroticized and attractive image of the other, progressively easily controlled by Wendland, Radu, in spite of occupying an essentially parallel position in the home of Hohenfels, is a more overtly destabilizing element. We see this particularly in a moment immediately following the beginning of Mâ's education. The scene is introduced by an intertitle stating "Prince Hohenfels, too, has returned from his trip to the Orient";[53] the juxtaposition of this sequence with the one immediately preceding it, where Mâ responds with delight and subordination to Wendland's gift of clothes and fabric, and the use of the word "auch," "too," draws attention to the very different outcomes of these two situations in which a foreign element is introduced into the Western home. In a long shot, we see Hohenfels enter his drawing room. Then we cut to a medium shot of Radu, hands raised in front of his chest, as though arrested in midprayer. Cutting back to a long shot, we see that he is kneeling in front of an altar-like arrangement of "Oriental" artifacts (a collection that, incidentally, shows little consistency, including a Buddha, a standing pharaoh, an Asian-style statue of an elephant, and a variety of vases and containers). In the next shot, we see Radu rise as Hohenfels, moving tentatively, approaches from the rear of the room. Hohenfels taps his servant on the shoulder, and Radu responds by clutching the dirty clothing he still wears and telling him: "I implore my god to show me the way to that disloyal woman!"[54] As Radu continues to stare into space, Hohenfels pats his shoulder comfortingly, shaking his head as the servant bows and exits the room.

The final scene and the contrast between the two moments depicting most clearly Mâ and Radu's respective adaptation to Western culture suggest both a kinship between the two foreigners' positions and a fundamental difference: Mâ can be controlled, transformed into a seductive image of the other that is functionalized in order to fascinate and entertain;

Radu, in contrast, is characterized as repulsive through his filthy clothes and uncombed hair, and his behavior—the superficial subordination to Hohenfels that only barely masks his true aim—emphasizes his inability to be integrated into Western culture. In other words, it is Mâ's appeal as desired image that enables her to become—to however limited a degree—an accepted part of her new environment. She might well challenge the structures of patriarchy through her active performance, but this challenge can be quickly neutralized by reintegrating her into an economy in which she is positioned as passive. In contrast, Radu challenges directly the primacy of the Western men who function as the masculine viewer's doubles. Witness the fact that, in spite of being a servant, the viewer sees him successfully manipulate his employer, and that he is able to assert power over Mâ—now technically Wendland's "possession"—merely through his gaze and his presence. Perhaps thence the ambiguity of Mâ's death; where Radu's represents the clear punishment of his evil, hers is both embodiment of Radu's effrontery and necessary removal of an object of desire that—despite her objectification—remains a threat. Thus, ultimately, both of these elements of the exotic must be neutralized: the film stages a confrontation with the dangerous other embodied in Mâ and Radu, capitalizing, through the former, on its power to fascinate and appeal to the viewer, while emphasizing, through the latter, how it threatens and is ultimately incompatible with Western culture.

Beyond expanding on the notion of the other, the death scene reinforces the identification of the woman with her inanimate image and the fatal power of Radu's gaze. As Mâ paces through her room, anxiously awaiting Wendland's return, she clutches her side as though in response to pain recalling the "wound" Radu inflicted on the painting: when he stabs her image in its side, Mâ's body suffers that pain. The identification suggests that Mâ's image has superseded the living agent; the fatal physical attack is aimed at the painting, which has become identical to, if not even more real than, the physical woman. At the same time, the fact that Mâ's "physical" death occurs as the result of Radu's fixed stare at her replicates the earlier attack in symbolic terms: his gaze is as dangerous and fatal as the physical act of stabbing; her image is as vulnerable as her body. That his gaze becomes murder weapon draws attention to the way in which, throughout the film, Mâ becomes the focus not of merely his hypnotic stare, but of a gaze that is fragmented and multiplied, ascribed to Radu, Wendland, and the audiences both within and outside of the film. In staging the fatal consequences of one part of this gaze, the film implicates the viewer in the violence done to Mâ and to the image of the desired woman.

As we see in the final scene, the gaze constructed as most explicitly powerful is that of Radu, who originally stages and controls Mâ. His dominance over her is figured in terms of hypnotism; much like the eponymous mountebank in *Caligari*, Radu is positioned as a madman with absolute control of his medium. Yet where Dr. Caligari uses his power to exact revenge on those who challenge him, Radu deploys his in order to affirm his possession of the woman whose image he initially constructed and controlled. As I noted, we might read the construction of Radu's powerful gaze as a reflection on the cinematic process in a variety of ways. In itself, the topos of hypnosis connects to contemporary discourses on the (potentially dangerous) effects of cinema. We see this even in the chance doubling of a key term from the film and its reviews: just as Radu has Mâ "under his spell," as she initially tells Wendland, so, as a critic stated in using that precise formulation, the film and Negri's performance in particular fascinated and controlled the audience.[55] Stefan Andriopoulos, in his examination of discourses focused on hypnotism and crime and their representation in cinema, draws attention to the influence of these discourses on the filmic medium. Andriopoulos notes that in *Caligari* "the undecidability that marks the medical spectacle of hypnotic fake crimes is transformed into a conflict between the internal story and the frame [and] the film's paradoxical narrative structure can also be read as a reference to cinema's suggestive power."[56] Similarly, in the ambiguity of Radu's power over Mâ and the thematization of the power of the gaze, we can see a direct connection to the way in which cinema functions. Andriopoulos also draws attention to the way in which the representation of hypnosis is taken a step further in Fritz Lang's *Dr. Mabuse, the Gambler*, where Lang represents the process of hypnosis in such a way as to position the viewer as his subject. Through the focus on Mabuse's face, his eyes looking into the camera, the film "forces the spectator to identify with Mabuse's hypnotized victim. The cinematic representation of hypnosis is thus transformed into a celebration of the hypnotic power of cinema."[57] In *Eyes of the Mummy*, strikingly, Jannings never looks directly into the camera and thus never directs his hypnotic gaze at the viewer; rather, we witness the hypnotist's gaze at his subject and are aligned with him through the use of point-of-view shots. In other words, in Lubitsch's film, we are implicated in the power dynamic enacted when Radu looks at and controls Mâ. Lubitsch's depiction of Radu's power of hypnosis not only references the "hypnotic power of cinema" but also implies an ambiguous power exerted through looking, one in which the viewer actively takes part in directing the desiring gaze at the screen.

Radu, throughout the film, remains the embodiment of dangerous power, dominating Mâ even once she has apparently escaped him. After fleeing with Wendland, she remains susceptible to his control, which is reimposed each time he sees her. Thus after Radu witnesses Mâ's dance at the *Varieté*, Mâ falls ill, victim of a mysterious sickness that confines her to her bed. Initially, after collapsing on the stage, Mâ is taken to her dressing room, where, once she finally returns to consciousness, she clutches Wendland, staring into space and telling him that "he lives in order to have his vengeance over me."[58] Although she recuperates, her illness returns after she encounters Radu while visiting Hohenfels with Wendland in a sequence in which the process of looking and the notion of image and real is further problematized. In a long shot, we see Hohenfels and Wendland in profile seated at either side of a small table, while Mâ's back is turned to the camera; her face and Wendland's are visible in the mirror above them. In that mirror, we see Radu enter the room through heavy curtains. The sequence cuts to a close-up of Mâ as her expression changes rapidly from enjoyment to fear, her gaze fixed in the mirror, then crosscuts between her and medium shots of Radu, who remains standing between the curtains and staring at her. As Wendland and Hohenfels continue talking, Mâ slowly rises from her seat; in the mirror, we see Radu staring angrily, then drawing back and closing the curtains. Mâ continues to rise and turns toward the camera (and the place in which Radu stood) as though hypnotized, much as she did when initially under Radu's control and when under the control of the music to which she danced so seductively. As her host and her husband rise, she suddenly loses consciousness. Mâ's response to Radu, acted out in her stiff posture and vacant stare, recalls the moment in which Mâ first awoke to find herself in Radu's captivity. Again, Radu "possesses" her through his gaze. Further, it links her possession directly to her eroticized performance, drawing on the identical body language as we saw in her response to the music at Wendland's party and during her performance at the vaudeville theater. By doing this, and by foregrounding a mitigated and indirect gaze—their eyes meet in a mirror and both are portrayed as reflected images to the audience—the sequence once again draws attention to the complexity of the power structures embodied in the relationship between viewer and cinematic object of the gaze.

As we have seen through the examination of Mâ's increasing passivity and, in particular, the role of the portrait in causing her death, her subjugation and downfall are the results of her function as the object of multiple gazes, those of Radu, Wendland, and the spectators within and outside of the film. Equally, however, the analysis demonstrates the particular power ascribed to Radu, who ultimately causes, most directly, her death. In a sense, this suggests that one of the transgressions of which Mâ is guilty, and for which her death serves as a punishment, is her initial act of fleeing her captivity. However justifiable her flight might be, it functions as the catalyst for her fate. In fleeing Radu's control and attempting to assimilate into Western society, Mâ violates traditional codes of behavior contingent on both gender and culture. As the exotic other who dares to try to access a new cultural setting and to abandon the domestic sphere for public performance, she stands in for the New Woman as a dangerously emancipated figure who challenges traditional gender roles. In escaping the repressive role of "conventional" woman that is embodied in her relationship with Radu, who controls every aspect of her life and persona, Mâ becomes an absolute "other" who threatens the stability of the social system into which she attempts to assimilate. In Hake's sense, she embodies a representation that goes back to early cinema, which is "present in the oscillation between conformism and subversion and the overarching sense of ironic detachment that lies at the basis of the films examined. The woman, in the process, comes to function as the discursive agent who negotiates these disparate influences and, at the same time, protects the claims of diversity: as a threat and a challenge."[59] Mâ, indeed, is "threat and challenge" to the social structures into which she is ultimately unable to assimilate, for her flight from Radu represents a decisive rejection of woman's subjugation to men and confinement in the domestic sphere. The tomb in which she was initially imprisoned suggests the severity of the limits imposed on women through conservative ideals of behavior; her subordination to Radu traps her in a sort of living death, prefiguring her death at his hands at the end of the film.

Whatever its intention, *The Eyes of the Mummy*, by tracing and performing the progressive objectification of what was originally introduced as a potentially threatening female figure, takes part in a process that, ultimately, victimizes and destroys its female object. It does so by averting what was originally a gaze that confronted and challenged. As the film progresses, Mâ becomes ever more completely the object of the desiring gaze, first in her trancelike dance, then in her portrait, finally in death; in all three moments, her eyes are closed. If we see Mâ—on the basis of sex and ethnicity—as representative of two types of "other" that posed a challenge to traditional notions of identity, then the end of the film—the moments in which Wendland and Hohenfels stand over the corpses of Mâ and Radu—represents the expulsion of two potentially threatening elements and the reestablishment of traditional norms and identities. Hake, in her analysis of early Lubitsch films, notes that Negri embodied a "kind of exotic, almost oriental eroticism" rooted in the specific shifts in contemporary understandings of gender and race.[60] The types of roles that Negri played—in so many of which she reaches a fatal end—emerge from a historical moment in which women are perceived to be threatening traditional power structures:

> The unbroken popularity of the vamp figure throughout the twenties, however, must be seen against the backdrop of women's emancipation and the feelings of disempowerment experienced by many men, especially in the lower middle class. While real women entered the public sphere and gained power in many formerly all-male professions, the vamp led her admirers into imaginary spaces where the unproductive excesses of sensuality could still be celebrated and where it was still possible to indulge in an unrestrained gender essentialism. Under these conditions, Negri came to embody woman as the ultimate Other. This also explains the numerous aggressive impulses against her.[61]

As Hake suggests, Negri, as Mâ, enables the viewer to experience both "unrestrained gender essentialism" and the spectacle of her punishment for her transgressive behavior. She challenges norms of behavior not by acting as a direct competitor to men on the field of employment but by embodying these "excesses of sensuality" that recast the threat in erotic terms, but nevertheless required her to succumb to the "aggressive impulses" that threat aroused.

And yet *Eyes of the Mummy* was a popular film not only with male audiences; indeed, if we look at the narrative itself, with its tragic arc and its "heroine's" ultimate "renunciation" of her transgression, it reads as the type of melodrama explicitly aimed at women. Can the power dynamics we have identified be transferred to woman-as-spectator, as well? Or can we shift our findings slightly to uncover the elements that would appeal to female viewers? In one sense, we can see the process Hake describes at work in the way the film appeals to women, as well. The process by which Mâ is "refashioned," for one, might aim to satisfy the desires of the female spectator as, in Friedberg's terms, "spectator-shopper,"[62] who "tries on different identities—with limited risk and a policy of easy return."[63] Viewing the spectacle of Mâ's "education"—her "fairy tale" story of being rescued from a life of captivity, followed by her new, lavish lifestyle and her elevation to celebrity—enables the female spectator her own escapist fantasy; this exotic figure, desired by the men around her, becomes an easy object for identification. Indeed, the moment in which we see her outfitted with an entirely new wardrobe of lavish clothes suggests the appeal of film as an embodiment of the process of shopping not only in the metaphorical but also in the literal sense. Harking back to Friedberg, this demonstrates an attention to a gaze that is both specifically female and empowered. As Friedberg notes, "new desires were created for her [the female flaneur] by advertising and consumer culture; desires elaborated in a system of selling and consumption that depended on the relation between looking and buying and on the indirect desire to possess and incorporate through the eye."[64] In the context of film, this process of the creation of a female consumer necessitates a female gaze powerful enough to "possess and incorporate through the eye." *The Eyes of the Mummy* seems to address itself to the women in the audience by offering the pleasurable opportunity to identify with a figure whose story is, at least initially, a fairy tale one, by exhibiting an alternate persona as well as a wealth of luxury goods that she may "try on" through her identification.

This identification, however, is ambiguous at best. On the one hand, the identification between the female spectator and Mâ serves a purpose both pleasurable and educational; she might well try on this exotic identity, but she must then "relive" its punishment in the moment of her on-screen double's death. On the other, we might ask whether the ending is not intended to appeal in some way to the female viewer as well. The film, after all, hints that Mâ is a danger not only to men, but also to women—recall the moment, during her performance at Wendland's party, in which she so entrances the men in the audience that we witness one ignore his female companion. Mâ is positioned as "other" not only because of her gender but also because of her ethnicity; as such she is distanced from the "typical" female viewer. The resolution suggests the removal of a danger that is already other than the self. The film seems to push the women in the audience not only to identify with Mâ but also to fear her, to see, in the end, her death as in some way necessary.

And yet another potential identification arises—namely, that of Mâ as embodying, in her status as the victim of Radu's hypnosis, the soldier who returns as the victim of war neurosis. I noted the ways in which hypnosis films took part in the discourse focused on defining the ways in which the process represented both a potential therapy and a danger to society. Considered in this light, we might trace Mâ's construction and ultimate demise as acting out the victimization of a generation of soldiers by the men who directed their actions and controlled their lives.

The Eyes of the Mummy, as we can see, is a far more complex film than it might initially seem, and it remains stubbornly resistant to a unified reading. In its performance of the way in which Mâ is constructed as object of desire, it acts out fundamentally ambiguous concerns, allowing the male viewer a fantasy of control and the female viewer one of freedom and empowerment, however temporary. Its multiple structures of identification demonstrate not only its appeal as escapist fantasy but also the complexity of gender dynamics and anxieties at the time. Mâ becomes a figure of simultaneous identification, desire, and fear for the audience as a whole. Particularly interesting is the way in which the film both critiques and replicates the power dynamics implicit in cinematic structures. Yet however problematic it might be that the film exploits that relationship between viewer and object, some critical dimension certainly is evident in a sort of surplus of focus on the dynamics of the gaze. The fragmentation of a single desiring gaze into those of Wendland, Radu, and the multiple levels and types of audiences, and the emphasis on the fatal consequence of the constellation embodied particularly in Radu's hypnosis and finding its end point in Mâ's death, reveal far too openly the power implicated in the relationship between spectator and object. Lubitsch's film explicitly thematizes the gaze and almost excessively plays with the positions of viewer and object, thus drawing attention to the structures at work in film. The film engages its viewers in a pleasurable process of looking and simultaneously implicates them in the desire and control embodied in said process. The slippage between the monster evoked in the title and the "real" Mâ draws attention to the structural similarities of the respective positions of "woman" and "monster" in film; indeed, it reveals the precise mechanisms by which woman, however aestheticized her image may be, poses a challenge to the active male gaze that must be neutralized. In staging the process of shaping Mâ into an image, the film reveals precisely that which is at its own core. The creation of Mâ's image—her costume, her trancelike dance, and, finally, her reduction to two-dimensional portrait—lays bare the artifice of the images projected for the viewer.

THREE

UNCANNY TALES (UNHEIMLICHE GESCHICHTEN, RICHARD OSWALD, 1919)

The Many Guises of the Dangerous Woman

RICHARD OSWALD'S *UNCANNY TALES* (*Unheimliche Geschichten*) premiered only a year after the release of *The Eyes of the Mummy*. While reviews were mixed, the film garnered praise for its innovation; in particular, at a moment in which Weimar Germany's artistic and cultural production was embodying the type of experimentation that would define it, Oswald clearly sought to shape a new approach to film. A selection of reviews compiled in *Film-Kurier* emphasizes the novelty of *Uncanny Tales*:

> *Berliner Tageblatt*: "Here for the first time a series of one-act films that aim for a very specific tone are presented. This is a new model. Here we effectively see the proof that thousands of extras and a monumental set are not necessary for an effective film, but rather that this can also be achieved in a different way." *B. Z. am Mittag*: "The ambition to find a way out of the same boredom of the movie drama is to be lauded. And the idea is certainly grasped correctly, even if, here, it is by far not acceptably realized."[1]

However mitigated the praise of such reviewers might be, they demonstrate that the film represented an experimental form, an attempt to push beyond the dramatic, narrative film and to create a new genre. Oswald, particularly by relying on a minimal cast and fairly plain set design, swam against the tide that was the sorts of *Sensationsdramen*—as, for example, *Eyes of the Mummy* and other Lubitsch films of the time, including *Carmen* and *Madame Dubarry*—that required "thousands of extras and a massive set." A reviewer in *Kinematograph* similarly emphasized the originality of *Uncanny Tales*, this time noting that the material of the piece—its focus on the uncanny—differentiated it from the "boring" dramas hitherto produced:

> These five one-act pieces show with astonishing clarity the area in which the success of film should be sought. Since the "Student of Prague" there has not, to my knowledge, been a film that dealt with such effective material. This is primeval cinema, and Richard Oswald was the destined leader whose talented hand was able to smooth the path and open new vistas that are bound to inspire admiration. How clearly the long-winded and, it must be stated, often also rather boring salon films and literary films, which still earn cinema many foes, pale next to the fantastic, the colorful whirl of these truly exciting events.[2]

In spite of such recognition, *Uncanny Tales* did not receive universal acclaim. In a perhaps characteristically ambivalent review in *Der Film*, one critic called the movie "an appealing attempt to transfer the literary form of the cabaret to the big screen," and deemed it "in sum and in individual parts a decided success"; at the same time, he noted that "in spite of the title, there is no consistent tone," and considered the frame story "generally unnecessary."[3]

Unlike *Eyes of the Mummy*, *Uncanny Tales* was not the product of a director attempting to establish himself in a new way. On the contrary, by 1919, Richard Oswald was already on his way to building a media empire. As a director, his works ranged from detective series to the *Aufklärungsfilme* (social/sex education films) that were one of his generic innovations, and he owned not only his own production studio but also a movie theater. Born in Vienna in 1880, he began to work as an actor before moving first to Düsseldorf, then to Berlin to take up positions at theaters there. In 1914, he became a screenwriter for Deutsche Vitascope. Success came fairly quickly, and, that same year, he directed his first film, *The Iron Cross (Das eiserne*

Kreuz). In 1916, he founded his own production company, Richard-Oswald-Film-Gesellschaft, and directed the first of the *Aufklärungsfilme*, *Let There Be Light!* (*Es werde Licht!*). Oswald, like Lubitsch would become, was an all-around film professional, first acting, then directing, producing, and writing or collaborating with others on the screenplays of his productions.[4]

Like Lubitsch, as well, Oswald had certain actors with whom he frequently worked and who became famous in the era in no small part because of his cultivation. The stars of *Uncanny Tales* are cases in point. The careers of both Reinhold Schünzel and Conrad Veidt took off after Oswald began casting them in everything from the moral dramas *Let There Be Light*, *Prostitution* (1919), and *Different from the Others* (*Anders als die Andern*, 1919) to horror films like *Night Figures* (*Nachtgestalten*, 1920) and entertainment pieces like *Uncanny Tales*; the actors played everything from homosexuals suffering at the hands of society to dramatic leads. In his career, Schünzel would move back and forth from acting to directing, have limited success as a director in Hollywood, and finally return to Germany in 1949; Veidt would become an even greater star, perhaps best known for his roles as Cesare in *The Cabinet of Dr. Caligari* and as the despised Nazi officer Strasser in *Casablanca* (Curtiz, 1942). Anita Berber, who began as a dancer and simultaneously fascinated and scandalized the public as much with her frequent turns as on-screen femme fatale as with her private life, was another one of Oswald's favorite casting choices, and acted in at least nine of his films. Like Pola Negri's in *Eyes of the Mummy*, Berber's roles in *Uncanny Tales* are fundamentally shaped and informed by her off-screen life: as Susan Laikin Funkenstein notes, "most writings on Berber from the 1920s, and even more recently, present her as scandalous, drug-abusing, tabloid fodder, and stories about her three failed marriages, antics in Berlin's gay and transvestite clubs, and well-known cocaine usage have been marshaled to justify such interpretations."[5] Where Negri became identified with the femme fatale simply by virtue of her non-German heritage and her on-screen roles, however, Berber gained this (dubious) distinction through the manner in which she staged herself. Berber gave expressive dance performances with titles like "Cocaine" (1922) and "Absinthe" (1925); while at first glance largely erotic spectacles, with Berber challenging existing laws on nudity in performance by dancing entirely unclothed,[6] "the Weimar dance and cabaret performances explored more substantive issues, among them women's social and cultural roles, national identity, technology and urbanization, and race and ethnicity."[7] Berber's performances in the various episodes of *Uncanny Tales* thus should be read in the context of her larger identity as performer, in which she openly flouted conventions of gender and morality.[8] Her mere presence on the screen is charged, raising issues of subversion, transgression, and excess that are bound up with her perceived sexual and personal identity.

In the framework of this book, *Uncanny Tales* is significant because it experiments with genre, thematizes the uncanny, and stages individual episodes that, however diverse they might superficially seem, coalesce around questions of gender and desire. Structurally, *Uncanny Tales* is an omnibus film, with five separate episodes connected through a frame story, and three main actors, Berber, Schünzel, and Veidt, taking the key roles in each episode. This was a new form, which we encounter again, in the Weimar canon, in Fritz Lang's *Destiny* and Paul Leni's *Wax Works* (*Das Wachsfigurenkabinett*, 1924), and which has certain interesting possibilities. Omnibus films[9] are generally made up of multiple episodes, often connected by a common theme or through a framing story and filmed either by a one or multiple directors. The term is rather loosely defined, so that at times any "episodic" film might be subsumed under it, and the term can be applied as early as D. W. Griffith's *Intolerance* (1916), where individual episodes taken from history are interwoven with the main story; more recent examples include *New York Stories* (Martin Scorsese/Francis Ford Coppola/Woody Allen, 1989), *Short Cuts* (Robert Altman, 1993), and *Cloud Atlas* (Tom Tykwer/Andy Wachowski/Lana Wachowski, 2012). Donald Haase suggests that two of the better-known omnibus films of the Weimar era, namely, the above-mentioned *Destiny* and *Waxworks*, might be related to Weimar Germany's reception of the *Arabian Nights*, and that "by invoking the narrative strategy of the *Nights*, these films thematize the filmmaker's role as storyteller."[10] He differentiates between the respective ways in which the films conceptualize the power of storyteller and of film, noting that in *Wax Works*, "the series of tales visualized for spectators by the writer and showman in the *Panopticum*—whatever threat of tyranny they may imply—are not told to defer death, as in the literary *Arabian Nights* and in *Destiny*, but to amuse a paying public in search of escape from modern reality."[11] Haase rightly points to the self-reflexive nature of the films as tied to the form itself. However, where *Destiny* draws on a model of the filmmaker as more akin to the storyteller and *Wax Works* in fact directly thematizes this notion through the device of the writer, *Uncanny Tales*, by foregrounding the act of reading in the frame story, shifts the emphasis onto the role of the spectator. I will discuss this element in more depth below, but it is significant to note the difference between the models proposed by Haase and that which we see here, for in *Uncanny Tales* the frame suggests an audience that is diverse and heterogeneous, given the multiple "readers" on whom the viewers are to model themselves.

The omnibus film is fundamentally self-reflexive because it plays with the structures of narrative and cinema, refiguring the ways in which a filmic narrative can be presented and drawing the audience's attention to the way in which it is constructed. To present viewers with separate episodes and challenge them to seek out the connections forces them to remain aware of the form itself and of the film as film. *Uncanny Tales* is no exception to this, for it, too, foregrounds its structure and the diversity of its components. The critic's estimation that there was no "consistent tone" in the five episodes is quite correct; the stories range from quite realistic over farcical to truly "fantastic." Four of the five interior narratives are based on literary texts; they are, in order: "The Apparition" ("Die Erscheinung") by Anselma Heine; "The Hand" ("Die Hand") by Robert Liebmann; "The Black Cat" ("Die schwarze Katze") by Edgar Allan Poe; and "The Suicide Club" ("Der Klub der Selbstmörder") by Robert Louis Stevenson. The final episode, "The Haunting" ("Der Spuk"), was written by Oswald himself for the film and is of particularly interest, given its negotiation between uncanny, ironic, and comedic tones and the fact that it was intended from the outset for the filmic—rather than literary—medium. With so varied a grouping of narratives, it is no surprise that each varies in terms of cinematography and approach to their respective themes. For example, only the second episode makes use of trick photography as a means of representing uncanny events; mise-en-scène and lighting, as well as editing, vary in accordance with the given narrative. The general appearance of the episodes might well be similar, drawing on the pantomime-style acting common to German films of the era and on expressionistic costume, makeup, and lighting, but the effect of these elements differs in each episode. Thematically, however, the narratives contain a common thread in that they thematize gender dynamics in a range of ways and demonstrate that examining these in Weimar Germany reflects on the ways in which both female and male identity were conceptualized, as well as on the shifting definitions of desire and the ways in which it is implicated in relationships between individuals.

In almost every episode, a woman becomes the object of two men's desires and thereby either threatens their friendship or positions them as antagonists to each other. In her function as the disruptive female figure within the recurring triangulations in the film, Anita Berber's various characters—acted by the character presented in the frame story as the "Dirne"[12] and thus immediately identified with sexual transgression—challenge and destabilize the male characters around her. She is both symbolic object of desire and narrative catalyst, driving the action in much the same way as Clover's "final girl" does in the slasher film. The triangulated relationships are never simple; rather, we might see Berber's characters as object of desire fought over by rivals as well as body through which homosocial desires are routed. Eve Kosofsky Sedgwick examines such triangulated structures of desire in *Between Men*, arguing that homosocial desires are frequently routed through women in order to avoid destabilizing the obligatory heterosexual system.[13] That is, male homosocial desire must be diverted through a triangulated third (female) figure in order to avoid crossing the narrow line separating behavior between men that is acceptable from such that is not. Sedgwick's notion of these structures of desires raises interesting questions for *Uncanny Tales*, particularly as its two male stars, Veidt and Schünzel, had starred together in Oswald's *Different from the Others*, a film that essentially argued against the criminalization of homosexuality and that had premiered only six months before *Uncanny Tales*. Certainly, just as Berber's scandalous behavior shaped her performances, so Veidt's recent turn as the homosexual victim of Schünzel's ruthless blackmailer would shape the two actors' characterizations. At the very least, we might see the strong bonds between the two men that are repeatedly interrupted or challenged by Berber's characters as more nuanced and complex than simple friendships or rivalries; rather, they, too, point to (masculine) gender norms that are being redefined, to masculine gender roles that are far less straightforward and absolute than we might think. Weimar Germany represented not only a space of increasing freedom for women but also one in which homosexuality, while certainly not fully accepted, was nevertheless increasingly visible and discussed. This undoubtedly forms a significant element of the background to *Uncanny Tales*.

Beyond presenting multiple takes on intimate relationships, *Uncanny Tales* reflects on the medium both because of the frequent shifts in the narratives that hinder the audience's "immersion" in the story and because the actors metamorphose from one character to the next. Actor and character are not conflated, as they might be in a traditional film; here, a central focus is precisely that Veidt, Schünzel, and Berber slip in and out of each of their roles, playing villain and protagonist, victim and temptress, depending on the given narrative. This emphasis on the virtuosity of the actors draws attention to the form and to the fictional nature of the images on the screen. The frame story that was deemed unnecessary by that critic in *Der Film* actually augments the self-reflexive dimension of the film; rather than bind together disparate episodes into a narrative whole—as, for example, the frame narrative serves to do in Lang's *Destiny*—the frame in *Uncanny Tales* focuses on the narrative form and the connection between the processes of reading and cinema. From the start the film explicitly raises questions of form and medium, inviting the viewers not to immerse themselves in the fantasy of the cinematic narrative but rather to confront it with an eye to its technical elements.

Given the structure of the film, it is difficult to analyze it as a single unit, and I will thus examine the framing narrative and each episode individually. Certain common threads emerge; in particular, regardless of the actual narratives, we see a certain level of playfulness toward or tolerance of the modern gender roles depicted in the film. That is not to say that *Uncanny Tales* does not demonstrate an anxious preoccupation with woman as an erotic object that is both desired and feared, but that this tendency is less absolute than in some of the other films examined in this book, and that the response to the anxieties raised by woman is, at least at times, less punitive. The ambiguity of the film's stance vis-à-vis changing gender roles becomes particularly clear in the final episode—perhaps understandably, given that it was scripted by Oswald himself, who again and again demonstrates in his body of work a nuanced and sympathetic understanding of the individuals behind the thorniest of the social issues of the time.

CREDITS AND FRAME NARRATIVE

The peculiar gender dynamics at play in the film are already suggested in the credits and the opening shots. In the credits, the three main actors' names are tellingly presented; each of their names forms one leg of a triangle. Immediately after the credits, we see a brief sequence, opening with a close-up of Veidt, then dissolving to one of Schünzel, then to one of Oswald. Again a dissolve, this time to a shot of all three, with Oswald between the two other men; he puts his arms around them and they begin to laugh. Although this convention of presenting the stars of a film and/or the director is not unique to *Uncanny Tales*, it is significant in that it not only draws attention to the film as film by presenting the individuals behind the fiction, but it also raises certain issues about the structure of film and its relation to other media. First, the introduction of the main actors: striking about this is that the actors are presented not in character, but as themselves, immediately undermining the illusion of the actors' identity with their roles. The inclusion of the director draws attention to the cinematic apparatus behind the images, reminding the viewer of the subjectivity guiding what will appear on screen. And perhaps the *exclusion* of Anita Berber is significant as well. If the frame story (and, to greater and lesser extents, the interior stories) is structured around the triangulation of the woman and the two men, made explicit in the presentation of their names, here she is absent, the triangular relationship instead imposed on the two male actors and the director. The shot of the three men suggests a closed relationship, an exclusively male group that shapes the filmic product. Reconsidering Sedgwick, we see a further complication of triangulated relationships; here, that between Veidt and Schünzel is routed not through a woman but through the man who directs the film and thus their actions, who essentially constructs the shifting networks of desire on screen. Berber, excluded from the shot of the guiding figures behind the film, is relegated to symbol, image, conflated, more so than her male counterparts, with her role as the "Dirne" that she is defined as in the frame narrative.

The self-conscious reflection on the medium of film that we see in the opening credits continues in the frame story, which begins with an intertitle announcing "Fantastical Prelude at the Antique Store" ("Phantastisches Vorspiel beim Antiquar").[14] The sequence opens with a long shot of a store cluttered with books and filled with customers leafing through the volumes. In the rear, slightly to the right of center, a life-size portrait of a woman is visible, with the label "die Dirne" above. Two similar portraits are visible at left and right of the frame, labeled "der Teufel" and "der Tod" respectively. The disorder of the shot is emphasized by the movements of the antiques dealer, who runs from one customer to the next, then jumps over his desk, before finally urging everyone out. Once the shop is empty, revealing the books filling shelves and stacked on surfaces throughout, the dealer runs to the front of the screen, where he sits on a table, picks up a book, and holds it to his chest, caressing it, before jumping back off of the table, running to another at the rear of the shot, climbing on this one, and extinguishing the light hanging above. We see him move toward the screen and out of the shot. The dusky store is lit in such a way as to highlight the portrait of the woman at the rear of the store, as well as the piles of books on the table at the front.

We then cut to a series of medium shots of the "portraits": first that of the woman, who raises her hand, opens her fan, and begins to wave it at herself; then that of the devil (Schünzel), who shifts slightly, then looks toward the right of the screen; and finally that of "death" (Veidt); he, too, shifts and nods toward the left. Next, we cut back to the woman, who smiles coquettishly and continues to fan herself, then to the two other men as they, again, acknowledge each other. From the start, questions of image and the gaze are raised. The portraits frame all three of the actors as visual and aesthetic objects, while their placement, with that of the woman at the center of the screen, privileges the female image as spectacle and suggests that she is interposed in the relationship between the two men. The shift from object of the viewer's gaze to active subject is initiated by the characters' gazes at one another, by the moments in which their gazes meet and precipitate the transgression of the containing frames. After this initial contact, the characters begin to move. We cut to a long shot of the shop and see first Veidt move out of the picture frame on the right of the shot, then Schünzel out of that on the left; both men approach the woman and help her out of her frame. The three of them, Berber in the middle, her two admirers flanking and watching her, walk to the table piled with books at the front of the frame. The theme of triangulation is already evident; the next two shots show her pointedly flirting with "the devil," while "death" menaces him, then embraces her as she turns toward him. The antique dealer's entrance interrupts their flirtation. As the woman and the devil laugh, Veidt grabs the old man, then pushes him toward the front of the screen, where he falls to his knees in front of Schünzel. The latter picks up the old man and rolls him over the table of books onto the floor and out of the frame as all three of the characters laugh. Having disposed of the "real" character, the three "living portraits" select the books that will become the stories on screen. Veidt and Berber sit close next to each other as they look at the pages of a book, Veidt caressing them, while Schünzel reads alone. After a series of shots of the three readers, the sequence fades out.

This "Fantastical Prelude" presents the setting to which the film will return as a way to segue from one internal story to the next, reminding the viewer of the imaginary nature of these stories and interrupting the viewing experience so as to break any semblance of reality and to undermine the viewer's "getting lost" in the images on the screen. The referencing of multiple (older) artistic media includes the medium of film in a group with painting and literature and thereby asserts its artistic value, so often challenged by social reformers at the time, and simultaneously differentiates it from these older art forms, stressing the innovation of cinema. That the three main figures are initially presented as portraits that "come alive" explicitly connects with early cinema, where viewers might relate to the moving images as though they were "photos come to life." As Gunning argues, this emphasis on the illusion of movement made the appeal of early film by presenting first a still image, then that image in motion; early film, he notes,

> strongly heightened the impact of the moment of movement. Rather than mistaking the image for reality, the spectator is astonished by its transformation through the new illusion of projected motion. . . . What is displayed before the audience is less the impending speed of the train than the force of the cinematic apparatus. . . . The astonishment derives from a magical metamorphosis rather than a seamless reproduction of reality.[15]

In its presentation of the lead actors, *Uncanny Tales* harks back to the uncanny moment of early cinema, drawing attention to the "force of the cinematic apparatus." Equally, the trope of reading a story that is then presented on the screen suggests an understanding of cinema as a narrative form that is related to the structure of the viewer's *Phantasie* (imagination); the frame suggests that as they read, the characters in the shop "see" the stories unfold "before their eyes," just as the viewer in the audience sees them unfold on the screen. This is further emphasized because Veidt, Berber, and Schünzel play the central roles in the interior stories, again undermining the semblance of on-screen "reality" and simultaneously reinforcing the notion that cinema is related to the personal experience of reading. Just as readers imagine themselves in the role of the literary protagonist, here the readers in the shop are transformed into the main characters of the texts.

The structure of the frame narrative was originally a literary one that enjoyed particular popularity in nineteenth-century German literature, especially in works, fittingly enough, that contained uncanny elements, such as Jeremias Gotthelf's "The Black Spider" ("Die schwarze Spinne," 1842), Theodor Storm's "The Rider on the White Horse" ("Der Schimmelreiter," 1888), and various stories by E. T. A. Hoffmann, who is invoked not only in reviews specifically of this film, as the progenitor of the frame-story form,[16] but also more generally in the era by those pointing to the fantastic and the uncanny as particularly apt subject matter for film and seeking to differentiate between material that befits literature versus film.[17] In literature, frame narratives often served to distance the reader from the story-within-the-story and to thus make the fantastic interior narratives more believable, even while injecting a level of subjectivity into them; mediated by the narrator, who is often presented in the frame in a realistic setting, the internal story becomes one that must be interpreted and tested for truth value by the reader.

The use of the frame narrative in *Uncanny Tales* draws on this literary device used most prominently in uncanny fiction in order to produce a similar effect in cinema, reminding the audience that the interior stories are being read and "relayed" to it by the three characters. At the same time, the fact that it is itself an uncanny frame shifts its significance from mediation of otherwise unbelievable narratives to connection of disparate ones; it draws together and unifies the tales, subordinating them to the framing story of the figures in the bookshop. Indeed, the frame narrative is perhaps more unequivocally uncanny than are any of the interior stories. Here, the paintings truly *do* come alive, with no explanation given or trickery revealed, just as, on screen, images shift into movement. That Oswald couches the frame narrative in literary terms—drawing a parallel between the process of watching a film and that of reading—suggests a view of cinema as structurally similar to the imagination; just as the reader might visualize the events narrated in a story, so the camera represents for the viewer a similar visualization of the text. And indeed, as noted, each of the episodes save the last is based on a previously published story. It is, of course, common practice to draw on literature as material for the screen, a practice, indeed, that was debated by film critics in Weimar, who saw in it a disregard for the peculiarities of the cinematic medium that could easily lead to missteps. One critic notes "that a true film can be written only in deferring to its specific technique, that the constant use of material taken from literature thus from the start strongly undermines film's effectiveness."[18] Yet the frame narrative of *Uncanny Tales* adds an additional twist: it binds together episodes of which most are based on literary texts and thematizes the *experience* of reading, drawing a parallel not between the two media but rather between the relationships connecting reader/spectator and word/image. In a sense, where the credits and introductory sequence of actors and director emphasize the directorial agency, the frame narrative effectively elides the same, suggesting, however idealistically, that the film depicts a very personal and subjective process rather than a single interpretation of a given text.

In this sense we can regard the frame narrative as the film's primary self-reflexive moment, one that draws attention to the structures of the medium and presents a possible model for the relationship between audience and image. At the same time, the frame introduces the cast in terms of specific types that speak to the iconographic figures of uncanny stories and to larger sociocultural constructions of gender identities: death, the devil, and the fallen woman. On one level, these types seem arbitrary in that they are not identical to the roles played by each within the interior narratives. Schünzel, the devil, is alternately a crazed ex-husband, a likeable detective, a cowardly Lothario, and, twice, a murderer—first of his best friend, then of his wife. Veidt, or "death," is twice cast as the likeable "other man," once as the victim of Schünzel's murderous rage, once as the crazed leader of the "suicide club," and, finally, as the tolerant and confident husband who averts his wife's infidelity through revealing her potential lover's inferiority. Neither Schünzel's devil nor Veidt's death are explicitly characters within the interior narratives, suggesting, perhaps, that the frame narrative assigns these identities to them not as a reflection on the stories but rather on the genre as a whole. Berber's role is slightly more apt; by labeling her as the

"Dirne," the frame narrative already suggests a certain level of transgression and moral guilt in each of the roles she takes on in the interior stories. In other words, the women in the interior episodes are never entirely victim, never entirely without guilt, but rather inherently occupy the latter position in the virgin/whore dichotomy that dominated representations of women from biblical narratives on. This is telling, given the period; with sociocultural emphasis placed on the sexual emancipation of the New Woman as representative of wider freedoms accorded to women in the era, the "Dirne" comes to stand in for emancipated woman in general. Still, the identification of the characters as specific types, while evocative of a general sense of the uncanny, does not seem to relate directly to the content of the interior episodes. We might speculate that the roles are chosen simply to fit the perceived personae of the actors: Schünzel's mobile features and peaked eyebrows certainly lend themselves to a Mephistophelian character, while Veidt, with his cadaverous face and his extraordinarily physical acting style, in which bulging veins and tendons so often take center stage, is equally well cast as death, and Berber certainly projected an image as sexually liberated, even depraved.[19]

Far from being unnecessary, the frame narrative serves as a primary self-reflexive moment, pointing to the importance of the specific medium and of the experiential dimension of the cinema. Identities in *Uncanny Tales* are fundamentally fractured; the film presents Berber, Schünzel, and Veidt not only as actors but also as the full range of characters and types. By thus pointing to the structures of specific media and to the constructed and artificial nature of cinema, the frame narrative, though brief, takes on primary significance in the film as a whole.

FIRST EPISODE: "THE APPARITION," ANSELMA HEINE

Once the frame narrative establishes the central trope of the film, we move quickly into the first of the five episodes. This piece plays explicitly with questions of gender and changing conventions of female behavior. The episode opens with a long shot of Berber walking on a path in a park when she is attacked, and Veidt's character, passing by, chases off the attacker. They depart together and, as they travel on a train, she relates her story, which is shown in flashback, explaining that the attacker is her ex-husband,

CHAPTER THREE

who is insane and continues to pursue her. They check into a hotel, where Veidt helps her to her room, clearly hoping for some intimate encounter, only to have her ask him to leave her alone, pleading illness. He joins his friends for an evening of drinking, then returns to the hotel—by this time fairly inebriated—and seeks her out. Instead of finding her, he discovers her room empty, windows open, wallpaper stripped and thrown onto the floor. Fleeing, he sees a mysterious man in the hallway; after the latter runs away, Veidt goes to his own room, considers the issue, then decides that he must mistakenly have gone to the wrong room. Preparing to depart the next morning, he asks the porter to announce him to the woman. Entering her room, he finds it just as it was when he left her there—wallpaper, tapestries, and furniture in their place—yet empty. A maid joins him and explains that there is no guest staying in the room, at which he seeks out the concierge, who tells him that he had in fact arrived alone and points to the guest book as proof thereof. When Veidt protests, various employees are assembled, all of whom confirm the concierge's statement. Dismayed, Veidt goes to the police, who also deny that he arrived at the hotel in the company of a woman. In the station, the woman's ex-husband appears and attempts to attack Veidt before telling the police officer that he must have hidden his wife. Again, the police officer insists that she was never in the hotel, and her ex-husband departs. We then cut to an exterior shot as a horse-drawn carriage moves slowly past, then Veidt sees and stops the man he saw in the hallway outside of the woman's room. Veidt convinces him to tell him what has happened, and the film then cuts to a flashback: doctors wearing masks fill the woman's room, then remove her body as the room is stripped. We then cut back to the man and Veidt standing on the street, as the former tells him: "No one was to find out that she died of the plague."[20] The man leaves, then Veidt moves slowly toward the camera, touches his forehead, then runs out of the frame; the final shot of the episode shows him in the park, eyes wide as he stops in front of a group of bushes then collapses on the ground.

This is perhaps the least "uncanny" of the episodes, for the ending so rationally explains the previous events as to remove any doubt in the viewer as to what actually happened. As one reviewer noted, the moment in which Veidt discovers the empty, destroyed room is effectively uncanny, but this is entirely reversed by the end of the episode.[21] In other words, the episode does not so much portray something truly uncanny but rather depicts an event that might be thus interpreted in spite of having a rational explanation, a narrative structure that we will see again in *The Hands of Orlac*. Indeed, the central conflict Veidt's character experiences revolves around the question of his sanity; is he the victim of a conspiracy, or has he, as the apparently objective witnesses around him assert, imagined his meeting and interaction with the woman? The narrative hinges on the question of real versus imaginary, on whether that which we see is indeed indicative of truth. The images the audience "witnessed" are drawn into question as well; do they represent the "real" events of the narrative or the false reality created by a diseased mind? Conceptually, the episode thus reflects back on cinema, revealing the complexity of the relationship between spectator and image. Further, it points forward to the ways in which this theme will continue to be developed in Weimar film, most notably in *The Cabinet of Dr. Caligari*, where the uncanny potential is maintained more consistently and the film's reflection on real versus imaginary remains more complex because there is, in the end, no absolute certainty, no fully satisfactory explanation of the narrative.

The explanation, in the end, seems, perhaps, too pat, too easy a way to resolve the questions the episode raises. In addition, Oswald does not fully exploit the potential to blur the line between the objective and the subjective. For example, he draws on very few point-of-view shots, though these would suggest that what is presented is mediated through the character's subjectivity. Instead, Oswald uses expressionistic sets and lighting in order to represent Veidt's character's disturbed psyche. This technique is particularly evident when Veidt discovers the empty room. Initially, he knocks at the door of the hotel room and we see a close-up of him as he looks up at the room number, then the camera tilts slightly up to show it. We then cut to a long shot of the hallway with him at the left, outside her door, before cutting to a long shot of the interior as he enters. The mise-en-scène contrasts strikingly with the rest of the episode, which is largely realistic. The wall at the rear of the shot is partially stripped of its paper, and the lighting emphasizes the whiteness of the stripped wall, of the mantel on the left, and of the curtains on the window at the right of the screen. Veidt's movements make clear that the setting is to represent darkness. We see him move to the wall and grope as though for the bed that originally stood there, then the shot dissolves to a medium close-up of him in front of the wall as he feels wires dangling loose. As he straightens up in shock, the camera moves with him, revealing the open window with the curtain moving slightly in the breeze. Veidt fumbles for matches and attempts to light one; we then cut to a long shot of the sky, clouds moving, yet faintly lit by the moon they are hiding. We next cut to a medium shot of Veidt, his face barely visible in the light from the window until he strikes a match and gazes around the room. The match goes out and he moves toward the window, and we cut back to a long shot, once again lit more thoroughly, as he looks outside. We then cut to a long shot of the sky as the clouds break open, then back to the interior, where Veidt reacts with shock to the now well-lit room, clutching his forehead, his eyes wide, as he moves away from the window. The shot dissolves into a longer shot of the same, and we see his actions repeated: he clutches his forehead, extends his arms, then runs to the door, nearly colliding with it before fleeing into the hallway.

The stripped, empty room becomes the physical representation of the uncanny moment and of Veidt's potential insanity. The viewer witnesses his groping in the dark and his dismay and horror at what he sees. The focus is, thus, not on the destroyed room itself, but on the man who enters it and is "destroyed" by its sight. Oswald films the scene in such a way as to ensure that we witness the moment of discovery, rather than sharing in it, thus the well-lit setting, even as Veidt feels his way in the dark. The expressionistic elements of the sequence—the chaos of the stripped walls and the dangling wires, as well as the shots of the clouds moving across the moon—further suggest that this moment is one that simultaneously impacts and represents the hero's interior state. What the sequence conveys is not the ambiguity of the images themselves but rather that of a mind that is potentially disturbed. For the viewer, the images remain unquestioned. We see no indications that they might, in fact, represent anything other than the "real" state of the room. They are, however, endowed with metaphoric significance, becoming manifestations of Veidt's interior disarray.

The discovery of the empty room precipitates Veidt's deterioration. Already, his frenzied flight and his subsequent attempt to explain the uncanny moment by suggesting that he simply went to the wrong room dramatize his loss of a stable sense of the real and contrast sharply with the mannerisms of the urbane man who, immediately before, met with his friends. His deterioration is accelerated when he is told, on the following day, that his meeting with the woman was imaginary. Veidt responds to this with mannerisms not unlike those of the insane ex-husband: his eyes are wide and rimmed darkly, and he collapses on the front desk of the hotel as they dispute the woman's existence. The episode thus constructs distinct parallels between Veidt and the ex-husband. After the former meets the woman, he becomes a sort of double for the latter, experiencing apparent insanity and thus forcing the reevaluation of the ex-husband's mental state. The parallels between the two men are made especially clear in the police station: as Veidt questions the police officer, we see the two men next to each other, framed symmetrically in a single medium shot; the symmetry links them. Further, both men inquire with the policeman about the woman and receive much the same response; he shows each in turn a folder, pointing out details for them, at which they are stunned, then depart.

Although the narrative hinges on questioning the relationship between real and imaginary/madness, the subtext to this thematic is focused on changing social mores regarding gender in general and marriage in particular. The catalyst for the experience is the conflict between the mysterious woman and her ex-husband; Veidt is drawn into an untenable situation because of his involvement with a woman who, in spite of being divorced, is nevertheless not "free" to enter into a relationship with him. On the one hand, the flashback in which we see the ex-husband's behavior toward her demonstrates his insanity. This sequence begins with a close-up of Schünzel, his face lowered; he then looks slowly up, raises his hands, and we see that he is holding a noose. The sequence then cuts to a long shot of the room: he stands at the rear, while she is seated at a desk in the foreground of the frame. The setting appears solidly bourgeois and thus emphasizes, by contrast, the husband's appearance—the dark circles under his eyes, exaggerated eyebrows, and maniacal smile. As she stares into space, then looks down at the desk in front of her, he approaches her from behind, then suddenly puts the rope around her neck and begins to pull. She jumps up and the two struggle, with her pushing him down onto the desk and finally cutting herself free with a letter opener. As he remains leaning on the desk, nonchalantly picking up a piece of food and beginning to eat it, she runs from the room, then the sequence fades out.

CHAPTER THREE

Schünzel's pallid face, exaggerated makeup, and fixed stare immediately code him as insane. Yet we can see, as well, hints of a critique of the woman: in her positioning in respect to him—her ignoring him as he stands at the rear of the room and the physical superiority implied when she pushes him onto the desk and frees herself from the noose—we see the suggestion that she is to be read as a New Woman, as markedly different from the traditional ideals of wife and mother. The fact that the man tries to kill her using a noose might be seen as a reference to legal execution, suggesting that she is being punished for some transgression and undermining her status as victim of inexplicable, murderous impulses on the part of her husband. And her explanation to Veidt—that "in spite of our divorce, he follows me everywhere"[22]—raises the issue of divorce, while simultaneously suggesting that she and her ex-husband remain bound together. This notion of a continuing tie is reinforced when Schünzel's character visits the police station to complain that she has disappeared; he continues to refer to her as his wife and seems to continue to have some level of legal standing.

That Berber's character functions as a representation of a sexually emancipated New Woman is evident in the scene in which Veidt accompanies her to her hotel room. Once the hotel staff departs, Berber removes her coat and hat and the two sit down at a table. The scene dissolves from a long shot of this tableau to a medium shot just as Veidt reaches for her hand and kisses it, then attempts to embrace her. She pulls away and rises, as does he, then the two kiss. Again she pulls away, this time clutching her forehead; he catches her as she sags, then they turn and he leads her toward the bed at the rear of the frame. After she asks him to leave her, pleading sickness, we again dissolve from a long shot of the two to a medium shot, as he kisses her hand, begins to leave, then returns and they embrace once again. Berber may well send away Veidt, but the scene makes clear that she is a willing participant in their encounter, interrupting it only because of her apparent illness. The dissolve from a long shot to a medium shot of the two together emphasizes the growing intimacy between the characters. Her character thus doubly challenges norms of female behavior, being not only divorced, but also happy to engage in an erotic relationship outside of marriage.

We can read the woman's transgression and emancipation as being at the root of the deterioration of both men who enter into relationships with her. Veidt himself, initially upstanding and apparently healthy, finds himself driven to insanity through the chance encounter with this desired—and desiring—woman; the parallelism between Veidt and the ex-husband's character suggests that the woman was, equally, the root of her husband's deterioration. She endangers him not only psychologically but also physically; as a victim of the "Pest," the plague, she is not only victim but also potential carrier of a contagion that has the potential to destroy society. Her interaction with Veidt's character thus endangers his life; the intimate moments they have shared, embracing on the train and in her room, exposed him to an illness that could prove fatal. The final moments of the episode emphasize the fact that even after her death, Veidt might be contaminated by his contact with her, for, once he has discovered her fate, Veidt's character clutches his forehead in much the same way that she did the evening before her death; he then flees into the park, his movements unstable, and literally keels over. While it is unclear whether we are to read this as representing loss of consciousness or death, the moment certainly conveys the character's complete loss of control, his status as passive victim of the attraction—and contagion—embodied in the woman he pursued.

One film critic, already presenting a generally negative review of *Uncanny Tales*, singled out this episode for particular denigration: "'The Apparition' by Anselma Heine was entirely incomprehensible to all."[23] And, certainly, as an episode designed to evoke in the viewer a sense of the uncanny, this episode seems to fall flat. The potentially metafilmic content of the episode—that drawing-in-question of the relationship between that which we see on the screen and that which "actually" happens—is only hinted at, and quickly gives way to a focus on the representation of Veidt's interior state. Yet in the context of this study, read with an eye to its reflections on gender norms, this episode is an interesting one. In this sense, the primary uncanny object is not the empty room but the woman herself, who enters Veidt's life mysteriously when he sees her in the park, then undermines his sanity and any notion of a stable identity, and finally threatens his very life. What makes her uncanny is, ultimately, her emancipation, the same quality that makes her dangerous. We might read her illness as a representation of the fundamental danger posed by emancipation and changing gender ideals to the masculine subjectivity represented by Veidt's character. The New Woman becomes a carrier of a "plague" that threatens to sweep the community and that must be suppressed and denied at all cost.

SECOND EPISODE: "THE HAND," ROBERT LIEBMANN

The transition between the first and the second episode is brief: we fade in to a medium shot of Veidt and the woman looking up from the book they have finished, to an intertitle designating the next story, to a medium shot of the devil, still cross-legged on the table with an open book in his hand. The transition brings the viewer back to the "real" frame in preparation for moving on to the next story: Veidt, Schünzel, and Berber are no longer the characters from the first episode, but rather the actors about to take on new roles in the second episode. This one again features Berber as a woman desired by multiple men: both Veidt and Schünzel, though friends, love her and decide to roll dice to see who will win her. When Veidt wins, Schünzel is enraged and strangles him. Several years later, Schünzel again meets Berber, who invites him to attend her first performance as a dancer. There, the haunting begins: he sees first Veidt's clawlike hand behind the curtain, then his face. Unsettled, he nevertheless accepts Berber's invitation to take part in a séance at her home. Seated around the table with her and two other men, he sees Veidt's hand next to his. Increasingly unnerved by this unwelcome guest, Schünzel leaves the table, but, after the other men depart, sees a series of visions of Veidt, culminating in footsteps that appear in the snow outside, leading toward the house. A final vision—which Berber also sees—appears: Veidt seizes his murderer and strangles him.

Even more than the first episode, this one is based on a triangulated relationship in which a woman acts as a disruptive element. It opens with a series of matted close-ups that fade into each other: first Berber's face, her chin propped in her hands, eyes and lips heavily made up, as she raises her eyebrows flirtatiously and looks first left, then right; then Veidt facing slightly right as he smokes; finally Schünzel looking toward the left. The sequence then cuts to a long shot of a table, with the three seated at center and facing the camera, Berber in the center. As a man and woman sitting on either side of them rise and move away, Veidt and Berber kiss, then another man approaches and asks her to dance, leaving the two men alone at the table. Both rise, moving toward the camera and out of the frame; we then cut to a long shot as Schünzel attempts to stop Berber from dancing. Veidt, seated at a table at the edge of the dance floor, rises and the two men stand on either side of her, clearly vying for her attention. When Veidt grabs her arm and attempts to pull her toward him, she shakes them both off and returns to dancing, while they remain at the front of the screen, both smoking and rubbing their hands, virtual mirror images of each other.

The opening immediately establishes a triangular relationship between the three; the sequence of close-ups suggests that the object of contention will be the woman. Her position—seated between them at the table—parallels the way in which she will come between them, undermining their friendship and leading to the death of both. And, again, she is figured as an emancipated woman: visiting nightclubs, embracing Veidt's character, and dancing with whomever she chooses. In the very first image of her, we see her power represented by the active desire implied in the suggestive looks she directs at the two men in turn. Indeed, they implicitly acknowledge both her power and her desire in the following moment, when they suggest that "she must choose one of us."[24] They decide, of course, not to leave the choice to her, instead gambling for the prize. This suggests a view of woman as material possession, as object of exchange between men; though they pay lip service to her empowerment, they nevertheless, in the end, undermine it. The two men thus oscillate between acknowledging her as emancipated and self-determining and imagining her as conforming to traditional values positioning woman as the desired—but undesiring—object. Their game, of course, ultimately reveals their error; neither man "wins" his desired prize, with Veidt ending up dead and Schünzel, though surviving, left empty-handed even before the haunting robs him of his life. From the first, Berber's character is fragmented into "real" woman, endowed with power in regard to the men who desire her, and passive image, the possession of which those same men see as possible.

The fatal danger in this episode again emanates from Berber; in the first episode the carrier of a "plague" that drives men insane, then threatens their very life, here, she again inspires dangerous jealousy. Veidt and Schünzel's characters are destroyed because they allow their desire to take precedence over their friendship. This is embodied in the primary uncanny element of the tale—namely, the haunting of Schünzel by the image of Veidt, in particular of his grasping hand. In the murder scene we see the simultaneous fascination and repulsion engendered in Schünzel by that hand. After he strangles Veidt and pries the latter's fingers from his sleeve, he lingers in the room, first pushing at the half-raised, grasping hand in order to lower it, then gulping the glass of wine Veidt had poured immediately before his death, finally lighting a cigarette and extinguishing the lights in the room. Only then does he depart, looking back toward Veidt's body several times. The hand that grasped hold of Schünzel and that will return during the moment in which Berber is positioned most explicitly as an erotic object—namely, during her dance performance—becomes a symbol of an unbreakable tie between the two men, forged through their friendship, then cemented in the murder.

The scene of the performance is notable not only because of Schünzel's vision of Veidt, but also because of its explicit staging of Berber. Schünzel attends after meeting her and accepting her invitation—an invitation that reinforces her agency as performer and marketer of her own image. We see her on stage from two different angles, one in which Schünzel is seated at front left of the frame, watching her, a second that suggests his point of view, in which the stage and the woman dancing fill the frame. Shots of her dance are crosscut first with close-ups of Schünzel watching and applauding, emphasizing the pleasure he derives from this experience. Then, however, we see a medium shot of a curtain with a hand reaching around it; the hand fades out, then we cut back to Schünzel's face, now shocked instead of pleased. We cut back to a long shot of Schünzel, now paying no attention to Berber dancing in the rear of the frame, then again to the hand on the curtain; this time it pulls it aside and reveals Veidt before hand and face fade out. Again a cut back to Schünzel, who this time covers his eyes in fear, then a shot of Berber dancing; just as she strikes her final pose, there is an iris in, then we cut to Schünzel, who faints.

This sequence is especially interesting: it raises questions of emancipation by emphasizing Berber's self-staging and her connection to the New Woman; it plays with the notion of visual pleasure by interrupting and obstructing the pleasurable experience of watching Berber's sensuous dance; and it problematizes the uncanny within the narrative, offering up two sites at which the haunting occurs: Veidt's specter and Berber's body. First the performance: in presenting one of Berber's dances, Oswald makes use of her talent and references her work outside of the film and her notoriety due to her frankly risqué and erotic performances. Both context and performance-within-the-film serve to align her with the New Woman and code her emancipation in specifically erotic and socially transgressive terms. Funkenstein notes the association between women's dance and her new freedoms: "In the Weimar era, the New Woman was fundamentally linked to dance. Unlike painting or literature, dance served as one of the few cultural loci dominated by women, and many cultural critics tied the New Woman's political and social emancipation to her physical liberation through expressive movement."[25] Berber's dancing thus expresses her role as emancipated New Woman and simultaneously points back to this emancipation as linked to the sexual, for it represents an explicitly "physical liberation."

The performance also raises questions of spectatorship and agency, reflecting back on the relationship between viewer and image. On one level, the dance works as Mulvey suggests such spectacle often does, to "freeze the flow of action in moments of erotic contemplation [that must then] be integrated into cohesion with the narrative."[26] In some sense, that is, the dance exists outside of the narrative proper, both pointing to the larger context—Berber's "real life"—and functioning as a moment in which the narrative energy is slowed. At the same time, the crosscutting between images of Berber's writhing body and the spectral body of Veidt reintegrates the performance into the narrative and undermines the visual pleasure it might engender. Both viewers—the viewer of the film and Schünzel, his on-screen double in this moment—are prevented from enjoying the performance by the images of the betrayed friend. The haunting body of the other man interposes itself between spectator and spectacle and puts an end to the apparently straightforward dynamics of the relationship between the two; thus the cuts from Schünzel to Berber's dancing body are replaced by cuts from the former to Veidt's haunting figure. The crosscutting between shots of Berber's performance and Veidt's ghostly appearance thus associates, even conflates, the two: both become objects of Schünzel's gaze, both pose a danger to the onlooker. In this sense, the appearance of the hand not only allows Berber's dance to "be integrated into cohesion with the narrative," as Mulvey might suggest, but also endows it with an excess value, with a power to evoke in the viewer a complex response that combines pleasure in looking and fear.

CHAPTER THREE

In problematizing the dynamics between viewer and image and conflating the alternately pleasurable and fear-inducing effects of the visual object, the scene of the performance constructs not one, but two uncanny objects: both Veidt's incorporeal presence and Berber's decidedly physical appearance become the vehicles of Schünzel's haunting and downfall. Veidt's appearance—insubstantial and disembodied—is as threatening as is Berber's erotic appeal. The pattern of tension evoked in the scene—Berber's performance that builds toward a final moment in which she "[falls] to the floor as if dead"[27]—foreshadows Schünzel's end even as it serves as a sort of representation of sexual release. Death and the erotic, the dead man and the living woman are thus conflated in this moment. In this, the relationship between the two men is necessarily complicated, invested with an erotic energy that suggests again the complex play of desire in the shifting triangles the film stages.

The doubling of the uncanny in Berber's body and Veidt's specter is developed further in the scene of the séance that Berber holds for Schünzel and two other (male) friends after the performance. Arrived at her home, Schünzel is unenthusiastic about a séance but allows Berber to pull him to the table, and he sits down beside her. The arrangement is presented in a long shot, with the cluttered room at the rear in darkness and the table, at the front of the frame, illuminated from above by a large hanging lamp. The four characters seated around the table are starkly lit, faces and hands highlighted against the dark wood, clothing, and background. Berber takes Schünzel's hands, which he has kept in his lap, and draws them onto the tabletop; the sequence then cuts to a medium shot of her, looking at Schünzel, then pans to him, before cutting back to the long shot of all four figures. And now the haunting resumes. In a medium shot of Schünzel, with the hands of those seated on either side of him visible on the table, we suddenly see Veidt's hand appear between those of Berber and Schünzel, fading in until it looks as real as the others. Even in death, Veidt threatens to separate Schünzel from the desired woman. Schünzel draws his own hands back, clenching them, then moves as though to hit the ghostly hand. Just as he does, it fades quickly out. We see the other figures' responses in close-ups: first Berber, a slight smile on her lips, then the two other men, each of them reacting with amusement. They coax him back into his seat, explaining: "If it is completely silent, we can even summon the ghosts of dead people."²⁸ When Schünzel demurs, Berber again pushes him to participate; in a close-up of the man, we see her move her face into the frame and next to his, looking at him mockingly before asking whether he is afraid. Her coercion has the desired effect and they resume the séance. Again, the film draws on trick photography for uncanny effect: as the four are seated around the table, the shot dissolves into one virtually identical, excepting that the man across from Schünzel is, this time, Veidt. Schünzel rises and grabs "Veidt's" head, and the shot dissolves back to the original characters, who react with consternation and amusement. The séance ends here, but Schünzel continues to be confronted by visions of Veidt: as he stands at the window, Veidt's superimposed image, his hand raised and grasping, fades in; when Schünzel flees to the other side of the room, his nemesis's ghostly head appears, magnified to fill half the screen, looking at its victim.

The scene of the séance might be one reason why one reviewer, fairly unimpressed by the film as a whole, praised this episode as the only truly "spooky" one.²⁹ In contrast to the first episode, the second confronts the viewer with images explicitly intended to convey that which the haunted character perceives. Oswald draws on a range of cinematographic means in order to depict the haunting, thus fulfilling the demands some critics made at the time that film should take advantage of its potential to represent the uncanny and fantastic in developing an aesthetic and artistic style: "Here visual representation can present fantasies such as could otherwise only be dreamed of or expressed in words. . . . All the transformations, mythical creatures, and magic that we read about in fairy tales and that must be replaced on stage by poor surrogates can now become seen reality."³⁰ The careful dissolves that allow one character to "turn into" Veidt, the superimposition of the image of Veidt's hand on the table, and his figure confronting Schünzel—all these moments draw on specifically filmic means to represent the uncanny. In this scene of the séance, we see an example of the ways in which fantastic film drew on and simultaneously developed cinematic techniques.

At the same time, the séance references a cultural discourse in which interest in the spirit world was coupled with a linkage between woman and the other. Barbara Hales analyzes the connection in Weimar culture between woman and the occult, noting that "the obsession in the Weimar press with women's involvement in the occult may be read as a sign of woman's perceived ambiguous position in society. New Women were at once described as careerists, mothers, sexual predators, and/or homosexual. This confusion led to an attempt to define the perceived manifestations of woman to make sense out of her ambiguous status."[31] Hales's analysis is apt: Berber's character is certainly ambiguous—dancer and self-staging performer, she dictates the terms on which she will function as object of desire. Her interest in the occult emphasizes her status as "other," based on an emancipation that is uncanny within the definitional framework of a society clinging to traditional norms of behavior and gender identity. Hales reads Berber's role in the episode as "a medium, who directs the spirit world both through her expressive dance and through the act of the séance. Berber's character awakens the dead using eroticized gestures. In this regard, her character must be considered in the context of the sexually liberated New Woman."[32] Hales is certainly correct in linking Berber's dance, her direction of the séance, and her erotic emancipation. Taking her analysis a step further, however, Berber's character seems to transcend the traditional role of the medium because she is not merely the passive vessel through which another agency communicates but rather the active instigator of the moment in which Veidt—himself robbed of his body—will enact his revenge. Berber indeed, as Hales notes, "*directs* the spirit world" [my emphasis], again transgressing, in this moment, norms of behavior that would dictate passivity. It is not only that she "awakens the dead," but also that she reendows the specter with physical power.

Indeed, in Berber's presence, the haunting reaches its climax; the confluence of the two uncanny elements—the desired, emancipated woman and the feared, avenging man—seems to increase the power that each holds respectively. Schünzel so desires Berber that even after the events at the performance, he accompanies her to her home; even after the experience of the séance, he remains there. Indeed, we might suggest that she fixes him first through attracting his gaze, then through deploying *hers*: recall that during the séance, he responds to her looks and her mockery by *not* acting on his fear. His desire for her holds him there and allows the haunting to escalate to his death. In this moment, again, Oswald visually represents the uncanny through trick photography. After the other guests leave, Schünzel staggers to Berber, wild-eyed, attempting to embrace (or cling to) her. When she shakes him off, we cut to a long shot of the room, with Berber standing at the front of the frame, spotlighted by the lamp, as Schünzel moves to the rear and looks out a window. We cut to him at the window, first averting his eyes, then looking back outside, then cut to a point-of-view shot of a lighted path below, where footsteps appear one by one in the snow, moving toward the house. We cut back to a close-up of Schünzel, now wild with fear, then to a long shot of the room. Berber still stands at the table, watching Schünzel as he staggers to a chair and sits down. Here, the shot dissolves to one in which Veidt is standing behind Schünzel and begins to strangle him. We cut to a close-up of Berber, who, clearly witnessing the ghostly attack, screams and covers her eyes, then back to a long shot of the room as Veidt drops Schünzel's body, before dissolving back to a shot that does not include Veidt. Berber moves slowly toward the rear of the frame; first in the long shot, then in a medium shot, we see her half-walk, half-crawl across the room. As she reaches the body, the camera moves to a close-up of her face, with a cross prominently visible at her throat, then tilts down to include that of the corpse. Berber moves out of the frame and the shot fades out on Schünzel's immobile face.

This moment in which Berber watches Schünzel's death is interesting both technically—for Oswald's use of trick photography, including the superimposed images of Veidt and the stop-action photography likely used to create the footsteps appearing in the snow—and thematically—in its development of the doubling between Berber and Veidt, between their respective functions as uncanny and haunting. The woman is both catalyst and vehicle of Schünzel's death; his desire for her precipitated his initial murderous act, then held him in the space—defined as hers—in which Veidt's ghost is able to destroy him. At the same time, we see an interesting reversal: Schünzel goes from spectator to spectacle, with Berber witnessing his death in much the same way that he witnessed her dance. To some degree, the dynamic functions similarly to the one Studlar suggests, with Schünzel embodying the masochistic male, effectively seeking out his just punishment from Berber, who takes on the role of the desired and maternal woman. Further, like in the dance, the presence of the impossible other that Veidt's ghost represents both fascinates and repels. Berber watches, covers her eyes (just as Schünzel did when he saw Veidt behind the theater's curtain), then looks again, unable to resist the fascination. Schünzel's death mimics her figurative death at the end of the performance, when she, too, collapsed and the spectacle ceased. We see, then, a shift in the construction of the relationship between image and viewer that points to the complexity of that structure. Initially, it is Berber who is put on display, first as the object of desire, later as the vehicle of Schünzel's haunting and death. Excepting in the opening scene at the nightclub, she is the sole woman depicted, destabilizing the relationship between the two men and ultimately precipitating, through her dance and her initiation of the séance, the return of Veidt as ghost. Yet the desire for her is dangerous, for it is through this need to possess her that Schünzel eventually becomes possessed; desire for the woman leads him to become, in essence, the passive object of Veidt's vengeance. This episode is perhaps the most interesting in terms of its conflation of issues of gender and terror. In the triangular relationship and the functionalization of Berber as the catalyst for Veidt's "return," we see clearly the ways in which anxiety about changing gender roles translates into the uncanny on screen.

THIRD EPISODE: "THE BLACK CAT," EDGAR ALLAN POE

The third episode, "The Black Cat," is based on a story by Poe and again centers on a triangulated relationship, this time focusing on an unsatisfying marriage, with Berber's character married to Schünzel's alcoholic, abusive husband. Veidt, as the urbane seducer, admires Berber in a bar and strikes up an acquaintance with Schünzel in order to meet her. The unhappily married woman responds to his advances, but her husband, after witnessing their flirtation, kills her and entombs her body in the basement. Veidt, suspicious of the other man's explanation that his wife has left to travel, returns with the police and they discover her body when they hear her black cat behind the newly plastered wall.

Cinematically, this episode does not draw on trick photography to convey the uncanny elements of the tale; quite understandably, as this tale is less focused on truly "fantastic" events than it is on a sort of karmic justice. The cat, as abused by the murderous husband as was the woman, becomes the vehicle by which his crime is revealed. Poe's story hinges on the cat's cry as that which reveals the murder; Oswald, working within the confines of silent film, tries to replicate the revealing moment visually by showing a close-up of the wall as its still-wet plaster begins to crumble. One reviewer praised Oswald's ability to reimagine an acoustic moment as a visual one: "Oswald shifted the acoustic effect to the visual very nicely here. In the film, it creates the intended effect much more strongly when, during the search of the house, the stucco suddenly begins to crumble and the wall to collapse at the site at which the corpse has been hidden."[33] Within the confines of the silent film, Oswald draws on the visual in order to represent that all-revealing cry of the cat, demonstrating both the challenges and the potential of the medium.

The thematic focus of this episode, like that of the first one, is a failed marriage; even more so than in the first episode, this narrative depicts the wife as justifiably estranged from her husband, and him as a straightforward villain. Perhaps this is because the wife's identification with the New Woman is not foregrounded, though she succumbs to Veidt's advances; rather, she is depicted as conforming to a traditional ideal of woman. From the first, the episode aligns the viewer's sympathy with her. The episode opens with a long shot of a bar, Berber standing in the center background, Veidt sitting with a companion in the foreground, and Schünzel, alone in the middle field, drinking. As she waits, apparently paying no attention to her surroundings, Veidt's character comments on Schünzel's attractive wife before approaching him. He thus initiates contact with her through her husband. Berber's suffering at the hands of her husband is reinforced when the episode next moves to a scene in their home, fading in on a shot of a black cat before dissolving to a medium shot of Berber, holding the cat and stroking it as she does needlepoint. Her husband enters the room and, after they argue, tries to hit her, then turns on the cat. As she looks at him in disgust, he caresses her hair, after which the shot fades out. Berber's character, from the start, contrasts starkly with her husband. Dressed in pale clothes and a hat, occupied in their home with traditionally "feminine" activities, and demonstrating her gentleness when she caresses the cat, she is here associated with the domestic sphere. The dissolve from the image of the cat to that of her is an interesting moment, suggesting a connection, even an identification between the two. The bond between woman and animal is so strong that the animal later exacts its dead mistress's revenge; at the same time, the animal—caressed by the wife, who is clearly starved for such attention and intimacies, kicked and abused by the husband—becomes a sort of stand-in for the woman herself. These two sequences—first in the

CHAPTER THREE

bar, then in their home—amply demonstrate that the viewer's sympathy should lie with the wife.

Having thus set the stage, the episode depicts Veidt's advances toward Berber. It is Veidt who initiates her indiscretion, and presumably is able to do so only because of her husband's neglect. She meets him in the bar a second time; again, the space is shown in a long shot, this time with Schünzel slumped at a table, five mugs in front of him, as the bartender attempts to shake him awake and Veidt watches from the rear. Through the windows forming the back wall, we see Berber approach, then cut to a medium shot of Veidt, who looks toward her, before cutting back to the long shot as Berber enters, then moves to Schünzel. When Schünzel rises and embraces her, she recoils; still, all three depart together. The meeting between the two is thus not engineered by her (though perhaps, to some degree, by Veidt, who does seem to exude an air of anticipation). Rather, she enters this decidedly masculine public space only out of necessity in order to find her husband.

Once in the couple's home, Veidt begins his seduction, aided, one might say, by the drunken husband, who encourages the drinking that facilitates the flirtation. We see the three framed in a medium shot, with Veidt and Berber seated at the table, Schünzel standing behind and between them as he pushes them to drink with him. Veidt's movements mirror Berber's: he sets down the mug just as she does, then both reach for and turn toward the other simultaneously, drawing apart quickly as the husband notices. Although the simultaneity of their respective gestures toward each other suggests mutual attraction, Veidt's behavior figures him as the pursuer, who purposely set out to form an acquaintance with her husband, waited for her to return to the bar, then engineered an invitation into their home. The progressive drunkenness of the husband and the other two characters' flirtation is shot in a single, long-duration shot: as Schünzel falls asleep, Veidt rises and moves around him to Berber, who responds with pleasure when he caresses her face and kisses her. Just then, the husband wakes up; he directs his anger toward Berber even as he amicably urges Veidt out. As she remains at the table, Schünzel menaces her with a chair; we cut to a close-up of her frightened face, then to one of her angry husband, then back to her as Schünzel reaches for the cat she holds. After Schünzel kicks the cat across the room, Berber attacks him, and, in their struggle, he strikes her with a mug and she falls, moving out of the frame. He throws two more mugs toward her—this is, presumably, the moment in which he kills her—then collapses on the table, eyes wide and shocked.

This scene places most, if not all, of the responsibility on the abusive husband. The marriage is portrayed from the start as fundamentally damaged—a fact that might be encapsulated in Veidt's wondering statement to his friend in the opening shot that "the drunkard has a pretty wife." The use of the long-duration shot of the three characters, spatially triangulated at the table, makes visible the triangulated relationship that is at the root of the tragedy; the wife, initially associated with a traditional domesticity, responds almost instinctively to the affection offered her by the other man only because her own husband does not allow her to inhabit the role of a wife. It is because of him that she enters the bar, rather than remaining in their home; he denies her physical affection, leading her to accept it from the other man.

Berber's relative innocence might be connected with the way in which the episode does not, in fact, linger on her "punishment." As I noted, Oswald elides the wife's death: Berber moves out of the frame just as Schünzel throws the mugs at her, and we see only his murderous actions. Equally, once dead, she virtually disappears from the diegesis. Oswald presents only one image of her dead body: when the husband carries her corpse into the basement, we see a long shot in which only a window and the stairs are lit. He descends with her face and arms dangling upside down, facing the camera and highlighted. This is the single moment in which her dead body is figured as aesthetic image; instead, the film replaces her image with that of the cat, in the violence the husband inflicts—we witness him kick and hit the cat multiple times—and in the moment in which the body is discovered. On one level, this again suggests sympathy toward the woman; the single image of her dead body functions to shock the viewer rather than to satisfy any voyeuristic interest in the woman's death. This sympathy is echoed in the public response to her disappearance. Veidt first suspects foul play when he returns to visit the couple and is told by the husband that his wife is traveling; once departed, we see a long shot of a wall, in front of which two men and a woman huddle, talking animatedly. As Veidt passes, he overhears them speculating that Schünzel has killed his wife. Returning to the apartment, he prefaces his accusations with "Alle Leute sagen," "everyone is saying," then departs and goes to the police. Public opinion becomes the deciding factor in revealing Schünzel's crime; surveillance by the population functions as a means of punishing the murder. The focus of public disapprobation is not the wife's transgression, but the husband's crime. A man, enraged and jealous, murders his wife; this is a scenario with the potential to be depicted in terms of a punitive fantasy, with her death figured as the fitting punishment for her transgressions, as we will see in the discussion of Artur Robison's *Warning Shadows*. Here, however, that fantasy is frustrated, further undermining the notion that her murder somehow befits her "crime." Indeed, in a sense, the episode entirely avoids focusing on the woman's transgression; the narrative energy is concentrated on the transgressions of the men in the story, primarily of the husband, secondarily also of the would-be lover.

Like her murder, the discovery of her body occurs off screen, with the cat—emerging from behind the wall—standing in for her corpse. Veidt and the police descend into the basement while searching Schünzel's house and initially do not find anything; then, we see a close-up shot of the wall from Veidt's point of view as plaster begins to crumble off of it, then a sequence of shots showing Schünzel's reaction as he struggles against the police and finally attacks Veidt. As the officers hold him back, Veidt picks up an ax and begins to break through the wall. In another close-up, we see the jagged hole in the plaster as the cat appears from behind it, struggling, then jumping to freedom. We might read this moment as one enacting Freud's "return of the repressed," the fundamental precondition of the uncanny that is evoked when the cat's cry reveals the murder. In hiding the corpse, the husband attempted to deny his own guilt as a failure in terms of his role as marital partner, as an alcoholic, abuser, and murderer. The crumbling plaster reveals that which he has tried to repress.

In the context of the focus on gender and the uncanny, this episode is interesting because it does not depict Berber as a dangerously emancipated woman. Where in the first episode we saw the suggestion that the woman's behavior might be at the root of her ex-husband's insanity, here, her actions certainly precipitate her murder, but they do not justify it. Rather, the focus is on the conflict between the two men, with her role merely being to set that conflict in motion. The disappearance of her body immediately after her murder, while avoiding her reduction to aesthetic object, equally emphasizes her functionalization; her corpse is proof not of a tragedy, but of a crime, and serves as the evidence that allows Veidt to assert his superiority over the other man. Read in this light, the entire episode can be recast as a meditation not on a failed marriage, but on a failed man. Schünzel and Veidt represent polar opposites, with the former embodying the negative, the latter the positive ideal.

FOURTH EPISODE: "THE SUICIDE CLUB," STEVENSON

Where "The Black Cat" conforms to the tendency of the film to thematize gender relationships, the subsequent tale differs both thematically and stylistically. In "The Suicide Club," as in the first and the final episode, the uncanny elements are revealed as illusionary. A reviewer in *Der Film* notes this as a positive trait: "Just as subtle is the self-irony with which the fourth and fifth pieces undo their uncanny effect."[34] Based on Robert Louis Stevenson's collection *The Suicide Club* (1878), the story had already been brought to the screen six years earlier by Joseph Delmont in his *The Mysterious Club* (*Der geheimnisvolle Klub*, 1913). In this piece, it is Schünzel who plays the role of the hero, with Veidt the thoroughgoing villain. Schünzel, a police inspector, is walking outside of a mysterious house when he finds a note, apparently written by a woman being held captive inside. He begins to investigate and insinuates himself into the building, where he discovers that it houses a strange club: the members daily draw from a stack of cards and the recipient of the ace of spades then dies in a strange process initiated when the club president's (Veidt) presses a sequence of buttons. After indeed drawing the ace of spades, Schünzel attempts to escape, then appears to collapse, dead, on the table, another victim of Veidt's murderous apparatus. Once Veidt returns, however, we discover that Schünzel has not succumbed; instead, he traps Veidt using the latter's own death machine.

As noted, the "uncanny" is tied, in fact, to illusion and technology; it is the result of the murderous machine, combined with Veidt's carefully staged spectacle. In this sense, the episode is related to the first and the last tales, both of which reveal the rational explanations behind their uncanny events. Thematically, this episode is strikingly different from all others in the film, for here a woman does not play a central role; even more so than in the previous episode, she serves simply to move forward the plot. The woman may be the catalyst for Schünzel's entry into the club, but only via the note he discovers and the contents of which remain unknown to the viewer. Instead, the emphasis lies on the way in which the members of the club—and Schünzel—are threatened by Veidt with a loss of agency, and the central conflict is that between the two men vying for control. From the outset, the focus lies on Schünzel's resourcefulness. The episode opens with a close-up of his face, then cuts to a long shot of a large room, furnished with wing chairs and small tables, in which several men, dressed in dark suits, are seated together, before dissolving into a slightly closer shot of the room, focused on two men who are comforting a third. The sequence then cuts to a high-angle shot of a parklike area; we see Schünzel walking, pausing to look upward, then continuing out of the frame. The camera tracks with him as he moves along the exterior of the building, then the camera pauses, and he continues out of the shot before we see him bend to pick up the piece of paper that has been dropped to him from above.

The opening sequence seems to suggest a specific point of view; the high-angle shot of Schünzel walking through the park might be read as representing the gaze of someone inside the house. Given that, immediately afterward the note is dropped for Schünzel, we might see that shot as representing the woman's gaze at him. Schünzel initially is merely wandering through the park; only when she sees and drops the note for him do his actions become oriented toward a specific goal. Her gaze at the man sets the narrative in motion. The woman's function as a catalyst for male action is quite different here than in the previous episode. There, she spurred Veidt to action because he desired her; it was in her role as aesthetic object that she was figured within that narrative. Here, instead, she is not the object of his gaze—she is as yet unseen—but rather the bearer of the gaze that imparts meaning to the male protagonist.

The note initiates Schünzel's quest for discovery. Investigating the city records, Schünzel finds that the building is supposed to be empty, and resolves to gain entry. He does so by simply climbing up the ivy that covers the building, yet, even as he manages to look inside, he himself is being watched. We see a medium shot of the back of his head as he looks through a window at the men gathered inside, juxtaposed with a close-up of another window as a hand slowly pulls back a curtain to reveal Veidt, who looks out, nods, then drops the curtain back in place. This reciprocal surveillance is made more complex when we see Schünzel climb a tree, then are shown a close-up, point-of-view shot of a young woman looking out a window. She is visible behind the separated panes of the window, against a backdrop that is similarly dominated by bars, a fact that suggests she is trapped inside the house. The shot fades out and we cut back to the close-up shot of Schünzel in the tree, looking inside.

The opening of the episode presents an interesting situation: the sequence is entirely dominated by male figures, yet the motivation for Schünzel's actions lies with the sole female figure; still, we see her only in that single image that suggests her imprisonment and carries echoes of fairy-tale narratives. At the same time, the close-up of her face peering outside is doubled in the close-up of Veidt doing the same; the sequence thus complicates the opening suggestion—that she is "directing" the action through her contact with Schünzel—and instead implies, through that moment in which Veidt looks outside and nods knowingly, that this is all a part of his plan. The thematization of the gaze that first appears through that ostensible point-of-view shot continues, with all three characters alternately watching one another.

Once Schünzel is inside, Veidt quickly discovers him. At this point the woman reappears; as Schünzel confronts Veidt, she runs into the room, clutching at the latter and begging him to release—and not kill—the other man. We see her face, starkly lit, in a matted close-up as she implores him, then cut to a close-up of Veidt's, equally stark against the dark background, as he remains impassive, then gestures her away with a shake of his head. We then cut to a long shot of the room, Veidt still seated at the front center of the screen, as Schünzel, smiling, attempts to calm her. A group of servants approach from the rear then takes the young woman away; at this, Schünzel reacts with shock and begins to follow her, only to be stopped by one of the servants. Schünzel pauses and turns back to Veidt, who explains: "The lady is my sister. You are in a club that one enters voluntarily, and voluntarily never again leaves."[35] This is the final moment in which we see the woman; she does not reenter the story, having served her purpose—to act as the catalyst for Schünzel's introduction to the club. With Schünzel inside, the narrative trajectory shifts to the "game" itself.

The game played by the members of the club is presented as exclusively male; the sister plays no part, consigned to her room by the orders of her brother. The process by which the "winner" of the game dies is presented as a mixture of uncanny and mechanized elements. Once Schünzel draws the fatal card, the other men quickly leave Veidt alone with his victim. Ceding his throne-like chair to Schünzel, Veidt demonstrates the workings of his "suicide-machine": pushing a first button confines the victim to the chair, pushing the second leads to his death. We see Veidt threaten to push that second button, then watch his hand push the third, which opens a panel in the wall beneath the large clock over the table. After telling Schünzel that he will die at twelve o'clock, Veidt releases him from the chair, walks through the panel in the wall, and leaves the other man trapped alone in the room.

The central tension in this episode arises from the subsequent sequence, in which Schünzel faces his impending death. Made up of short-duration shots, the sequence builds toward Schünzel's anticipated death, alternating between close-ups of his face as he looks up at the glowing numerals of the clock, medium shots as he searches for an escape route, long shots of the fatal room, and—perhaps most alarmingly—close-ups of the face of the clock and of Veidt's eyes, lit only by a strip of light that leaves the rest of his face in shadows as he watches his victim. At one point we see Schünzel make a desperate bid for salvation; he rises, runs toward the clock carrying a chair, then climbs onto it and turns the minute hand back to eleven thirty, yet when the sequence cuts to a medium shot of Schünzel laughing in relief, the clock visible above him, we see the minute hand rapidly advance to its original position. As the minute hand inexorably advances, Schünzel sits down in the throne-like chair, the camera tilting with him to maintain his position in the center of the shot as he first sits, then rises again, clutching his chest before collapsing on the table. The sequence cuts to a close-up of the clock, now showing twelve o'clock, then tilts slowly down as a panel opens and Veidt approaches from the rear. We cut to a long shot of the room as Veidt enters and approaches the other man, who is stretched motionless on the table. An intertitle gives us his laconic statement: "The shock has killed him."[36]

Oswald builds the suspense effectively in this sequence: Schünzel's pacing and his fruitless search for an escape route, all depicted beneath the giant clock ticking mercilessly toward the moment of his death, are calculated to affect the viewer. As one critic noted, "when Reinhold Schünzel, watching the large clock, counts the few minutes that remain before his death, when the hand continues to advance and the clock finally begins to strike twelve without any sign of a savior, one truly does hold one's breath."[37] Oswald equally skillfully reverses the tension instilled in the audience, for Veidt's actions and threats against Schünzel are suddenly turned back on him by the supposed victim. As Veidt sits down in his chair, laughing, we see an intertitle quoting Veidt's previous explanation of the machine, that when he presses the button, his victim cannot rise. We cut back to a long shot as Veidt looks shocked, then Schünzel jumps quickly off the table. In the next shots, Schünzel mimics Veidt's earlier words and actions, pointing to the second button as though to press it. As Veidt sits trapped in his chair, Schünzel presses the last button, opening the panel in the clock; we then cut to a medium shot of the two men as Schünzel takes a card out of his wallet, then to a close-up of said card, identifying him as "Artur Silas, police inspector." With a jovial wave at Veidt, Schünzel departs.

If the episode represents a conflict between two men vying for control, then the ending resolves it in favor of self-determination and the forces of law and order; though Veidt appears to have undermined Schünzel's agency, ultimately we see that this was illusory. In his status as the president of the "suicide club," Veidt challenged masculine agency, seizing power over life and death, even over an individual's desires—for the members of the club are there "by choice," yet are not allowed to leave. With the woman present only as the initial catalyst for the action—as a sort of bait aimed to ensnare the next victim—the emphasis is squarely on the constructions of masculine subjectivity and identity. The hero—resourceful, courageous, and able to overcome a menace that is figured in both mechanical and supernatural terms—represents the individual that is able to triumph in the modern world. His role as part of the police suggests a benign state that enables and supports the individual.

At the same time, given the multiple moments in which we see characters watching one another, the staging of the "death" as a sort of voyeuristic spectacle, and the notion of being "spellbound" by the machine that evokes such strong emotions in its victim, we necessarily see an element of reflection on cinema itself. Schünzel's interest in the club is initiated by the note, then solidified once he peers through the windows and sees the men—and the single woman—inside. Schünzel is not only the bearer of the gaze but also its object, of the point-of-view shot at the opening and of Veidt's gaze. Indeed, as Schünzel seeks desperately to escape from the room in which he has been imprisoned, Veidt takes on even more explicitly the position of the viewer, embodied in his eyes staring out of the darkness at the other man's actions and clearly experiencing pleasure in watching his agonized behavior. This suggests a complex understanding of the respective roles of viewer and image, who oscillate between active and controlling agent and passive object, subject to the whims of the "director." Indeed, even the latter is not purely the guiding conscious behind the images on the screen but rather occupies an equally ambiguous position; witness Veidt, whose rules structure the club and who thus holds the power over life and death, but who eventually finds his power undermined and himself at the mercy of a new "director." The ending comes as a release: the third button pressed, Schünzel opens the door to the outside world, letting light into the darkened, menacing chamber and liberating the audience from its "captivity."

FIFTH EPISODE: "THE HAUNTING," OSWALD

Where the fourth episode minimizes the role of the woman, the fifth and final piece once again places her at center stage. This episode again centers on a marriage in trouble. Berber, married to Veidt, feels neglected by him. When a flirtatious nobleman, Schünzel, is injured and brought to the castle, she is quickly seduced by his attentions, in spite of his obvious exaggeration of his own qualities. Recognizing the situation, her husband devises a plan, telling his wife that he must leave on an urgent errand and consigning her to the baron's protection. While the two flirt over tea, a number of uncanny events suddenly happen: pictures begin to move up and down the wall, the chandelier descends and ascends spontaneously, and suddenly dark figures enter the room, menacing the wife and the baron. The latter reacts with terror. When the husband appears, she is relieved and their relationship restored.

More so than in the other episodes thematizing a woman's infidelity, here Berber's flirtation is not condemned but rather viewed as a result of her husband's failings. The opening shot of the episode shows a medium close-up of her, dressed in Rococo-style clothes and powdered wig. As she smiles coquettishly into the camera, then pouts and turns away, the sequence dissolves to a medium shot of her before cutting to an intertitle: "I, a young woman—it's ridiculous! I sit here entirely abandoned. My husband focuses on everything—except on me."[38] This opening not only introduces the central problem but also the tongue-in-cheek tone that the episode takes toward the topic, perhaps most clearly expressed in the rhyming intertitles. We see immediately that the plot of the episode hinges not on the wife's near infidelity but rather on the husband's neglect, and we are reminded that men, too, must fulfill a specific role in marriage. Veidt's character is portrayed as unaware of his wife's needs, while she is represented as feeling—quite rightfully—ignored. After the opening intertitle, we see a long shot, with Berber, at the front of the frame, seated alone in a darkened room. She calls over a servant, then sends him away, disappointment obvious in her mien; she then rises and walks to the rear of the room before moving out of the frame. In this brief moment, mise-en-scène reinforces the sense of her as being neglected. Dressed in a white dress with a powdered wig, moving from the front to the rear of the shot, her figure is isolated in the large, dusky space, visually representing her isolation in her relationship. Her husband is introduced immediately after this. In a medium shot, we see him bent over papers at a desk, looking up as Berber moves into the frame, then kissing her before she moves out of the frame again, temporarily mollified. The camera lingers on Veidt as he turns back to his work, then the sequence fades out. By opening with the image of the young woman, isolated and lonely, the episode establishes sympathy for her in the viewer. Her subsequent dalliance with the injured guest is thus positioned not as fundamentally immoral but as a result of her specific situation.

Of all the episodes, this is the most playful, in terms of its depiction of the relationship between the wife and their guest and of the "uncanny" events that lead to the couple's reconciliation. When he is first carried into the castle, the man is unconscious; in a long shot of the room, we see the wife, clapping her hands excitedly at the prospect of a guest, then rising as two servants enter from the rear, carrying the baron between them. After they seat him in a chair at the front of the frame, Berber dismisses them, then lifts one of his arms and lets it fall again before sitting down next to him. Schünzel's character is introduced as a literal plaything for the lonely woman, unconscious and doll-like. Her behavior emphasizes her

CHAPTER THREE

guilelessness in the way she approaches him. Still, as the episode progresses, it depicts the relationship between the wife and the visiting baron explicitly in terms of sexual transgression, staging a series of visual double entendres. We see him acting out his prowess in a significant way. In a long shot, we see the wife sitting at the lower left of the screen, while the baron pantomimes battle, pulling out his sword, then telling her: "Fear is a stranger to me. The fire of man's courage strengthens my limbs. Just yesterday, I vanquished a lieutenant with a smile in hand-to-hand combat."[39] The bombastic verse not only emphasizes Schünzel's pretension but also references the physical in a way that takes on erotic overtones when viewed in the context of his subsequent interaction with Berber. As he mimes inflicting a deadly thrust with his sword, the wife puts her hands to her mouth, obviously impressed. The baron wipes his sword lightly, then nicks his finger while attempting to put it into its scabbard. Enlisting the help of the wife, he holds the sword as she takes its tip and helps him replace it; at this moment, Veidt enters from a door at the rear. The sequence then cuts to a slightly high-angle close-up of the wife's face, level with the baron's groin, as she guides the tip of the sword into the scabbard, then cuts to a long shot as he forcefully inserts it and steps away from her. Seeing her husband behind the baron, the wife embraces and tells him: "This man has courage! Close to him every woman would feel steeled. It's entirely different when I see you, you, who is lacking everything to be a man."[40] The sequence cuts to a long shot of the couple embracing and the baron turning away, sucking at his injured finger, then from a medium shot of the latter to a medium close-up of the couple.

The exchange is overtly suggestive, with the sword standing in for the phallus and Schünzel's supposed fencing abilities for sexual prowess. At the same time, it constructs the wife as gullible, being taken in by the man's behavior where the viewer is not—Schünzel's pained response to his nicked finger contrasts starkly to Veidt's confident tolerance of his wife's dalliance. This confidence in his own masculinity is not even affected by her statement to him, though she questions his masculinity in the most direct terms, with her suggestions that "he lacks everything that would make him a man." The episode constructs the couple clearly through these opening scenes: the young woman is naive, immature, and not very smart, while her husband is tolerant, responsible, and understanding of her failings. The viewers are aligned with Veidt's character; aware of his neglect, yet equally aware of his responsibilities as a nobleman, they recognize his behavior as the root of his wife's transgression without condemning him. What makes the husband likeable is his tolerance and his intelligence. His response to the situation is playful, yet again demonstrates his intellectual superiority. Thus we see him in a brief shot in which he, seated at his desk and surrounded by his three servants, outlines his plan to reveal Schünzel and win back his wife's affection. The servants' amused reactions emphasize the playfulness of the moment.

Veidt's plotting demonstrates his awareness of their guest's questionable behavior, again suggesting an intellectual superiority on his part even while emphasizing his tolerance of his wife's failings. When Veidt tells his guest and his wife that he must temporarily leave, the sequence opens with a medium shot of Schünzel and Berber sitting on a sofa, the baron caressing the wife's hand. The camera tilts up to show Veidt approach, leaning against a doorframe to their rear, looking down at them with a knowing smile. As he steps down into the room, the wife quickly takes her hand out of that of the baron, while the latter noticeably increases the distance between the two. Veidt leans to kiss his wife, then tells them: "They call me away urgently on an important mission. I place my wife in your protection."[41] The baron reacts with obvious pleasure, clapping his hands lightly as Veidt departs, then leaning toward the woman. The triangulated relationship between the three characters is starkly drawn: the wife is the disputed object of desire, depicted as slightly childish and susceptible to the flattering attentions of the baron only because of her own boredom and feelings of being neglected; the baron, lecherous and dishonest, is no match for Veidt's husband, whose trickery will serve to reveal the other man's dishonesty and regain his wife's admiration.

Once the husband has departed, the uncanny events commence. The sequence begins with the wife preparing a table, covering it with flowers as she awaits her guest. When he approaches from the rear of the frame, she first turns away, then gives him her hand, which he kisses while bowing with a flourish. They sit down and she pours tea for them, then the sequence cuts to a medium shot as he grasps her hand and leans to kiss her shoulder and to a close-up as he kisses her again. The camera thus draws in more closely as their intimacy increases. This potential transgression is, however, interrupted by the haunting. In a long shot of the two seated at the table, we see the portraits hanging on the wall at the left of the frame slowly begin to rise. Both of the characters initially react with fear, then, as the wife cowers at the table, the baron rises and draws his sword, pointing it toward the pictures that now descend to their original place. They sit down again, then we cut to a close-up of the baron as he rapidly drinks a glass of wine. Again the long shot, with the baron rising and bending to kiss the woman; again, the portraits begin to rise along the wall, and this time the baron tries to shield himself with his ornate chair. The uncanny events only escalate after this. As they sit down again, the chandelier begins to descend toward the table, interrupting the baron's attempt to again kiss her and prompting him to draw his sword and feint toward the offending light fixture before cowering against the fireplace as the chandelier rises back to the ceiling. And, finally, two cloaked shapes enter the room, circling the table slowly and prompting the baron to lose consciousness. As Schünzel's character falls out of his chair, Veidt enters at the rear of the frame and the shot dissolves to a medium shot of him as his wife runs to him and he tells her: "A courageous man! Through his actions, he demonstrated courage that I lack. To flirt with my wife—that courage is courage that I don't have."[42] As two of the servants approach, laughing, he gestures them away and the shot dissolves to a close-up of the couple; she kisses him passionately, then puts her head on his shoulder as he utters the final lesson of the episode: "You feel love toward me igniting? When a woman kisses her husband one has to call that a tale that truly is entirely uncanny."[43]

The uncanny takes on a very different quality from the other episodes; here, it is quite obviously trickery, intended to reveal the baron's dishonesty and cowardice and restore the marital relationship. The events that interrupt the baron's advances toward the woman are, as the audience is quite aware, tricks that the husband planned and executed. Indeed, the camera work reveals quite clearly the mechanisms behind these "special effects"; the strings on which portraits are raised and lowered are certainly not hidden to the viewer of the film. The uncanny, here, is performed in order to evoke a specific response, to expose the baron's credulity and cowardice and thus undermine his masculinity. His reaction—the fact that he draws his sword as though he were confronting a flesh-and-blood enemy—reveals him to be fundamentally out of step with modernity, for it demonstrates his superstition and his recourse to older models of masculinity that are no longer applicable in a world in which reality can be mechanically manipulated. The baron contrasts sharply with Veidt; where the baron mistakes the mysteriously moving objects for things possessed, Veidt harnesses the potential of special effects and deploys them to demonstrate his intellectual superiority. This staging of the uncanny events points back to the film as a whole: there, too, the uncanny is staged with the aim of provoking specific reactions in the audience; there, too, what might strike the viewer as uncanny is the result of trickery, of the playful use of narrative and medium. The final episode then draws attention to the medium itself, emphasizing the disjuncture between the image and reality. In this sense, we might see Veidt's character as a representative for the director; witty, intelligent, and confident, he stands in for Oswald, whose direction has shaped the diegesis of the film as a whole, just as the husband's "direction" of the "haunting" leads to the intended resolution of the situation.

Thematically, the episode approaches sexual mores and roles far more playfully than do the previous; far from punishing the wife for her transgression, it suggests that the husband was to blame. The wife's flirtatious behavior is not condemned; rather, the episode implies that the erotic relationship based in mutual admiration and attention needs to be actively maintained within the marital relationship. Ultimately, the episode proposes a very different model of marriage than the conservative one, openly articulating this in the husband's comment that what is truly uncanny is "when a woman kisses her husband." This statement reveals a concern with and awareness of the ways in which, for women, marriage can be an unsatisfying institution; unappreciated and neglected by her husband, her desire for and affection toward him quickly fall victim. Indeed, the episode is equally progressive in its acknowledgment of sexual desire in women. Berber's flirtation with Schünzel is an outgrowth of her unsatisfied erotic drive; this desire is not eliminated or denied but rather redirected toward Veidt at the end of the episode. At the same time, Veidt's final lines reflect back on the content of the film as a whole and point again to the very definition of the uncanny. In the statement that this very domestic ideal—this "heimliche" situation of a woman embracing her husband—embodies precisely that which is "unheimlich," we see reference to Freud's original definition of the term. And, in this moment, we see a pointed reference to the notion at the basis of much of my analysis: that the "everyday" relationship between man and woman, the gender norms and dynamics that underlie culture's conception of itself, are themselves haunted by the uncanny, by that which we repress and deny. Any step outside of common norms of behavior—be that through the continuing existence of an erotically charged relationship between a husband and wife, as here, or through a broader emancipation from repressive gender norms, as embodied in the New Woman—thus embodies that uncanny that must be masked behind the uncanny narrative, behind the artificial trickery like that Veidt's embattled husband employed.

The final piece thus stands as the thematically most progressive of the five; we see a nuanced, modern understanding of the marital relationship. It is certainly not an ideal depiction—Berber's wife is far too silly to qualify as the ideal of an emancipated woman—but it nevertheless demonstrates sympathy with women who transgress norms of behavior by emphasizing the responsibilities that their husbands have toward them. The brief closing frame continues in such a playful vein: we return to the opening setting of the bookstore, where the shopkeeper tries to explain his experience to the policemen he has summoned. Unconvinced, they depart, leaving no witness when the portraits each make a final "statement": Berber slowly turns her head toward him, then sticks out her tongue, while Schünzel blows smoke into his face, precipitating the shopkeeper's frantic flight. The last moment again draws attention to the cinematic form and the technical skills of the actors. What triumphs, in the end, is the "trickery" of cinema: the pictures, though apparently once again contained, retain their life and the potential to reemerge from their frames at any point.

THE FILM AS A WHOLE

What we see after examining the frame narrative and the individual episodes is how diverse the film as a whole is. Oswald stages the uncanny in a range of ways, from overt trickery, to that which is, in the end, revealed to be very much based in the real, to that which can only be called supernatural. This diversity is a quality the genre of the omnibus film was uniquely able to explore and represents an attempt to cater to the audience's desire to experience a range of emotional responses. Particularly in a film designed—at least in part—to frighten, the variation in tone and content was viewed as effective; as one critic noted, "skillfully adapting to the needs of the film audience, only the first three pieces aim to frighten."⁴⁴ In this shifting between moods and themes, *Uncanny Tales* resembles more closely the *Varieté* (vaudeville) or a theatrical presentation of sketches than it does our modern conception of a feature film. Still, we can identify certain thematic strands that recur. As the title suggests, we see a preoccupation with the uncanny in all its permutations. If we consider the uncanny as revealing, per Freud, that which has been repressed, we can point to the content of each episode as revealing something about the hidden anxieties that dominated German culture at the time. Thus we might read "The Apparition," with its thematization of the plague and its depiction of Veidt as a victim of a conspiracy of silence, as reflecting fears of pandemics (perhaps tied to the worldwide lethal flu outbreak of 1918–20) and of the individual's increasing powerlessness in a modern society; "The Hand" as connecting to the interest in spiritualism and the occult that emerged in Germany in the early twentieth century; "The Black Cat" as engaging with questions of insanity and criminality that were particularly pressing after the national trauma of the First World War; "The Suicide Club" as asserting individual agency and the power of self-determination to a population whose sense of this had been undermined by war and modernity; and "The Haunting" as engaging with questions of reality and appearance that were raised by the developing medium of film. The episodes touch on a range of fears that dominated society at the time. These fears are bound up intimately with modernity; they represent the precarious position of the individual in a sociocultural setting that had undergone and continued to undergo rapid and fundamental change. And we see these fears and anxieties reemerge throughout Weimar in cinematic and cultural production, with the themes and types we find in *Uncanny Tales* reemerging again and again. Veidt's confusion of reality and imaginary has its doubles in *The Cabinet of Dr. Caligari* and in *The Hands of Orlac*; Berber as medium bears some resemblance both to *Caligari*'s Cesare and the doctor himself; Schünzel's two turns as failed husbands—first insane, then murderous—point toward the jealous rage of the husband in *Warning Shadows*.

Just how determinative of the era are the fears we see expressed becomes more clear when this version of *Uncanny Tales* is compared to Oswald's own remake from 1932. In that film, Oswald did away with the innovative episodic structure but retained two of the episodes used here—"The Black Cat"

CHAPTER THREE

and "The Suicide Club"—and wove them into a single, (relatively) cohesive narrative. The precise way in which Oswald reworked the film is interesting and bears at least brief examination, particularly as it draws attention again to the peculiarities of the original *Uncanny Tales* and points to the ways in which the position of film and the construction of gender changed over the course of the thirteen years between the respective releases.

Oswald's second version of *Uncanny Tales*[45] (*Unheimliche Geschichten*, working title: *Der Unheimliche*) premiered in Berlin in September 1932. This version focuses on a reporter, Frank Briggs (Harald Paulsen), who pursues a man (Paul Wegener) who murdered his wife and hid her body behind the cellar wall, seeking him out first in an insane asylum that has been taken over by its inmates, then in a suicide club. Oswald's film was greeted as a successful return to the type of uncanny film that had been so popular in the early years of the Weimar Republic. Reviews explicitly pointed back to the silent version and saw the film as a renaissance of earlier thematics. One reviewer in *Film-Kurier* stated that "Richard Oswald has again taken up his 'Uncanny Tales,' with which he was so successful during the era of the silent film, adapted to the sound film,"[46] and suggested that this tendency pointed to a continued interest in the uncanny: "In our time, which, in spite of its new objectivity, again and again focuses on transcendental things, the uncanny film has risen anew."[47] Another reviewer similarly suggested that the film connected to early cinematic narratives and praised Oswald for seeking out such "unusual" material.[48] Striking about both reviews is the implication that the cultural setting of the late Weimar Republic was one in which audience interest had moved away from the uncanny narratives that were so common in the late 1910s and early 1920s; so much so, indeed, that Oswald's film—which was, essentially, simply a rescripting of his earlier film—was viewed as an innovation.

We find in the two versions of *Uncanny Tales* fundamental differences that reflect not only the way in which society and culture developed, but also the distance between cinema in 1919 and 1932 respectively. The 1932 film opens with a scene of Briggs and his girlfriend (Mary Parker), who is a performer; as he drives her to her next engagement, he hears screams from Wegener's character's house and stops to investigate, sending her on her way. Meanwhile, Wegener, an inventor, is angered by his wife (Roma Bahn), who confronts him in his basement workshop and who he kills after her cat destroys the model of his "suicide machine." When Briggs later returns to the house with the police, they discover the woman's corpse behind the wall of the basement because Wegener accidentally sealed the cat in with the body. Wegener flees and is pursued by Briggs to a wax museum, where the two men struggle between the figures of famous murderers, brought to life by mechanical means. Wegener escapes to an emergency room, to which Briggs, injured in the struggle, follows him, only to find that he has been transported to an insane asylum. The hero follows him there and demands to see him, then discovers that the asylum has been taken over by its inmates. Briggs manages to free the imprisoned doctors and reimpose order. Some time later, Briggs goes to investigate a purported suicide club and finds that its president is the murderous husband. After drawing the ace of spades, Briggs is scheduled to die, but feigns his own death, imprisons Wegener's character in the machine he himself invented, then releases the grateful members of the club, with words of condemnation for Wegener and encouragement for the disillusioned members.

The most striking change from the early to the late version is the elimination of the frame story: where 1919's *Uncanny Tales* presented the internal episodes as structurally similar to literature, thus reflecting on the way in which film functions, the 1932 version attempts to create a single, coherent narrative. The characters no longer move between roles, drawing attention to themselves as actors, but are identified with a single character. Where, for example, Conrad Veidt shifted between romantic rival, evil leader of the suicide club, and tolerant husband, implicitly pointing back to his role as actor, here, Paulsen is only and always the stalwart reporter, while Wegener's murderous acts all stem from what is portrayed as the criminal insanity motivating his character. The critic in *Film-Kurier* defined contemporary society as interested in "the transcendental" despite its dominant position being rooted in "new objectivity"; this cultural orientation, diametrically opposed to the expressionist tendencies of early Weimar, is illustrated in the very different approach Oswald takes in 1932 to depicting the uncanny.

Indeed, by removing the frame narrative, Oswald reshapes the film fundamentally, adapting it to a cultural setting in which cinema increasingly aimed for verisimilitude, for a representation of "reality" in a way that deflected attention from the cinematic apparatus. The uncanny is subordinated to the adventure tale: every plot element in this piece is explicable based on Wegener's insanity; gone are the playful attempts to reflect on varying "types" of uncanny experiences. In its earlier incarnation, Oswald's film drew on the frame narrative depicting the uncanny event of paintings coming to life and connecting to the conception of cinema as living images both to distance the viewer from the interior episodes by furnishing a "rational" explanation for them and to suggest a structural similarity between the public experience of cinema and the private one of reading. The experience of watching a film, there, was explicitly structured as parallel to the process of imagining the images of a textual narrative. Without the frame narrative, *Uncanny Tales* reads like classical cinema; the process of watching a film and the dynamic relationship between viewer and images are no longer explicitly referenced. The narrative attempts to impose a logical explanation for the uncanny events depicted, thereby shifting, as a reviewer noted in *Der Film*, to an exploration of criminal insanity: "What is terrifying and uncanny in this film is based on human imagination and fantasy.... The uncanny yields finally to the sphere of criminal insanity, which is solved by a very much rational young man."[49] No longer does Oswald aim to exploit the audience's awareness of the cinematic apparatus, to build on the viewer's awareness of the medium; instead, he creates a piece that aims for a seamlessly voyeuristic effect, where the audience can become immersed in the images unreeling on the screen and forget the technology and manipulations underlying the film.

At the same time, we might see this fundamental shift as reflecting a very different relationship between viewer and film. Where, in 1919, *Unheimliche Geschichten* drew on the notion of cinema as inherently uncanny, as the simulation of life on screen, in 1932, the audience would have been far more inured to the experience of watching a film. And, like in his version of *Alraune*, which I will discuss later, Oswald does little to exploit the uncanny potential of sound. We might see this as a peculiarity of Oswald's cinematic style; at the same time, it supports the suggestion Robert Spadoni makes in his discussion of the uncanny in early sound film, that "technical changes combined with the waning of the novelty of sound film to effect a steady down-turn in medium-sensitive viewing."[50] Early sound film might well have carried the potential to be uncanny simply by virtue of its components, yet it did so only for a very brief time, and Oswald, in his second *Uncanny Tales*, made little use of this peculiarity. The effect is to lull the viewer into a unified viewing experience, to eliminate the breaks and disruptions that characterized so many of the earlier pieces and that forced the viewer to reflect on the films as film.

Thematically, too, this version of *Uncanny Tales* enacts a characteristic shift. Where the earlier version foregrounded gender and relationship dynamics, this one is dominated by a strong male hero who single-handedly unveils and successfully pursues the murderer. This new emphasis on the male figures as the driving force in the film is evident in the working title of the film, *Der Unheimliche (The Uncanny One)*,[51] which presumably refers to Wegener's antagonist and thereby directs attention to the relationship between his character and that of Paulsen. The women in this version of the film take on even less central roles than they did in the earlier version. We see only a few female figures that are in any way significant, and even they are given minimal screen time and character development. Women appear in roles that can be described more as a part of the mise-en-scène than as active figures in the advancement of the narrative. Thus we initially see Briggs in a car with his presumed girlfriend, who disappears from the narrative after Briggs begins to investigate Wegener; we see Wegener's wife, whom he quickly murders and who then is shown again only as a corpse; we see a few women who are inmates of the insane asylum, characterized chiefly by their obvious insanity and thereby adding to the sense of the "uncanny" surroundings; and we see a woman who is a member of the suicide club and whom Briggs, in the end, encourages to seek out life rather than death. All of these women conform far more to the notion of women in film as passive, aesthetic objects than did the women in the films I have previously analyzed.

To return to the "original" *Uncanny Tales*, what is interesting about it and what becomes even clearer when we compare it to the later version is that it addresses cultural anxieties through narratives that coalesce around relationships between men and women: failed marriages, flirtations, and potential love affairs; strong male bonds disrupted by emancipated women or illicit passions. We see this pattern again and again in films of the era; woman, whether threatening, inspiring, desired, or feared, functions as the site at which not only her own changing role, but also sociocultural changes quite outside of gender, are confronted, imagined, and dealt with. In Oswald's first *Uncanny Tales*, the women at the hearts of the stories drive

CHAPTER THREE

men to insanity or to action and are functionalized to represent the disruptive sociocultural element that has the potential to inspire everything from murder to creative success. In this sense, however sympathetically Oswald might figure Berber in her various roles, woman nevertheless tends to be presented as a "passive" character, in that the focus is not so much on her actions as it is on those she causes men to take. At the same time, because of Berber's life off screen, the characters she depicts share a common association with sexual transgression and active erotic desire. In this, Berber in her many and multiplied guises represents the full range of emancipated woman, and thereby the full range of the ways in which she threatens masculine subjectivity.

FOUR

WARNING SHADOWS (SCHATTEN: EINE NÄCHTLICHE HALLUZINATION, ARTUR ROBISON, 1923)

Transgression, Abjection, Projection

1923 FINDS US IN a very different cultural moment than the one in which *Uncanny Tales* premiered four years before. It marks the endpoint in the early, crisis-ridden years of the young republic, which had seen political turmoil and the lingering effects of the war and was now facing rampant inflation. By the time Artur Robison's *Warning Shadows (Schatten: Eine nächtliche Halluzination*[1]) premiered in Berlin on October 16, 1923, the republic was nearing the peak of the crisis that would be resolved through the introduction of the *Rentenmark* in November. The mark was virtually worthless, with a dollar buying 25.2 billion.[2] The issue of *Film-Kurier* that reviewed Robison's new movie on October 17 sold for 5 million. Yet inflation certainly did not halt the accelerating development of the German film industry. Beyond the sheer number of works produced during this time, a proliferation of industry journals and magazines is testimony that those involved in cinema felt they were taking part in a momentous process, in no less than the creation of a new form of art. What the deepening economic crisis did was to bolster the cultural anxieties coalescing around gender and identity that had been dominating Weimar society since the birth of the republic. In Robison's *Warning Shadows*, we see an extreme example of the reaction to this complex of fear, desire, and disavowal.

Robison took an active part in the debates surrounding the medium. Indeed, given his work, it is surprising that so little is now known about him; so sparse is the biographical data available that the biography on filmportal.de, the website the Deutsches Filminstitut (German Film Institute) maintains, notes that it is "based on contradictory short portraits from the 1920s that cannot be checked."[3] Born in 1888 in the United States as the son of German immigrants, he returned to Germany with his family seven years later and studied medicine before giving up his career as a physician and turning to the theater. Robison's birth and early migration set the tone for his subsequent life: he moved frequently between Germany, other European nations, and the United States. His early experiences as a stage actor were in the United States, then, in 1914, he returned to Germany, where his interest in film was sparked. He directed a number of films in Germany, the United States, and Switzerland before *Warning Shadows*, his best-known piece. After its release, he worked for a time in London, where he filmed parts of UFA's *Looping the Loop* (1928) and followed that film with *The Informer* (British International Pictures, 1929), his first sound film. In the early 1930s, he again worked in Hollywood, this time for Metro-Goldwyn-Mayer, before returning to Germany in 1933. He died there two years later, while completing his version of *The Student of Prague* (*Der Student von Prag*, 1935).[4]

Robison is certainly not a household name when we think of Weimar film today. He was nowhere near as prolific as were Lubitsch and Oswald, for example, nor have as many of his films survived. And, while the actors he cast in *Warning Shadows* were a talented and diverse group, they, too, are less well known today. Fritz Kortner, who plays the lead, was a prolific actor from 1915 on, and though many of his roles were in films that are today lost or largely forgotten, they were nevertheless hits at the time and do include starring roles in films like *Satanas* (Murnau, 1920), *The Hands of Orlac* (Wiene, 1924), and *Pandora's Box*. Ruth Weyher, the flirtatious wife, had frequent roles in films throughout the 1920s and even briefly worked as a producer, for the 1928 film *What's Wrong with Nanette* (*Was ist los mit Nanette*, Holger-Madsen). Alexander Granach, the traveling entertainer, was another prolific actor whose career took him from roles like that of Knock in Murnau's *Nosferatu* to those in Hollywood films like *Ninotchka* (Lubitsch, 1939) and *Hangmen Also Die!* (Lang, 1943). And Gustav von Wangenheim, frequently cast, as here, in the role of the handsome young lover, is perhaps best known for his role as Hutter in *Nosferatu*, but he acted steadily throughout the 1920s before fleeing Germany once the Nazis rose to power.

The relative unfamiliarity today with Robison and with the actors he cast in *Warning Shadows* serves to remind us how limited our understanding of Weimar film production remains and how much is left to discover. Even admitting that we have access to only a limited amount of the era's filmic production, the emphasis on a small number of films and directors who are considered canonical has led to a view of Weimar cinema that is far from complete. The fact that Robison is not known as widely today as are directors like Lang, Wiene, or Lubitsch is less a reflection on his artistic ability and his significance to the developing medium than it is on the circumstances of his career and the vagaries of a historical era that saw so many of its cinematic production lost. In fact, the reception of the film, as well as the critical writings that focused on it, demonstrate Robison's active participation in an attempt to cultivate film as an autonomous and respected art form and suggest that he was very much engaged with the technical development of the medium. Indeed, when *Warning Shadows* premiered in 1923, it was almost universally hailed as a major step in the development of film. In July of 1923, a reviewer in *Kinematographische Monatshefte* called the film "an artistic accomplishment that will show German film new paths, help spread its reputation in all countries of the world."[5] In the October/November issue of the same journal, Paul Hildebrandt hailed the film as one "that for the first time proves even to the harshest opponent of film: here there is a new genre with its own rules, in which the utmost can be achieved just as in painting, sculpture, music, etc.,"[6] and he compared it favorably to certain films that were already considered artistic masterpieces:

> We have in the meantime seen the films by Wegener and were able to point to the singular significance of this reformer of the feature film; we saw good historical films like "Madame Dubarry" and "Anna Boleyn," we learned through the films by Svenska that there is an element in the homogenous closeness of Swedish farming culture which makes film there a priori, so to speak, superior to

German film; we found in "Caligari" and "Nosferatu" a fantastic-uncanny note struck most strongly—and yet "Schatten" is far superior to all of these films, because it combines all of their virtues into one and gives us virtually the greatest that has thus far been accomplished, perhaps even the utmost attainable.[7]

High praise for a film that has certainly not enjoyed the esteem of such Wegener classics as *The Golem*, let alone Wiene's *Caligari* and Murnau's *Nosferatu*. The review was the second review of the film in *Kinematographische Monatshefte*—this fact alone, as the author notes, was unprecedented[8]—and spanned a full four pages, analyzing and praising the film's technical achievements. Hildebrandt was especially impressed that Robison had dispensed with intertitles, relying not on text but purely on the visual in order to advance the narrative and clarify characters' emotions and responses. *Warning Shadows* became a symbol of film's potential as an independent and valid artistic medium. Hildebrandt saw this innovation as both revolutionary in terms of the development of the medium and especially appropriate to the thematic of the film:

> In nearly all reviews I found praise for the lack of intertitles, thus for the fulfillment of a demand that was raised in 1917 at the meeting in Stettin.[9] That *Warning Shadows* is yet understandable, indeed, that intertitles would here only function as a disturbance, is, based on what I have said, because primitive urges are easily represented mimetically, therefore speak directly through the image to the viewer; that intertitles would here only interfere is due to the sphere in which the film plays: in the fantastic, with which the rational cannot coexist.[10]

Hildebrandt makes clear that the development of the medium's conventions was a topic of discussion for artists and critics invested in advancing cinema's status as an art form equal to, yet independent of, other artistic media. We can see Robison's film not only as entertainment but also as a direct intervention in that debate. In this sense, the content seems to Hildebrandt virtually secondary, other than through its status as "fantastic" rather than "rational." Indeed, his review essentially elides the actual content of the film in favor of focusing on technique and effect. Addressing the central hallucinatory episode, with its sadistic depiction of the wife's murder, Hildebrandt argues that the viewer experiences this as representing the fantastic, rather than the real, within the film:

> But at the same time, the author spares us the most extreme: that terrible tension that would let this film be experienced as a work of art, but not as *the* work of art, the last possible one. We already *know* through the frame narrative that all of these terrible things, the murder of the wife, the husband's growing insanity, the brutal acts of the suitors, are not anything real. It is "the other side of their beings" that emerges—symbolically represented by the fact that, under the influence of the entertainer, they suddenly appear on the other side of the table. Through this process space is created for the most monstrous things, for a dream world, a world of blind drives, of most extreme possibilities, in which passions play themselves out without inhibitions, without touching us in our souls as *realities*, but rather as *truths*[11] (his emphases).

Hildebrandt's interpretation of the frame narrative's effect and of the relationship between it and the interior, hallucinatory episode is a fascinating reflection of the way it might have been read at the time. On one hand, he suggests that the viewers would interpret the characters' actions as occurring in a "dream world," as representing not "Wirklichkeiten," not real events, but rather "Wahrheiten," deeper truths. To Hildebrandt, in other words, the film is doubly removed from the viewers; these are not real events that they witness, but rather representations of representations, cinematic images of symbols. On the other hand, Hildebrandt's own interpretation of the viewing experience implies the significance of the events represented. His notion that the frame narrative creates a space in which "passions may play out without inhibitions" intimates that those "monstrous things" that occur in the hallucinatory episode represent desires and anxieties that cannot be acknowledged openly. In this sense, even without addressing directly the *content* of that hallucination, Hildebrandt's review lends credence to this analysis, for it draws attention to the significance of these events to the viewer's psyche.

The review is also interesting because it suggests that *Warning Shadows* was one of a small group of films that were regarded as true artistic masterpieces and that it inspired a good deal of debate among critics and, one would presume, among the viewing public as well. Robison himself, spurred by criticism of the idea of films without intertitles, articulated his programmatic reflections on the medium. In an at times very personal exchange in *Der Film-Kurier*, he countered an argument by Walter Jonas in favor of the use of intertitles. Jonas had challenged the notion that "the good film, the only true film, is the film without intertitles."[12] Jonas anticipated the arguments of those in favor of films without intertitles:

> I can already hear the answer: first general phrases like "optical experience" . . . "figuratively seen" . . . "visual" and whatever other little words there are that are always raised at the right time when terms are lacking. But then the actual argument comes, the only one: text is something that is borrowed from literature, and film is something entirely independently understandable, is optical, has nothing to do with other genres of art, not with the epic, the theater, music, or painting.[13]

Jonas did not see in these arguments the attempt to advance cinema as a medium; the very tone of his statements—condescending, even mocking—suggests that, to him, filmmakers and critics who would follow these injunctions were simply misguided. He viewed film as more closely related to theater than to the visual arts because of its dependence on chronology and suggested that denying film the use of the written word would impoverish the medium. In a final, fairly antagonistic jibe at those who would aim for films that were "pure" because they dispensed with intertitles, he noted: "It is symptomatic that the obsession with the film without intertitles was born in Germany, for here it has always been usual to limit organic growth through rigid theories, through pointless speculations by overly smart people, without any relationship to life; first the (only half thought-through) doctrine, then art (see expressionism)!"[14]

Jonas's disdain for the "obsession with films without intertitles" suggests an understanding of the medium as separate from such theorization. His central emphasis was on the narratives rather than on the possibilities of film as an independent medium, hence the emphasis on its similarity to theater. In spite of himself, he implied that film had some artistic status by comparing it with a more established artistic movement—namely, expressionism. Clearly, however, Jonas had little respect for that, either. Indeed, Jonas seems to suggest a divide between the artistic film and the film that appeals to and fulfills audience demands; in this, he articulates a question that plagued the film industry at the time and that, to be sure, continues to be posed in relation to modern cinema.

Judging by his response, which was rapid and heated, Robison took Jonas's accusations personally, though perhaps not very seriously. He brushed off Jonas's qualifications to reflect on film, directing his statements "less to the author, who will let it roll off his back with the superiorly smiling gesture of the enviable one with a solid skull—and with the secret titillation at having been taken so seriously—than to the reader who is occupied with other things and who does not yet have a position on the film without intertitles."[15] Noting that the vast majority of films would continue to use intertitles because producers "must, in accordance with average taste, produce entertainment films and, secondly, because only a few themes are suitable to be presented in pure, wordless films,"[16] Robison implied that those films that do eschew intertitles represented a development and refinement of the medium, rather than functioning as mere "entertainment." He, like Jonas, seemed to accept the differentiation between "Unterhaltungsfilme"—films aimed to entertain, to cater to that "average viewer"—and artistic films, those that embody "pure filmic representation." Robison undermined Jonas's suggestion that film constitutes a "composite art form," even as he argued that, were it such, it would not necessarily need to include text: "To call film a composite medium is an old and superficial definition; to call it a composite of image and word is nonsense. And, even if one were to accept the analysis that 'film is a mixed art,' this would not prove that it must necessarily include a linguistic component."[17]

Robison's rebuttal is a passionate—and at times arrogant—reflection of his self-estimation. To him, the "average reader" and, presumably, movie patron is at once superior to Jonas and the representative of an "average taste" that is, at its basis, opposed to the artistic development of film. He himself, as a director who produced a film without intertitles, takes part in that "pure, word-less film composition" that he sees as the epitome of cinematic art. His reflections are deeply personal, suggesting that directors who strive to create these "pure" films are part of an avant-garde, even while avoiding any mention of his own foray into that model, for nowhere does he reference *Warning Shadows*. This did not escape Jonas, who had the last word in the debate that the editors of *Film-Kurier* suggested was eliciting "on this overly personal level only few objectively productive perspectives."[18] Jonas noted that with *Warning Shadows*, the "Drachentöter" ("dragon slayer") Robison was himself the director of one of "two truly successful attempts to create films without intertitles."[19] Oscillating in tone between mocking and conciliatory, Jonas stated that he never intended to suggest that films without intertitles should not be produced, but rather simply spoke against "the attempts at a monopoly on the part of proponents of the film without intertitles"[20] with the aim of undermining the notion that "film with intertitles = entertainment, film without intertitles = art."[21]

This exchange between Robison and Jonas gives us an understanding of the ways in which debates about the development of film played out in the era and a more rounded of image of Robison himself. It makes clear just how much Robison's focus lay on the form of the piece, on its function as representative of a step in the development of cinema, and it reveals the way in which theories of film were growing up around the industry in the era. This is striking, for, in concentrating on the form of the work, the discussion pays little attention to the film's peculiar narrative. And the narrative of *Warning Shadows* is certainly a peculiar one, essentially depicting in the most sadistic terms the brutal punishment of a woman whose behavior challenges traditional gender norms. *Warning Shadows* takes place in a single night and centers on a man (Kortner) who is consistently undermined by his flirtatious and perhaps adulterous wife (Weyher). While entertaining four of the woman's admirers, including a young man who seems to be her lover (von Wangenheim), the husband becomes increasingly enraged by her attention to the other men. During the meal, a traveling illusionist (Granach) entertains the assembled party with a double feature: first a shadow-puppet play focused on an adulterous wife; then a second, metaphorical shadow play, in which the guests appear to take part in a communal vision or hallucination and act out their desires through their "shadow selves." In this hallucinatory episode, the husband witnesses his wife's dalliances with her young admirer and, in response, acts out a sadistic, punitive fantasy, having her bound by servants and forcing her assembled suitors to kill her. Freed from his madness by her death, the distraught husband is quickly dispatched by the suitors, who unceremoniously defenestrate him. The hallucination having culminated in its fatal end, the party awakens. The entertainer's presentation has worked as intended: the young wife, cured of her flirtatiousness, has eyes only for her husband, and the suitors depart.

This is the narrative that film critics of the time largely ignored in favor of their focus on the technical peculiarities of the film, a narrative in which central significance is given to a murder that, as we will see, carries both sadistic and erotic overtones. This blind spot continues, as well, in modern analyses of *Warning Shadows*. The film has inspired surprisingly little scholarly attention and almost none focused on gender issues. As with so many Weimar films, subsequent analyses have tended to be shaped by Kracauer's reading, which hailed *Warning Shadows* as "among the masterpieces of the German screen"[22] and as one of a small group of films that "aimed at endowing rational thinking with executive powers"[23] during the post–World War I period. To Kracauer, the film staged a sort of "magical therapy [that] recalls model cases of psychoanalytical treatment."[24] Kracauer's emphasis was thus on the resolution of the film; the outcome of *Warning Shadows* as a "model case of psychoanalytic treatment" is one in which the conflict is addressed and resolved, the marital unit repaired. As such a cinematic representation of psychoanalysis, *Warning Shadows* could be grouped with films like Pabst's *Secrets of a Soul* (*Geheimnisse einer Seele*, 1926), where the process and outcome of analysis is an explicit part of the narrative. Kracauer's reading also points to the thematization of hypnosis that here, as in *Eyes of the Mummy*, references its function in contemporary psychological treatment. To Kracauer, the enactment of violence in *Warning Shadows* is entirely secondary and serves only as a necessary therapeutic component.

Subsequent scholars have similarly focused on the resolution of the film. Frances Guerin interprets the central hallucinatory episode as an experience that allows the characters to resolve their irrational urges and emphasizes its positive effects on the husband, arguing that "the husband as hero journeys to the edge of reality—here, into the illusory uncertainties of representation—and returns having resolved the conflicts that plague him."[25] James C. Franklin, in his examination of the function of the shadow in *Nosferatu* and *Warning Shadows*, also ultimately stresses the manner in which the hallucinatory episode serves to constructively enable the characters to reconcile their own dangerous desires: "This confrontation with their own dark drives permits a final rejection—or perhaps it is a Jungian assimilation—of these impulses in the film's happy ending of loyal friendship and marital reunion."[26]

Certainly these scholars are quite right in suggesting that *Warning Shadows* frames its narrative as an experience that leads to a sort of psychological and moral progress. And they do suggest the significance of gender roles and relationships within the film, in that they acknowledge the central importance of the relationship between husband and wife. Yet what interests me in the context of this study is how *Warning Shadows*, in its depiction of that central conflict, engages with and represents anxieties emerging out of the specific sociocultural moment, and, through its depiction of the woman at the center of the narrative, takes part in the development of cinematic conventions focused on gender, the gaze, and power. The context of the film, we must recall, is a society that has been traumatized by war and by five years of subsequent poverty and instability. If there is a perceived "winner" in this new society, it is woman, who gained rights and privileges through the experience of war and the institution of the Weimar constitution that have fundamentally changed her status in relation to men. Already in *The Eyes of the Mummy* and *Uncanny Tales*, we have seen the way in which female emancipation was coded as sexual transgression and punished with either death or reassimilation into a more traditional heterosexist structure. In *Warning Shadows*, we see perhaps the most extreme of the punitive fantasies, for assimilation is achieved only because the woman experiences— and the spectator witnesses—her death. In this sense, what we see are not the characters coming to terms with what Franklin called "their own dark drives,"[27] but rather a reenvisioning of woman's emancipation in terms of sexual excess and transgression, and a fantasy of return to a previous model of social roles and hierarchies that is embodied in an ostensibly powerful male gaze. This is the conflict at the heart of *Warning Shadows*: the clash between traditional social and marital roles and those theoretically allowed by a new society, the clash between woman as passive object, subjugated to first father, then husband, and woman as active subject.

The conflict is acted out not only on the level of narrative but also on that of cinematic structure. This analysis of the film will reveal that *Warning Shadows*, both through the narrative wherein the adulterous wife is reconciled with her husband only after "experiencing" her own murder and through the structural peculiarity that comments on the relationships between viewer and objects of the gaze, responds to shifting gender roles in Weimar culture. On one level, the film works to restore male power by subjugating the threatening woman on the level of narrative and of structure. The male subject regains power by reasserting a model of gender roles that denies woman her newfound freedoms—here coded as sexual—and repositions her as passive object. Yet even as it does so, *Warning Shadows* undermines the stability of that power, laying bare the fundamentally limited control the viewer exerts.

To examine the film, I will first turn to its self-reflexive moments in which it reflects on the medium and to the way this aspect of the film shapes our reading of the gender problematic. I will then examine the construction of the relationship between the husband and wife, in which the husband's increasing loss of power is quickly—and violently—reversed. The details of the narrative and cinematic presentation of the conflict suggest a gaze that becomes representative of masculine power, on the part of character and spectator. Equally, the contrasting constructions of the wife and the maid suggest that active female power is the potentially destabilizing and dangerous element. In this sense, *Warning Shadows* represents another point in the development of the filmic trope of masculine viewer and passive female object, a constellation emerging out of the sociocultural need to reassert a power perceived as having been undermined. And yet, at the same time, the film reveals the fundamentally mitigated power accorded the spectator. The dynamics in the film construct an ostensibly powerful gaze even as they undermine an active spectatorship. Here—in the complicated and multiplied constructions of seeing and the ambiguous power assigned to the process—we can trace the way in which cinema developed gendered structures in response to cultural anxieties.

In terms of the structures of the gaze, *Warning Shadows* superficially seems to act out a fundamentally conservative model, aligned with that articulated by critics like Mulvey, wherein the woman figures as passive object of a controlling male gaze. Yet when we look closely, we see moments of slippage and ambiguity that suggest a more complex structure at work and that problematize any straightforward reading of power dynamics. For one, as we will see, *Warning Shadows* presents a female lead who explicitly stages herself as object of desire, and who does so fully self-consciously, unlike Mâ in *Eyes of the Mummy*. In her analysis of early German cinema, Heide Schlüpmann offers interesting ideas on the ways in which those films empowered the female spectator and the actor who became her double. Regarding the former, she suggests that "the 'danger' posed by the cinematograph around this time was not just that female audiences would gain insight into the erotic pleasure of men but also that it enabled women's self-perception. The prejudice of a gender-specific self-reflexivity as formulated by Jean Paul—'only man, not woman, looks at himself'—was shaken."[28] To Schlüpmann, a woman's role as actor represented an explicit assertion of agency:

> The actress had always been a "modern" woman.... She appropriated for herself, like a man, a public, self-determining existence and engaged in an experimental relationship to the world.... Onstage, actresses had to hide their intrinsic modernity beneath the presentation of images of women constructed by men. Film, in contrast, gave them a chance for self-representation in the sense of an emancipation from these images: no dramatist, no director determined their performance before the camera.[29]

On one hand, Schlüpmann's analysis of the way in which film enabled women to enact, in their performance, "self-representation" that was tied to "emancipation" is not entirely applicable to a film like *Warning Shadows*, where there was, indeed, a director who "determined their performance." The business of film had certainly changed by the time Robison made *Warning Shadows*. Yet Schlüpmann's analysis offers intriguing insight into such later films, opening up the ways in which we might conceptualize the position of the female spectator and that of the wife who so consciously stages herself. For, if the notion of "women's self-perception" was a prospect that caused consternation such a relatively short time earlier, then certainly here, in a film that allows women to regard their double as she stages herself and engages in an act of the sort of "self-representation" that Schlüpmann regards as emancipatory, the position of the female spectator might be more empowered than would initially appear. By emphasizing the conscious quality of the wife's self-display and directly thematizing the process, the film suggests a dimension of power in this act, undermining the notion that the object of desire is fundamentally *object*, passive and deprived of agency. By putting herself on display the woman challenges the men around her, threatening their control and their hitherto stable positions, and this potential for empowerment is extended to the female viewer. The cinematic strategies that work to control the woman-as-object—the ways in which she is subjugated to a gaze that attempts, however incompletely, to control—are then an expression not of a preexisting and universal power structure, but of a desperate response to the challenge she poses.

Indeed, if the process of self-staging takes on such a central role, what does that say about gender categories in general? If this identity of transgressive woman, as "New Woman," is a performance rather than an expression of a "real" essence of identity, then how does that shape the construction of the gaze, of the relationship between image and spectator? Even during the era, we see an awareness of the problematics of gender, a suggestion that gender identity is not an expression of a natural essence, but a performative quality. Thus Joan Riviere argued that gender entails a "masquerade," posing a key question: "what is the essential nature of fully developed femininity? What is *das ewig Weibliche*? The conception of womanliness as a mask, behind which man suspects some hidden danger, throws a little light on the enigma."[30] Interestingly, when considered in connection with *Warning Shadows*, Riviere began her remarks with the analysis of a patient of whom she found that "the explanation of her compulsive ogling and coquetting—which actually she was herself hardly aware of till analysis made it manifest—was as follows: it was an unconscious attempt to ward off the anxiety which would ensue on account of the reprisals she anticipated from the father-figures after her intellectual performance."[31] We see, in the wife in *Warning Shadows*, this sort of "compulsive ogling and coquetting." If the wife represents the feared New Woman—but does so through staging herself and performing transgressive behavior that is embodied in her open exhibition of desire and sexuality—then does this image she projects conform to her "real" identity, or does it act, as in Riviere's case, as a sort of "mask" that hides an even more terrifying prospect—namely, "intellectual" or social power? And, if this image of femininity is a performance, what about the men that surround her? Gender as performance implies the denaturalization not only of femininity but also of masculinity. The husband's assertion of sadistic power, the admirers' lecherous gazes, and the ostensible lover's devotion—these, too, would then constitute performances. If we consider the characters' actions and desires as components of masquerade, then the stability of the various power relationships—and of the notion of a gendered, powerful gaze—is further undermined. And indeed, from the start, the film emphasizes the sense of characters as constructed, as acting out types instead of "true" identities.

The film begins with a theatrical sequence in which the characters are introduced to the viewer. The opening shot shows a small stage, curtain still drawn, with a candle on the floor in front of it; a hand then reaches from behind the shell-shaped cover of the prompter's box, takes the candle, and the curtain opens to reveal a blank screen. The film draws attention to itself as film, emphasizing its status as art, separate from the real; what will be presented is a shadow play on multiple levels. The individual characters—presented as anonymous types, that is, "the woman," "the man,"[32]—are introduced in a series of shots that emphasizes the techniques on which the film draws. Thus, after the curtain opens, we first see the silhouette of two hands covering the screen, after which their shadows move apart and the husband, Kortner, stands before the screen. He looks toward each of the stage wings before his image dissolves into his silhouette, which pantomimes listening, then moves off stage. Similarly, the woman, introduced next, first moves onto the stage and stops at its center, then gestures toward someone off stage before putting her finger to her lips. The shot then dissolves to her silhouette, which is quickly covered by that of the hand; when the latter completes the "wiping" motion across the screen, the wife has disappeared. The remaining introductions of characters work similarly: the "youth" (and the wife's ostensible lover) moves to the center of the stage and picks up a sword before the shot dissolves to his silhouette, which is again "wiped away" by the shadow of the hand; the three admirers approach stage center and make gestures outlining a woman's body before they are covered by a silhouette of the wife's head; and, finally, the two male servants arrive, move toward the faint silhouette of a woman's body (apparently that of the maid) that appears between them, then fade to their silhouettes and disappear. The final two characters are presented in a way that breaks from this pattern: the maid simply walks across the stage, after which a man—the "entertainer"—rises out of the prompter's box, looks after her, tips his hat at the camera, then follows her off stage.

This opening sequence touches on the crux of the narrative—namely, the dangerous consequences that follow when a woman acts on and gains erotic power. The young man is clearly a competitor for the husband, and the phallic symbol of the sword emphasizes the sexual nature of the competition. The lecherous behavior of the three suitors again suggests sexual competitiveness, which is immediately tied to the woman when the figures of the men dissolve into a silhouette of her head. This dissolve is particularly interesting as it suggests a sort of reciprocal relationship between the men and the woman: they are preoccupied with her beauty, yet she, too, literally has the men "on her mind." The servants, too, are implicated in a power relationship in which a woman's body functions as object of attraction and desire. And, equally, woman's sexuality takes center stage in the introduction of the maid and the entertainer, drawn as he is by her beauty to literally chase her off the stage. The introduction thus figures female sexuality—and its problematic effect on men—as being at the center of the narrative action that follows.

At the same time, the sequence draws attention to the constructed nature of film and to the role the director takes in guiding actions and creating characters on screen. The repeated use of trick photography—the dissolves that make the characters appear and disappear in front of the projection screen—references and accords central significance to the technical possibilities of cinema. The "shadows" of the title are, as the sequence reminds the viewer, a fundamental part of film, where shadows are projected and manipulated at the behest of the director. The construction of the sequence, in particular its stagelike framing, again reminds the viewer of the medium. As Sabine Hake notes, "two commonly used metaphors for the act of showing in films from the early teens are the stage curtain and the stage set. . . . [These] invariably draw attention to the staging conventions that govern the cinema as a whole."[33] Certainly this sequence does what Hake suggests; referencing the theatrical heritage, it reminds the viewer from the outset that the film is film, that it is not a "simple" replication of reality but a carefully composed piece of art. In this, it harks back to earlier cinema, where the linkage between theater and film still seemed more direct, yet it does so within the context of a film that self-consciously attempts to advance the medium as an independent art form. Given this tension, we might see the opening sequence less as a reference to theater than as a reminder to the viewer of the divergence between cinema and the real; in other words, these opening moments already raise the central theme that will emerge through the screenings-within-the-screenings, the double shadow plays within the shadow play that is the film.

The opening is also important because it introduces the entertainer, who serves as an on-screen double for the director, for, from the first shot, in which the hand reaches for the candle, the viewer is aware of some specific subjectivity guiding the manner in which characters are presented. When the entertainer then gets out of the prompter's box and onto the stage, he retains this ability to guide the narrative even as an active participant. With this, the film points forward to the double interior shadow play, where the entertainer will take on the role of director within the narrative as well. And yet again, the question of gender is raised and the absolute authority of the "director" is undermined, for the woman who crosses the stage distracts him and he interrupts his projection in order to follow her. In other words, the opening sequence introduces the peculiar status of woman-as-cinematic-image: she may function to distract, to break the viewer's—and even the director's—concentration. What this moment suggests is an acknowledgment on Robison's part that even the subjectivity of the director may be mitigated and undermined by his own desires and anxieties.

This self-reflexive moment in the opening of the film introduces the question of how cinema functions, a question that will recur throughout *Warning Shadows*. Again and again, the entertainer will present his "moving shadows" to various audiences by creating shadow animals with his hands for the servants, projecting a shadow-puppet play for his hosts, and, finally, manipulating their own "shadows" into that traumatic fantasy. Indeed, the entertainer's ability to direct and manipulate that which we as the audience see should lead us to question every element of the film, including the ostensible happy ending; might we see that, too, as something he has contrived for us? Fundamental to the way in which we as viewers are pushed to interpret the film are the complex structures of the relationships depicted. Before returning to the significance of the entertainer's role, let us consider how the film constructs the various relationships between the husband, the wife, and the viewer.

From the start, *Warning Shadows* appears to address itself to a masculine viewer, aligning the audience with the husband. After the brief sequence in which each character is introduced, the narrative proper opens as the entertainer, seated by a fountain in the courtyard of the couple's house, watches the young man, who approaches the house and is dismayed to see the silhouette of the couple apparently embracing inside. The sequence immediately cuts to the interior, where the wife is, in fact, refusing to kiss her husband and urging him out of the room. As the servants show in the young man, the husband goes to his wife's bedroom, presumably to await her. Here, the sequence is interrupted by what is either fantasy or memory, a shot in which the husband carries his wife to an ornate, almost throne-like chaise, then orders her maid away and kneels at his wife's feet. After the wife's three other admirers arrive at the house, all under the watchful eyes of the entertainer, the scene cuts back to the husband and dissolves to the second fantasy scene; this time, the wife is alone in a stylized garden when the magnified face of the young man appears superimposed next to her. Then the faces of the three admirers appear below her and their hands reach lecherously toward her before her image fades out.

Both narratively—by depicting the wife's duplicity—and structurally—by showing glimpses of the husband's interior life—this opening sequence aligns the viewer with the husband, forcing the audience into the position of a man who will be progressively disempowered, but then will experience his fantasy of revenge. This alignment is reinforced through repeated point-of-view shots in the following section, where the husband witnesses the event that precipitates his growing fury toward his wife. As the wife preens in front of a mirror in the main room of the house, the three admirers stand between her and the door to the room; one of them traces the outline of her body in the air, much as he did in the opening sequence (fig. 3). The sequence then cuts to a shot of the door into the room, where the husband sees the shadows that appear to show his wife's body being caressed by the men around her (fig. 4), before cutting to a reaction shot of the husband, then back to a point-of-view shot of the door. Although the viewer is aware of the divergence between the actual events taking place in the room and the husband's interpretation thereof, the sequence nevertheless aligns viewer and husband and serves to justify his subsequent behavior. This alignment is strengthened when the husband finally joins his wife and her guests. Still in the hallway, he is joined by the younger of the two servants, whom the wife has admonished and slapped after catching him

CHAPTER FOUR

FIGURE 3. Shadow play. What really happens

leering at her. The servant, in an apparent act of revenge against her, nods in response to the husband's questions, confirming his interpretation of the events occurring in the room. The husband then intervenes: he opens the door, enters, and closes it behind him, and the scene cuts to what appears to be a point-of-view shot of the theater-like room, with the woman beneath the proscenium, flirting with the other men. By presenting the husband's perceptions of the scene, the sequence works to align us with him and emphasizes the problematic nature of his wife's behavior.

Even while emphasizing the husband's point of view, the film establishes an antagonistic relationship between the viewer and the wife. She is repeatedly depicted as duplicitous and vain. On one level, the wife appears to conform to women's expected role; she is the object of desire and contemplation, both for the men within the film and for the viewer. We see her preening in front of the mirror as her admirers watch her, first in a medium close-up, then in a long shot, the camera emphasizing the fascination with both face and body. As the group gathers around the dinner table, she is positioned in the middle, with light falling squarely on her, again drawing attention to her function as object of contemplation. And we witness her dancing, first with the men, then alone, staging herself as an erotic spectacle. Yet for all this, the film does not allow a simple identification of the wife as a passive object of contemplation, for she clearly actively wields her power to enthrall. As she preens in front of the mirror, she seems aware of the effect her actions have on the men watching her. Indeed, she chooses to whom she will display herself, as becomes clear when, even as she poses for her admirers, she catches the younger of the two servants watching her and responds by slapping him. The wife controls not only who her audience

FIGURE 4. Deceptive appearances

is but also how it will view her, a fact that is emphasized by showing her arranging her image as she stands in front of the mirror. In transcending the traditional status of passive object, the wife further undermines her male viewers, subordinating them to her control. Although she exerts her power by manipulating the sexual desires of the men around her, the wife has gained a position that challenges husband—and viewer—on all levels, in terms of sexual and, by extension, social power.

As the wife's power increases, that of her husband diminishes. This becomes particularly apparent as the group gathers at the dinner table. Her husband, angered at the open flirtation between his wife and her admirers, spills a glass of wine, at which his wife rings a bell to summon the servants. No one responds, as the servants are distracted by the entertainer, who has managed to insinuate himself into the house and is demonstrating his shadow plays in the foyer below. The husband then rings the bell himself and, when he, too, receives no response, goes in search of them. The shots of him descending the stairs and confronting his servants are crosscut with shots of the admirers gathering around the woman, whose flirtation escalates in her husband's absence: she raises her glass to toast her young admirer in a gesture that will later become more intimate when she allows him to drink from her glass even as her husband watches. This crosscutting of his ineffective commands with her flirtatious behavior emphasizes his double humiliation in this moment in which his summons go unanswered; he finds himself unable to control not only the servants but also his wife.

What is at stake is quickly established through the characterization of the two central characters. The wife's transgression of social boundaries, embodied in her possible infidelity and flirtatiousness, enables her to gain power, while symbolically castrating her husband. The remainder of the film works to resolve this issue. The central mechanism for regaining this power is through the staging of the fantasy of punishment within the hallucinatory episode that is guided by the entertainer. Allowed to enter the room and entertain the guests, he begins by performing a shadow-puppet play that echoes the conflict between his hosts; in it, he presents the story of a man who witnesses his wife cavorting with her lover. The entertainer then moves to a far more disturbing shadow play. He sets a hallucinatory fantasy in motion by manipulating the assembled party's shadows; the characters disappear and reappear on the opposite side of the table, essentially themselves now in front of the "screen" represented by the blank wall, themselves the subjects of the illusionists "warning shadows." Almost immediately, the wife leaves the room; meanwhile, her admirers distract her husband, enabling her ostensible lover to follow her. Once alone, the two embrace, then she pushes him away and he falls to his knees in front of her, echoing the husband's memory of his relationship with the woman and reinforcing the power she wields through their physical positions.

This is the fatal moment in the film, as the husband, who has followed her, sees their reflection in the mirror outside her door and witnesses them embracing as the young man leaves her. Ordering his servants to bind his wife and bring her to him, the husband enters his study and begins selecting swords, testing their blades suggestively. In the context of Weimar culture, where Freudian theory was a widely circulated discourse, the moment is particularly significant. Freud argued that swords are (one of the many) symbols for male genitalia;[34] he further suggested that the multiplication of symbolic representations of genitalia stands for the concept of castration.[35] Given the framework of *Warning Shadows*, where the characters experience a dreamlike hypnotic state, we can see this moment as drawing directly on Freudian notions regarding the anxieties formative to male subjectivity, suggesting, again, that the husband has been symbolically castrated through his wife's assumption of power over him. The decor of the study reinforces this notion, as the room is dominated by a large painting of a woman, identifiable through her dress and distinctive hairstyle as the wife and literalizing the manner in which her image dominates her husband.

Although the scene reminds the viewer of the husband's lack of power, it also suggests that he will soon be restored to his "proper"

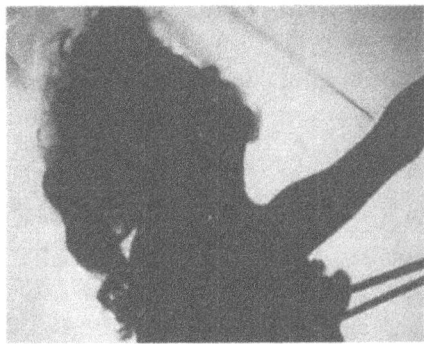

FIGURE 5. A suggestive death

position, for the shots of the husband in his study are crosscut with those of the servants finding, chasing, and finally tying up the wife. This demonstrates the beginning of the process by which he will regain control over the woman. And, indeed, once he has returned to the living room, it becomes clear that the husband has regained his dominant position through initiating his wife's punishment, for, when he again rings a bell to summon his servants, they respond immediately, bringing in his wife, now bound and disheveled. This sequence, in which the servants bring in the woman and tie her down on the table and the husband then forces her admirers to take swords and murder her, reveals most clearly the film's erotic investment in the wife's punishment. Throughout, close-ups of the wife's frightened face are crosscut with shots of the youth and the admirers, who are simultaneously frightened and spellbound by the sight of the prostrate woman, as well as with shots of the younger servant, who hesitates and watches the scene with obvious relish before departing the room. A long shot of the woman tied to the table, displaying her disempowered body fully while her husband gestures toward her with his sword, leads in the murder. We then see a sequence of short shots as the youth tries to disarm the husband and the latter forces him to the ground, crosscut with close-up reaction shots of the increasingly desperate woman. The sequence culminates with a shot of the woman as the shadows of the three armed admirers move toward her, then cuts to a close-up of her silhouette as her body writhes when the three swords fatally pierce her chest (fig. 5), before cutting to a long shot as she falls, dead, onto the table. The husband appears released from his madness through her death; he briefly leaves, then returns with flowers from the garden. The youth and the three admirers then attack him, forcing him to the window, and we see a quick shot of his dead body on the cobblestones below.

This episode ostensibly functions as a cautionary tale, acting out an escalation of the action that leads to the deaths of both of the central characters. Yet the presentation of the events belies such a reading; the sequence reads more like fantasy than cautionary tale, staging the punishment of the wife in a way that emphasizes the voyeuristic pleasure it engenders. The wife's abasement is initiated in a moment in which she is particularly aware of her power; exiting her room after the young man has left, she pauses to look at herself in a mirror, only to be grabbed by one of the servants. Twice she manages to struggle and get away. Caught for the third time, she tries to save herself by pleading with them and offering them her jewelry, but the younger of the servants—the man she earlier humiliated with a slap across the face—pushes her to the ground before binding her, making explicit through their respective physical positions the reaffirmation of masculine control. And the film continues to linger on the details of the wife's humiliation once her husband has her brought in and tied down on the table. The frequent cuts to close-ups of her face as she watches the young man struggle with her husband and realizes that her fate is sealed suggest a sadistic enjoyment of her fear. The scene of punishment takes on explicitly sexual and sacrificial overtones as the wife is tied down to the table in front of all assembled. Her abasement is particularly extreme given that in being made helpless and put on display before the men, her previous empowerment through her function as object of desire is reversed; it is now associated with her humiliation. She remains an object of the men's gaze, yet one that has been reinserted in the normative structure, no longer actively staging herself as object, but passive and victimized. Indeed, her function as object of desire for the men around her is heightened in her disempowered state, as is made clear by the fact that admirers and servant continue to gaze on her helpless body in fascination. The wife's abasement goes hand in hand with an increase in her husband's power. Most obviously, he directs the actions of servants and admirers, manifesting power not only over his wife but also over the male figures and the viewers, who are a captive audience to the scene. In punishing his wife, the husband blots out whatever power she had, a fact that is made manifest by the manner in which, visually, he effaces her, as his head on multiple occasions blocks the audience's view of his wife. And the final moment of the punitive fantasy—the moment in which the suitors move toward her with swords drawn—takes on distinctly sexual overtones. If the wife thus far has represented uncontrolled female desire and emancipation, the mode of her murder suggests that it can—and must—be mastered through male reassertion of phallic power, represented through the multiple swords stabbing the woman's body.

In contrast to the wife's death, that of the husband is quick. Where her death is staged as an erotic scene, focusing on her suffering body as object of desire, his is so quick as to forestall any level of voyeuristic enjoyment. If anything, the sequence is far more invested in his apparent breakdown, showing him rending his hair and weeping over his wife's corpse. We might see this as demonstrating the real reason why the man dies at the end of the episode: not because he has committed a murder, but because he has not entirely regained his power by doing so; he continues to be "subordinate" to his wife. The two deaths eliminate both destabilizing elements: the empowered woman and the weakened man.

This reading of the fantasy is reinforced once the narrative shifts from the hallucination back to reality. From a shot of the visitors immediately after they have forced the husband out of the window and watched him fall to his death in the courtyard below, the camera tracks back to show that the image is, in fact, projected onto the screen behind the table. Husband, wife, and guests are still seated around the table and awaken to the entertainer, who returns to the original shadow-puppet play. Recall that this play thematized an unfaithful wife; in its culmination, the husband kills his wife's lover and forgives her, while she, who had hitherto been quite open about her affair with her lover, takes on a newly subservient role. Thus the moral of the hallucinatory fantasy is reinforced; sexual and social dominance is restored to the husband, and, with the wife taking on an ostensibly more "natural" role, the crisis is averted.

The parallelism between the shadow play, the hallucinatory episode, and the film as a whole suggests the instructive nature of film; just as the wife in the puppet play subordinates herself to her husband, so does the flesh-and-blood woman. At the end of the performance, the wife and guests follow the husband's lead when he applauds the entertainer. As the latter repacks his puppets and prepares to leave, the admirers, and then the youth, exit as well. The wife, significantly, does not acknowledge any of

CHAPTER FOUR

FIGURE 6. Order restored

the men, save the entertainer, whom she bids farewell by chastely allowing him to kiss her hand. Unlike previously, all of her attention is focused on her husband, whom she repeatedly embraces. Once the couple is alone, the older servant enters the room to open the drapes and is startled—and pleased—to see the couple happily together. The two then move to the window and the scene cuts to a point-of-view shot of the courtyard below, where the preparations for a market are being made, before cutting back to a medium exterior shot showing the couple opening the window and standing together. We then see the entertainer in the courtyard, as he watches the three admirers depart. Subsequently, the scene cuts to a long shot in which the youth is visible, before moving to a close-up of him as he looks longingly up at the woman in the window. A close-up reaction shot shows her ignoring the youth, her eyes fixed on her husband (fig. 6), before the sequence cuts back to a shot of the disappointed youth exiting the courtyard. After again cutting to a close-up of the couple in the window, the sequence shows the peculiar departure of the entertainer: he chases after a pig that has gotten loose, then jumps onto its back and rides out of the courtyard as the villagers respond with laughter before continuing their business. The final shot emphasizes the reestablished domestic ideal, cutting again to a close-up of the happy couple framed in the window.

In this final sequence, the relationship between husband and wife is presented as a traditional image of domestic bliss. The opening of the drapes, letting in the morning sun, suggests a new beginning for them, emphasized by the older servant's surprise at their new closeness. The moment in which they stand framed in the window establishes them as a distinct and naturalized unit. When the youth looks back up at the couple, the wife responds by turning away from him and looking at her husband adoringly. This moment in particular, with the couple framed in a tableau suggesting a sort of natural unity, and the woman looking up at her husband while he looks slightly past her, represents a reestablishment and reification of traditional gender roles. The moral orientation of the film is reinforced by the scene on which they gaze: the reconciled couple stands at the window of their grand house, regarding the villagers gathering for a market in the square below. This tableau points back toward an earlier, conservative social ideal, positioning the man as superior of not only his subjects but also his obedient wife.

Thus far I have focused on *Warning Shadows* as thematizing anxieties coalescing around shifting gender and power relationships and resolving said anxieties through a narrative that reasserts traditional norms. How does this thematic strand connect to the way in which the film structures the relationship between viewer and object? As I suggested earlier, the narrative focus on the need to eliminate the destabilizing potential of the emancipated wife is echoed in the structure, which imposes a process of identification and objectification that positions the woman as passive object. I noted the way in which the construction of female objects of desire as potentially destabilizing and the structures of identification between viewer and male characters apparently work in a similar way to that Mulvey outlined in her analysis of classical Hollywood film. The two female characters—the wife and the maid—function as objects that arrest the gaze of audience and characters, whereas the viewer is, as I have discussed, aligned with the husband. What is dangerous about the wife is that she stages herself, in marked contrast to the maid, and, in doing so, undermines the spectator's ability to "possess" her. Recall Studlar's estimation of Dietrich in the von Sternberg films, where "possession of the performer through the gaze is really nonpossession."[36] From the start, the maid is constructed as unthreatening, even as she functions as an object of desire. Within the narrative we first see her from the point of view of the entertainer, who watches as she opens the door to the visiting admirers. In this moment, the film cuts from a close-up shot of him looking at the door to a long shot through the doorway as the maid takes the guests' coats, after which one of the men raises her chin and moves as though to kiss her; the older servant closes the door just as he does so, blocking the view of the action, and the entertainer approaches the closed door and leans toward it as though to listen. The presentation of the maid as the object that initially draws the entertainer's—and the viewer's—gaze is emphasized by the mise-en-scène, in that the doorframe emphasizes her appearance.

That the maid functions as an object of desire capable of arresting the gaze of the men around her becomes even clearer once the entertainer has entered the house and is explaining his art to the older servant. In a close-up of the two men, we see him pause in his conversation and stare fixedly toward the right of the screen; we then cut to a medium-long shot of the stairs as the maid descends. Initially, only her feet are visible, then, as she descends and the camera tilts slightly upward, she enters the center of the shot, pauses, takes out a mirror and begins to fix her hair. We then cut back to a long shot of the older servant and the entertainer, just as the latter drops his bag and runs toward her. The next shot again shows the maid, with the entertainer standing a few steps below her, visibly admiring her and attempting to caress her legs before being pulled away by the two male servants.

This moment enacts the fascination exerted by the woman as object of desire, the way in which her appearance can interrupt all action, leaving the male viewer effectively powerless, in thrall to his desire. The slow tilt of the camera, allowing the viewer to initially see only her legs as she descends, serves to fetishize her body. Her form becomes the primary object of the viewer, divorced from any specifics of her persona. The moment is made all the more significant because the character who is so suddenly stopped in his tracks by the maid's appearance is the entertainer, the on-screen stand-in for the director. This suggests an awareness of the crucial position women occupy within the visual economy of the film; they have the power to seize the viewer's gaze, to distract even the guiding intelligence behind the images on the screen.

And yet the maid, in marked contrast to the wife, is not presented as a figure that endangers and challenges the male viewer. The crucial difference in the way the two women are positioned lies in the fact that where the wife actively stages herself, the maid is positioned by those around her. This distinction becomes particularly clear during a sequence in which the maid and the servants are preparing a screen for the entertainer by nailing a sheet to the wall behind the table. We see the maid and the younger servant in a medium-long shot, she standing on a chair and attempting to attach a sheet to the wall, he standing at her side, admiring her legs. She turns and must twice gesture for him to give her the hammer before he does so, never interrupting his contemplation of her legs. The sequence then cuts to a medium shot of the table as the wife sits down, surrounded by her admirers; she then gestures for one of them to get her fruit from the tray in front of her and he quickly complies. We then cut back to a brief shot of the maid and the younger servant, who continues to stare at her legs even after she hits his finger with the hammer as he holds a nail for her, before returning to a shot of the wife and her admirers. The crosscutting between the two situations emphasizes how differently the two women are positioned. Where the maid is a passive object, holding the man's attention without in any way actively attempting to do so, the wife aggressively seeks to draw the gazes and attentions of those around her. Further, the fact that the shot of the maid emphasizes only part of her body connects back to the entertainer's reaction to her; again, hers is the female body fetishized, fragmented so as to render her more passive. In this way, she stands in stark contrast to the wife, who is positioned by the camera as an active object at the center of the screen and of the action she directs. By thus contrasting the positions of wife and maid as active and passive objects of desire respectively, *Warning Shadows* demonstrates the danger active objects of desire pose to traditional power structures.

Even as it addresses the central role that the female body as object of desire plays in film, however, *Warning Shadows* reveals the complexity of the power dynamics involved in the relationship between spectator and image, for, though it expresses the husband's increasing control in terms of taking possession through the gaze, it reveals the limitations thereof. This is especially evident in the repeated play with point-of-view shots, wherein the viewer takes part in the frustrating experience of seeing only a part of what he looks at. For example, when the couple and their guests are initially seated at the dining room table, we see a medium frontal shot of the husband and the wife; the wife then leans toward screen right (where her ostensible lover is seated), moving out of the frame, and the husband looks toward her. His expression suggests that something untoward is occurring, but the viewer cannot immediately see what this might be. The sequence then cuts to a medium shot in profile, so that we can see her talking to the other man; again, however, our view is blocked, first when the husband leans forward to look at them, then when the younger servant steps between husband and wife in order to pour wine from a heavy carafe. This moment enacts the loss of power associated with a limited viewpoint: so long as the husband's view is blocked by the servant, he is denied full knowledge of—and control over—the events. The viewers are forced to reenact this experience, when the wife moves outside of the frame and when their view is blocked first by the husband, then by the servant. Here, the film implicitly reveals the power associated with the gaze (by staging a loss of power predicated upon partial and limited vision) even as it draws attention to the way in which film manipulates the gaze.

This ambiguity in the relationship between the apparently powerful spectator and the image is repeatedly evident in the film. Again and again, *Warning Shadows* thematizes the potential for vision to mislead, the ways in which the image can be manipulated and misinterpreted. Consider the multiple moments when that which a character—and the audience—first sees is quickly proven to be other than it appears: the apparently blissful kiss the young man witnesses that turns out to be no more than a false projection on the drapery, the scandalous embrace the husband sees silhouetted on the door that is no more than a lewd shadow play. Vision in *Warning Shadows* is everywhere mitigated, indirect, routed through shadows, reflections, and visions. The gaze is repeatedly multiplied: the spectator watches a character watching what is, ultimately, a fantasy, an image rooted not in the real, but in deception, trickery, or artistry. The resolution of the film is no more real than the hallucinatory episode, a fact that is underlined when the scene of traditional domesticity veers into farce as the entertainer rides off on a pig. The film constantly draws attention to itself as film, not only through the thematization of the "cinematic" episodes of the two shadow plays, but also through elements of mise-en-scène such as the living room in which the characters meet, with its spatial layout reminiscent of a stage. And the central, fantasy episode, staged as a sort of communal experience of hypnotism, references a complex discourse focused on trauma, hypnotism, and cinema. Andriopoulos has traced the discourses linking cinema and hypnotism in Weimar Germany, and he notes in connection to *Dr. Mabuse, the Gambler* that in the film, through the alignment of the viewer with the victims of the criminal mastermind, "the cinematic representation of hypnosis is thus transformed into a celebration of the hypnotic power of cinema."[37] Kaes points out that hypnosis—likened specifically, by Ernst Simmel, to the process of watching a film—was one treatment for war neurosis and trauma.[38] *Warning Shadows*, through depicting the story-within-the-story as a hypnotic vision guided by the entertainer, reflects back on the process of film itself and undermines the potential empowerment that might be drawn from the experience of "taking control of" the image through the gaze.

The ambiguity of the viewer's empowerment in relation to the image connects to contemporary reflections on film. Recall that Hake notes the way in which cinema was conceptualized as representing an experience allowing both for control and passivity: "The notion of visual pleasure, despite its association with excess and self-deliverance, confirmed the male spectator as the center of meaning production and the master over time and space, taking into account his desire to surrender control to an outside source, if only temporarily."[39] Even as it allows for the fantasy of "the male spectator as the center of meaning production," *Warning Shadows* satisfies and comments on this "desire to surrender control," revealing film's ability to guide and manipulate perception. While contemporary critics like Mulvey, Doane, and others have postulated a powerful, active gaze that is gendered masculine as the dominant force in the experience of cinema, *Warning Shadows* suggests a far less definite structure. In one sense, it conforms to the structures Mulvey identified, constructing an apparently powerful, masculine gaze that exerts power over a female object made passive; yet it exceeds the parameters of those structures, as well, by constantly drawing attention to its own technical manipulation, to the "trickery" at the root of the medium. The process by which the female object is subjugated to the gaze serves only to temporarily distract the spectators from their own passivity. The presentation of the maid—and her ability to arrest, through her mere presence, the gaze even of the entertainer, who functions as a stand-in for a directing authority—points to the woman's body as a sort of narrative interruption, as a cinematic element capable of drawing attention away from the viewer's limited control. In this sense, the female body becomes functionalized, serving as the object that allows the viewer the fantasy of control within the cinematic experience.

And the limitations of the imagined authoritative male gaze are further made clear by the inclusion of the entertainer. Underlying the fantasy of a reestablishment of control on the part of the husband is the constant awareness that there is another subjectivity guiding the actions and reactions we see on screen. The entertainer directs the husband as much as he does the wife. In film, man and woman are equally the objects of a director's work as they are the subjects of their own performance. The entertainer encourages and facilitates the ways in which the spectator sees and mis-sees what is projected onto the various screens; he anticipates the characters' reactions and guides them according to a narrative he has constructed. His character, in other words, functions as a constant reminder that masculine power is here not absolute, that it, too, is undermined and mitigated. And the moments in which we see his concentration waver—the opening in which he chases the maid off the stage, the moment in which, after being admitted to the house, he is shown spellbound by her appearance—emphasize that his, too, is an authority that is limited and subject to distraction; the entertainer/director is as much at the mercy of his own desires and fears as is the viewer.

On one hand, on the level of narrative, where the brutal punishment of the wife leads to her emerging from the hallucinatory episode as a passive object and contains her behavior within traditional gender norms, and on the level of structure, where the camera works to align the viewer with male character and enables both to take control of the wife as passive object of the gaze, *Warning Shadows* acts as a response to the anxiety resulting from the era's changing gender norms. It overtly enacts a fantasy allowing the return to outdated social hierarchies and restabilizing a male subjectivity that perceived itself as under attack. *Warning Shadows* appears very clearly to demonstrate the way in which films of the era address themselves and appeal to a male viewer traumatized by his confrontation with modernity. On the other hand, though the overt relationship between viewer and image positions the former as exerting power over the latter, *Warning Shadows* repeatedly draws attention to the mechanics of cinema—through the staging first of the shadow-puppet play, then of the hallucinatory episode that is couched specifically in terms of a cinematic projection—and thus undermines and reveals that overt relationship and reflects on the specific aims of its own cinematic techniques. In other words, given that *Warning Shadows* self-consciously refers to its own medium and the mechanisms at work therein, we can see that the film deploys these mechanisms to reinforce the core of the narrative—namely, the potential to reassert control over the destabilizing social element—here the transgressive woman—through distinctly filmic means. In this way, the film reveals that it constructs the acceptable positions of women and men, as well as the relationship between viewer and image, so as to offer the male viewer a fantasy of the power to control and objectify women. The fact that this is fantasy becomes abundantly clear through the repeated reference to the filmic apparatus. The audience is repeatedly reminded of the way in which woman serves to distract from the powerful gaze that is revealed to be limited and mitigated, the powerful viewer who is shown to be manipulated by the very images over which he appears to exert control.

In theoretical terms, *Warning Shadows* is a film in which the structures of the gaze are rendered in their full complexity. While we can isolate certain dynamics that appear to prefigure those that scholars like Mulvey have found in classical Hollywood film, such structures are here functionalized in a unique way. I suggest that *Warning Shadows* purposely plays with the notion of a powerful gaze, that it does indeed enact the empowerment of the (male) viewer but simultaneously reveals the fantastic and ephemeral quality of that empowerment. Instead, the audience witnesses and takes part in a process that shifts and reshifts power structures; every position, from the wife staging herself to the desiring suitors to the vengeful husband to the canny entertainer, entails both power and weakness, both agency and passivity. Indeed, this ambiguity is extended to the audience: *Warning Shadows* demonstrates the way the viewers are both powerful bearers of a gaze that takes control of the images on screen and passive consumers of these images that are staged in such a way as to manipulate desires and fears. The film makes use of cinematographic structures in order to comment on cinema itself. In this sense, *Warning Shadows* deemphasizes a gendered audience, for it casts the viewer, to some degree, as a part of a mass, with little individual agency.

Perhaps it is quite correct that so many of the reviewers and critics downplayed the content of the narrative of *Warning Shadows*; ultimately, the punitive fantasy of the film is not only a response to social fears but also a key element that serves to engage with the structure of the medium. The transgressive wife certainly stands in for a set of social changes that were subsumed within the specter of female emancipation and embodies a challenge to masculine power. In depicting the "fate" to which her behavior leads, *Warning Shadows* performs a fantasy in which women who attempt to step outside of the boundaries of socially inscribed, conservative gender roles are brutally punished. And, through the positioning of women as passive objects and through the power relationship between viewer and object, *Warning Shadows* inscribes the same "punitive" and controlling process on the level of cinematic structure, inaugurating a trope that contains and arrests the female subject. Yet even as it does so, the film undermines the reality of this structure, always reminding the viewers of the cinematic apparatus that guides their perception and interpretation and presenting the unsettling idea that the control afforded them is, in fact, as much an illusion as are the pictures unreeling on the screen.

FIVE

THE HANDS OF ORLAC (ORLACS HÄNDE, ROBERT WIENE, 1924)

War Trauma, Injury, and the Return to a Changed World

ROBERT WIENE'S *THE HANDS* of *Orlac* premiered in Berlin on September 24, 1924, less than a year after Robison's *Warning Shadows*. Yet so much had changed in the Weimar landscape by the time Wiene's film was released and the films are so stylistically and narratively different from each other that they seem far more removed than those eleven months might warrant. In February of 1924, the state of emergency that had been imposed the previous November was lifted. This was the beginning of an era of stabilization, of Weimar's "Golden Twenties." It coincided with an artistic shift from expressionism to *Neue Sachlichkeit*, the "New Objectivity" that was often manifested in a move away from the anxious preoccupation with madness and the irrational that characterized so much of the immediate post–World War I period. Cinema took part in that shift: the mid- to late 1920s would bring fewer films like *Caligari* and *Nosferatu*—anxiety-filled reflections of the limitations of the individual in an irrational world—or even like *Uncanny Tales* and *Warning Shadows*—alternately

CHAPTER FIVE

playful and punitive representations of the subject's response to a changing environment, couched in terms of the uncanny. Instead, film shifted to a focus on "reality"; the dangers to the individual were more likely to be the "real" dangers of a modern world than the mystical threats hiding beneath its deceptively rational surface. Thence the beginning of the *Straßenfilm* ("street film"), the genre Karl Grune's *The Street* (*Die Straße*, 1923) inaugurated and that perhaps was best epitomized in Pabst's *The Joyless Street* (*Die freudlose Gasse*, 1925), a genre that focused on the dangers life "on the streets" and the attractions and debaucheries of the city posed to the upstanding bourgeoisie. In film, the central focus was more likely to lie on the "real" darkness in human life, not madness or psychological trauma, but the harsh conditions of daily life, the effects of poverty, illness, and despair.

Against the backdrop of this moment, *The Hands of Orlac* stands as a sort of transitional work, straddling cinematic expressionism and New Objectivity and drawing on themes and stylistic elements from both movements. We can see in the film a concern with madness, with the psychological deterioration of the eponymous hero, yet the "resolution" to this process is found in science; the medical and criminological establishments intervene and save Orlac. As a film that draws on and essentially acts out the shift from expressionism to New Objectivity, *The Hands of Orlac* is especially interesting. In its navigation of the topics of war, masculine trauma, and female emancipation, we find parallels to the earlier films thus far discussed side by side with shifts in the way in which these themes are addressed.

By the time he released *The Hands of Orlac*, Robert Wiene was already well known. Born in Breslau in 1873, he studied law and later was awarded a doctorate before working at a Viennese theater. His work in cinema, as screenwriter and director, began in 1912, after which he made films steadily. With the release of *The Cabinet of Dr. Caligari*, Wiene had an international hit. This is the film for which he is best remembered, a film that has weathered the years and figures among the few best-known examples of Weimar cinema; indeed, this is the film we might see as having defined cinematic expressionism, embodying both the style and the content that modern scholars view as definitive of the movement. Certainly not all of Wiene's films were as successful—his *Genuine* (1920), for which many had high hopes given its release immediately after *Caligari*, was, if not a failure, then only a mixed success.[1] Still, Wiene enjoyed continued acclaim, founding Lionardo-Film in

1922, then taking on creative leadership of Pan Filme in Vienna in 1924. His career began to falter only after the rise of National Socialism. In 1934 he fled to England, then on to France, where he hoped to collaborate with Jean Cocteau on a sound version of *Caligari*. That goal unrealized, Wiene was again given the opportunity to direct in 1938, this time a spy thriller, *Ultimatum*. He died before the final work on the film was completed.[2]

The Hands of Orlac was Wiene's first production for his Pan Filme. The film, based on Maurice Renard's "Les Mains d'Orlac," which was published in 1920 and translated into German in 1922,[3] tells the story of Paul Orlac (Conrad Veidt), a world-famous pianist who, returning from his final concert tour, is involved in a train accident. Orlac survives the accident, but with severe injuries to his hands. At the urging of his wife, Yvonne (Alexandra Sorina), Orlac's doctor replaces the pianist's mutilated hands with those of Vasseur, a man recently executed for murder. The operation seems a success, but Orlac's recovery is fraught; he becomes convinced that his newly attached hands maintain a life of their own, combating him for their control and inclining him to violence. Wrestling with his body and struggling for mental stability, Orlac also strives to preserve his social status and to save his marriage, for the new hands make it impossible for him to continue his career as a pianist. Events escalate when Orlac approaches his estranged father for help and discovers his corpse; all indications seem to point to his having been murdered by Vasseur's hands, in other words, by Orlac himself. Already despairing, Orlac is then approached by a man (Fritz Kortner) claiming to be the executed murderer, who tells him he was revived by having his head reattached (much like Orlac his hands) and orders him to bring him a million marks or he will tell the police that Orlac must have killed his father. As bleak as the situation might seem, *The Hands of Orlac* does not deny the audience a happy ending. With the help of the maid Regine (Carmen Cartelieri), who had originally conspired with the blackmailer, the police uncover that the plot to frame Orlac and to drive him to madness was masterminded by this Vasseur, who is in fact not only an imposter, named Nera, but also the real perpetrator of the murder for which the donor of Orlac's new hands was executed as well as of the murder of the elder Orlac. Orlac's hands are thus not those of a murderer, after all, and, with his name cleared and his mind put at ease, Orlac can reconcile with his wife.

CHAPTER FIVE

This topos—of the murderous body part that transforms its new "owner"—is certainly the stuff of horror films. *The Hands of Orlac* was remade in Hollywood as *Mad Love* (Karl Freund, 1935) and as *Hands of a Stranger* (Newt Arnold, 1962), and was also remade in a joint British and French production as *The Hands of Orlac* (*Les mains d'Orlac*, Edmond T. Gréville, 1960); more generally, the topic of murderous limbs figures in films like *The Beast with Five Fingers* (Robert Florey, 1946) and *Body Parts* (Eric Red, 1991). The fear these films express—that "foreign" body parts might retain and transmit the qualities of the individuals from whom they were taken—seems to be a fundamental human anxiety even today.[4] In the context of Weimar in the mid-1920s, it connects back to the realities of war; with the maimed bodies of former soldiers now a common part of the social landscape, the fantasy of being able to make them "whole" again—and the fears such a possibility would raise—is understandable. And it reflects on the way in which we connect the body and psyche, in which we see the one as intimately bound up with and fundamentally inseparable from the other. No matter how rationally Orlac's doctor might insist that "the head and the heart guide the hands," the viewer can certainly identify with this problematic at the center of the film.

After it premiered in Germany on September 24, 1924, Wiene's film had its general release there on January 31, 1925. Reviews were generally positive, with one critic noting that it represented the hoped-for advent of Viennese cinema: "The hope that there would soon come out of Vienna a great film went unfulfilled for a long time before this one, directed by Robert Wiene for Pan-Filme, was released."[5] And, again, critics raised the question of the development of the medium when reviewing the film, with one calling it "one step on the path to the artistic film."[6] It was certainly not viewed as a perfect piece; the ending, where the film veers from uncanny into realistic with the introduction of techniques of crime detection, was seen as disruptive: "Why must this mysterious stranger suddenly turn out to be a trivial criminal drawn from the police logs of the daily newspaper, after the viewer has already prepared himself to view him as a sort of 'revenant'? And do you also know that such a reversal in the mood can endanger the film's success with the audience that you desire so strongly?"[7] *The Hands of Orlac* thus disappointed precisely where it shifted from expressionism toward New Objectivity. In keeping with the new thematic emphases that the New Objectivity would bring, *The Hands of Orlac* reverses the originally uncanny orientation, effectively forestalling any ambiguity. Unlike in a film like *Caligari*, for example, the audience is left with few questions regarding the "reality" of Orlac's experience. Instead, Wiene's film works much more as did, for example, the opening episode of Oswald's *Uncanny Tales*; there, Veidt's character similarly faced a mysterious incident (the disappearance of his traveling partner) only to find it explained away by a very "rational" reason (her death from the plague); there, too, the critics were disappointed by this turn, which seemed to detract so much from the effect of the piece. Still, overall, *The Hands of Orlac* was received positively in Germany. Veidt, who plays the title role, was already famous for his depictions of tortured characters, most notably the somnambulist Cesare in Wiene's *Caligari*; his performance as the tortured artist garnered particular notice, though some German critics complained that he tended to veer into a caricature of himself: "Unfortunately his performance is not always free of self-consciousness, of that famous Conrad-Veidt note that has already become a sort of cliché."[8] Quite right: the film abounds in shots of Veidt's face, veins throbbing in his forehead, mouth twisted in despair, as well as of his hands, which, with their visible tendons and tortured movements, seem to take on a life of their own, looking quite convincingly as though they are "alien" appendages. And yet, in spite of his at times overly mannered acting, Veidt's performance dominated *The Hands of Orlac* to such a degree that it overcame the American market's general skepticism toward the film when it was shown there three years later: "Were it not for Veidt's masterly characterization, 'The Hands of Orlac' would be an absurd fantasy in the old-time mystery-thriller class."[9]

As with *Warning Shadows*, contemporary reviews of the film demonstrated a tangible reluctance to deal with the film as a whole. Their focus on the mood of the film and the actors, on the shift from uncanny into realistic, neglected, or perhaps repressed, the violence Orlac exhibits toward others, especially his wife. Indeed, though much of the problematic of the film coalesces around questions of trauma, subjectivity, and gender, reviews once again paid little attention to these themes. Equally, while some reviewers touched on the artistic value of the film, they did not fully analyze it in terms of its significance as a piece emerging at a moment of stylistic transition. I will here focus on this, on the ways in which *The Hands of Orlac* points back to the trauma of World War I and of the individual in a changed world, acting out an unconscious violence directed toward the threatening other represented by woman, even as it functions to represent the stylistic shift occurring at the time. Emerging in the moment in which the early crisis years of the young republic gave way to a relative stability and in which the haunting images of expressionist films ceded primacy to the pragmatic realism of New Objectivity, *The Hands of Orlac* can be viewed as much as a hybrid as is its eponymous hero. It is at once expressionist—focused on the apparently deteriorating mind of Veidt, that quintessential expressionist actor—and not—emphasizing the rational explanation through the resolution to the story; at once film of terror—in its evocation of the mystical, of the dead walking again—and melodrama—in its thematization of the love story that underlies the narrative. I consider this peculiar hybridity here: how does the film accommodate these competing tendencies?

On its surface, *The Hands of Orlac* may seem far removed from a war film, and its hero—the injured artist, so sensitive as to be unable to touch his wife with the hands that seem to represent his changed self—certainly does not conform to the stereotype of the soldier returned from combat. Yet it takes little closer examination to identify the markers that point inexorably back to the experience of war and suggest that the physical and psychological trauma resulting from the experience of the train accident stands in for that resulting from challenges to male subjectivity on multiple other fields.[10] Seen in the context of the society scarred by World War I and by the early, crisis-ridden years of the young republic, Wiene's film dramatizes the plight of the masculine subject confronted by war and modernity. Orlac's hands, functioning simultaneously as parts of his body and as "alien" appendages, become a multilayered signifier of physical, psychological, moral, and social trauma. Orlac embodies the masculine subject faced with multiple challenges: the experience of war and the destruction wrought by physical combat, the return to a new society in which his own role is fundamentally altered and women have taken on new power and been granted new rights, and the confrontation with a modernity that signifies an absolute break with the past and leaves him attempting to bridge the gap between past and future. Thus the three fronts on which Orlac must assert himself: that of the body, physically altered and newly limited; that of his marriage, in which he no longer occupies the hitherto stable role of provider; and that of his relationship with his father, a generational conflict that threatens him and must ultimately be "resolved" in such a way as to allow him to move forward.

From the beginning, the film suggests the equation of Orlac's trauma with that stemming from the experience of war and ties it inextricably to shifting gender roles. *The Hands of Orlac* opens with a medium close-up of Yvonne, half-reclined against the high headboard of a bed, arms and head swathed in a white gown and veil and legs covered by a dark blanket. A smile on her face, she slightly raises the letter in her hand and lowers her eyes to it: "My beloved! In 24 hours I will be with you and will take you in my arms. My hands will caress your hair and your warm body will shudder in my embrace."[11] She stares unseeing toward the camera as she lowers the letter, her chest heaving. After a brief sequence showing Orlac performing at his last concert,[12] we cut to a second sequence that takes place after those promised twenty-four hours. This one is very different, fading in on a long shot of that same room, lit so that the foreground remains in shadow, while Yvonne, standing slightly off center as her maid helps her dress, and the headboard of the bed on which she earlier reclined are highlighted. The maid runs to the rear of the room, then returns with a jacket that she helps Yvonne into. The sequence cuts to a medium shot of the two women as the maid notes that there are yet two hours before the train is scheduled to arrive. Yvonne finishes tying the collar of her jacket, then urges the maid away, and we cut back to the long shot of the room as both women run from center to the mirror at the left rear, apply final touches to Yvonne's wardrobe, then run toward the exit at the right front.

This opening sequence raises immediately one of the crucial problems at the heart of the film—namely, Yvonne's vacillation between her role as a passive, traditional wife and that as an active (and eroticized) agent. Her activity as she prepares to go to meet her husband—running back and forth across her room, imperiously directing Regine—contrasts sharply with her static position as she reads his letter. The camera work itself—the use of the extreme long shot, compared to the tight framing in the opening moment—emphasizes a move from a constrained and decidedly domestic space to a space that grants her the potential for further action. And yet, even in that first, private moment, there is a suggestion of transgression; Yvonne's visible physical response to the prospect of Orlac's return and his articulation of her desire—his anticipation of her "warm body" that will "shudder" under his touch—points to an active female desire and sexuality that does not conform to traditional gender ideals. Yvonne is neither the passive woman waiting for her husband's return nor the woman rendered maternal and representing the comfort of a stolid, unerotic domestic sphere; instead, she is the wife-as-lover, her response to Orlac's letter pointing toward her own active and visible physical desire.

Even as it introduces the gender trouble at the heart of the narrative, the opening scene symbolically references the experience of war that will play a central role in the film. The reliance on the letter as a form of communication, as well as its expression of the anticipation of a reunion, parallels the experience of couples separated by the husband's deployment. Certainly, Orlac is no soldier; in fact, his artistic profession appears as far removed from that as possible. Still, the film establishes an absolute link between Orlac's profession and his identity and highlights the necessity of physical wholeness in practicing his work, a notion that would resonate with former soldiers, whose postwar identities were deeply bound up with their status as soldiers and who were equally dependent on their (often compromised) bodies. Further, the letter Orlac sends to Yvonne already suggests a fragmentation of his identity; we move from the "I" to his "hands" to "his embrace"; even in writing to his wife, and before his injury robs him of his physical wholeness, Orlac ascribes a special status to his hands. Initially "present" only via his absence, Orlac's introduction to the viewer is significant; we see him in a slightly high-angle medium close-up, seated at the piano and looking down at his hands as he plays, a positioning that equates his subjectivity with his hands. The subsequent fade to a close-up of the hands moving across the piano keys emphasizes their centrality to his sense of self. Further, the camera's focus on Orlac's hands points back to the letter. On one hand, the moment again suggests a fragmentation of the body that predates the accident; on the other, it implicitly suggests a kinship between the erotic relationship with his wife and his activity as musician, a theme that will continue throughout the film.

The suggestion that Orlac and Yvonne's situation stands in for that of the (absent and oft-injured) soldier and his waiting beloved is strengthened by the depiction of the train accident. This is the moment that represents the initial trauma Orlac suffers, the primary catalyst for his subsequent decline. The accident unfolds with terrifying speed. Initially, we see a single shot of a passing train, before cutting to Yvonne, who is preparing for her husband's arrival. The film then cuts back to a shot of train tracks, then to one of a train moving toward the camera, before showing a switch operator. Immediately after this, we cut to two trains passing each other, then one suddenly, rapidly, runs off the tracks. The accident itself takes only a few seconds; it is the aftermath[13] that dominates this scene, with short shots of the wreckage, of men pulling bodies from the cars, and of the victims, many of them women and children, rapidly crosscut with shots of Yvonne hearing of the accident and commanding her driver to take her to the site. The scene of the accident is confused, dominated by the wrecked cars, torches, a spotlight that is trained blindingly into the camera, and the silhouettes of the rescuers. Once at the scene, Yvonne quickly takes action, searching in the wreckage until she locates Orlac and has him transported from the site.

Two aspects of the scene are particularly significant. First, we can read the train accident as symbolic of war, an equation that is emphasized by the imagery of the casualties and the confusion of the scene. In his discussion of the treatment of war neurosis, Freud draws an explicit connection between the traumatic effects of war and those of railroad accidents.[14] This suggests that the parallel would be familiar to the contemporary viewer. The sheer chaos of the cinematic moment is emphasized by mise-en-scène and cinematography: frames are cluttered, angles are askew, and the smoke, spotlights, and torches suggest confusion.[15] The chaos is furthered through the rapid cuts—some shots are so rapid as to become virtually subliminal—as well as through the skewed angles and chiaroscuro lighting. The shots of the casualties of the accident—a woman's body swinging upside-down into the frame, a crying child accompanied, significantly, by a young man in a military-style uniform—bring to mind the casualties of the recent war. The train accident reads much as one might imagine the aftermath of battle. Second, crosscutting scenes of the accident with Yvonne's actions—her immediate, active response to news of the accident, and her determined search for Orlac at the site—furthers the crucial conflict that coalesces around gender roles. With Orlac incapacitated, Yvonne decisively sheds her previous passivity and takes control. She commands her driver to take her to the scene of the accident, then alights quickly and without his assistance from the car; further, she takes the lead in the search, climbing alone into the mangled cars until she locates Orlac and summons her chauffeur. Once a group of men come to help her remove him, she directs them as they carry him out, then waits, embracing him, as they fetch a gurney. What becomes clear in the scene is that the train accident functions as the source of both physical and psychic trauma. On the one hand, as a metaphorical representation of war, it is the very real event that leads to Orlac's injury and thereby threatens his ability to return to "civilian" life. His hands mutilated, he becomes like so many of the soldiers who returned, scarred by war, from the battlefield. At the same time, the accident is the catalyst for Yvonne's newfound activity; she moves from the narrowly circumscribed domestic sphere in which she was initially presented, transgressing the traditional boundaries of her role as wife and thereby threatening Orlac's identity.

Her active intervention in the situation continues in the next sequence, in which she takes her husband's injured body to the hospital, where she instructs the doctor, upon hearing of the severity of his injury, to save his hands at all costs. It is here that the circumstances that will lead to Orlac's "haunting" first arise. The scene opens on a long shot of the doctor, lying in bed and slowly beginning to stir in response to the servant standing in front of him. It cuts to a medium shot as the man sits up and the servant reminds him of the impending execution of the murderer Vasseur, whose body will be delivered to the clinic. The doctor rises and begins to prepare, but his preparations to receive the corpse are interrupted by the servant's announcement of the accident: the clinic will be receiving both the murderer's corpse and the pianist's injured body. Informed of the medical preparations surrounding Orlac's arrival, we next see Yvonne as the sequence cuts to a long shot of a room, in the foreground of which she leans heavily on a table. When the doctor enters through a door at the rear of the frame, she straightens, reaches her arms imploringly toward him, then stumbles in his direction. We cut to a long exterior shot of two hospital employees and the chauffeur as they lift the gurney with Orlac's inert shape out of the car and carry him inside, then fade in on a long shot of the dimly lit reception area, where Yvonne is collapsed in an armchair, apparently sleeping. She starts up and we cut to a close-up that lingers on her rigid posture and wide, unseeing eyes. The doctor enters with news of Orlac's injuries, initially focusing on the injury to his head, which, he announces, may well be survived. In response, Yvonne appears relieved; in a close-up we see her turn slowly away from the doctor, smiling in relief and closing her eyes. Yet the true blow is yet to come, as the doctor announces that Orlac will lose his hands. This prospect appears to affect Yvonne far more severely than did that of his head injury; in a close-up we see her smile slowly fade, her eyes widen as she stares unseeing toward the camera, then a look of horror transforms her face. In a long shot of the doctor standing, with Yvonne seated in the chair, she pushes herself heavily up and reaches her arms toward him, imploring: "Save his hands! They are his life! Save his hands! They mean more than his life to him!"[16] Yvonne remains standing, arms rigidly outstretched toward him, as the doctor considers her plea, then she moves to him and collapses against him, clutching at his neck and chest before falling to the ground, where she remains, leaning against the armchair and weeping. As the doctor continues to consider, we see a point-of-view shot of the executed murderer's body being removed from a carriage outside, then a close-up of the doctor, clearly conflicted, but finally telling Yvonne that he will try to comply with her plea.

On one level, this sequence simply moves the narrative forward through the introduction of the body of the murderer who will be the source of the uncanny new replacements for Orlac's mangled hands and of the doctor who will undertake the operation. Yet the visual details in this brief sequence—in particular, the parallelism between the presentation of the murderer's body and that of Orlac—shed further light on the conflict that threatens the latter. Both bodies are shown inert, motionless objects that are manipulated by those in whose charge they are: Orlac's body is as passive as is the corpse of the executed man. The accident and his incapacitation represent the moment in which he loses all control over his own destiny, and his fragmented body represents on the most basic level his loss of agency. And just as it emphasizes Orlac's incapacitation, his new status as the object of the actions and decisions of those around him, the scene makes clear who has assumed control over his passive, injured body, for it places Yvonne at center stage, lingering on her distress and framing her image in an oddly and strikingly eroticized way. Much like in the opening moments of the film, where the erotic and desiring dimension of her character was highlighted, so here, through her movements—the heaving chest, the trembling, and the dramatically expressive gaze—she is portrayed in a manner that stresses the physical. Her clothing disheveled and torn, she is shown with arms and shoulders bare, in a state of near dishabille. Her appeal to the doctor, underlined by her physical contact with him, again places the emphasis firmly on her body. But she is more than erotic object of the camera's eye and the spectator's gaze. Even in terms of the physical, she has transgressed the norms of behavior, moving outside of the private yet still situating herself as object of desire. In this, as in virtually all of the films I have thus far discussed, sexual emancipation and transgression stands in for more general emancipation. And this is the moment in which Yvonne decisively seizes control over her husband's destiny, determining what course of action will be taken and pushing the doctor to try to save her husband's hands. In Clover's terms, Yvonne takes on the role of the narrative catalyst, advancing and determining the action.

The film's emphasis on Yvonne's transgressive empowerment continues in the sequence following the apparently successful operation. Here, even with the reintroduction of a now conscious Orlac into the diegesis, Yvonne maintains her position of control, and camera work and mise-en-scène serve to emphasize Orlac's objectification. The sequence begins with a medium shot of Orlac, heavily bandaged and reclining in his hospital bed with Yvonne leaning over him, as the medical staff enters. We cut to a close-up matted shot of Orlac, who looks on with little comprehension, as the doctor grasps Yvonne's hand in his, telling her: "Here you have your husband back. Now he is in your charge."[17] His statement explicitly relegates Orlac to her protection; she has been publicly designated his guardian, usurping the role the husband traditionally occupies. The phrasing is significant, suggesting that he is little more than an object that can be "returned" to her and placed in her "custody."[18] Indeed, the arrangement of Orlac's body on the bed, where it seems to virtually vanish into the mattress, suggests a lack of substance, reducing him further from the virile, capable man he originally was. His passivity becomes his dominant quality in this scene, as his injured body is "unwrapped" by the doctor and his assistants. The reunion between Orlac and Yvonne, who reenters the room once the doctor has removed the bandages, reflects on the respective role each plays and introduces the uncanny element that will progressively challenge Orlac's sanity. We cut from a long shot of Yvonne as the doctor guides her into the room to a slightly high-angle, close-up, matted shot of Orlac reclined against his pillow. Through his position and his clothing, he recalls the opening image of Yvonne: the hospital gown echoes her own earlier dress, while the bandages recall the white headdress she wore. In other words, Orlac is explicitly aligned with that first image of an as yet passive Yvonne, emphasizing the reversal in their roles. We then cut to a long shot as Yvonne hesitates until the medical staff leaves, then moves slowly toward the bed. In a medium shot, we see her kneel next to her husband, then lower her face toward his. An intertitle relays her compliment to him: "You have such beautiful, shining eyes . . . I can't look at them enough . . . and such soft hair."[19] We cut to a close-up of the two, Orlac looking up at her with half-closed eyes as she gazes at his face, then turns her head slowly toward his hands: "Your hands, your dear hands will take care of me."[20] We cut from a matted close-up of Orlac's slightly discomfited face to a medium shot: as she continues to look at his hands, he raises them slowly. Back to a matted close-up as, startled, Orlac looks toward the door, then to a medium shot as he begins to rise, visibly frightened, while his wife continues to caress his bandaged hands. In a long shot, we next see him staring at the window above the door, where an apparently disembodied head has appeared, and then cut to a close-up of the same. As Yvonne remains transfixed by his hands, Orlac reacts to the eerie sight: "There, there's a head back there . . . it's looking at me, at my hands,"[21] and adding, when Yvonne turns and sees nothing: "He's laughing at me! Death is laughing at me!"[22]

This sequence is a significant one, emphasizing the reversal of the traditional roles assigned to husband and wife and linking this reversal to the introduction of the uncanny element. The explicit parallelism between the way in which Yvonne was initially portrayed and that in which Orlac is represented suggests that he has taken on the passive role hitherto assigned to her. Orlac's immobility and his positioning vis-à-vis his wife—who leans over him, occupying a spatially and symbolically superior position—underline this, as does the manner in which Yvonne takes the erotic lead in their relationship. Recall how, in the opening letter, it was Orlac who expressed his desires for her; here, she is the one whose hands caress his body, and she openly positions him as a passive object of a desiring gaze, giving him compliments that seem more fitting to the rhetoric employed by men toward women and that, indeed, reference her desire to "look at" him. The moment demonstrates how fundamentally Orlac and Yvonne have exchanged roles within their relationship: Orlac is now the passive object of his wife's active gaze and desire. And, by linking Yvonne's definitive assumption of an active role with the beginning of Orlac's "haunting," the sequence ties her to the ghostly apparition and effectively constructs her empowerment as itself uncanny.

Indeed, the disembodied head that appears to Orlac, demanding back its own limbs, is already connected to Yvonne, for it has that information she has withheld from her husband. Both Yvonne and the ghostly head have control over and information about Orlac; as such, both draw attention to the way in which his body and psyche are now fragmented and incomplete. In becoming mutilated victim and medical patient, Orlac has been not only turned into a passive object but also rendered fundamentally fractured: the new hands do not replace his own and thereby make the body whole, but instead draw attention to an invisible yet all the more potent lack. The identity crisis brought about by the transplant points to the impact of "invisible" scars of traumatic events, another element that suggests the film's symbolic representation of war trauma. Orlac's perception of this lack is complicated, for even before he knows what has happened to his hands, he seems haunted by the sense that something is amiss. His reaction to the face in the window makes clear that his fears stem not only from the external events but also from an internal awareness that, somehow, he is no longer identical to the man he was before the accident, the man whose subjectivity was inextricably bound up with his hands. Rather, he feels himself an object of ridicule, certain that the unknown face is laughing at him and convinced that it is looking at his hands—a measure of his (perhaps unconscious) awareness of having been irrevocably changed by his experience. That these changes will fundamentally affect his own identity and his relationship with his wife is made clear by the final shot of the sequence, where Orlac averts his eyes from the door—and Yvonne—as she stares uncomprehendingly at him.

After the appearance of the ghostly head, Orlac's sense that something is wrong with his hands continues to grow. In the following sequence, he reclines on a balcony, bandaged hands rigid as he looks suspiciously at them. When the doctor emerges and leans over him, Orlac looks up, raising his hands and articulating his fears: "Tell me, what is wrong with my hands? What are you hiding under these bandages?"[23] As the doctor and his assistants remove the wrappings, Orlac looks on fearfully, staring at each hand as it is revealed. In a long shot, we see him still scrutinizing his hands as they rest on his knees; when the doctor rises, he asks: "Will these hands be able to play again as they once did?"[24] We see a medium shot of Orlac's back as he looks up at the doctor, whose authoritative figure dominates the frame and whose answer seems calculated to deny Orlac any concrete information: "In a healthy body, there lives a healthy spirit. When your hands are healed, your spirit will show itself to mankind through the skill of your hands."[25]

On one level, the sequence demonstrates Orlac's sense of a fractured self and a loss of power; he realizes immediately that, under those bandages, "they" are hiding something from him. This notion suggests a profoundly damaged consciousness: he is no longer aware of and in full control of his own body. On another, the doctor's statement—his suggestion that the health of the spirit finds expression through the hands—is one that, as we will see, undermines the ultimate "resolution" of the film. For the suggestion might also be read in the negative: if the actions taken by those hands are not "healthy," then that, too, would represent the sickness of the spirit controlling them. As the film progresses, Orlac is troubled by the violent impulses he feels, actions that he becomes convinced emanate from those alien hands; yet the doctor's statement already suggests that these impulses must necessarily be rooted in Orlac's own psyche, must, in other words, stem from the resentment and anger he feels toward Yvonne as a result of his loss of power.

Orlac's discomfort is a manifestation of his fragmented subjectivity that further increases when his suspicions are confirmed by the information Yvonne has thus far kept from him. In the night before his release from the hospital, Orlac receives a letter informing him of the origin of his "new" hands. The moment is presented within a sequence that highlights the isolation Orlac experiences and emphasizes the uncanny dimension in his psychic dissolution. The hospital room is initially rendered in an extreme long shot, with his bed at the left of the frame spotlighted, his body dwarfed by the high ceilings. A cloud of smoke seems to billow down from the ceiling, filling the right half of the frame, before giving way to the superimposed image of Kortner's face, which is in turn replaced by a fist that fills the frame and moves threateningly toward Orlac's body. We cut to a medium shot of his bed as he starts up as though from a nightmare. After examining the room, Orlac is just about to recline again when he discovers a note on his bed: "His hands could not be saved. Dr. Seral replaced them with the hands of a dead man, the hands of the murderer Vasseur."[26] Orlac's reaction is immediate; horrified, he clambers out of the bed, holding his arms outstretched as though to keep the alien hands as far away from himself as possible, then collapses on the floor.

The dream elements that haunt Orlac and that are introduced in this sequence represent the first overtly uncanny elements of the film, the first use, that is, of trick photography, here of superimposition. The billowing smoke is not only an atmospheric element but also points back to the smoke that dominated the scene of the train accident and thereby to the traumatic event at the root of Orlac's deterioration. At the same time, it functions as a symbol of how the true source of Orlac's new hands and of his fragmented psyche is obscured; confined to his bed, the passive object of the doctor's treatment and Yvonne's decisions, he cannot see the truth clearly. The looming face of Vasseur references Orlac's vision of the same peering into his hospital room and raises anew the question of whether that first image represented a hallucination (Yvonne did not see it) or a manifestation of the real. Perhaps most interestingly, the giant fist that pushes Orlac down against his bed functions as an expressionistic representation of his own disempowerment, visually representing his sense of being treated as a passive object and referencing again the central symbol of his loss of power, his "own" hands, bandaged and inactive. The whole of this sequence is designed to suggest his isolation and to cast doubt on the border between the real and the imaginary.

In Orlac's actions once he receives the letter, we see clearly how the crisis he is experiencing is bound up with the sense of the loss of his identity. Immediately after his dream, still holding his hands stiffly out from his body as though to emphasize their alien quality, he confronts the doctor. His question implies that the information he received in the letter was a confirmation (rather than a revelation) of the alien nature of his hands: "So it's true? I have the hands of a murderer?"[27] In one sense, this query concerns Orlac's specific situation; he now "has," attached to his own body and identity, the hands of another. In another, it references the experience of the soldier returning from war, who must come to terms with actions that, outside of the context of the battlefield, would be criminal; herein the split that Freud suggests, between the ego as it existed before the experience of war and that new identity, bound up so inextricably with the process of killing. Orlac, his body apparently still unchanged excepting for those new, murderous hands, represents on a physical level the psychological split that characterized and destabilized so many former soldiers.

That this crisis is bound up with and implicated in his now damaged relationship with his wife becomes clear as Orlac prepares to be released from the hospital. In a long shot, we see an assistant helping Orlac into his coat; Orlac remains virtually immobile as though to emphasize his objectification. The contrast between the opening moment, in which Orlac plays the piano and is thus characterized in terms of rapid action and physical skill, and this one, in which he barely moves and becomes almost childlike in his dependence on the assistant, serves to underline the radical change he has undergone because of his traumatic experience. As the assistant directs Orlac to put on his hat and then leaves, we cut to a medium shot of the pianist, still immobile, his psychological isolation made visible in the framing and in his static posture. He slowly raises his hands a few inches, saying: "These hands may not touch any living being."[28] The significance of this moment is emphasized by a cut to Yvonne and Regine preparing for his arrival, after which we cut back to Orlac, who tries to complete his preparations for his return to his home and his ostensible reintegration into this previous life by putting his wedding ring on his finger. In a high-angle close-up, we see him try twice to force the band onto his finger, which is far too large for it, then cut to a medium shot as he pockets the ring, despair evident in his expression. The depiction of this moment—in which that "alien" finger hardly moves, becoming virtually inanimate as he tries to fit the symbol of his previous life onto it—again emphasizes the radically changed relationship Orlac has to his body. Symbolically, the moment draws attention to the fundamental damage that has been done to his marriage; his previous identity undermined by his traumatic experience and the loss of his hands, Orlac is literally no longer the man who married Yvonne.

Orlac's return home reaffirms the link between his previously stable roles as pianist and as husband and the way in which both have been disrupted. The sequence begins with a wide interior shot of Yvonne awaiting his arrival.

CHAPTER FIVE

The frame is cluttered, with blossom-covered branches in the foreground partially obscuring the action. Orlac enters on the left, yet does not move toward her. When Yvonne approaches him, holding a flower toward him, he moves only slightly, but then stops and remains immobile. Here, the "masculinity" of Yvonne's newly active role is again emphasized and extended into her relationship with her husband. He becomes the one who is awaited by the ardent lover and for whom the home has been prepared with aesthetic flourishes; the flower that she proffers him as she tries to initiate physical contact shifts her definitively into the role that would ordinarily be reserved for the man. The erotic dynamics of Orlac's relationship with his wife become further complicated when the sequence next cuts to Orlac in another room, approaching his piano. In a medium shot, we see him caress, then kiss the lid of the piano before sitting down and raising the cover off the keys as Yvonne enters. Like in the initial concert scene, we cut to a close-up of Orlac's hands on the keys as he begins to play, then immediately see a medium reaction shot of Yvonne as she looks away from him. Orlac stops playing and closes the lid onto the keyboard. We then, as in the previous scene, return to a long shot of the two as Yvonne moves toward him and embraces him; as before, Orlac raises his hands as though to caress her, then lowers them again, remaining immobile. This sequence is a crucial one, with implications both for the relationship between the spouses and the construction of Orlac's subjectivity. On one level, the scene explicitly links Orlac's sense of identity as pianist with that as man and husband; his touch has become ineffective in relation to his wife and to his art. His private and public roles are inextricably bound up with each other; unable to fulfill the one, he can no longer act as the other. At the same time, the fact that he caresses and kisses the piano emphasizes an erotic dimension to his profession. Ursula von Keitz rightly notes that this moment constructs Orlac's musical virtuosity as being specifically erotic.[29] This further problematizes his relationship with his wife, for it suggests that from the start there was something "odd" about their relationship, in that his erotic desire and energy was never wholly reserved for her. Woman and instrument thus come to be linked, insinuating that when Orlac's bond with Yvonne was yet undamaged, it was one in which she became an object that he manipulated, an extension of his own body and subjectivity that he "played" just as he played the piano. His subjectivity now undermined, we can read his failure in the attempt to play as symbolic of his failure with Yvonne—recall

FIGURE 7. Stylistic oddity

the letter, in which he anticipated his hands moving over her body and her body responding, just as the piano keys respond to his touch. And Yvonne's response to his failure to play as before—her physical turn away from him—is a metaphor for what is essentially her rejection of the man he has become.

There is another dimension to Orlac's shattered identity: he responds to his sense of disempowerment and his certainty that his new hands are shaping his psyche not only, as in this previous scene, with a reluctance to touch Yvonne but also with an aggression that escalates once he discovers more information about the ostensible origin of his hands. He seeks out information by buying newspapers that present the details of the murder case. This moment is stylistically interesting: in a static long shot, we see a newsstand that is little more than a window in a wall covered entirely with newspapers, with only the head of the saleswoman visible inside the opening (fig. 7). He takes his purchase into a basement bar, where, increasingly agitated, he reads the relevant article: "The murderer Vasseur in court. Vasseur still denies everything, but is condemned by the fingerprints which were found at the scene of the crime. The stiletto has a sign of an X on the handle, and on it one found Vasseur's fingerprints. Thus it was proven that Vasseur was the murderer."[30] In a close-up, we see Orlac's face over the newspaper, then he looks up and we cut to a long shot of the room. The shot blurs and dissolves to a blurred close-up of a fist holding a dagger marked with an X, then moving away from the camera and striking at the body of a man barely visible in the background, before the hand, this time empty, is held again in front of the lens. We cut back to a long shot of the room as Orlac starts up in horror, clenching and unclenching his own hands.

CHAPTER FIVE

This moment is especially interesting in terms of the film's style. Juxtaposing the expressionistic representation of the magazine stand, with its newspaper-covered front suggesting a vaguely sinister quality to the public presentation of information, and of the dark, dingy bar into which he descends with the objectivity suggested by the scientific methods used in the criminal investigation, it neatly embodies the way in which the film can be situated somewhere between expressionism and *Neue Sachlichkeit*. The magazine stand visually represents the dangerous quality of the information Orlac finds, which will precipitate him further into his crisis, while the bar could be viewed as a hell of sorts, where his identity is further challenged. Orlac's vision of the murder—again drawing on stylistic elements that are at odds with the fairly objective overall representation—is significant, for we can read it as simultaneously an effect of his fear at the fragmentation of his identity and a sort of fantasy rooted in the anger and hostility his traumatic experience engendered.

The information he gains in no way reassures Orlac; rather, it serves as yet another step in his apparent psychosis and as the catalyst for his escalating violent impulses. He returns home immediately after finding the articles, and we see him enter, then stop and recoil, as the film cuts to a close-up of a dagger lodged in an interior door, its hilt clearly marked with an "X." He stumbles back, then moves toward and grabs the dagger. We then cut to an extreme long shot of the piano room, as Orlac sits down on the sofa, still grasping the dagger, then to a medium shot as he holds it, saying: "I feel him take possession of me, of my shoulders, my brain, cold, frightening, and terrible."[31] As he continues to grasp the dagger, seemingly both drawn to and repulsed by it, we cut to a close-up of the maid looking on unseen, then back to Orlac, who suddenly rises and, lifting the lid of the piano, hides the dagger inside. He is only momentarily relieved, for he stares at his hands, then pushes each sleeve up before clutching at his chest. In a close-up, we see him stare angrily at his limbs, their veins raised and knotted, saying: "Damned hands!"[32] Yet even once hidden, the dagger seems to have a magnetic effect on him, for, shortly after this scene, we return to the image of Orlac in the room, this time moving toward the piano with his arms outstretched, as though his hands are pulling him. He removes the dagger and closes the lid of the piano, and we cut to a shot of Yvonne in bed, sitting up as though startled. We then cut back to an extreme long shot of him holding the dagger, moving into the shadows at the rear of the shot, before we again see Yvonne, first getting out of bed, then listening at the door. Again, we cut back to Orlac, who raises the dagger and then pantomimes a violent stabbing. As Yvonne enters the room and witnesses his actions, he attempts to conceal the dagger behind his back, then backs away from her as she moves toward him, and finally orders her out: "Don't come near me—go!"[33]

These two scenes develop the notion that Orlac's violent impulses stem from his traumatic experience and are directed most consistently toward his wife, who embodies the threat to his previous identity and power. Information is represented as dangerous; because of it, the dagger that Orlac finds is not merely a weapon, but a suggestion of his own guilt. Modernity—represented through the dissemination of information in the newspapers, as well as through the crime-solving techniques that were used to "prove" Vasseur's guilt—is not a rational force that combats madness, but a contributor to Orlac's decline. The very sight of the dagger inspires in Orlac a fantasy of violence, where his body mimes the murderous act that represents an urge both frightening and attractive. And though the violence is represented as abstract, we can read it as directed toward Yvonne. The crosscutting between his pantomime of violence and Yvonne awakening links the two; if there is an object of his hostility, it is not the anonymous murder victim, but rather Orlac's own wife, whose will led to his current situation. His angry exhortation that she not come near him implies not only a conscious desire to protect her from the urges he recognizes in himself but also the realization of his murderous urges toward her.

The shots of Orlac's hands that dominate this scene take on a very particular cast in the cultural context of Germany after the First World War. Within the narrative of the film, the scene acts out Orlac's perception of his hands: alien appendages that control him, that literally lead his helpless body to actions he would otherwise not take. Yet such apparently external control is never simply that in this era. Consider two other seminal films from the era: F. W. Murnau's *Nosferatu*, the first of many cinematic retellings of Bram Stoker's *Dracula* (1897), and Fritz Lang's slightly later *M* (1931), which focuses on a child murderer. In *Nosferatu*, as the vampire leaves his home in order to enter the room of his victim, we see a similar focus on his hands, as though they, like Orlac's, are pulling him toward his victim. The two scenes are, indeed, strikingly similar ones, with Orlac essentially reenacting that pose of the "sleepwalker" drawn inexorably toward the desired victim. In *M*, as the child molester and murderer whom the urban underworld has hunted down cowers before the kangaroo court and attempts to explain his actions, he similarly uses his hands as he states: "But I, can I act any differently! Don't I have that damned thing inside me? The fire, the voice, the torture? I always feel it, someone is after me, but it's I myself who is chasing me."[34] In both of these films, the hands come to represent not an external will being imposed on the monstrous figures but rather an internal compulsion toward violence, a compulsion that might, as in the case of *M*'s murderer, be at odds with conscious drives and desires, but nevertheless stems from within. Although the narrative of *The Hands of Orlac* suggests that it is an external will that is driving the man, seizing control of him and undermining his volition, the moment is ambiguous and can be interpreted more in line with these other films as demonstrating an internal urge—an interpretation that is supported by the revelation at the end of the film that the hands Orlac has been given are in fact not the hands of a murderer.

The source of Orlac's hostility toward Yvonne is rooted, as I have suggested, in his inability to reassume his former position and her assertion of activity and power. Yvonne's social and sexual transgression is twofold. Socially, she challenges her husband's role not only by taking on responsibility for his health but also for their economic survival. It was Yvonne who pushed the doctor to replace Orlac's mutilated pianist's hands. Two further scenes expand on the economic dimension of her new role. In the first, we see a long shot of Yvonne, seated facing the camera; behind her, there is a line of men identified as their creditors.[35] In response to her pleas for more time, they initially shake their heads slowly and as one; finally, when she asks for just a single day more, they grudgingly nod. In this brief moment, Yvonne essentially undermines Orlac's identity further, not only because she takes on a responsibility previously held by her husband, but also because, in approaching the creditors, she implies that he cannot do so himself. This notion that Yvonne has taken on a role ordinarily reserved for her husband is developed when she visits Orlac's estranged father in order to plead for his help. In a shadowy medium shot, we see Yvonne in quarter-profile standing in front of a heavy door, hesitating before lifting the massive knocker. We cut to a medium shot framing the door at the center as Yvonne waits and the door slowly opens.

The elder Orlac's servant peers out, his face and white hair highlighted, as Yvonne draws away fearfully. After looking her pointedly up and down, he steps outside and we cut to a close-up of his unmoved face. In a medium shot of the two, Yvonne gestures toward the interior of the house, then the sequence cuts back to the close-up of his face as he first smirks, then shakes his head, saying: "I'm not allowed to let anyone see him, certainly not one of you."[36] In a close-up, we then see the two of them, Yvonne pleading and folding her hands beseechingly, then moving closer to him, her hands on his chest, as she begs him to let her enter. After several glances at her face, which is quite close to his, he finally relents, nodding, and we cut to a medium shot as he gestures at her to follow him inside. The dusky hallway with its arched ceiling is shown in a long shot as the servant leads Yvonne toward its end. We then cut to a long shot of a large room, with table and chairs in the foreground and a throne-like chair on which Orlac's father, his face highlighted, is seated. The servant enters through a door at the left front of the frame and Yvonne follows the servant slowly. We cut to a medium shot that reveals the dais on which the elder Orlac's chair rests; as the servant ascends and goes to stand at his master's right shoulder, Yvonne remains on the ground, supporting herself against the wall and looking at the two men. The sequence cuts between medium shots of all three and medium close-ups of Yvonne as she pleads their case: "Paul cannot play anymore. We are threatened by poverty. He has no idea yet. Help us!"[37] When the elder Orlac remains unmoved, she runs up the steps and stands by his chair, beginning to weep: "He's your son, your own flesh and blood. You can't just abandon him."[38] We then cut to a close-up of the man's face as he responds: "I no longer know my son and his wife. I have no family!"[39] He refuses to engage further with her and Yvonne finally follows the servant out of the room. The scene fades out on the man seated alone in the room.

In approaching first the creditors and then her father-in-law, Yvonne seizes the responsibility ordinarily reserved for her husband. She does so entirely without his consent, which is emphasized by her statement to the elder Orlac that "Paul has no idea." However dangerous information might be, it nevertheless represents power, and Yvonne's actions thus further undermine Orlac, for she denies him a full understanding of the situation and thereby places herself in the position of his guardian. Further, as in her interaction with the doctor, Yvonne stages herself as erotic object in attempting to persuade her father-in-law to help them. She touches the servant in order to convince him to let her see his master; once inside, she moves ever closer to the man as she begs him to support them. Although her actions are aimed at protecting the couple's livelihood, they nevertheless represent a transgression of her previous role. She has decisively taken on the role of economically and sexually emancipated woman, bypassing her husband's authority and taking on the responsibilities that would, before his traumatic experience, have been his.

Beyond developing Yvonne's new status as an emancipated woman, the scene is significant when viewed in the context of a culture in which generational conflicts are bound up not only with normal development but also with the experience of war. The mise-en-scène works to align the elder Orlac decisively with an older tradition; Gothic architecture and the almost medieval austerity of the room in which he receives Yvonne position him as the representative of an outdated—and hostile—tradition. If this moment embodies the fantasy expressed postwar through the *Dolchstoßlegende* ("legend of the stab in the back"), holding, among others, the older generations (represented by the commanding officers) responsible for the injuries to and deaths of the young soldiers on the battlefield, then it serves to reaffirm that suspicion; the father refuses to help, even when his son is faced with personal and financial ruin. Further, the elder Orlac's cry that "I no longer know my son and his wife" suggests a fundamental break between the generations, a shift in Orlac and Yvonne's personae that so changes them as to lead to an absolute estrangement. We might read this as underlining the new social and gender roles embodied in Yvonne's activity, and so vastly removed from the traditions represented by Orlac's father.

The representation of Yvonne's newfound activity expresses the ambivalent response to women taking on new responsibilities and thereby building new relationships during and after the war. With Orlac incapacitated by the accident, Yvonne becomes the primary provider, exceeding the boundaries of her former identity as his wife. In this she acts out the reality of the women left behind by their husbands at war, and of those whose husbands returned incapacitated; they, too, found themselves in the position of having to provide for their families. Her move from the domestic spaces in which she is situated before the train accident into a public space signified by her interaction with the doctor, the creditors, and Orlac's father suggests a second transgression: she is no longer figured as the object exclusively of Orlac's desires, but also of the desires of these other men. Already in the opening scene, she takes on a decidedly erotic role; this is not the traditional, maternal, staid wife of a film like *The Street*, but rather a figure who bears much more resemblance to Lubitsch's Mâ, who exhibits herself openly on stage, and to the wife in Robison's *Warning Shadows*, whose illicit desires threaten her marriage and her husband's sanity. Yvonne's physical response to the letter from Orlac, her repeated depiction with heaving chest and rolling eyes, and her caresses of his prone and still bandaged body in the hospital suggest an active desire that is incommensurate with the traditional role of wife. More problematically, as she moves outside of the private sphere in her attempts to secure their financial survival, she draws on her seductive abilities in her interactions with other men. While pleading with the doctor to save Orlac's hands, she approaches and virtually embraces him; in their subsequent interaction, he repeatedly takes her hand in his. In her encounters with the creditors, she is positioned in front of them as though on display. In these public interactions, we can read Yvonne as representing the New Woman, newly active, escaping the domestic sphere, and functioning as an erotic object not only for her husband but also for the other men she encounters. Orlac, metaphorically doubly castrated through the loss of his former social and financial status as well as through his marital impotence, exhibits hostility toward her not because of an external will embodied by the alien hands, but rather because she represents a threat to his social and sexual superiority.

Orlac's hostility toward Yvonne thus seems rooted in a perceived loss of sexual potency caused by Yvonne's empowerment. The way in which emancipation contributes to Orlac's fragmented identity is equally evident when we examine the maid, Regine. Regine serves as the epitome of the weak woman, so deeply in thrall to a man—the devious Nera, who has orchestrated the original murder and staged the "haunting" of Orlac—that she will conspire with him to destroy her employer. Earlier, she attempted to break free from Nera's power, writing a letter to him that asserted: "I can't listen to it anymore, can't bear it. I don't trust you anymore, even if you were to kill me. I can't obey you any longer."[40] The phrasing is already weaker; it is not that she "will" not do these things, but rather that she "cannot." And even this limited determination is short-lived. Immediately after the sequence in which Yvonne visits the elder Orlac, we cut to a long shot of Regine standing in front of a motionless, cloaked figure, raising her hands and trembling as she states: "Forgive me! I promise never to disobey you again."[41] We then cut to a long shot of the two, this time with the man standing behind her, revealing himself to be Nera. Regine remains immobile as he stares at her and we cut to a close-up of the two, her face still, his eyes fixed on her as he threatens: "I'll go to his father tomorrow myself, if you can't convince him to do so."[42] She turns to meet his eyes and he continues to stare at her until she again turns away, breathing heavily, her shoulders slumping. We cut to a slightly more straight-on close-up; as Nera continues to stare at her and give her orders, his face poised over her bare shoulder, Regine arches her head back, then slumps forward. Her pose and movements are ambiguous; we can read them as stemming either from fear or from pleasure. Indeed, Nera appears to have a virtually hypnotic effect on Regine, recalling the control that Radu holds over Mâ in Lubitsch's earlier film. Regine's subordination to the will of Nera complicates the reading of the film further. If a strong-willed and active woman—like Yvonne—poses a danger to Orlac's sense of self, here a weak-willed, passive woman endangers his life. Perhaps the desire that both women display functions as the destabilizing element; we might read Regine's "enslavement" to Nera as contingent on illicit desire, her acts in conspiring with him as the outgrowth of female desire run amok. Like Yvonne, she is portrayed not as maternal and domestic, but as driven by passions and responding to erotic needs; in this, both of them represent the view of the New Woman as defined by her transgressive sexual emancipation. Further, Regine's betrayal of her employer breaks a fundamental rule of a more traditional worldview in which the home—including the servants—represents a single, familial unit. In transferring her loyalty from her employer to a man she desires, Regine undermines traditional notions of her role as a domestic.

Regine functions as the medium of another's will, just as Orlac sees himself as the medium of that of the "murderer." We see this in Regine's subsequent interaction with Yvonne, for immediately after her meeting with the man, the maid approaches her mistress in order to suggest that Orlac himself visit his father. In a medium-long shot echoing the constellation of the elder Orlac on his throne with his servant half-hidden at his right ear, we see Yvonne seated at a table, as Regine, behind her, counsels her. Yvonne responds negatively, but Regine persists until the other woman slumps forward onto the table, weeping, and her maid departs. The servant's insinuations have their effect; later, after Orlac enters the room, Yvonne begs him to approach his father for help. As so often before, his wife draws on her physical power of persuasion to convince him, throwing herself on his chest, before releasing him. In a long shot, we see her step away from and turn her back toward him, shrugging before she sits back down and explains: "He turned me away, even though I pleaded with him desperately."[43] She begins again to weep, as Orlac remains standing, his only response the agitated clenching and unclenching of his hands. The influence that Regine (and, through her, Nera) exerts on Yvonne touches again on questions of subjectivity and agency, undermining the notion of a distinct and independent will as much as does Orlac's sense of being haunted by his new hands.

On one level Regine functions simultaneously as a foil to and an alternate for Yvonne as emancipated woman: she is fundamentally weak and becomes subject to a man's will; at the same time, she acts out desires that position her as, paradoxically, sexually emancipated. On another, Regine's interaction with Orlac draws attention to the notion that the failure of the relationship between husband and wife is a result of Yvonne's new power. On the orders of Nera, the maid approaches Orlac as he is seated on a sofa in an attempt to "seduce his hands."[44] In a sequence of medium shots, we see her approach him, kneeling next to him on the ground, then crawling closer before grasping his hand and kissing it. We then see a sequence of close-ups: first, Orlac starts and pulls his hand out of her grip, then pauses, reaches toward her and caresses her head, first with one, then with both hands. A close-up of his smiling face demonstrates his pleasure in this interaction with the maid. We then see a close-up of her, suddenly worried as his hands caress her more roughly. She finally pushes his hands away, saying that they hurt her, "like the hands of a murderer."[45] What is telling is that Orlac, unable to caress or even approach his wife, is quite happily able to do so to the maid. The latter, by virtue of her social position, is figured as inferior to him, a fact emphasized by the spatial positioning, as she kneels and crawls toward him. With the maid, Orlac feels secure in his superiority and is able to react toward her "as a man." Significantly, however, here, too, his initial caress turns to aggression; his identity destabilized through

Yvonne's newfound activity and dominance, he exhibits aggression toward all women, as representations of the one who purportedly undermined his own position. Nera and the maid—as well as the narrative of the film as a whole—conspire to convince both Orlac and the viewer that the alien appendages are guiding his immoral behavior. Yet, ultimately, the resolution of the film undermines this suggestion that his aggression stems from the hands that represent something "other" than his subjectivity.

Superficially, the resolution of the film restabilizes Orlac's identity. After being confronted by the supposed "Vasseur," who demands money in return for not accusing him of his father's murder, Orlac, at Yvonne's urging,[46] goes to the police. His story—shown in flashback—is initially greeted with skepticism and the prosecutor wants to arrest him, but the police inspector who headed the investigation of the elder Orlac's murder intervenes and tells Orlac to bring the money to his blackmailer. He does this, entering the basement bar, shot in a dusky long shot, alone. Once he gives the money to the criminal, four officers run from the rear of the frame, their guns aimed at the blackmailer; as he rises, the inspector and the prosecutor descend the stairs into the bar. After identifying their quarry as the notorious criminal Nera, who until recently worked in the clinic, the inspector proceeds to strip off the elements of his disguise, first unbuckling and removing the attachments that were to resemble prosthetic hands, then revealing and unceremoniously stripping off the line of tape that served as the "scar" of Nera's supposedly reattached head. This process is presented in a medium close-up that shows clearly the inspector's confidence and Nera's acceptance of having been discovered. The almost cordial behavior between the two men contrasts sharply with the previous expressionistic presentation of the villain, emphasizing—as does the fact that this moment is shown in a single, fairly long-duration shot—the rational and objective processes behind the apparent haunting; the shot—itself eschewing the cinematic "trickery" enabled through editing—reveals the parallel trickery within the narrative.

Yet Orlac is still not out of danger, for Nera asserts that though he may be a blackmailer, the murderer they seek has Vasseur's hands, and reveals that those hands are now those of Orlac. Just as the prosecutor moves to arrest Orlac, disaster is averted. Regine and Yvonne enter and, as the sequence cuts between slightly high-angle medium shots of the room, with the police clustered in the front of the frame and Orlac frozen against the wall at the rear, and medium shots of Regine huddled against the wall on the steps descending into the bar, Yvonne runs to embrace her husband and her maid reveals that Nera is the true murderer. She wavers for a moment when Nera briefly reasserts control over her. After he tells her to be silent, we cut from a medium shot of Regine with the image of Nera superimposed behind her to one of Nera, staring at her as he did before. But the inspector is able to break the hold over her, ordering her to reveal the full conspiracy. She does so: Nera, Vasseur's former friend, took wax imprints of the latter's fingerprints and had gloves made with these. He committed the murder for which Vasseur was executed and then killed the elder Orlac in hopes of framing his son. Orlac, comprehending that "if Vasseur was not a murderer, then my hands are innocent,"[47] seems to be "healed" of his identity crisis. We cut from the moment of his realization to a medium shot of Yvonne, who backs slowly against the wall and thereby into the shadows before swooning and falling to the ground. Orlac, still examining his hands, moves toward her, before we cut to a final medium shot of the man, framed alone, caressing and examining his hands.

This final moment is abrupt, and in fact is only one of two quite different endings that exist. In both versions, the ostensible resolution to Orlac's crisis of subjectivity fails to put an end to all of the questions raised. The hands, after all, were not in fact those of a murderer; the murderous urges that so unsettled Orlac and that found expression in the rejection of and hostility toward Yvonne are rooted not in the alien appendages but rather in his own self.[48] Regardless of the "innocence" of the hands he has been given, Orlac's identity, after all, has been irrevocably changed; his body is still a hybrid one, his hands—symbol of his livelihood and of his will—are still those of another man. Further, the passivity that threatened him persists; again, Orlac requires the active intervention of a woman in order to be saved. At the same time, in those final shots, where Yvonne retreats into the shadows and loses control of her body, we see the suggestion of her return to a more traditional role that would enable him to regain his power. The final shot of Orlac alone stresses an individuality and independent agency that points to itself as the defining characteristic of the "healthy" masculine subjectivity. In this reading, the "solution" to the crisis of masculine identity

CHAPTER FIVE

FIGURE 8. The New Woman effaced

precipitated by changing social and gender norms would be tied to a return to prewar mores; the aggression Orlac exhibits toward the (temporarily) emancipated Yvonne, this would suggest, is an innate part of his identity that emerges in response to female empowerment.

The alternate to this ending[49] perhaps even more clearly represents Orlac's return to his former role: Yvonne faints, and it is Orlac who guides her out of the bar in which the resolution occurs. The next shot—an exterior shot in which Yvonne swoons and her husband catches and carries her to a bench—suggests that all is now well. Former gender and social positions are reaffirmed, it is Orlac who is once again dominant within the public sphere and who functions as the protector for his wife when her body fails her. This next-to-final moment in the film, combined with the final shot—a close-up of Orlac's and Yvonne's faces, with his hands first caressing and then covering Yvonne's face (fig. 8)—presents the notion that once again he will take the lead in their relationship, with the reaffirmed man literally "effacing" the New Woman.

Striking about both endings is an ambiguity that serves a distinct purpose—namely, to present the inescapable difficulties arising from female emancipation in the years following the First World War. The film suggests that the crisis of male identity precipitated by the changed social arena with which returning soldiers were confronted surfaced as aggression directed toward the women who appeared to be usurping social roles formerly reserved for men. At the same time, while acknowledging that a return to previous power hierarchies might seem a solution to this crisis, it hints that such a rigidly patriarchal hierarchy is a relic of the past that must be overcome in order to move forward. What we thus see in *The Hands of Orlac* is a dramatization of a sort of double trauma that fragments masculine subjectivity in the years after World War I and that emerges in the hostility Orlac exhibits toward his wife. The primary trauma is that inflicted on body and psyche by the traumatic event, here by the train accident that stands in for the experience of combat. Like the soldier returning from war, Orlac's body is maimed, his livelihood threatened by his injury. The hands that replace his destroyed appendages become symbols of the trauma stemming from the experience of combat and physical mutilation. But the hands do more. The film, as Klaus Kreimeier notes, focuses on "the dissolution of the unity of body and psyche, body and soul."[50] The hands of alien origin represent this fragmentation; they penetrate the mind of their new owner, irritating him, destabilizing him, and driving him mad. They haunt Orlac in the same way that war memories trouble veterans. In the fantasy of the film, the hands, not Orlac, are the source of violence—a split mirroring that of soldiers who return home as both heroes and killers, praised for their deeds and tormented by their guilt. This ambivalence in returning soldiers triggers what Freud calls an "Ichkonflikt," "ego conflict," in that it represents a confrontation between the "Friedensich" and the "neues kriegerisches Ich," the formerly unified "peace ego" and the newly emerged "warlike ego";[51] the return from the war front thus results in just such a fractured subjectivity as we see in Orlac. Equally, the physical symptoms associated with this internal conflict—the nightmares, flashbacks, and "tremors and paralyses"—are just such symptoms as we see in Orlac.[52] The hands resist Orlac's command, thus representing that sense of loss of physical control traumatized soldiers exhibit. Because they are no longer under Orlac's control, his new hands prohibit continuing his career as a pianist, propelling him out of the social structure in the same way as the returning soldiers were. Orlac's traumatic injury functions as a metaphor for the plight of returning soldiers who must come to terms not only with the physical and mental scars of war but also with a society in which their previous social position and their very livelihoods are under attack.

But the trauma Orlac's experience and injury brought about is not the only source of his crisis; rather, it is coupled with the psychic trauma precipitated by the shifting roles assigned to husband and wife, man and woman after the train accident. On the level of the plot, the accident becomes the catalyst for a crisis of Orlac's identity, which emerges in his increasing hostility toward his newly active wife. If Orlac symbolically represents the soldier, who returns from the war front irrevocably changed, Yvonne, in turn, embodies the homeland that is no longer *Heimat*, but rather home front, a site of struggle, a location of deep-rooted tension. Yvonne represents an emancipated and active woman who manages to escape the domestic sphere and who thereby functions as a catalyst for war trauma, deepening the psychic wound and catapulting the man into an identity crisis that is easily identifiable as a crisis of masculinity. The theme at the heart of the film is precisely this masculine identity crisis emerging out of the experience of war and manifesting itself specifically in a desire to reassert prewar gender positions.

Read in these terms, the elements of the narrative take on new significance. The central question that haunts Orlac—that of moral guilt, embodied in his fear of the violent urges he recognizes in himself and of the possibility that he might have murdered his father—finds an easy answer in the tale of betrayal that emerges in the film's mystery plot. Orlac apparently maintains his innocence not only because the hands are retroactively found innocent of committing murder in the past, but also because his present violent inclinations turn out to be based on the whispering of a blackmailer and murderer, the man who calls himself "Vasseur" but is actually Nera. As a representative of that generation who returned from war having killed, Orlac is relieved of his responsibility; his actions stem not from an innate immorality but rather from an outside power acting through him. Nera's plan to frame Orlac—and, in particular, the complicity of Regine, the supposedly loyal servant—echoes common conspiracy theories of the postwar period, particularly the *Dolchstoßlegende*.[53] In the odd narrative of *The Hands of Orlac*, where the bulk of the action revolves around Orlac's hostility and violent urges, only to present a shocking reversal that serves to assert his innocence in the end, we see a simultaneous staging of two fantasies that dominated post–World War I culture: that of exculpation, put forth by the prewar ruling class, and that of revenge against this class, who had cold-heartedly thrown millions of soldiers into lost battles before it finally abandoned them altogether. This reading makes sense of one element of the film that does not quite fit neatly into the narrative and the import of which is oddly elided—namely, the relationship with and murder of Orlac's estranged father. As a symbol of a past social order, his abandonment of

Orlac during Orlac's time of need can be easily read as paralleling society's neglect of that generation that returned from war broken and in need of help. The elder Orlac functions as a symbol of a ruling generation that sacrificed its young, yet itself survived—and profited from—the carnage of war. The murder of the father thus is more than a plot device; it is an act of revenge against that generation and the social order for which it stands.

In addition to its symbolic import, *The Hands of Orlac* is interesting in terms of its stylistic elements, for it enacts a transition in terms of stylistics and of the experience of watching film. Stylistically and narratively, we can see this as a film situated at the intersection between expressionism and New Objectivity. The mise-en-scène vacillates between the expressionistic, embodied in the jarring images of the aftermath of the train accident, the depiction of Orlac's nightmare and his vision of the murder, the stylized newsstand, and the moody interiors of the house and the bar, and the objective, represented by the doctor's offices and the daytime outdoor scenes. The acting, too, seems split. Where Veidt, Sorina, Fritz Strassny (as Orlac's father), and Paul Askenas (as the elder Orlac's servant) draw on the broad gestures and exaggerated facial expressions characteristic of pantomime acting, the actors portraying the medical staff and the police act in a far more naturalistic and muted manner. In many ways, this confrontation between the two stylistic directions is fundamental to the uncanny quality of the film, for it confuses the viewer's expectations. The audience is forced to question whether the events on screen are to be read as depictions of a "reality" in which an executed murderer could indeed return from the grave and his hands could truly haunt their new "master," or as one in which Orlac's diseased and damaged psyche misinterprets the quite rationally explicable events around him. As I suggested, *The Hands of Orlac* is thus as much a hybrid as is the reassembled body of the hero, combining elements of the two cinematic styles and drawing on these in order to destabilize the viewer and emphasize its uncanny effect.

Beyond functioning as a bridge between these two approaches, we can interpret the film as enacting a shift in the mode of watching film, in the way in which the audience approaches the image on the screen. Where films like *Warning Shadows* and, to a lesser degree, *The Eyes of the Mummy* build on and amplify the inherently uncanny confrontation between viewer and double on the screen, between individual and the "ghostly" semblance of life, *The Hands of Orlac* moves toward refamiliarizing the image on the screen. The presentation of elements that initially appear uncanny but are then revealed to be based on very objective science or trickery parallels the ever more cinematically savvy viewer's understanding of the technological processes at the basis of the medium. Just as Orlac's haunting is revealed to be the effect of his traumatic experience and of the machinations of the would-be blackmailer, and the uncanny appearance of the "reanimated" head is shown to be no more than a trick a criminal who is very much alive employed, so the audience by now is aware of at least the basic processes underlying the images projected onto the screen. That is not to say that the film entirely demystifies the cinematic process; indeed, in a sense, the ultimately unsatisfying ending works to suggest an uncanny surplus—both in terms of narrative and medium—that cannot be fully explained. Orlac's hostility toward Yvonne, his sense of a fractured identity and of personal disempowerment that finds its release in his violent urges, are not fully resolved by the film's rational ending; he received the hands not of a murderer, but of an innocent man, thus his "haunting" cannot be reduced to a pseudo-medical effect of the transplant.[54] Nor can we ascribe his actions solely to the influence of the criminal Nera, for Orlac's psychological deterioration begins even before the other man approaches him. Although it does so in a very different way than, for example, *The Cabinet of Dr. Caligari*, the resolution of the film leaves crucial questions open, suggesting that no narrative could fully explain the uncanny events depicted in the film. This maintains an uncanny quality in the experience of watching the film: some level of mystery must remain; the viewer must still be able to gain entry into the cinematic experience through a decidedly irrational suspension of disbelief.

In terms of the development of cinematic representation of women, Yvonne's initial transgressive activity and desire and the resolution of this problematic through her final return to passivity and her husband's concomitant return to the position of active agent represent an interesting step. In her active function, Yvonne exceeds the role that many critics see as traditionally assigned to the female characters in film. For example, Mulvey suggests that classic Hollywood cinema prescribes an active male protagonist who is capable of "forwarding the story, making things happen,"[55] and a female figure whose "visual presence tends to work against the development of a story line, to freeze the flow of action in moments of erotic contemplation."⁵⁶ She argues that the pleasurable experience of film emerges from the identification between viewer and the "more perfect, more complete, more powerful ideal ego" embodied in the male protagonist.⁵⁷ Yet in *The Hands of Orlac*, the possibilities of identification are very different. Here it is Yvonne who functions to "make things happen"; she prods the doctor to undertake the fateful transplant, she visits Orlac's father and pushes her husband to do the same, thereby enabling the attempted blackmail, and she ultimately urges her husband to go to the police, resulting in the proof of his innocence. In this sense, she is a figure far more similar to Clover's "final girl," or even, in spite of the fact that she is determinedly *not* depicted as a mother, to Studlar's powerful maternal figure. Orlac, in contrast, is in no way an embodiment of an image of the self that is, in Mulvey's words, "more perfect [and] more complete"; quite the contrary, he embodies the (male) viewer's primal fear, the male body castrated, objectified, and mutilated. If we think of the experience of watching a film as based on a set of identifications and disavowals, the male viewer's identification with the "protagonist," Orlac, is one with a fractured, disempowered identity, forced into the position of a passive object, both as the incapacitated injury victim and the focus of his wife's active desire. Again, we might see him as superficially aligned with the structures Studlar postulates: to identify with him involves identifying with a man who has taken on a "feminized" position. Yet this stems from more than a universal psychic structure. Instead, we see the depiction of a male subjectivity that sees itself as being under attack. In Germany in 1924, Orlac represents quite fittingly the male subject fractured and destabilized by the experiences of physical injury (the war), the loss of previous social position (changing gender roles), and economic instability (hyperinflation). Driving the film is the necessity to recreate the wholeness of the protagonist and thereby that of the viewing subject. In regard to this, the ambiguity of the ending is, again, an important quality, for it does not allow for the certainty of such wholeness, instead suspending the viewer in an uneasy identification with a protagonist who may well have superficially escaped his crisis, but whose psychological split has not been entirely remedied. If anything, the only clear "progress" made in reestablishing a more "comfortable" identification is that the active role taken by Yvonne is disavowed in the end; the fact that she faints and, perhaps even more so, the final image (in some versions) in which Orlac covers her face with his hands and hides it against him first relegates her again to passive object and then entirely denies her representation.

To shift the ways in which the characters of Orlac and Yvonne function, we can consider them in terms of the suggestions that Doane makes about a different set of films—namely, what she calls American "1940s films of the medical discourse."[58] In the opening chapter, I discussed her contention that these films equated female undesirability with illness and the process of healing with a woman's return to the position of desired object;[59] ultimately, these films pushed the female spectator to take on a masculine position. Doane's notion of the ways in which sick and healthy bodies connect to gender, agency, and spectatorship raises interesting questions when we examine *The Hands of Orlac*. How do the stakes change when the diseased body is male, rather than female? In the films she examines, Doane suggests woman-as-patient is "not spectacular but symptomatic," and her body has "both a surface and a depth."[60] Orlac as a patient may well be "symptomatic," but he is, equally, "spectacular," his body put on display to doctor, wife, and viewer, his agency relinquished to those who control his fate and interpret his symptoms. The gaze at Orlac is never only masculine; indeed, if we recall the many moments in which Yvonne looks at him, we might suggest that there is a desiring and powerful female gaze that identifies most astutely the significance of the symptoms he displays. On one hand, the film seems to equate Orlac's illness with his becoming an object of the gaze; the male body objectified, by the powerful gaze of a woman no less, is as much a result of disease as is the female body empowered. At the same time, this constellation essentially opens up a space for a gaze that is feminized, for the viewer's gaze is aligned most closely with that of Yvonne. And this "feminized" spectator position is effectively carried through to the end. Recall the final sequence, where we see a close-up of the couple's faces as Orlac caresses, then covers Yvonne's face before the shot fades out;[61] here, Yvonne's "loss" of the gaze coincides with the dark screen that signifies the end of the film and, in effect, the viewer's relinquishment of a spectatorial position. We may well be able to isolate certain incarnations of the male gaze, in particular in the doctors and the policemen who ultimately "solve" the mystery of Orlac's haunting, yet these figures are secondary ones, and their "solutions" to the problem of Orlac's "unruly" body are unsatisfying at best. The representatives of the law, in particular, appear so late in the film and present a solution that is so incongruous and unsupported that, even if they might be intended to embody a scientific or "masculine" gaze, they merely draw attention to its ineffectiveness. Perhaps thence the oscillation between the uncanny and the melodramatic in the film. Orlac's affliction renders his body—and that of his active wife—uncanny in terms of traditional social norms, yet at the same time, it offers to his wife a level of agency and power that she cedes only in the final moment of renunciation. In terms of the gaze, *The Hands of Orlac* might be uncanny because it stages and aligns the spectator with a feminine gaze. In doing so, it further undermines some crucial preconceptions about film, for here, the desiring and possessing gaze is *not* de facto a masculine one. Rather, *The Hands of Orlac* suggests that the construction of such a masculine gaze is addressed to and intended to resolve very specifically the dilemma of the masculine identity fractured, maimed, and disempowered.

Even more so than the other films I have thus far examined, *The Hands of Orlac* draws attention to the ways in which male subjectivity is challenged, even under attack in this period, for the effect of the traumatic experiences of war and of the return to a changed society on the masculine body and psyche are foregrounded. Orlac—his body damaged, his psyche fragmented, and his social and economic position radically changed—becomes a clear representation of the veteran, who faces seemingly insurmountable challenges when trying to reintegrate into family and society. In this film, we see plainly the multiple traumas that find their expression in hostility directed toward emancipated woman, who represents most clearly the radically changed position of the male subject. The fantasy of return—the notion that body and psyche can be entirely healed, that the individual can reclaim his former position—is played out in a manner that is unsatisfying enough to suggest that it is, indeed, no more than a fantasy. Questions are left unanswered, and Orlac's recovery reads as little more than a narrative device. On the one hand, *The Hands of Orlac* articulates a bleak reflection on a male subjectivity fragmented and traumatized by its confrontation with modernity; on the other, it problematizes the notion of a compulsory male gaze and opens up a space for a female and feminized spectatorial position. This might be the ultimate in the uncanny: the notion that the woman—on screen or in the audience—might, too, be the bearer of a determining gaze, might desire and possess through her look, and might do so not by taking on the role of the male viewer, but as woman herself.

SIX

A DAUGHTER OF DESTINY (*ALRAUNE*, HENRIK GALEEN, 1928) AND *DAUGHTER OF EVIL* (*ALRAUNE*, RICHARD OSWALD, 1930)

From Dangerous Hybrid to Self-Sacrificing Woman

THIS CHAPTER BRINGS US to the last years of the Weimar Republic, and to two very different filmic adaptations of a story in which a fatal woman takes center stage: Henrik Galeen's and Richard Oswald's respective versions of *Alraune* (1928 and 1930). By the time Galeen took on his project, which would premier in January 1928, Germany was a very different place than it had been just a few years before. The economic stabilization that had already begun when Wiene's *Hands of Orlac* premiered in 1924 was well established. As economic upheaval and the initial open political and social chaos of the early years of the republic faded into the past, filmmakers distanced themselves more and more from the expressionistic material and style that had been so prevalent in the late 1910s and early 1920s. Still, Galeen's movie and Oswald's later remake to varying degrees hark back to those early, conflict-ridden years, when that which unreeled on the screen inside the "refuges" of the movie theaters often seemed directly symbolic of the chaos outside.

Both films were based Hanns Heinz Ewers's *Alraune* (1911), the fairly well known story of an "artificial" woman who fatally endangers all the men around her. Ewers was a prolific writer of everything from satirical cabaret pieces to fairy tales, uncanny and horrific stories to screenplays, including *The Student of Prague* (*Der Student von Prag*, Wegener/Rye 1913).[1] *Alraune* is built around the myth of the mandrake, a root that sprouts from the earth beneath a gallows in the moment in which a hanged criminal's sperm enters the earth, and which brings to those who possess it fortune and wealth, yet at a price. Taking his inspiration from the legend, a scientist, ten Brinken, attempts to create what he sees as a "living mandrake," and inseminates a prostitute with the sperm of a hanged murderer. The child resulting from this experiment and raised by him, Alraune, inherits her mother's promiscuity and her father's immorality, causing the deaths of numerous men around her and, in the novel, finally committing suicide.

This theme of unnatural beings, figures that appear human, yet ultimately are unmasked as the "artificial" beings they are, was a fairly common one in films of the Weimar Republic. From Otto Rippert's *Homunculus* series (1916) to the various incarnations of the *Golem*, including the coproductions by Paul Wegener with Henrik Galeen (1915) and with Carl Boese (1920), the topic of artificially created life was the central trope in films that implicitly posed the question of how human subjectivity is formed. While these early films focused on the creation of male bodies, later ones shifted to narratives in which the body created was female, in which the story essentially represented a rescripting of the Pygmalion myth, with the woman painted as a monstrous and dangerous figure. The traumatic effect of changing social roles and gender norms found expression in narratives focusing on the dangerous impact of these powerful—yet unnatural—women. In these narratives, we see two thematic strands intertwined: power that is masculine is embodied in the fantasy of man as the creator of woman, while that which is feminine finds expression in the artificial, idealized creation that inevitably turns on its creator. The most well known example of this tendency is Fritz Lang's *Metropolis*, where the mad scientist, Rotwang, quickly loses control of his creation, but these two versions of *Alraune* present interesting reworkings of the theme.

Ewers's novel was filmed a number of times between the late 1910s and the early 1950s. While it is difficult to specify exactly how often, as there were at least six films titled *Alraune* or something similar and the earliest versions appear to be lost, the large number of versions is evidence of the popularity of the material. Indeed, in 1919, two studios—Luna and Neutral—produced films titled *Alraune*, a fact that ended in a lawsuit, with each studio attempting to assert its rights. In April of 1919, *Der Film* reported the outcome of the trial: "Luna declared that its *Alraune* was based on the novel by Hanns Heinz Ewers and thus is the real first *Alraune*-film, while Neutral asserted that they acquired the manuscript, the narrative of which is based on the legend of the mandrake, for a film called *Alraune* in April 1918 from the author F."[2] Neutral's version—later given a longer title, *Alraune, the Hangman's Daughter, Called Red Hanne (Alraune, die Henkerstochter, genannt die rote Hanne)*—had little to do with Ewers's story, but Luna's version was the first of several that exploited the lurid content of the novel, and was followed by the 1928 and 1930 versions by Galeen and Oswald, both starring Brigitte Helm as the eponymous vamp, as well as one from 1952 starring Hildegard Knef (dir. Arthur Maria Rabenalt).[3]

The versions from 1928 and 1930 are interesting for a number of reasons. Both focus on a threatening, emancipated woman who embodies a sexual power and immorality that is, as one critic writing about Galeen's version stated, "beyond good and evil."[4] Ten Brinken, the mad scientist who masquerades as her uncle, is ultimately destroyed by his own creation. The basic narratives of the two films are largely identical, but the ways in which they do differ—in terms of narrative and cinematography—are crucial in that they point toward changes in the positioning of women and developments in the medium. Narratively, the respective endings suggest very different approaches to neutralizing the threat the transgressive woman poses: either to force woman to abdicate her active erotic power and conform to a more conservative definition of woman or to punish her transgression with death. Indeed, the two films approach their respective narratives within the frameworks of different genres—the uncanny "fantastic film" and the melodrama respectively—thus further shifting the ways in which gender is conceptualized. Cinematographically, the different ways in which Alraune is represented as object of desire and as dangerously active subject reflect a shift in conventions of the medium that can be tied to the move from silent to sound film and to the rapidly changing social environment.

The character of Alraune, the seductive yet dangerous vamp, has her predecessors not only in the artificial women of Weimar film, but also in a line of similar female figures in German culture stretching further back, from Frank Wedekind's Lulu[5] to Lang's evil robot Maria[6] on to von Sternberg's Lola-Lola.[7] We might see Alraune as the pinnacle of the trajectory along which the women in the previous films are located; she embodies all those dangerous characteristics that we have seen in Negri's Mâ, in the women in *Uncanny Tales*, in Yvonne of *The Hands of Orlac*, and in the flirtatious wife of *Warning Shadows*, but to a far greater degree, for these traits are what define her. Helm's Alraune represents a combination of the other, the erotic, the transgressive and the seductive—indeed, she seems to combine all those threatening traits into a single figure who represents simultaneously her male creator's fantasy and his undoing. David Davidson, in his analysis of the female figures in G. W. Pabst's *Pandora's Box* (*Die Büchse der Pandora*, 1929), von Sternberg's *The Blue Angel* (*Der blaue Engel*, 1930), and François Truffaut's *Jules and Jim* (*Jules et Jim*, 1961), suggests that they represent the end point of a development in which woman's symbolic value shifts in response to a changing sociocultural environment; to him, Lang's doubled Maria represents "the fierce struggle between the old iconography and the new, between the 'safe' sexuality of the 'pure woman,' who exists outside of time, and the threatening sexuality of the 'amoral woman,' whose rise is linked to the depersonalization and dynamism of the Industrial Revolution,"[8] while Pabst's Lulu and von Sternberg's Lola-Lola stand for "'real women;' these figures' searing sexuality and moral coolness tacitly suggests an inner duality."[9] We might locate Alraune at the end point of this development, among Pabst's Lulu and Sternberg's Lola-Lola; a "real woman" who is, paradoxically, fundamentally "unnatural," whose very creation challenges nature as well as the structure of society. She, too, represents the changed construction of woman, tied closely to modernity and characterized by active and dangerous sexuality and fundamental amorality. Her very existence becomes testimony to the tension between nature and modernity; hers is an origin fundamentally unnatural, rooted in the scientist's arrogant attempt to create life and thus to seize the role reserved for nature or god. Alraune, like the women Davidson discusses, functions as a projection of the male psyche, embodying the desires and fears of ten Brinken; at the same time, she is the projection of her cinematic "creator(s)," the director, camera, and the actor herself who shaped her image as literal projection onto the screen.

CHAPTER SIX

I include the actor among the group that becomes the cinematic creator of Alraune because she represents an active subject that is too often erased by notions of directorial control and because, in the two versions of *Alraune*, we see a single actor embody the titular character. Both Galeen and Oswald cast Brigitte Helm, who had rapidly risen to fame after her starring role as the two Marias in Lang's *Metropolis* (1927) and had been signed to a ten-year contract with Ufa. Her role as the title character in Galeen's *Alraune* came after starring turns in G. W. Pabst's *The Love of Jeanne Ney* (*Die Liebe der Jeanne Ney*, 1927) and Karl Grune's *At the Edge of the World* (*Am Rande der Welt*, 1927). *Alraune*, in which she returned to a role much closer to that in *Metropolis* than those of the "boring, well-behaved girls"[10] she portrayed in the intervening films, cemented her status as enigmatic femme fatale, both in films and in the popular imaginary. In a sense, the role that Helm played in the two version of *Alraune* determined her subsequent career and colored the manner in which the movie-going public viewed her.[11] And, though Alraune is no automaton, as is the "evil Maria" Helm played in her film debut, we can see her as an extension of the same, as a character that embodies similar anxieties. Andreas Huyssen suggests that in Lang's film, Rotwang's creation of the robot Maria represents an attempt to master nature: "By creating a female android, Rotwang fulfills the male phantasm of a creation without mother; but more than that, he produces not just any natural life, but woman herself, the epitome of nature. The nature/culture split seems healed."[12] At the same time that woman comes to stand in for nature, she symbolized technology, again as imagined by man: "The film suggests a simple and deeply problematic homology between woman and technology, a homology which results from male projections: Just as man invents and constructs technological artifacts which are to serve him and fulfill his desires, so woman, as she has been socially invented and constructed by man, is expected to reflect man's needs and to serve her master."[13] Both Marias in Lang's film are fundamentally other, occupying the roles of virgin and vamp simultaneously constructed by and threatening to men.[14] That woman becomes both fantasy and danger to man is represented through the initial construction of the robot Maria, the fascination of the male characters with her body (most clearly demonstrated in her striptease), and the climactic burning scene, where her flesh disappears, leaving only the mechanical interior behind. This process is constituted, Huyssen argues, through the male gaze:

> It is male vision which puts together and disassembles woman's body, thus denying woman her identity and making her into an object of projection and manipulation. What is interesting about Lang's *Metropolis* is not so much that Lang uses the male gaze in the described way. Practically all traditional narrative cinema treats woman's body as a projection of male vision. What is interesting, however, is that by thematizing male gaze and vision in the described way the film lays open a fundamental filmic convention usually covered up by narrative cinema.[15]

Huyssen's analysis of *Metropolis* sheds an interesting light on the two versions of *Alraune*, in which Helm's role appears at times to hark explicitly back to her turn in Lang's film. Here, too, we see the topos of an artificially created woman: ten Brinken, like Rotwang, attains the male fantasy of creating "without mother," for the body that bears the child that he engineers is virtually effaced within the narrative of the film. Even more than in *Metropolis*, in *Alraune* this life created by man is not simply the appearance of life, but is real, a body not built out of metal and endowed with life through electricity, but living and breathing. And yet Alraune is constructed as male fantasy, both inescapably attractive and desired and, through these qualities, fatal to those who fall under her spell. Further, like *Metropolis*, both of these versions of *Alraune* reveal the constitutive role of "male gaze and vision," simultaneously catering to a desiring male gaze of characters and audience and revealing the power structures implied in this gaze.

What is especially interesting about the two versions is how each constructs Alraune as the object of desire and embodiment of the fantasies and fears of the men around her, and what kind of identifications each suggests. Further, comparing the two versions sheds light on the impact of the changing medium. A comparison of the films raises important questions: what was it about this narrative, with its focus on the dangerous, "unnatural" woman, that made it so popular at the time? What does it suggest about gender and identity, about the way in which both are constituted in a performance and about the relationship this performance has to an individual? *Alraune* draws attention to the constructedness of the woman at the heart of the narrative: an "artificial creation" by virtue of her origin, she is doubly "artificial" because she is simply a character being played by Helm, and triply so because that performance is filmed and projected, one more step removed from the real. That the film was produced twice in such a short time only heightens that sense of artifice and suggests that it caters to certain dominant sociocultural fears and desires focused on women, identity, and transgression.

ALRAUNE 1928: HENRIK GALEEN'S VERSION

Although the details of Henrik Galeen's life are not precisely documented, by the time he directed *Alraune* he had already established himself as a screenwriter and director. His best-known works are ones that draw on the uncanny or the mystical as central features; together with Wegener, he wrote, directed, and acted in the first version of the *Golem* (1915) and apparently had some part in Wegener's 1920 version (*The Golem: How He Came into the World/Der Golem, wie er in die Welt kam*),[16] then wrote the screenplays for the classic *Nosferatu* and for Paul Leni's *Waxworks* (*Wachsfigurenkabinett*, 1924). In 1926, he directed the second version of *The Student of Prague*, another film based on a novel by Ewers, this time starring Conrad Veidt. In Galeen's version of *Alraune*, the narrative emphasis lies on ten Brinken's transgression of the laws of nature and on the "blasphemy" that the artificial creation of a child embodies. Galeen takes liberties with Ewers's story: here, Alraune, being raised as the niece of ten Brinken (Paul Wegener), runs away from her convent school with a young man, Wolf (Wolfgang Zilzer), who is enamored with her. After meeting a group of circus performers on a train, she joins them, acting as assistant to the magician who becomes her lover. When ten Brinken finds her, she agrees to go away with him. Surrounded by admiring men, she falls in love with a young viscount (John Loder) and is devastated when ten Brinken refuses to accede to their marriage. While her ostensible uncle sleeps, she discovers the journal in which he has noted his progress on the "experiment" she represents. Enraged, she is tempted to strangle him, yet decides, instead, to have her revenge by making him suffer. She embarks on a calculated campaign to make him fall in love with her, ultimately leading him to lose his money at a roulette table and then telling him that she is leaving. Ten

Brinken, driven mad by her behavior, attempts to kill her, but is disarmed at the last moment by his nephew, Frank Braun (Ivan Petrovich). With ten Brinken ruined, Alraune begs Braun to take her away, saying that she wants to become "a human being" in order to be able to truly love another.

Galeen assembled a cast of well-known actors, though Helm and Paul Wegener are the only two with name recognition today. While *Alraune* was certainly a star vehicle for Helm, it seems equally apt for Wegener, whose career had been made in films that were fantastical and uncanny, from his starring turn in *The Student of Prague* (*Der Student von Prag*, 1913) to his classic *Golem* (*Der Golem, wie er in die Welt kam*, 1920). Indeed, recall that he would later play a similar role in Oswald's second *Uncanny Tales*, as the insane inventor who murders his wife and thus becomes the intrepid journalist's quarry. His presence speaks to that element of the story that is uncanny, to that mystical excess that is not explained by the "science" behind creating Alraune, even as it quickly characterizes ten Brinken as a fundamentally evil character. Indeed, both Wegener and Helm, who had so recently starred in *Metropolis*, seem like they were eminently suitable to creating a film that capitalized on the uncanny quality of the narrative.

And yet the mixed response to the film suggests that Galeen was not able to realize the full potential of both narrative and cast, with one critic noting that he attempted to mix social commentary and realism with the fantastic in a way that undermined the final product:

> There were two possibilities: to depict the path of a wanton woman who drinks red blood and remains childlike in spite of all the suffering that she causes. For this, the constructive mixture of the semen of a hanged man and the womb of a whore is not necessary. Or the story becomes an uncanny one, a cinematic fable, with uncanny light- and shadow-effects. . . . Henrik Galeen, too thorough, tries to combine two stylistic types. An "Alraune" is not, however, generated from this experiment.[17]

This review points to one of the central issues arising in this present study: why films that focus on a woman's destructive power—on that "path of a wanton woman"—so frequently are framed as "uncanny stories" and "cinematic fables." Yet the critic's reading draws attention to one major difference between the other films I have examined and *Alraune*: where the earlier works mask their preoccupation with questions of female sexuality and emancipation behind their respective uncanny narratives, *Alraune* concentrates openly on the fatal power wielded by the woman. It is Alraune herself, sexually liberated and demanding, actively desiring, and willing to take that which—or those whom—she wants, who is openly figured as the primary, uncanny element. In her analysis of the film, Valerie Weinstein notes that narratively and stylistically, *Alraune* fuses the uncanny and the rational in order to represent its subject matter:

> Science and the horrific narrative merge thematically and stylistically as the film progresses, and the imbrication of horror and realist claims, superstitions and science, is accompanied throughout the film by the use of techniques associated with Expressionism and the New Objectivity. This mixture of styles in *Alraune* highlights the event the film locates at the intersection of superstition and science: genetic crossbreeding. Alraune is a product of this genetic crossbreeding. . . . Styles and structures typical of the horror film render her monstrous, as strategies with realist claims locate her in the spectators' real world.[18]

The uncanny quality of the emancipated and empowered woman is not displaced onto another horrific element but located squarely within the female body. Alraune is both the desired body and the object of horror. The critic certainly recognized this quality of the film and, in depicting it as a problematic one, suggests that the "experiment" was unsuccessful. Yet the criticism points toward an interpretation very much in line with Weinstein's reading and toward a metafilmic dimension to the piece, an equation of the title character with the process of filmmaking itself; just as ten Brinken is not successful in his creation of "an Alraune," so Galeen's movie functions as a flawed creation. In considering the self-reflexive significance of Galeen's *Alraune*, this is one dimension we will examine.

That first review is representative of others in that it identifies the dual focus in the film, the framework of the uncanny, medieval legend that gives shape to what is, effectively, a tale of social realism. Further, this reviewer mentions Frank Wedekind's scandalous *Lulu* plays, comparing Alraune to "Lulu, the Biblical snake."[19] In this, too, the reviewer was not alone; another called Alraune the "spiritual relative of Wedekind's Lulu."[20] This is significant, suggesting already a certain interpretation of Galeen's title character. Wedekind's dramas—two connected pieces, "Earth Spirit" ("Erdgeist," 1895) and "Pandora's Box" ("Die Büchse der Pandora," 1902)—focus on a sexually promiscuous woman, with the respective halves detailing her rise from prostitute to society girl and her subsequent fall and death at the hands of Jack the Ripper. Lulu functions as a sort of proto–femme fatale, a woman who acts on her every desire and thereby on her true nature. In referencing Wedekind's Lulu, the reviewers of Galeen's *Alraune* focus not on the film character's "unnatural" origins and on her creator's transgression of scientific morality but rather on an "evil" within her that is rooted in the "natural," going back to the biblical fall—she *is* the biblical snake rather than its victim, embodiment of woman as *inherently* immoral and dangerous to men. With this, they reflect an anxious preoccupation with woman's status at the time: on the one hand, any woman who challenges and endangers men, acting out and projecting an active eroticism, must necessarily be "unnatural"; on the other, this dangerous quality is positioned as the defining characteristic of woman from the very moment of her (biblical) creation.

Galeen's film certainly acts out this ambiguity. Superficially, it functions as a simple, Frankensteinian tale, focused on the figure of a mad scientist who is punished by his own creation for overstepping the boundaries nature dictates to science. Yet the iconography of the film suggests a more complex significance. In its depiction of a woman whose power over the men around her is fatal and must be contained, *Alraune* reveals the anxieties of this cultural moment in which gender roles and power hierarchies were being redefined. Further, through the depiction of Alraune as wielding a power based on the gaze of men at her and, importantly, her reciprocal gaze at them, the film reflects on the dynamics of the medium, on the way in which the gaze functions as a part of power hierarchies that structure—and are revealed—in film.

On the narrative level, Galeen's film emphasizes ten Brinken's culpability, painting him as a mad scientist in the tradition stretching from Dr. Frankenstein to *Metropolis*'s Rotwang, from the creator of the Golem to that of the homunculus. Like his predecessors, ten Brinken oversteps the boundaries of morality, violating, as his nephew tells him, "nature and all that is most worthy and fine."[21] The legend of the mandrake figures prominently, suggesting a Faustian dimension to ten Brinken, who seeks fortune through his "living mandrake" but underestimates its destructive power. Thus the opening intertitles relate briefly the outline of the legend, stating ominously that "the magic power of the mandrake root could bring luck—but it could also bring suffering and torment to anyone who tried to own it," before cutting to the brief opening sequence, in which a man climbs toward a gallows on which a hanged man still dangles and begins to dig beneath the body. This image is then immediately juxtaposed with Professor ten Brinken, who lectures a group of young men on his plans to "conduct scientific research into this old superstition" regarding the mandrake. Galeen's use of the legend foreshadows ten Brinken's inevitable downfall. The final scene—a long shot in which ten Brinken, financially ruined and abandoned by Alraune, turns away from the camera—reinforces the narrative arc focused on the punishment of his character. As the final intertitle states, "he who had violated nature suffered the hell of loneliness and insanity." In this most superficial narrative strand, Alraune herself is little more than an object, the embodied proof of ten Brinken's scientific experiment gone mad, and the victim both of his unscrupulous actions and her unfortunate genetic heritage.

Yet the visual representation of the film works almost defiantly against the basic narrative of the mad scientist. In the iconography of Galeen's film, Alraune functions as the center of a network of gazes that structures the shifting power dynamics between the main characters. She is far from being a passive object; rather, like so many of the women we have examined, she actively stages herself as object of desire. Even more, her gaze onto the men around her is a powerful one. This dangerous power that Alraune wields ultimately comes to represent her greatest "sin," her transgression of norms of behavior and of the structure of classical film. Like the earlier films I have examined, Galeen's *Alraune* problematizes the notion that the role of woman in film is to function as the object of the male gaze of both character on the screen and spectator to the film. At least for a time, Alraune becomes the bearer of the gaze and the object of the male gaze only insofar as she stages *herself*. The male spectator is ultimately released from the uncomfortable position in which this reversal catches him when Alraune begs Frank to "make her human," suggesting that her empowerment and independence are qualities that ultimately place her outside of a "natural order" and that, in order to be "human" (and thereby a "real" woman), she must become the object of masculine power. In spite of this resolution of the issue in favor of a male-dominated power hierarchy, Galeen's film nevertheless problematizes the power structures at work in film, suggesting that the relationship between subject and object, viewer and image, is one in which both positions offer some level of power.

The first sequence in which Alraune is introduced begins as a fairly straightforward characterization of her questionable character. It opens with a close-up of a bowl with a fly crawling on its lip. Only after showing the bowl from two different angles does the scene cut to a medium profile shot of Alraune as she watches the fly. Twice more we cut between the fly on the bowl and Alraune, who watches it intently before finally flicking it into the liquid. The sequence ends with a lingering shot of her, still in profile, as she bends, nearly motionless, over the bowl, presumably examining the fly as it drowns (fig. 9). Weinstein notes that this moment, along with several others in the film in which Alraune "is in direct physical contact with disgusting vermin," functions through what Noël Carroll calls "horrific metonymy" to associate the girl with said vermin: "she is akin enough to them that they do not disgust her."[22] While this is certainly a significant point, what is equally important about this sequence is that it establishes the way in which Alraune will be represented. First, there is her silence. Utterly alone during the sequence, she barely moves and says nothing. Throughout the film, it is striking that only a few of the often excessively wordy intertitles articulate Alraune's words. The second significant element lies therein that she is shot only in profile, averting her eyes from the camera. In itself, this might not be significant; however, throughout the film, Alraune carefully controls her gaze onto those around her, and it is the reciprocation of their own gaze—her acknowledgment of their presence specifically through focusing her gaze on them—that those men whom she destroys desire. Further, the fact that what she is looking at is a living being in its death throes—which she herself has caused—suggests the dangerous quality of being the object of her gaze. The introduction of Alraune thus raises the central problem that she poses to the system of norms determining relationships between the genders and points to the potentially deadly power of the gaze.

Alraune's first (human) victim is Wolf, whom she convinces to steal from his father and run away with her, then abandons. While her teacher

CHAPTER SIX

FIGURE 9. Death examined

and classmates prepare a birthday celebration for her, Alraune sits in her room, watching out the window until she hears Wolf whistle for her and sees him on the roof of another building. Once outside, their interaction is shown in a sequence of fairly long-duration, medium shots. The emphasis is on the interplay of their gazes, and the moment, in spite of its dramatic repercussions, draws on only two intertitles. We see Wolf on the left, looking at Alraune, who is visible only in partial profile as she returns his gaze. Wolf is speaking quickly to her; the intertitle relates his statement as: "I cannot do it to my parents." Immediately, Alraune turns away from him, first averting only her eyes, then turning her back on him entirely. Wolf attempts to force her to look at him by moving from her right to her left shoulder, but she turns away again. As Wolf continues to speak quickly, she begins to move away and he grabs her arms to stop her. We see Alraune facing into the camera while Wolf stands behind her, still trying to catch her gaze until he gives in and tells her "I'll do everything you wish!" Only now does Alraune reward him by looking at him. Two issues are particularly significant in this sequence. First, we see Alraune's power to overcome her admirers' moral boundaries. She disturbs that most fundamental relationship between child and parents, convincing Wolf to betray his own parents. Perhaps more interestingly, we see the first instance in which her gaze at a man becomes that which he seeks out, that which satisfies his desire. In looking at Wolf, Alraune acknowledges and seems to promise herself to him. As the figure who exerts her power thus over the men around her, she resembles closely Studlar's maternal: she embodies the fantasy of "the loving inflictor of punishment"[23] who "exercises the authority of the pre-Oedipal mother whose gaze forms the child's first experience of love and power."[24] In this sense, Wolf and the other men who desire her represent the masochistic spectator that Studlar theorizes, who "is desiring, but helpless, the passive recipient of the pleasures which the mother controls through her presence or absence. . . . The masochistic gaze leads to the male's subjugation to the female, not his control of her."[25]

The idea that the men around her desire Alraune's gaze is reinforced by her interaction with the various men she meets when she and Wolf flee the convent together. In the first important sequence, we see Wolf and Alraune sitting across from each other in a train compartment, drinking champagne. A young man moves into the hallway, smoking, and shots of his face are crosscut with point-of-view shots of Alraune's face, visible through the open door of the compartment. Realizing that he is there, she first starts, then, still watching him, takes a sip of champagne. At this moment Wolf, sitting across from her, realizes that she is no longer returning his gaze; angry, he closes the blinds to interrupt the exchange of looks between Alraune and her new admirer. There follows a moment that seems to present a temporary reversal of the earlier dynamic: now, Wolf averts his eyes from her, while Alraune caresses him until he relents and they embrace. Like earlier, the reciprocation of the gaze takes on the function of reward; the crucial difference is that, where Wolf had to agree to Alraune's wishes in order to be rewarded with her gaze, she forces him to respond to her without ceding any control to him. She does so by staging herself as precisely that which Wolf desires from her: caressing his arm, embracing him, essentially acting out the part of his lover. Wolf's jealousy when Alraune looks at the stranger in the hallway reveals his awareness of the value of her gaze, even as he remains subject to its power.

A second encounter suggests that the conflict at the heart of the film revolves around this apparent reversal, around the putting on display of a male figure for a dominating female gaze. As Wolf sleeps, Alraune watches as a group of circus performers boards the train. She is joined in their compartment by a magician, who, when Wolf awakens and angrily leaves the compartment, prevents Alraune from following him by performing a series of magic tricks. Implicitly, the magician is putting himself on display for her, becoming the object of her gaze, though her power is mitigated initially because he is able to manipulate her by drawing her gaze to his hands and the various items that he makes appear and disappear. During his final trick, however, Alraune regains the upper hand. He conjures a mouse, then puts it on her ankle. As the mouse scurries up her leg, the sequence cuts to a close-up of his face as he watches her, then to a close-up of hers as she catches his gaze and reciprocates it. As he comments on her fearlessness, the sequence cuts between medium shots of their faces and lingers on hers as she stares back at him and into the camera. Here, even as she becomes an object of his gaze by virtue of her fearless reaction to the mouse, she simultaneously fixes him with her gaze, deriving pleasure from his reaction, which is both impressed and horrified. The moment of intimacy this represents is interrupted when Wolf reenters the compartment and a struggle ensues between the two men. Here, the men fighting over Alraune become a spectacle watched not only by her but also by the circus performers, who gather to look on. The final shot of the sequence is again of her face, as she watches them with obvious enjoyment. Again, Alraune makes the men around her the objects of her gaze, and derives pleasure—and power—from doing so.

The most significant example of this constellation wherein a man desires to be the object of Alraune's gaze, and wherein her withdrawal of this gaze represents the moment of his ultimate downfall, is Alraune's relationship with ten Brinken. Once Alraune discovers her origins and decides to avenge herself by making him fall in love with her, he goes from being the bearer of the gaze—observing and thereby controlling his "creation"—to being its object. This becomes clear as soon as Alraune reads the book in which he has noted the progress of his "experiment"; enraged and humiliated by her discovery, she enters ten Brinken's room as he sleeps. The book represents Alraune's ultimate objectification: she is the specimen that is examined and tracked by its creator. Her discovery leads Alraune to attempt to reverse this relationship in which she is the passive object of ten Brinken's machinations. We see a medium shot of her as she moves toward the camera and it tracks back into the room. Cutting between medium, high-angle shots of ten Brinken, still asleep, and medium and long shots of the two, Alraune bent over him, the moment emphasizes the shift in power: it is now Alraune who dominates him, her spatial position representing her momentary superiority. We then see a series of close-ups of their faces, then linger on a close-up of ten Brinken's head and chest as the shadows of Alraune's hands, clawlike, approach his throat as though to strangle

A Daughter of Destiny and Daughter of Evil

him, then are pulled away. Throughout the sequence, ten Brinken remains asleep, the passive object of Alraune's gaze, vulnerable to her power. He has gone from possessing her—as creation and as "child"—to being possessed by her. In this moment, she reasserts her power: within the narrative by determining ten Brinken's fate through her decision to destroy him, and within the cinematographic structure by the way in which her movements determine those of the camera.

As in so many of the films examined, the primary way in which Alraune exerts power over ten Brinken is by staging herself as the object of his desire. We see this clearly in a later scene, where it becomes evident that even as she positions herself as the object of his desiring gaze, she does so actively, suggesting a level of agency. In the grand hall of a hotel, Alraune plays Ping-Pong, surrounded by male admirers, while ten Brinken sits alone, jealously seeking her gaze. Victorious, she joins him, but quickly turns her back on him, pulling out a powder compact and ostensibly examining herself. The sequence then cuts to an extreme close-up of the mirror, shot from her point of view; at first, her eye is visible in it, then she shifts the case until ten Brinken's face is visible as he watches her (fig. 10). We then cut back to a medium-long shot of the two of them, then to the mirror as she shifts it slowly back to reflect her eye. What is remarkable in this moment is that it presents the second dynamic at work in the play of the gaze, complicating the seemingly straightforward structure in which man is always and only the bearer of the gaze onto woman by recognizing that even as he watches, he is being watched. The moment openly acknowledges that there is power in staging the self as object of desire in a way that the other films I have examined do not. Alraune stages herself consciously, deploying a gaze made doubly powerful in that it allows her to objectify the man at whom she looks and to control and manipulate his gaze. She is, ultimately, the victor in this power struggle, a fact that is perhaps foreshadowed when she wins the Ping-Pong game.

What this network of gazes suggests is that Alraune exerts her power by appropriating a powerful gaze that takes control of its object in a way that reverses dominant models. The men she controls are deeply invested in this relationship; indeed, they appear to experience their objectification as constitutive of their own subjectivity. In this, they occupy the sort of masochistic position that Studlar identifies as rooted in the maternal

CHAPTER SIX

FIGURE 10. Convoluted gazes

and as central to cinema. In the absence of Alraune's determining gaze, they experience ruin, the "loneliness and insanity" to which ten Brinken is doomed. Yet the power that Alraune holds is by no means depicted as unproblematic and must ultimately be undermined in order to reestablish a dominant, phallocentric model. As in *The Hands of Orlac*, the identification between (male) viewer and on-screen double is problematic in *Alraune*, for the central male figure, ten Brinken, does not function as a figure of identification. Instead, Galeen's film introduces another character, Frank Braun, who functions as the hero with whom the viewer might identify. Frank's first encounter with Alraune is an indirect one: ten Brinken shows Frank first a photograph of Alraune, then the book in which he has recorded her development. From a medium shot of the two men, Frank staring intently at the photograph, the scene cuts to a close-up of the image of Alraune, looking into the camera, then back to the two men as Frank puts down the photograph and turns his attention to the written record. Unlike the other men who become the victims of Alraune, Frank first encounters her as image, suggesting that from the start, he represents a subject position that allows the viewer to exert control over Alraune. He never positions himself as the object of her gaze, never seeks out her gaze as an acknowledgment of his own existence, and thus avoids becoming her victim. This position of power is reinforced because he has access to the information about Alraune's creation; from the first, he knows more about her origins than she does. Frank thus becomes a figure through which the spectator may assert power; he remains "outside of" the narrative, present only in the opening and at the very end of the film, and acts as a disinterested observer. Frank, in other words, takes on the function of a distanced viewer, critically engaging with the narrative—just as he casts an evaluating eye on Alraune's photo and the story of her creation—but not becoming personally involved in it.

The close of the film reinforces the reading of Frank as enabling the spectator's gaze to be dominant and defusing the danger Alraune's assertion of control posed. In the final shots, Alraune flees ten Brinken, who, after losing his money at the gambling tables after she slipped away, has returned to their rooms to find her preparing to leave him. Insane with jealousy, he grabs a knife and chases her outside, but Frank disarms him. The sequence depicting the struggle between the two men is important. It moves from a long shot in which all three are shown, Alraune slumped against a wall, the men struggling in front of her, to a brief shot in which she watches them, then back to a long shot as she averts her eyes and Frank pushes ten Brinken against the wall opposite her. It then crosscuts between close-ups of Frank, of ten Brinken staring into the camera, and of Alraune, eyes still closed. In a long shot, we then see the tableau shift as Frank turns from the now disarmed and suddenly unthreatening ten Brinken to Alraune, who, eyes still closed, seems in danger of fainting and staggers toward Frank. As ten Brinken watches, she collapses in Frank's arms, asking him to take her away and help her to become "human" and capable of love. Significant here is what is missing. Alraune does not look at Frank; there is no exchange of gazes, he merely glances at her and then looks one final time at ten Brinken, who backs away fearfully. The emphasis is shifted to Frank as the bearer of the gaze, which explicitly represents power. He disarms ten Brinken simply by staring him down and effectively takes possession of Alraune in the same moment. She, in contrast, no longer wields a powerful gaze, instead submitting entirely to Frank's dominance.

The framing moments in which Frank appears establish the male gaze as the determining one, defusing the danger caused by the identification between the viewer and the male characters that are objectified—and figuratively castrated—by Alraune's gaze. With this resolution in mind, we can read Galeen's film like so many films from the era, as an anxious depiction of women's emancipation as a direct threat to male subjectivity. In this trajectory, Alraune embodies the "vamp" that comes to stand in for the specter of the New Woman and must ultimately give up her powerful role and conform to more conventional gender norms. The "unnaturalness" that

Alraune is accused of due to her origins becomes a fitting shorthand for the "unnatural" qualities of emancipated woman.

Her unnatural origin and the "monstrous" qualities that result from it are why Alraune is not simply just another Weimar vamp, but rather one in the line of women I have examined whose emancipation is rendered in uncanny terms. I noted that unlike in some of the other films I have discussed, Alraune is the primary uncanny object. She is uncanny not only because of her "unnatural" origin, but rather because the film repeatedly blurs science and magic and associates Alraune with the latter. Weinstein argues that Alraune's status as product of science recedes, and suggests that Galeen quite purposely constructs her as uncanny through cinematic means: "Alraune's origin as the product of artificial insemination alone would not render her monstrous in Carroll's sense. Instead she would merely represent a new and unfamiliar reproductive technology. . . . It is the shift from biological to technological and fantastic parentage that leads us to read Alraune's origins as monstrous: her 'fantastic biology' blends these normally distinct identities."[26] As Weinstein notes, Galeen's identification of Alraune with the mandrake root—not only through her name but also through a sequence that shows ten Brinken's treasured root dissolve into Alraune herself[27]—as well as his suggestion that she functions as "the reaffirmation of primitive animism [and] the all-powerful animistic fetish"[28] are central to the way in which the film depicts the woman as uncanny, as the monster who challenges and threatens the masculine subject both on screen and off.

Yet this reading of the film as one that unequivocally portrays emancipated woman as monstrous and that stabilizes this monstrosity by reassimilating her into a dominant patriarchal order seems unable to exhaust the potentially subversive moments in which the power of her gaze is thematized, and which run counter to the idea of an easy resolution to the problem. In particular the moment in which she staged herself even while watching ten Brinken's response suggests a repositioning of woman vis-à-vis the male gaze, a conscious self-objectification that works to empower woman. It suggests an added dimension to the relationship critics like Mulvey define: if the male gaze is the medium through which he takes control of the image of the female, reasserting dominance over her and thus over her as symbol of castration, and if this act serves to effectively construct male subjectivity as occupying this imaginary position of power, then the woman's awareness of this process, and her conscious staging of the self in such a way as to manipulate the process of his construction of subjectivity, problematizes a simple, phallocentric power hierarchy, and suggests a very real dimension of power to taking on the position as image. Because the process of staging herself is a *conscious* act on Alraune's part, the power relationships associated with the gaze become more complicated and no longer easily fit into a model that equates woman with passive object, man with active bearer of the gaze. In Studlar's terms, the performance of femininity, the staging of the self, precludes absolute "possession" of the woman as object. This is not to say that the types of power wielded are entirely the same, but it does suggest a level of agency in the process of creating "the image of woman" in film. In this sense, we see in Galeen's *Alraune* a continuation of the theme already introduced by Lubitsch in his *Eyes of the Mummy*, but here developed in a very different way. Where Mâ's status as performer represented a highly mitigated power, with her agency in staging herself repeatedly undermined by her trancelike movements and her susceptibility to Radu's hypnotic gaze, Alraune's performance is staged entirely by herself. Far from being controlled by an outside force, she directs and manipulates the men around her; once she has determined to punish ten Brinken, she does so purposefully and effectively. Alraune may well be shown giving up her power to stage herself in the final moments of the film, when she submits to Frank, but even this is not entirely convincing. Is it truly a new beginning for the woman, an acceptance of the role of submissive wife? Or is it yet another moment in which she manipulates the men around her, playing to that which they desire in order to retain power over them? Ultimately, Galeen's *Alraune* leaves unanswered the question of who, in the end, holds the upper hand and thus points toward far more complicated power dynamics in film.

If we shift the terms of our reading slightly, we can see that like so many of the films we have examined, Galeen's *Alraune*, too, can be viewed as a reflection on the cinematic medium. Keeping in mind Alraune's status as a sort of hybrid, the product partly of technology, partly of some obscure and mystical "magic," the analogy between woman and film implicates the industry in the production of similar fusion projects: the movie that unreels on the screen might well be no more than the rational product of a set of scientifically explicable and technologically based steps, yet it retains a certain excess value, perhaps locatable in the effect that it has on the viewer. In an era in which the audience might well be accustomed to the experience of film, in which the uncanny effect that early films had simply by virtue of the novelty of seeing apparently static images "come to life" had surely decreased, Galeen's *Alraune* might be seen as an attempt to rekindle that uncanny response, itself blending science and magic, realism and expressionism in order to undermine the notion of any clear boundary between the categories. In thus refusing to fit clearly into these categories, the film—like Alraune herself—challenges the viewers' preconceptions and draws attention to the potentially uncanny in rational life.

OSWALD'S VERSION: *ALRAUNE* 1930

A scant two years after Galeen released his *Alraune*, Richard Oswald's version premiered, again as a vehicle for Brigitte Helm, but this time in the form of a sound film. That the remake should appear so soon was not particularly unusual, as such recycling of popular hits guaranteed a certain level of success. In the words of one reviewer: "'Alraune' as a sound film— Ufa decided to make this film for the certain success in theaters and because of the great role for Brigitte Helm."[29] Indeed, in his discussion of filmic remakes, one critic remarked that Oswald's decision to remake *Alraune* was unusual only because he retained Galeen's lead, noting "that this is the only case in which the lead role was played by the same person in both versions, which, after the first great success of Brigitte Helm, actually seemed natural."[30] Even more so than in Galeen's version, Oswald's was a vehicle for Helm, in spite of the fact that the cast was rounded out with a roster of well-known names. Ten Brinken was played by Albert Bassermann, who had been famous as an actor in theater before breaking into film, where he had a steady supply of roles first in Germany, then in Switzerland, and finally in Hollywood, and who would be an Oscar nominee for best supporting actor in Hitchcock's *Foreign Correspondent* (1940). The romantic male lead went to Harald Paulsen, who would play the hero in Oswald's second version of *Uncanny Tales*. Like Bassermann, Paulsen had started in theater and transitioned to film very successfully, and tended to play the role of charming, likeable men like Frank Braun in this version of *Alraune*.

A Daughter of Destiny and Daughter of Evil

As the countess, Agnes Straub was another famed theater actor who would have been well known to the viewing public. And ten Brinken's mistreated assistant, Dr. Petersen, was played by Bernhard Goetzke, an actor perhaps best known today for his role as Death in *Destiny*, but who had worked steadily throughout the era of silent films.

Oswald had thus assembled real talent for his remake; nevertheless, the focus remained firmly on the role of Alraune, exploiting as much as possible Helm's popularity and her status as femme fatale gained from her role in *Metropolis*. And yet the Alraune Helm plays here is quite different from the one she played two years earlier. Oswald differentiates his version from Galeen's *Alraune* not only by following more closely Ewers's novel in that, here, the eponymous woman ultimately commits suicide, but also by compressing the action, eliminating any depiction of Alraune's youth and instead showing only her creation before moving forward seventeen years to the point at which she returns to ten Brinken's home. Where Oswald diverges most markedly from the literary and cinematic predecessors is in stylistics and in the fundamental motivation of his Alraune. Stylistically, Oswald eschews any real reference to expressionism, instead attempting to take advantage of the new possibilities the medium presented in its acoustic elements. His markedly realistic mode of filmmaking has its parallel in the narrative emphasis on the realistic elements of the story; this Alraune is not the uncanny product of a process half-scientific, half-magical, but the victim of ten Brinken's ambition and overreaching. Brigitte Helm's own words regarding Oswald's remake are telling. In an article in *Filmwelt*, she noted that her initial dismay at Oswald's plan was mitigated once she realized how differently the director envisioned his Alraune: "He created a new Alraune, one completely different than her old prototype: instead of the evil, libidinous school girl a young creature, innocent in the face of her doom, spreading disaster; instead of the woman taking revenge through demonic, evil actions the loving, knowing woman who commits suicide because she does not want to share the curse that lies upon her with the man she loves."[31] Helm seems to grasp quite clearly the way in which the two films—despite sharing their underlying narrative—fundamentally differ; where the first was indisputably an uncanny film, trading on its depiction of a creature portrayed as "evil," "libidinous," and "demonic," the second shifted into melodrama, depicting the unavoidable doom of a woman in love, "cursed" not through any fault of her own, but because of the egomaniacal arrogance of her creator. What is especially interesting about Oswald's *Alraune* in the context of this study is that it demonstrates how the sociocultural environment had shifted: women's emancipation is no longer hidden behind narratives of the uncanny, displaced into the "monstrous," threatening figures on the screen, but rather reformulated as an inevitably tragic impulse, as a state as unnatural as is Alraune herself.

The narrative of Oswald's version is fairly simple, in spite of his addition of a subplot that has ten Brinken conspiring with his main patron, the countess, in a campaign of "Kindesunterschiebung," supplying children to unknowing families in need of heirs (including the countess's own husband). The film begins with a group of students that includes Frank Braun visiting the latter's uncle, ten Brinken, who tells them about the legend of the mandrake. As the scientist discusses his advances in artificially "creating" rats, Frank suggests that a truly worthwhile endeavor would be to create a human, then intimates that he could supply a woman to act as mother. After introducing his uncle to Alma (Brigitte Helm), a waitress and singer at a bar, Frank removes himself from the situation, yet ten Brinken continues the experiment with the help of his colleague Petersen and the countess. The film then moves into the future, introducing Alraune (Helm), the product of the experiment, who has been raised as ten Brinken's niece and has recently returned from school to live with him. Immediately, Alraune takes casualties: first the chauffeur, who dies in a car accident after she pushes him to drive ever faster and more recklessly, then the countess's daughter, whose engagement is dissolved because of Alraune's interference, then Wölfchen, Petersen's son, who drowns while getting flowers for Alraune. Finally, ten Brinken himself becomes her victim, making advances towards her, which she rebuffs in disgust. At this point, Frank returns from Africa, and, in spite of initial reservations, begins a relationship with his "cousin." With the discovery that ten Brinken has been embezzling money to support his (and Alraune's) luxurious lifestyle, however, the household collapses, and after Alraune refuses to flee with him, ten Brinken commits suicide. Initially, his death appears to free her and she makes plans to return to Africa with Frank. However, in a confrontation with the countess, who is angry that she has lost her fortune to ten Brinken, Alraune discovers her origins. Reading ten Brinken's record of his "experiment," she is shocked to find the list of those whom he considered her victims, last among them Frank. In an effort to save the man she loves, she commits suicide.

Beyond the differences in the narrative of the two films, Oswald's version, by virtue of being a sound film, necessarily functions in a different way. Where Galeen's version represents the power structures in the network of gazes between the characters, Oswald's complicates this through the addition of sound. Although his Alraune, too, stages herself for the desiring gaze of the men around her, even while exerting her own power through her gaze at them, this power structure competes with that embodied in her speech. The camera tends to linger on Helm's image, framing her as the desired object by emphasizing her near immobility; this serves to exploit Helm's characteristic stillness[32] and to emphasize her function as erotic image. At the same time, we can locate her objectification not only in her abdication of a powerful gaze, but also in her move from using imperative and declarative language to posing questions; where Alraune initially controls the men around her through commanding them to do their bidding, she is later silenced, abdicating her position of power to Frank.

It is striking that Oswald does not draw on the potentially uncanny effects of sound in support of the narrative. As I have discussed, Spadoni has examined the way in which the audience perceived early sound film as uncanny in a way that harked back to early silent film in general.[33] To Spadoni, the very development of the Hollywood horror genre is tied to the rise of sound film,[34] for it draws on an inherently uncanny quality of the projected body as the source of speech: "In particular, something seemed to be wrong with the status of the human figure on sound film. This figure could seem ghostly—or uncanny—a perception founded on the return to the foreground of general viewer awareness of cinema's artificial nature."[35] The horror genre, Spadoni suggests, drew on a quality of sound films that—however temporarily—rendered the figures on screen inherently monstrous: they conformed to Carroll's notion of category violations in that "these figures could seem both alive and dead at the same time."[36] In this, the characters in early sound films effectively mirrored, through the technological peculiarities of the medium in that moment, the fundamental split Alraune embodies: as a product of both science and "magic," as a creature both "natural"—in that she is a biological organism—and "unnatural"—in that her natural origin is effectively

CHAPTER SIX

erased by eliding her birth in favor of an emphasis on her "creation" by ten Brinken.

And yet Oswald's film nowhere exploits this uncanny potential, instead eschewing any hint of expressionistic atmosphere and content in favor of a solidly realistic depiction of the events. Unlike in Galeen's version, Helm's Alraune is here not a hybrid creature whose effect on men carries hints of an almost mythological allure, but rather a woman whose attraction seems predicated on her appearance and her open flouting of gender norms. The same director who, eleven years before, strove to exhaust the range of uncanny effects in his *Uncanny Tales* here recasts an uncanny story as pure melodrama. Mihaela Petrescu points out that this incarnation of Alraune met with only mixed success: "One reviewer, for instance, complained that Oswald's film was monotonous and artificial, that it bordered on parody because it was unintentionally comical, and that viewers laughed throughout the entire evening."[37] Petrescu argues that this response was partially because of the efforts of director and actors and partially because "the status of the vamp, a media-creation designed to allure and frighten viewers with its intense seductiveness ever since its debut in silent film, was changing."[38] Beyond this, I would argue that Oswald, trying to navigate the new possibilities of the medium and the stylistic tendencies of the moment, fails to render the same complex power relationships through the voice, as did Galeen through the gaze. In other words, the earlier version of *Alraune* was uncanny at least in part because its dynamics of gender and power were couched in terms of the building blocks of cinema, acted out through patterns of displaying and looking at the body that are basic to the medium. In contrast, Oswald's vacillation between vision and speech as indicators of power undermines the uncanny metafilmic effect of his *Alraune*, while his foregrounding of Alraune's potential for change and her ultimate self-sacrifice shifts the generic framework of the film from terror to melodrama. To trace these fundamental changes, I will first examine certain elements Oswald does retain from Ewers's original story and Galeen's silent version, and will then turn to the generic shift we see enacted, in which Alraune's depiction as vamp leads inexorably to her downfall.

Oswald essentially only retains one uncanny element from the original story—namely, the background of Alraune's creation. Here, as in Galeen's version, ten Brinken is a sort of mad scientist; at the same time, even this representation is mitigated, for the man's madness is tied directly to an immorality that is solidly rooted in the real, specifically the economic. Ten Brinken is introduced as a respected scientist, seated at his heavy desk. His conversation with the countess, however—focused on her having paid him for his "procuring" her daughter—conflates financial gain, science, and the creation of life and undermines his respectability; even before Alraune, ten Brinken has been "playing god." The prominently placed skull on his desk is a telling prop, not only as a traditional symbol of the doctor, but also as a means of mirroring ten Brinken, for the skull is positioned so that when the sequence cuts to a medium-long shot of the two, it functions as a virtual reflection of ten Brinken. This associates him with death and foreshadows his later suicide. The moment serves to introduce and characterize ten Brinken as well as the countess, who becomes an active participant in the experiment of creating Alraune and who, later, will precipitate her downfall. Her body language is telling: she remains standing throughout the sequence, looking down at ten Brinken and only once leaning to his level. Her association with wealth—and the suggestion that she has essentially "bought" her relationship with ten Brinken—is emphasized not only when she tells him that her husband has paid the promised fee for their child, but also when she gives him money. Indeed, ten Brinken directly comments on the financial nature of their relationship, saying: "My scientific experiments necessitate immense resources . . . otherwise we would never have known each other."[39] From the start Oswald depicts both ten Brinken and the countess as morally questionable, and directly links this quality in them to the man's work and to the financial gain he derives from this. We see none of the mystical reflection on the creation of life that we saw in Galeen's version—ten Brinken is, here, culpable not because he counters certain spiritual imperatives but rather because of his very human flaws of avarice and megalomania.

We see a similar distancing from mystical content in the way in which Oswald's version of the story introduces the legend of the mandrake. As ten Brinken and the countess talk, the scientist's nephew, Frank, arrives with friends in order to extend their birthday congratulations. Just as Frank begins to congratulate his uncle, he is interrupted by the sound of breaking glass. The sequence cuts to a close-up of Frank's hand reaching for a knobby root amid shards of glass. Frank's comments suggest an uncanny sort of agency on the part of the root: "This thing here fell down and smashed one of your old, valuable vases."[40] Here, the camera pans left, from Frank holding the root, to ten Brinken standing behind the seated countess. This is the moment in which ten Brinken introduces the legend of the mandrake; he explains:

> That is a mandrake, also called a mandragora. A magical root, according to superstition it brings her owner happiness and wealth, but unhappiness and death, if he is separated from it. The legend of its creations is strange. In that moment in which a hanged man breathes his last, the earth receives his last power. Through the coupling of human and earth, these roots come into being. Precisely that humble root was, for me, the basis of my experiments on artificial insemination.[41]

The moment foreshadows ten Brinken's eventual downfall; not only does the root, apparently through its own volition, fall and destroy his "old, valuable vase," but also ten Brinken references the power that the mandrake holds over its owner. In this sense, the presence of the root points back to Galeen's *Alraune*, where, as Weinstein noted, Alraune was not only associated, through what Carroll calls "horrific metonymy," with various types of vermin, but also with the root, pointing to its (and her) function as "the reaffirmation of primitive animism [and] the all-powerful animistic fetish."[42] If we see the root as an inanimate double for Alraune, then this scene already characterizes her as active and dangerous. It is fitting that the word for "root" is, in German, feminine; thus the speech he makes, referring to the danger that the root, "she," poses, might well be read as already pointing toward Alraune's dangerous power.

And yet the uncanny potential of this moment is not developed; indeed, the mise-en-scène of the film seems to deliberately work against any such reading. Unlike Galeen's version, which presents the legend in an expressionistic opening scene, here it is framed as pseudo-scientific, particularly through ten Brinken's suggestion that his own scientific experiments focused on artificial insemination are a sort of continuation of that legend. The legend becomes secondary to the scientific discourse, functioning only as a way to articulate an aim framed as rational and connected not to a traditional notion of the magical but rather to modernity. This continues in the subsequent moment, in which Frank spurs ten Brinken to move from experimenting on rats to doing so on humans. We see the men in the laboratory, where Frank suggests that the artificial creation of life would be worthwhile if he could create a human—"a living mandrake"—rather than a rat. Depicting ten Brinken in the setting of his laboratory ties him explicitly to the realm of science. In one sense, the rats become the doubles of the Alraune to come, ten Brinken's creations and the object of his classifying and defining gaze as much as she will eventually be. Their common origin in the laboratory suggests something grotesque about Alraune in that they share a common creator; yet, again, she is not likened as explicitly to vermin as she is in Galeen's version, for there is no direct visual linkage between rat and woman.

Beyond this minimal reference to the original, mythical origin of Alraune, Oswald's version shifts the focus so decidedly onto the scientific as to obscure any uncanny subject. One way in which he does so is by depicting in detail the machinations necessary in order to create the girl. Showing the steps ten Brinken and Frank take in order to create Alraune emphasizes not the mystical origin of Alraune and, thereby, of woman-as-vamp, but rather ten Brinken's exploitation of women and the untenable position of women who act outside of gender norms dictating a domestic, maternal ideal. It is Frank who has identified the "mother" for their experiment: Alma, a performer (and perhaps a prostitute) in a local bar. After joining ten Brinken and Petersen there, Frank commands the owner to have Alma sing. Oswald presents the performance in a way that aims to exploit its erotic potential, shooting Helm's Alma in a medium-long shot with the musicians behind her and the audience in front of her in shadows. With her white blouse and pale hair, the viewer is immediately focused on her body as she sings and sways seductively. The emphasis is firmly on Alma's body as object of desire; thus the sequence cuts from the shot of her entire figure to a medium shot of her face and torso, then tilts down until we see only her waist and legs, encased in a tight, reflective black skirt. It then cuts to a close-up of her face, again shot in soft focus; significantly, her features are shadowed, so that we do not see her eyes and thus have no sense of her emotional response as she sings. The sequence continues to alternate between medium-long frontal and profile shots, always placing Alma at the center of the frame, and close-ups of her face.

The presentation of her performance establishes Alma as an object of desire and emphasizes her physical presence. She is exclusively object of the gaze; we rarely see her eyes clearly in the close-ups, nor do we get a sense that she is looking at specific members of the audience when she performs. In addition, the song she performs suggests that she herself views her body as a commodity and that her relationships with men are exclusively economic. The lyrics are telling:

> When men cheat on me
> it's a pleasure for me
> I find a new one
> there are so many of them.
> When men leave me
> I can never hate them
> I'm not used to anything else
> it leaves me cold.
> I even thank them
> that it lasted so long
> and because of that I feel
> almost honored.
> You can have me
> you can have me
> regardless, who you are.
> I only care whether you have money.
> If I love a man
> to whom I belong
> as though it were the first time
> if I want to hold him
> he leaves me standing there
> who cares![43]

Superficially, this song says much about the way in which Alma is presented—as a woman who will simply "look for another one" if men betray her, who is willing to offer herself to anyone, "whoever you are," as long as they have money. Yet two moments suggests a greater complexity to her character: when she sings that when she loves a man and wants to "hold" him, he leaves her, we see a close-up of her face; for a moment, she is not the indifferent, bawdy bar singer, but appears moved. Perhaps this is due to the fact that this is the sole moment during her performance when, during a close-up, we can clearly see her eyes, as she looks upward and we see light reflected in them, suggesting tears. We get a glimpse of Alma as a tragic character, as the victim of the men who love and leave her; she is a victim of a society in which a woman has little economic power and finds herself at the mercy of the men who desire her. This figuring of Alma as a commoditized body is suggested again when, once she has bowed and blown kisses to the applauding audience, she takes a tray from the bar owner and begins to collect tips and sell postcards, presumably featuring her image. As she moves around the room, we see a medium-long shot of her approaching a well-dressed man seated alone; after he demonstratively puts a few bills on her tray, he takes her arm and attempts to pull her onto his lap. She shakes him off, steps away, and turns her back on him, to which he responds with surprise: "What? What's the problem? Don't act like that!"[44] Alma responds by hitting him and walking quickly away; as the camera pans right to follow her, the audience laughs. In not only performing, but also selling her own image, Alma has become a commodity; at the same time, her response suggests an attempt to assert control over her body and to differentiate between the image—which he has purchased—and the body—to which, her actions suggest, his money does not entitle him.

Ironically, of course, Alma will soon entirely lose control of her body, becoming merely the vessel for ten Brinken's experiment. She joins the men at their table; when she presents her tray to ten Brinken and he takes out his wallet, Frank reaches over and removes a bill. In a medium shot, framed by the curtains of the private table with the men seated on either side, Alma, centered, reacts with surprise; he has given her a hundred marks. Given the moment immediately preceding this one, perhaps Alma should be aware that with his money, Frank is not just rewarding her performance or buying a postcard, but rather attempting just what the previous customer attempted: to buy Alma. The amount of money, however, is so large that Alma seems content to enter into this unwitting transaction; when Frank pulls her onto the seat next to him, she happily joins them. This moment

CHAPTER SIX

figures woman as commodity, for sale to the highest bidder. And, though Alma might believe that they have purchased no more than a few hours of her company, this is the moment in which she entirely abdicates control. Shortly thereafter, we cut to a medium shot of Alma and Frank alone at a table, with her head resting on his shoulder. He urges her to have another drink and, after she complies, hands her a pen and tells her to sign her name to the papers before her, then repeats slowly as she obeys: "Alma Raune." As she giggles, reminding him of how obedient she has been, he kisses her perfunctorily, then picks up the signed piece of paper and waves it to ensure that the ink has dried before putting it into his pocket, putting on his hat, and rising to leave, ordering Alma: "come along, my child!"[45] Alma's loss of control is represented in her drunken state, as well as in her surrender to Frank, whom she has obeyed and whose address to her—"my child"—pointedly references her lack of agency. The scene drives home a notion that the female body is pure object, capable of being "signed away" by the individual. Alma's signature is also of interest, given the word play evident in her name: she is, in a sense, already an "Al(ma)raune," identical to the child she will bear, a suggestion driven home by Oswald's casting of Brigitte Helm for both the mother and the child. That excess syllable—"ma"—references the maternal body, hinting at Alma's true role, which ten Brinken will usurp.

This sequence in the bar not only demonstrates just how unethically both ten Brinken and Frank act in undertaking the experiment, but also points to the dilemma of "emancipated" woman, with emancipation here, as so often, coded as sexual; in the depiction of Alma, woman's liberation is portrayed not as a positive potential, but rather as a condition most likely to end in the sort of sordid existence she leads. Further, the moment suggests an absolute divide between such sexual liberation and the maternal, a divide that will be confirmed by Alma's unremarked-upon death during childbirth: Alma Raune as an individual will be eradicated through her transformation into the maternal body; her morally questionable characteristics will be reincarnated in her daughter, on whom they will act as a curse she can escape only in death.

With the mother supplied, the next sequence sketches out—very briefly—how ten Brinken acquired the necessary sperm for his artificial insemination. In a medium shot, we see Petersen and another man standing in a shadowy hallway as the doctor passes on ten Brinken's thanks for the other man's help. Two officers then enter, one on either side of the condemned man whom they lead in front of Petersen; the camera pans right with them as they turn into a hazy room, at the rear of which a gate opens to reveal a gallows and two figures waiting to undertake the hanging. The condemned man stops and struggles briefly, but the officers force him to continue on, as Petersen and the other official move into the frame, silhouetted against the gallows as they walk toward them before the shot fades out. We can read this as the strongest critical moment in the depiction of ten Brinken and his experiment, for here the violence involved in the creation of Alraune is visually represented; ten Brinken not only usurps a woman's control over her body, but also, through his cooperation with the executioner, becomes complicit in the man's hanging. The fact that the man struggles humanizes him, denying the viewer any simple characterization of him as a criminal rightly condemned to death. At the same time, the sequence and that before suggest the genetic basis to Alraune's flawed persona; she is, indeed, the daughter of "a prostitute and a murderer," the result of the pairing of two such individuals, made doubly immoral and unnatural by virtue of the unnatural process that creates her.

We see in the opening segment of the film how Oswald, even while referencing the uncanny background to his *Alraune*, shifts his emphasis from the uncanny-expressionistic into the melodramatic-realistic mode. The emancipated woman is not a threat that must be masked through her representation as uncanny, but rather a doomed creature from the start. This notion of sexual and erotic emancipation as a fatal flaw is further developed in the depictions of Alraune's victims, which demonstrate the way she stages herself as erotic object while simultaneously revealing her own suffering when this staging claims victims among the men who admire her.

The way in which her active desire is dangerous to both others and herself becomes most clear in Alraune's relationships with Wolfgang, ten Brinken's colleague's son, and with Raspe, the chauffeur. This is the content anchoring the sequence with which the central part of the film opens: seventeen years have passed, and Alraune, now on the cusp between girl and woman, is once again in ten Brinken's home. Alraune is introduced initially in a sequence in which she lies on a couch, her back to the camera, playing with a doll, while her young admirer, Wolfgang, sits at a desk facing the camera. The conversation between the two is significant, characterizing the girl as cold and unfeeling. After she asks Wolfgang whether he has completed his essay, he rises and tells her that he cannot work because he constantly thinks of her. Unmoved, still playing with the doll in her hands, Alraune asks why he thinks of her. When he confesses that he loves her, she responds coolly, telling him "But I don't love you."[46] We end with a medium close-up of Wolfgang, wringing his hands and lowering his gaze. The sequence immediately suggests Alraune's lack of empathy and feeling for those around her. The initially idyllic scene of the two young people alone in a room shifts to one in which she demonstrates her cruelty toward those who love her. The doll she plays with while so unfeelingly rejecting Wolfgang stands in for the men with whom she will "play," and whom she will destroy. And the use of sound in the scene is interesting; while we see Wolfgang speak, we only hear Alraune, whose face remains turned from the audience. That Alraune's face remains averted denies the viewer the pleasure resultant from seeing her. Instead, we hear her voice, the second mechanism by which she exerts power over the men around her.

The full extent of her power becomes clear in the following sequence, which begins with a long shot of the dark foyer and stairs of the house. We hear the sound of footsteps and see the chauffeur's wife approaching, met halfway by Jakob, the butler. The sequence cuts to a medium shot of the two, her face well lit, as she explains that she and her husband want to quit. When he asks her why, she responds angrily: "Don't ask as though you don't know what's happening in this house! Who is leading the regiment here, since that young woman is back from the boarding school? I can't stand anymore what she's making the men into. . . . Puppets!"[47] As she continues up the stairs to Alraune's room, the chauffeur's wife expresses the danger of the situation: "We're leaving in time. Before it's too late."[48] The woman's words point clearly to the issue at stake: Alraune's control over the house—and her power over men, whom she turns into her "puppets"—is that which endangers those around her, an influence that must be escaped "before it is too late." That her assumption of power usurps a role ordinarily reserved for men is suggested by the rhetorical question as to "who is leading the regiment"; the evocation of the purely masculine military sphere as symbol for the home, which Alraune has infiltrated and disrupted, suggests again her transgression of women's acceptable roles.

A Daughter of Destiny and Daughter of Evil

Just how absolute Alraune's power over the men around her is becomes clear when, after having told the chauffeur's wife that she would accept their resignation, she immediately reverses her decision and demands that the man take her for a drive. In a medium shot, we see the chauffeur working on the car as his wife approaches and tells him they may leave. Just as they embrace, another servant knocks at the window behind them and announces to the chauffeur that Alraune wants to go for a drive. Although his wife begs him to refuse, he complies, demonstrating the way in which Alraune disrupts the relationships around her. Her appearance in the sequence immediately after is equally telling. From off screen, we hear her respond to the wife's command that he not continue to drive her: "Why not?" The sequence cuts to a medium shot of Alraune, looking toward the camera, hair covered by a dark, tweed cap, then back to a shot of the couple. The wife's face is frightened, that of her husband immobile, as though he were entranced by the girl's appearance. We cut to a medium profile shot of the two looking toward Alraune before panning right to show her in profile, then left as she moves toward them. As she pauses, the camera stops, framing her at the center of the shot. The framing again constructs Alraune as object of the gaze. The chauffeur's confused response to her asking whether he is ready demonstrates her effect on the men around her; we hear him off camera, saying first "yes," then "no," attempting to tell her that the motor is broken. The camera again moves with Alraune as she approaches them, and, framed in a medium shot, stares at him, his wife relegated to the shadowy background of the shot. He is unable to resist her fixed stare, finally looking away and telling her that the car is ready. The sequence then cuts to a slightly high-angle medium shot of the car as first the chauffeur, then Alraune get in; she extends her arm along the top of the seat, as though marking her possession of the chauffeur even as his wife stands by. We then cut to a medium shot of the car as it begins to drive, panning slightly as they depart to show the wife left behind and lingering on her before the scene fades out.

The powerful gaze that Alraune casts on the men who admire her is evident here; indeed, in depicting the chauffeur losing all resolve under the effect of her gaze, the film endows her with an almost hypnotic power. The figure pits her directly against the man's wife, figuring her yet again as the vamp who threatens marital bonds. She exerts her power through her gaze, her body, and her voice: training her desiring and commanding look at the chauffeur, while simultaneously figuring herself as an erotic object and posing a question that pertains not only to the drive, but also to larger desires. "Why not" take the drive, why not succumb to her gaze and to the desire for her.

The result of Alraune's assertion of her power is the drive they take, presented so suggestively as to reveal how her power derives from her sexuality. The sequence, set in a grassy, wooded area, begins with a fade-in medium shot of the chauffeur, standing and looking off screen. When the camera pans right, we see that he is looking at Alraune, who is shown in a medium shot, seated in the grass, staring into space. As though feeling his look, she glances toward him, then away, and rises; the shot remains steady for a moment, so that we see her legs as she walks toward the camera and off screen. Here the framing refers back to the presentation of Alma, who was presented similarly while singing. The visual fragmentation of the dangerous female body not only serves to emphasize her function as object of contemplation and desire but also fetishizes that female body. Once Alraune moves out of the shot, the camera pans rapidly back to the chauffeur, who is still watching her, demonstrating the fatal attraction she exerts on the men around her. The sequence then cuts to a long shot, with the chauffeur in the background as Alraune moves toward the camera; again, the camera moves with her, maintaining her as the focal point of the shot, until she pauses. The camera pans slightly right to show a small stream, bridged by two narrow strips of wood, then pans back to show Alraune with the chauffeur now standing behind her. She glances at him wordlessly, in response to which he picks her up. We next cut to a medium close-up of the two, the man cradling her against him, her arms around his neck, as they look at each other. The camera moves with them as he begins to carry her away; the shot then fades out.

Like the sequence showing Alraune and Wolfgang, this one is superficially idyllic, but it contains a sinister element. The silence that dominates this scene shifts the focus even more decisively to Alraune as erotic image. The chauffeur's reaction mimics the viewer's response to the filmic image; he is rendered speech- and powerless, simultaneously passive spectator and participant through his response to Alraune. And the scene is suggestive of an intimacy that goes far beyond what is shown, for the gesture of picking her up, followed by the fade-out, insinuates that something else has occurred in the moments between this one and their reaching the car; the fade-out stands in for the potential sexual encounter. The location is also important. I have touched on the way in which Alraune is figured simultaneously as "unnatural," as stepping outside of the prescribed gender norms, and as connected with nature, as embodying, in her amorality and sexuality, woman as original sinner. Here the film points to the latter quality, suggesting, through her contemplative silence, some primitive connection between woman and nature.

The conclusion of the sequence suggests yet another characteristic of Alraune, for in it she becomes tied to a fatal modernity embodied by the car that becomes the mechanism for the chauffeur's death. The deadly end to the interlude between Alraune and the chauffeur begins with a fade-in to a long shot of the car. Alraune runs toward it from the rear of the shot, joined by the chauffeur, who helps her in before himself climbing behind the wheel. The drive is initially represented through point-of-view shots of the rapidly passing scenery and the speedometer indicating the increasing speed of the vehicle. As the cuts become more rapid, we see close-ups of a spinning tire, a sign warning of construction ahead, and a policeman writing what is presumably a ticket as they pass. The sequence then cuts to a medium shot of the two framed behind the windshield, with Alraune exhorting Raspe to drive "faster, faster." This is the sole dialogue in the scene, and it accompanies the ever more rapid montage of shots of the wheel spinning, the passing scenery, the speedometer (its needle indicating that it has reached the maximum speed, 180 kilometers per hour), and Alraune, her face ecstatic as the wind blows her hair. The faster they drive, the more urgent her voice becomes, and the more rapid the cuts, until individual shots are virtually indistinguishable. The sequence ends by cutting back and forth between the chauffeur and Alraune behind the windshield and ever closer shots of a construction vehicle; we then cut back to the two as Alraune screams, we see a flash of light accompanied by the sound of the vehicle crashing, and the screen goes dark.

This sequence can be read as at once a depiction of the dangers of modernity and as a stand-in for an illicit sexual relationship. Alraune's physical response to the experience, her exhortations to drive "faster, faster," and the end in the crash and explosion, all figure the moment as symbolic of a fatal physical and erotic experience. Indeed, the use of montage can be tied to this connection between Alraune and modernity; the very form

CHAPTER SIX

itself connects to the technological and cinematic development that is a crucial topos in *Alraune*, moving away from earlier German film's emphasis on "camera movement and composition (over montage)"[49] and pointing toward a new conception of the self and its connection with this modern world.[50] Alraune is conflated with the modernity represented by the car and the experience; like the vehicle, she pushes the men around her into a situation in which the changing environment becomes their undoing. The fact that Alraune emerges unscathed aligns her with this fatal modernity and also emphasizes her unnaturalness. We see this in ten Brinken's reaction to news of the accident. In a long shot of the hallway in their home, we see Alraune enter through the door at the rear and move listlessly toward the front of the shot. The camera pans slightly to the right to show ten Brinken exit his laboratory, then rapidly back so that the two are framed symmetrically. His words to her are uttered in an ambiguous tone: "Nothing happened to you?"[51] She merely shakes her head in response and moves out of the frame; the shot remains focused on him as he watches her climb the stairs, her steps audible. Ten Brinken's statement is not merely an expression of relief but also of surprise, calling attention to how strange it is that Alraune was unharmed by the fatal accident.

Alraune's reaction to the accident expands our understanding of her character because it suggests some level of emotional response, in spite of her apparent cruelty, and a reliance on relationships with men not as reciprocal, but as a means of self-realization. We see her reaction in the following brief sequence, which opens with a medium shot of Wolfgang, still seated at the desk in Alraune's room; the camera then moves to the right and we see the door open and Alraune slowly enter through the arched doorway that frames her. Wolfgang immediately utters her name, but she does not respond. As she moves to the sofa and sits, Wolfgang approaches her, again calling her name. The sequence then cuts to a medium high-angle close-up of her face against the pillow, Wolfgang's head visible as he sits next to her. After glancing at him, she looks away, then commands him: "Tell me that you love me."[52] His response—"Alraune, I love you"[53]—are the final words in the sequence.

This is a poignant and ambiguous moment. On one hand, her apparent composure characterizes her as surely as does the repeated depiction of her as virtually immobile: again, she is unnatural, an unmoving and unmoved statue rather than a "real" woman. On the other, her need for reassurance from Wolfgang—her command that he tell her he loves her—points to her need for affirmation and affection. We see evidence that her demeanor masks an awareness of some need within her, a sense of herself as different from those around her. This will become more evident as the film progresses, through her desire for and simultaneous fear of knowledge about her background.

The ambiguity in Alraune's response to her effect on men reaches its climax in her relationship with Frank, where she finally recognizes her "fatal" power and chooses *Entsagung*, self-sacrifice or renunciation, in order to try to save him. Her downfall is ultimately figured not so much as a punishment for her fatal power over those around her but rather as a result of her desire, emerging from her relationship with Frank, to abdicate this power. Where, in Galeen's *Alraune*, her relationship with Frank is one in a line of potentially "true" loves, Oswald presents the relationship as the first one in which she experiences emotional attachment. Perhaps this is partially rooted in the circumstance that Frank, aware of her "unnatural" origins, is initially anything but drawn to her. Their first encounter occurs when he, having returned to Germany after seventeen years in Africa, tries to visit his uncle, who refuses to see him. As he leaves, Alraune stops him. He responds to her off-screen interpellation by turning toward her, and she enters the shot. The scene cuts to a medium close-up of the two; when she explains that she is ten Brinken's niece, rather than his daughter, and that her parents are dead, Frank quickly looks away from her, then he asks her to repeat her name, reacting with such obvious shock that she asks him what has so startled him. His discomfort—clearly stemming from his knowledge of her background—finds expression in the fact that he avoids looking at her and quickly tries to leave. Frank's reaction—so unlike that she usually evokes in men—startles her, and she attempts to reassert control, forcing him to look at her by repeating his name, then suggesting her awareness of his discomfort: "Why do you want to leave so soon, when I followed you?"[54] Her statement articulates a difference in the constellation of this relationship when compared to her previous ones; here, she is not the object of a man's pursuit, but the pursuer. From the start of their interaction the balance of power is shifted, with Alraune repositioned as the desiring woman, rather than as the desired object.

The shot remains static, focused on the two as Alraune attempts to make a connection with Frank by emphasizing their purported familial relation.

CHAPTER SIX

She asks him whether he knew her parents and seems disappointed when he replies in the negative, then interrupts herself to say that "we're related and must say 'du' to each other."[55] Frank's reaction—he merely repeats the word "related"—contains an irony that the viewer is aware of, but that Alraune does not grasp. The imbalance in their relationship—the fact that Frank is privy to knowledge about Alraune that she herself does not have—is perhaps one of the reasons why she is not able to control him in the same manner she does other men. The remainder of their interaction suggests some attraction to her on his part: the sequence cuts to a medium shot as she asks him when they will see each other again, and he tells her that he will wait for her that evening in the park. As she moves out of the frame, the camera lingers on him as he watches her go. Ultimately Frank, too, sees Alraune as an object of desire; his gaze visibly following her echoes an earlier episode in which ten Brinken did the same. Yet unlike almost all of the men who fall victim to Alraune, Frank knows more about Alraune than she does about herself. Further, the relationship she alludes to in initiating contact with him—the fact that she believes them to be cousins—is, of course, false; indeed, Frank is implicated in the "creation" of Alraune, as it was he who supplied ten Brinken with Alma, her mother.

We might also read Alraune's mention of their being "related" in a different way; the word also suggests, after all, "similar." Perhaps this realization is the impetus for Frank's interest in her. In her statement, Alraune unconsciously suggests that she, like Frank, can change. His self-imposed exile to Africa, after all, came on the heels of his involvement with ten Brinken's experiment. The moment in which he is initially reintroduced stresses the change in his character. This brief sequence opens with a long shot of a ship at sea, then cuts to a medium-long shot of Frank on the ship's deck, talking to a member of the crew. Already, Frank's appearance contrasts with what we saw earlier; where in the opening scenes he wore a conventional suit and a dark hat, here he is dressed in a lighter, loose, tweed suit and wears a less formal hat. In addition, in earlier scenes, we saw Frank only in darker settings: in a shadowy *Biergarten* in the opening scenes of the film and in the windowless bar where he procured Alma. On the ship, he leans against a white wall, and the lighting suggests bright sunlight. This is borne out in his encounter with Alraune. Frank has quickly left the darkness of his uncle's house after the latter refused to meet with him, and Alraune meets him in the outdoors, again in bright daylight. Setting and appearance suggest that Frank's moral sense has changed radically.

Frank views his development similarly. On the ship, he tells the crew member how eager he is to be back in Germany, stressing that he has been gone seventeen years, and pointing out, when the other man suggests that much will have changed, that he has himself changed. He alludes to this again at the home of ten Brinken. Already, he looks markedly out of place as he waits in the foyer: his light-colored coat contrasts sharply with the darkness of the hallway and the dark suit of Jakob, the servant. Once informed that ten Brinken will not see him, Frank inquires as to how Jakob is doing; his response, again, stresses the manner in which things change over time: "A lot has changed here."[56] And in response to Alraune's questions, he emphasizes how long he has been gone.

Frank's interest in Alraune increases only after she mentions the way in which they are "similar,' and thus appears rooted in his realization of the potential for a human being to change. This belief enables him to trigger a genuine change in Alraune, as well as in their environment. Initially, the encounter with Frank precipitates a shift in Alraune's demeanor that becomes visible when she, shortly after meeting him, goes in search of Wolfgang, then hears that he drowned at the countess's ball. We see Alraune, seeking out Petersen, in a medium shot, hesitating outside of the door to his office; the sequence then cuts to a medium shot of the door as it opens and she slowly steps inside. We then see a medium-long shot of Petersen, flanked by two officers investigating ten Brinken for embezzlement; he rises angrily, asking her what she is doing there, then releases a tirade against her, blaming her for his son's death and posing the question that will torment her when he asks her if she knows who she is. The sequence cuts to a close-up of Alraune's face, her eyes wide and looking toward the camera, as Petersen continues: "You are a—"[57] We cut back to Petersen, who stops speaking, straightens, then collapses and buries his head in his arms on the desk, before we cut to a medium shot of Alraune, who turns and runs out of the door.

Unlike in the earlier scenes, Alraune is not presented as an object of desire; even the close-up shot of her face is focused more sharply, emphasizing her horror at Petersen's words and her vulnerability. Petersen's statement suggests that she can never be fully human, particularly when he

CHAPTER SIX

begins to tell her "who" she is, using the word "ein"; the neuter article divorces her from her natural gender and suggests that he will describe her as an inanimate object.

Alraune's reaction to the news of Wolfgang's death thus suggests a level of emotion in her that was not evident before and that might be traced to her meeting with Frank. A brief scene, set in ten Brinken's home several months after the scientist commits suicide, confirms this. The scene comprises a single long shot, set in the ornate drawing room where ten Brinken previously acted on his sexual desire for Alraune. This time, however, the lighting suggests daylight entering the room. A maid stands at the center of the room, listening to the sound of a man singing from off screen, as Jakob enters. Their exchange is significant: in response to her saying "Father Jakob, the house here is a real singing club,"[58] he remarks: "My dear child, it was not always like this. Even six months ago there was little song here."[59] Already, the use of familial titles—"father Jacob" and "my dear child"—suggests a newfound camaraderie in the home, a notion that is further emphasized by the maid's use of the term "Gesangsverein," singing club, which implies a community of people. The fact that the formerly dark, foreboding building, where most scenes were set in the windowless foyer or in rooms only half-lit, is now not only well lit but also filled with singing, further stresses how much Frank's presence has changed the environment.

Frank's influence is visible again when we next see him with Alraune eating breakfast outdoors at a table surrounded by flowers. Alraune's attire—a loose, white dress that covers her shoulders—is markedly different from what she wore in previous scenes. Her first action is to ask Frank whether he would like more milk in his coffee; when he assents, she pours it for him. She next asks him to tell her more about his farm in Africa. Here, we cut to a medium close-up of the two, Alraune looking at Frank, who is in profile at the front of the screen. Spotlighting emphasizes Alraune's paleness, yet in a very different way than it did, for example, at the countess's ball; her face and hair appear natural, while the draping of the dress is anything but revealing. Her gaze is fixed on Frank, yet he does not meet it. Alraune's contribution to the conversation consists entirely of questions. After Frank tells her about the beauty of his farm, she asks him whether he feels "Sehnsucht," "longing," for it, and, when he responds that he has built a new life there, she looks away from him, visibly upset, before asking him whether he intends to leave. When Frank tells her that he wants them both to go, she asks first whether he truly wants to take her, and then when they will depart. The conversation between the two appears to indicate a shift in Alraune's behavior, in that, previously, she uttered commands or declarative statements, whereas she here asks questions. In a sense, this suggests that Alraune has lost (or renounced) a certain level of power; here, it is Frank who holds the power to disappoint her, as becomes clear by her reaction at the thought of his leaving. Indeed, Frank's statement indicates that he intends for her to change further: "You will be very happy there, Alraune. You will forget everything, everything."[60] If, in the past, Alraune was ten Brinken's creation, here she becomes that of Frank; he states decisively that she will be happy, and suggests that by allowing her a new beginning, a chance to "forget everything," he will, in essence, recreate her.

Perhaps it is the change that Frank has brought about in Alraune that leads to her self-destruction. Her new subordination to him becomes particularly visible when he leaves to discuss legal matters with Manasse and prepare for their departure on the following day. In a long shot of the terrace, we see Alraune still sitting at the table. Frank takes her hand and kisses it, then gets up and enters the house. As he goes, Alraune watches him, a clear reversal from earlier scenes, where she exerted power over those around her by figuring herself as the object of their gaze. The sequence then cuts to a medium close-up of Alraune at the table, her hands folded. Left alone, Alraune is at the mercy of the countess, who arrives to demand the money she lent ten Brinken. Their conversation demonstrates clearly Alraune's progressive loss of power; once Alraune tells her that she has nothing to do with her finances and the countess should talk to Frank Braun, her guardian, the older woman moves to the center of the shot and turns to face the camera. The shift reinforces Alraune's subordinate position. We then cut to a medium close-up of Alraune, shot over the countess's shoulder; again, the older woman's height and presence dwarfs the younger woman. And Alraune's denial of knowledge about her uncle's financial affairs equally draws attention to her powerlessness; it connects not only to her inheritance but also to her origin, a fact that is made clear by the countess's subsequent words: "You don't know what you are, either, do you? You're a cuckoo. I was there. Your dear Frank had the funny idea to artificially produce people instead of rats. . . . You're just the result of one of ten Brinken's experiments. You daughter of a whore and a hanged man."[61]

The moment reveals a weakness in Alraune: her desire to know about her origins. Several moments earlier the film hinted at this. Thus, upon meeting Frank, she asked him whether he knew her parents and was disappointed when he told her that he did not; equally, when Petersen used a similar construction, asking her angrily whether she knew "who she is," Alraune's reaction demonstrated, like here, a desire to know and a fear of knowing, a sense, perhaps, of something inherently "unnatural" in herself. The body language is crucial: as the countess confronts Alraune, the latter repeatedly attempts to draw herself up but is unsuccessful, until, at the final revelation that she is the "daughter of a whore and a hanged man," Alraune cannot even meet the countess's eyes, and lowers her head entirely when the older woman leaves.

Spurred by the countess's words, Alraune seeks out ten Brinken's lawyer, Manasse, who gives her the record of her origins. When she tells him that the countess has revealed the experiment, Alraune uses the term "aufgeklärt," which we can read as alluding not only to general knowledge but also to knowledge that is potentially fatal: sexual knowledge, referencing again the biblical fall and drawing a connection between Alraune and the construction of woman as implicated in man's fall from grace. This is furthered by Manasse's words as he gives her ten Brinken's notebook: "Then you'll know everything."[62] Alraune hesitates when she takes the book, demonstrating that she, too, realizes the danger of "knowing everything." Yet she cannot resist the information; immediately after her meeting, we cut to a high-angle close-up shot over Alraune's shoulder, showing her reading the page on which ten Brinken had noted her "victims." The camera then shows a closer view of the page, with the names clearly visible, and Alraune moves her hand to cover Frank's name, saying "Nein, nein, du nicht," "no, not you." We then cut to a close-up of her as she looks up from the book and toward the camera, lingering on her somber expression before the shot fades out. Already her decision seems made, her *Entsagung* decided: she will do anything to keep Frank safe.

Her final encounter with him makes her determination clear. The sequence begins with a long shot of a room where Frank sits at a desk; the camera follows him as he rises, whistling, then turns on a gramophone, playing the song to which she danced at the countess's ball, where she had acted out her role as femme fatale and estranged the countess's daughter from her fiancé. It then pans slightly right to show the glass doors behind him, and we see Alraune outside. We then cut to a close-up of her as she enters, pausing to look at him, before cutting to a long shot as she approaches him and puts her hand on his shoulder. When he greets her and asks her where she was, she pauses, responding only to his joking comment that he thought "the countess might have eaten her" with a light "she almost did." Frank moves out of the shot to pour glasses of wine; when Alraune joins him at the desk, the camera moves with her, keeping her centered. She does not respond to his toast to their anticipated departure, nor to his reflections on where they will go. As Frank moves around the room, scarcely paying attention to her silence, the camera follows him, before cutting to a close-up of Alraune as she watches him. We cut back to a long shot, then to a medium shot as he bends toward her and asks her whether she is not looking forward to their departure. She finally answers in the affirmative, yet her response barely registers with Frank, who suggests that she must not be able to imagine it, as she knows so little of the world, unlike him: "But I, I became a new man out there."[63] She finally speaks, saying that he has not yet kissed her; we then cut to a medium shot of Frank facing the camera, with Alraune's head visible in front of him, as he caresses her hair and bends to kiss her before kneeling in front of her. The sequence cuts to a close-up of Alraune as she strokes his head in her lap and murmurs again "not you" as though to affirm her decision.

The repetition of the song to which she first danced establishes it as a leitmotif for Alraune, or, perhaps, for her downfall, for it is associated with the scandalous ball, with ten Brinken, who, himself desiring her, hummed it as he tried to seize her after the ball, with Alraune's understanding of her danger to Frank, and, later, with her death. Close-ups of her in this segment, while again shot in soft focus, emphasize her vulnerability: her hair is loose, her gaze pensive as she looks at Frank. Certainly, she remains an object of contemplation, made more passive by her slow movements and her relative silence, but she is framed markedly differently from before, eroticized not by her active staging of herself but rather through her abjection. She fascinates because she has become a hopeless figure; indeed, her death has been so heavily foreshadowed that the scene reads almost as a death scene. The viewer, thus, derives pleasure from what amounts to a moment of absolute self-sacrifice. Frank, by contrast, is the dominant figure, unaware of her concerns, convinced of his plan to go away with her. The emphasis is on him as the active figure, the one who determines the course of action, who "became a new person." Alraune is denied this possibility, suggesting a more fatalistic reading of her character than that of Frank; she becomes a "new person" only through her self-sacrifice, which we witness most strikingly as she caresses him one last time, even as she articulates her decision to save him.

That this final scene between Frank and Alraune effectively functions as her death scene is even more evident when we examine her actual death, which the final sequence presents in a strikingly aestheticized way. After the scene between the two of them, we see a long shot of darkness broken by a door opening and Alraune's silhouette exiting the room. As a slower version of the "fatal" song begins, we cut to a long shot of the stairs, spotlighted only in their center, so that, as Alraune descends, she moves from shadows into light and back into shadows. Initially, the camera remains static, so that we see first only her bare feet below a white gown and black robe, then her pale face; once she fills the frame, the camera tilts slowly downward to maintain its focus on her. The shot then dissolves to a close-up of waves capped with white foam, then cuts to a long shot of a lake surrounded by trees silhouetted against the sky, the rising (or setting) sun casting a line of light on the water's surface.

In this final sequence, Alraune is, for only the second time, presented entirely alone;[64] there are no other characters for whom she functions as a fatal object of desire present. Her silence represents again her loss of her power. At the same time, she remains an aesthetic and erotic figure, the image over which the viewer exerts control. She has moved, in other words, from being a transgressive and actively self-staging agent toward becoming a safer figure, woman as object rendered absolutely passive. Yet the moment is an ambiguous one, for, in choosing suicide, Alraune makes a paradoxically active choice. And the final two shots—of the waves and the placid lake—are interesting; denying the viewer the actual sight of her death, they suggest that woman as image cannot be entirely passive, and they imply some level of activity in the staging of the self as desired object.

A Daughter of Destiny and Daughter of Evil

What we see in Oswald's *Alraune* is a very different specter of female emancipation: still as a potentially lethal danger to men, but, even more so, as a fatal, tragic flaw within the woman herself. Alraune as emancipated woman undermines the traditional social structures that figure men as hierarchically superior. Her erotic power is an active one that renders the men around her helpless and ultimately drives them to their deaths. In her fundamental shift at the end of the film, we see the suggestion that the pleasure she took in her power was not true pleasure, a fact already hinted at in one moment in particular, when, after ten Brinken succumbs to his desire for her and attempts to kiss her, she rejects him and flees to her room. There, we see her seated in front of a mirror, her gaze directed away from her own reflection, as though in an attempt to separate herself from her body as object of desire and from the fatal appeal it has for the men around her. Seen in this way, we can read the film not as the story of an immoral, fatal woman whose mystical power over the men around her figures her as monstrous, but rather as that of a woman who oversteps social norms and endangers the men who desire her even while attempting to discover her place in the world. In this reading, her discovery of her unnatural origins—which leaves her unmoored, without a past that would ground her—becomes as much the cause of her death as is her desire to protect Frank. Thus Alraune's suicide become a complexly significant moment; it is at once the moment in which she seizes power, directs her own destiny, and escapes ten Brinken's control, and that in which she acts out a social prerogative that figures her—by virtue of her emancipation and her lack of any sort of traditional familial ties—as unnatural. Paradoxically, it is the moment in which the fundamentally unnatural woman—her unnaturalness embodied in her activity, her desire, her fatal effect on the men around her—is made natural through her *Entsagung*, her assumption of the role of self-sacrificing woman through the act of suicide.

In the context of the development of the medium, we see certain elements in Oswald's film that parallel those in Galeen's version. Thus the camera works to reinforce Alraune's unnaturalness: through the use of lingering, long-duration shots that emphasize her immobility, close-ups that draw attention to her face as more flawless than seems humanly possible, and framings of her body—especially with her back bare—that eroticize her even as they render her statue-like. In Oswald's film, the eye of the camera seems to represent the desiring eye of the viewer: seeking to exert control over her as object, to render her passive and motionless. At the same time, like Galeen's version, Oswald's undermines this process, depicting again and again the effect of *her* gaze at the men around her; she, too, exerts control, fixes the men who become her objects of desire, and robs them thereby of power. Yet the addition of sound adds a dimension through which her power is expressed; in interpolating the men around her, in deploying the imperative, she renders them doubly disempowered. The very different endings might, in a sense, connect to the different qualities of silent and sound films. Galeen places the emphasis on Alraune as fallen woman, as victimizer, only reversing this in the final moments of the film, where Oswald invests more energy in presenting her changed persona. Galeen's ending suggests that Alraune abdicates her power, subordinating herself to Frank, while Oswald's implies a seizure of power, however limited. Both suggest that Alraune's active gaze must be averted, yet the later version equally strives to silence her, emphasizing a powerful dimension in her speech and denying her this.

I noted that Galeen's version of Alraune suggests some degree of a powerful, feminized gaze, however problematically; in the later version, gender is bound up with viewing in a very different way. Instead of emphasizing the dangerous quality of Alraune's power and the punitive dimension to the narrative even while presenting the model, however disparaged, for a powerful female gaze, Oswald's *Alraune* works as a melodrama, appealing specifically to a female viewer through its staging of a woman who is empowered and who acts on her desires. On the one hand, Oswald's *Alraune* does not construct a notion of female agency as potent as that of Galeen's version; on the other, we can read Oswald's film as speaking to a specifically female experience. As Petro notes, "for female audiences, who were only just beginning to be addressed as spectators, the film melodrama almost certainly provoked an intensely interested and emotional involvement, particularly since melodramatic representation often gave heightened expression to women's experiences of modernity."[65] Oswald's *Alraune* seems to appeal to the female spectator far more directly and pointedly than did Galeen's. Perhaps this is one reason for (or one effect of) the way in which the uncanny potential of *Alraune* is minimized in the later version. This Alraune, in spite of her active desires and apparent amorality, is no "uncanny body"; she is not constructed to engender fear in the female spectator (as she might in the male viewer), but to speak, in some way, to women, to allow them to identify and empathize. As Petro argues, "To theorize female subjectivity in Weimar requires that we revise notions about perception and spectatorship in the cinema and explore the ways in which modernity was experienced differently by women during the 1920s. . . . In psychic terms alone, we may say that women did not share the male fear of the female body, and thus did not retain the same investment in aesthetic distance and detachment."[66] The notion that "women did not share the male fear of the female body," when considered in connection with Galeen's and Oswald's respective versions of *Alraune*, suggests the very different appeal that each held and the reason why they differ so strongly in their evocation of the uncanny. In the earlier version, structured in such a way as to build on Alraune as dangerously emancipated, as a woman whose active desire and whose manipulation of the men around her proves fatal to the men who succumb to her, she must necessarily be an uncanny figure: she is, again, the female body made unfamiliar through its empowerment. Thence the emphasis on her uncanny origins, the echoes, in her portrayal, of the threatening robot Maria from *Metropolis*. There, Alraune was constructed as a specter that would haunt the fearful *male* viewer, familiar yet defamiliarized, desired yet threatening.

In the later version, by contrast, Alraune, in spite of her "unnatural origins" and her ability to fascinate the men around her, is primarily depicted as a woman in the process of developing, learning the extent of her powers, seeking out her origins, and ultimately giving up her life for the man she loves. In this, she represents a sort of (negative) developmental model for the female spectator, acting out fantasies of empowerment. Indeed, in this context, even her "unnatural origins" become a measure of her independence; however much her lack of a true "family" might be construed, in the end, as contributing to her self-destruction, it simultaneously allows her to construct both herself and a fantasy of a "better," absent origin. Alraune, in other words, enables the female spectator to live out the ultimate sort of emancipation, divorced from constraining familial ties and predicated on her own desires.

This is not to suggest that Oswald depicts Alraune as an ideal; rather, she oscillates between being a figure of identification and/or fascination and one of danger. This indeterminacy connects Oswald's *Alraune* even more strongly to the genre of melodrama. In her discussion of Detlef Sierck's *Final Chord* (*Schlußakkord*, 1936), Sabine Hake notes the ways in which melodrama was fundamentally bound up with the female viewer's experience: "The power of the melodramatic found expression in the close attention to female problems; the emphasis on social and racial difference; the tension between individual and community; the fascination with decline and degeneration; and the reliance on standard melodramatic elements like the inevitability of guilt, the ubiquity of suffering, and the impossibility of happiness."[67] Hake suggests that Sierck draws on the conventions of the genre not only in service of affirming the traditional female maternal ideal, but also, paradoxically, in order to explore the fascination exerted by the woman who falls outside of that role:

> The validation of traditional gender roles in the narrative does not account for the intense interest with which Sierck, through his portrayal of Charlotte, indulges in a fantasy of female eroticism unburdened by the demands of motherhood. Whereas the character is punished for her transgressions [actor Lil] Dagover's sheer presence as an image that articulates the pain of difference undercuts such punitive strategies.... The camera focuses on the spectacle of the desiring woman not only to witness her inevitable destruction, but also to celebrate her resistance to external determinations and simplistic explanations.[68]

Hake articulates quite clearly the ambiguity that figures so often in melodrama, where the depiction of a transgressive woman as fascinating spectacle competes with the need to contain and punish her. This ambiguity, Hake notes, is how Sierck's film addresses the gender problematic at its center: "Confirming Fredric Jameson's observation that narrative is a privileged medium for the articulation of social conflicts and that ideological positions are always contested, the problem of female eroticism is therefore 'resolved' through a strategy of simultaneous articulation and containment."[69] Considering Oswald's *Alraune* against Hake's notion of the way in which melodrama allows this articulation of both fascination and containment makes clear how here, too, we ultimately see a "validation of traditional gender roles" and the "inevitable destruction" of the "desiring woman." The later *Alraune* conforms quite clearly to the concerns and conventions of melodrama. And yet—as in Sierck's *Final Chord*—we can see that Oswald simultaneously dwells on and "celebrates" Alraune's difference, that he, too, stages her as "a fantasy of female eroticism unburdened by the demands of motherhood." Indeed, even more than *Final Chord*, where the transgressive woman is directly contrasted to a maternal ideal, *Alraune* dispenses with a maternal dimension to its "heroine." Herself the product of an "unnatural" origin, her mother reduced to "vessel" and quickly erased from the narrative, Alraune seems entirely removed from the maternal. She ultimately embodies *only* the fantasy of femininity separated from maternity, and is thus particularly potent as a figure that represents empowerment and emancipation for the female spectator and doubly destined to self-destruction.

THE TWO VERSIONS

The two version of *Alraune* are examples of the way in which the Weimar film industry recycled and reworked narratives, much as modern film industries do, and demonstrate the effect of significant changes in film technology and in the sociocultural environment. Where Galeen's *Alraune* emphasizes its uncanny elements and stages the transgressive woman as simultaneously empowered and unequivocally dangerous, Oswald's shifts the genre from uncanny tale to melodrama. In one sense, this is a strange choice; particularly because of the advent of sound, Oswald might have been able to capitalize on a renewed sense of the uncanny in film. In another sense, Oswald's reworking of the generic frame represents a direct address to and acknowledgment of the women in the audience. Alraune is a complex figure of identification and disavowal for a viewership recognized as mixed, if not as predominantly female. And even as the two films point to a shift in the way the spectator was conceptualized, so they demonstrate the changes in the sociocultural environment, where the semantics used to define and justify woman's position were rapidly changing. Thus where early Weimar culture confronted women's emancipation as a newly codified reality and opposed the dangerous, desiring, and empowered woman to the traumatized and multiply *disempowered* returning soldier, late Weimar

CHAPTER SIX

Germany needed to find new ways in which to represent the dangers of women's liberation. In a transition that points toward the gender roles that would become normative in Nazi Germany, we see, in Oswald's version of *Alraune*, the suggestion that emancipation renders a woman dangerous to men *and to herself*. Emancipated woman, in Oswald's vision, has no choice but that of self-destruction; she can prove her femininity only, paradoxically enough, by recognizing her own incommensurability with "natural" social structures and destroying herself in service of a greater good.

CONCLUSION

THE FILMS EXAMINED IN this study are signposts of sorts, points of entry into an understanding of Weimar cinema's never entirely neat and coherent development. Born out of the destruction of World War I and poised on the edge of ruin in its early years, Germany came full circle by 1933 and again faced crisis, of a very different sort than in the founding years of the republic, but equally traumatic and with even more devastating effects to come. It seems at times impossible to believe that Weimar Germany existed for less than fifteen years, from the moment of its proclamation on November 9, 1918, to Hitler's ascendance to the post of chancellor on January 30, 1933. How radically did German culture change during this brief time, how fundamentally different was the society of the 1920s than that before the First World War, and, equally, how different was Weimar at its "decadent peak" than in the moments that marked its end. The rapidity of social and political change was paralleled by the radical developments that marked cinema; there, too, films made during the immediate postwar years seem light years removed from those produced at the end of the republic.

And yet we can see in the films examined the way in which cinematic conventions and narrative tendencies built on and evolved in a process that was shaped by technological advance and sociocultural change. Films like Oswald's version of *Alraune* point not exclusively toward a universal imperative that figures woman's desire as incommensurate with society and requires its repudiation, but rather emerge out of the responses to formative sociocultural anxieties and to new developments in cinematography that we already see developing in *Eyes of the Mummy* and other films of that time. Whatever preexisting tendency there might have been to position woman as the aesthetic object of contemplation, the very modern ways in which this was done within the context of cinema represents not merely

Conclusion

the "natural" progression of a universal trope but rather a process shaped and defined by historical and cultural events. We can see the vital trauma of Germany's experience in the war and of its changing sociocultural environment during the Weimar Republic as a catastrophic impact that shaped the ways in which identity would be conceptualized thereafter. And while this book focused narrowly on film of the Weimar Republic and thereby on the ways in which cinema of that era was implicated in and symptomatic of the crises of identity with which the new nation grappled, it raises questions about the relationship between self and the screen, subjectivity and the image, that are equally important in looking more broadly at film. How does cinema become a site of simultaneous conformity and disruption? How does it reflect and work against the type of radical social change that evokes anxiety in the audience even as it celebrates and contributes to that change? How does it speak at once to such a range of spectators, satisfying those who look to it as a source of escapism as well as those who hope to see it as an impetus of further change?

In broad terms, what these films demonstrate is the changing way in which German cinema addressed the thorny issue of gender during the era. I traced the trajectory from the immediate post–World War I period, when films dealt far more overtly and violently with emancipated women, figuring them as a threat to traditional gender roles and norms and, thereby, to masculine subjectivity, to the end of Weimar, where transgressive women were dealt with by being "fixed" as erotic object and also by being represented as ultimately themselves seeking out traditional roles. In other words, where the early Weimar vamps—from Lubitsch's Mâ to Robison's flirtatious wife, from Oswald's multiple incarnations of Anita Berber to Wiene's Yvonne—had to be wrestled into submission, the vamp of late Weimar realized her own unhappiness—which stemmed directly from her erotic and social liberation—and willingly, even eagerly, subordinated herself.

Yet this overt trajectory represents a simplification of sorts. Indeed, these films raise a number of questions and problematize the very notion that we can trace a fully coherent narrative of the way in which the female image is developed and functions in the films of the era. One of the questions at the heart of this book asked why Weimar Germany's meditations on gender dynamics were embedded again and again in stories of the uncanny. What made these types of films so appealing to the audience? I have suggested that the connection between gender and the uncanny underscores the difficulty of dealing with changing social norms directly, the need to couch them in terms outside of the real. These uncanny narratives masked most effectively the dominant uncanny object—namely, woman as equal, as emancipated and empowered, as active and desiring. And this image is one that we can see as uncanny not only to the male viewer but also to the female, albeit for different reasons. On one hand, she challenges male subjectivity and agency, standing for the maternal made uncanny, the return of the female body as superior and destructive. At times, she becomes, in other words, the pre-Oedipal desired maternal that Studlar sees as formative of masochism and central to cinematic pleasure. On the other hand, she confronts the female viewer as an equally uncanny image, for she represents to her a sense of possibility that is not inferior to that of man and that suggests the return to a moment before she was made to realize the limitations tied to sex. These uncanny female bodies, these unruly women who threatened and needed to be suppressed, were symbolic of fundamental cultural shifts, of a world in which the self was uprooted and redefined. The films might have appealed because they responded more broadly to the terrifying newness of modernity, to a world in which everything was changed, in which what seemed familiar and known was actually different, defamiliarized, irrevocably transformed. Uncanny films might have been an answer as much to the immediate trauma of the war and the unfamiliarity of a social environment in which women and men suddenly inhabited new roles as they were to a world fundamentally turned on its head, in which an unceasing progress had radically impacted the individual and would unavoidably continue to do so.

Perhaps this is why these uncanny films populated theaters during such a specific era and lost significance toward the end of the Weimar Republic: they spoke most effectively to the historical moment that we might see as defined by defamiliarization, in that everything that would previously have been a basis on which to define the self was undergoing radical change—from government to social and familial hierarchies, from the real landscape of the nation to the imaginary landscape of the culture, from the technologies that reordered work to those that constructed new forms of entertainment. As the Weimar Republic stabilized and the population became accustomed to the effects of modernity on life, cinema turned increasingly

Conclusion

away from narratives that drew attention to the strangeness of this new world and toward those that examined it in terms of the real, that cast a "rational" eye (of the camera) at its effects. What makes the uncanny films of the era so remarkable is that they are the products of a moment in which key elements of the cultural background—the effects of the war, the stage of modernity, the social status of men and women, and the technical possibilities of cinema—converged in a sort of alchemy that allowed all of these disparate pieces to be expressed at once. Thence the ambiguity, the multilayered and multifaceted narratives, the ways in which these films contradict themselves and resist single, unifying interpretations; they embody the nature of the moment, itself wrought by ambiguity, contradiction, and change.

In spite of their historical specificity, these uncanny films contributed to a lasting iconography; the women who haunted these films left their legacy to cinema as it developed internationally throughout the twentieth century. We might see traces of them in the femmes fatales of Hollywood film noir and the beautiful victims of Universal's horror films, even in those (few, yet increasing) heroines of today's films that resist the role of romantic lead and step outside of the mold of the "good girl." And we equally see the development of the visual language to which these films contributed. The ways in which film is structured, in which it situates viewer and image and constructs positions of power and passivity even as it represents a space of multiple identifications and viewing positions, builds on the types of cinematic tropes inaugurated in these films in service of simultaneously reasserting power over and celebrating the potentially threatening images on screen.

That is not to minimize the limitations of these unruly women and the ways in which they were dealt with—violently and permanently—in the resolutions of the films. For the women that populate these uncanny narratives were fundamentally symbolic, the embodiments of potentials pushed to their extremes. However threatening those images of woman were, they represented as much the specter of modernity as they did the reality of life. Not every woman in the Weimar Republic could be viewed as a New Woman—far from this, the vast majority of women hewed to a more traditional, circumscribed role. Even those women who had moved into the workplace were more likely to do so out of necessity than out of a

Conclusion

desire for independence. The unruly women in these uncanny films are as much an articulation of the fears (and desires) associated with the effects of modernity as they are representations of the real. Perhaps this ambivalent function factors into the ways in which these films appealed to female and to male viewers. The woman empowered, transgressive, and modernized is multiple things to multiple viewers: she threatens the male viewer by suggesting a female power that challenges gender hierarchies and identity even as she represents an illicit desire; she represents, to the women in the audience, the possibility for the expression of desire and a model for a new sort of self-assertion and self-expression even as she undermines in a terrifying manner the ways in which they have hitherto defined their selves and their lives. While my analyses of these films have shown that there exists an overt narrative that often serves to reassert a conservative ideal at the expense of the transgressive woman, I have equally tried to trace the moments of excess that suggest that these overt narratives are more ambiguous than they might seem. Even in enacting the reaffirmation of conservative gender roles and power hierarchies, these uncanny films undermine them by pointing to their fantastic nature. In the end, the powerful men and "domesticated" women are as much uncanny figures as are the transgressive and transgressed-against figures that cede the screen to them. The pleasure in these films might result from the shifting power dynamics, from the representation of other potential identities, however much those alternatives might be foreclosed in the end.

The suggestion that these cinematic women served as a way to foster more fluid understandings of gender roles, even when they were ultimately "punished," seems borne out by the way in which the representation of women changed as the Weimar era drew to a close and once the Nazis rose to power. Indeed, the terrifying potential of these images becomes manifest in the social politics of Nazi Germany, where the New Woman ceded cultural space to woman-as-mother, whose sphere of influence was reduced to *Kinder, Küche, Kirche*.[1] We should ask whether the changes in the cinematic representation of desiring women that we see as the Weimar Republic nears its end already point toward—and perhaps contribute to—their increasing absence from screens after 1933. Does not Brigitte Helm's second incarnation of Alraune—as self-sacrificing woman who chooses death in order to save the man she loves—find her doubles in so many of

Conclusion

the "heroines" of Nazi cinema, where transgression was so often punished or contained? Does the development she represents—that shift that builds on the suggestion that the woman empowered, desiring, acting as subject was not the "return of the repressed" (and thereby fodder for uncanny representation), but rather the tragically misguided impulse that would inevitably end in female self-abnegation—suggest a cultural response to the dangerous woman that would be carried to its inevitable and oppressive conclusion in Nazi Germany? Scholars have amply demonstrated that we cannot read even the most overtly ideological Nazi films without considering potentially transgressive moments,[2] and yet there, in films like Detlef Sierck's *Final Chord* (*Schlußakkord*, 1936)[3] and his *La Habanera* (1937),[4] we might say that the unruly woman is no longer the same complex figure simultaneously desired and feared, symbolizing at once the hopes and the anxieties raised by modernity, but rather one that must be decisively overcome in the end. In the uncanny films of the Weimar era, the suggestion that emancipated woman was unnatural was one that was drawn on, yet simultaneously undermined through the very form of the cinematic narratives. In the context of the Nazi era, perhaps we can suggest that that "unnaturalness" became her defining characteristic, that which, progressively, led to her disappearance from any representation. Tracing the remnants of these images of female power into the Nazi era, we see that what is horrifying is no longer the specter of female emancipation, but the way in which that emancipation is closed off, the decisive suppression of women's empowerment.

Adding to the complexity of these cinematic vamps is the fact that they are never only the representation of woman-as-individual, nor even of "woman" as imaginary type, as specter of modernity, but rather point back to the medium itself. In the visual economy of these uncanny films, the uncanny female body stands in as well for cinema; her emancipation, modernity, and transgression stands for the artistic and technological possibilities of film, the ways in which it was changing the definition of culture and art, expressing the historical moment on screen, and redefining notions of the self and the other, of the real and the imaginary. The woman on screen, in other words, was simultaneously object and symbol of the cinematic eye. And, as the medium became familiarized, as it ceased to foreground its peculiar status between real and imaginary, the ambiguity and

Conclusion

multiplicity with which she was invested in her function as medial symbol decreased.

Another question these films raise is how we might bring them into dialogue with the ways in which scholars have tried to conceptualize the dynamics of power expressed in film and the gendering of image and viewer, both in films of the time and more broadly. Janet McCabe discusses female spectatorship in early Weimar film as exemplified in Lubitsch's *The Oyster Princess* (*Die Austernprinzessin*, 1919), noting that "pervasive consumerist fantasies and commodified versions of the feminine self"[5] were central motivations for the pleasure women took in the cinema and suggesting that a varied audience was a central concern of Weimar film industry: "The industry was interested in building a heterogeneous yet stable audience for its products, and did so by managing knowledge about, and producing representation for, them. . . . The German film industry recognized an imagined female audience and set about producing, circulating, and popularizing a set of modern identities in the process of attracting this audience."[6] McCabe's analysis speaks to the sort of multiplicity and ambiguity this analysis has identified in these films, a quality that opens up a space for identification as well as for distantiation, for she recognizes the pragmatic need for the films of the era to appeal to as broad an audience as possible. And her suggestion that women took pleasure in the "consumerist fantasies and commodified versions of the feminine self" displayed in films like *The Oyster Princess* is equally applicable to some of the films discussed in this book. Recall the scenes of Mâ's transformation at the hands of the European seamstress. But given these uncanny films' close engagement with the anxieties precipitated by Weimar modernity and their concomitant use of the image of transgressive woman as symbolic of social change, the position of the female viewer as consumer is only one part of a complex and multilayered figuration of female spectatorship. While the overt narratives of these films often seem to appeal most directly to a male spectator who perceives himself as disadvantaged and his position as under attack, alleviating the threat to that viewer by reassimilating or obliterating the dangerous woman on screen, we have seen the competing strands that celebrate female desire and agency, act out female potential, and construct a powerful female gaze within and directed at the cinematic image. Rather than being presented only two possibilities, of either taking on an uncomfortable alignment with an implied, universal male viewer, or being marginalized and experiencing the pressure to recognize the self as pure image, the female spectator is offered multiple additional subject positions: to identify with a woman who stages herself actively as paradoxically active object of desire; to "take possession of" the array of identities and luxuries displayed on screen; even to "judge" and revel in the punishment of a woman constructed as "other" than she, as too transgressive, too immoral.

This is not to suggest that these multiple possibilities are embraced unequivocally; certainly, we see the recognition that they pose a danger of sorts. Yet the ways in which the female spectator is appealed to and the woman on screen is constructed contest the absolute gendering of the gaze as male and the image as female and speak to the pleasures of spectatorship for a broad range of identities. Petro pointed to the "blind spot" in criticism of Weimar film: "it is the existence of a female spectator, and the function of representation for mobilizing her desires and unconscious fantasies, that analyses of the Weimar cinema have repressed or ignored in order to reproduce the same story—the story of male subjectivity in crisis—which is then taken to be the story of German history or culture itself."[7] What we see in these films is that in spite of the significance of that "male subjectivity in crisis," they acknowledge the female viewer and work toward "mobilizing her desires and unconscious fantasies" (or conscious ones!). From *Eyes of the Mummy* to *Alraune*, these films address themselves to more than that "wounded" male subject. Indeed, we might suggest that the female subjectivity to which they speak is equally as fragile, as potentially traumatized, as is the male, and speaks equally to the cultural moment in which her sense of self was being redefined. Does the death of Mâ not cater just to the injured man but also to the woman who perceives Mâ, exotic and desired, as direct threat to her own position? Does the murder of the flirtatious wife in *Warning Shadows* not reaffirm more bourgeois notions of morality and behavior that many of the women in the audience likely held? Even as they appeal to woman-as-spectator, these films point to the impossibility of constructing "her" as a single, unified entity; the *real* women in the audience were a disparate group, with different backgrounds and futures, a wide range of beliefs, hopes, and fears.

What I hope to have accomplished is not only to reclaim certain "lost" films that would add to the understanding of the complexity and range

Conclusion

of Weimar film, but also to reveal their ambiguity, the ways in which they connect to and engage with the changing sociocultural background. These films that so often appear naive or even primitive to today's viewer are not only documents of the historical and cultural moment, grappling with the monumental changes occurring in society and in cinema, but also complex representations of the ways in which the medium tried to stretch its own boundaries and appeal to the population. And even as they represent the products and expressions of specific moments and appeal to a historically bound, though diverse, audience, the cinematic strategies and tropes of these films have shaped those that exist even today. Overtly, they have contributed to the ways in which film deals with its dangerous women. Techniques such as the lingering close-ups on women's faces and bodies, the inclusion of performances, whether explicit—like the dances we see Pola Negri, Anita Berber, and Brigitte Helm perform—or implicit—like the ways in which the wives in *Warning Shadows* and *The Hands of Orlac* are framed as erotic objects of contemplation, and the multiple depictions of situations in which the unruly and desiring female body is "domesticated" and controlled via a masculine on-screen double—have factored into modern cinematic tropes and conventions. And yet the complexity of the women populating these films remains the hidden undercurrent that should be considered Weimar film's legacy to modern cinema. Underlying even the most "conventional" depictions of women in film are these disruptive heroines, these troublesome women who challenged conservative norms of behavior and aggressively overstepped the boundaries that had heretofore circumscribed their lives. The dangers they posed to the status quo, their active challenging of dominant social mores, directly shaped the mechanisms of control with which cinema responded. Whether she is framed as vamp or romantic lead, femme fatale or maternal body, woman in film—the way in which she is framed and controlled, the activity she is allowed, and the limitations she finds imposed on her—always relates back to those original forebears, to the transgressive women that populated Weimar film and so essentially shaped and changed Weimar culture and society.

NOTES

Introduction

1. Anton Kaes, Martin Jay, and Edward Dimendberg, preface to *The Weimar Republic Sourcebook*, ed. Anton Kaes, Martin Jay, and Edward Dimendberg (Berkeley: University of California Press, 1994), xvii–xx, xvii.
2. As Jan-Christopher Horak and Jennifer Bishop note, the vast majority of émigrés from Nazi Germany were Jewish ("German Exile Cinema, 1933–1950," *Film History* 8, no. 4 [1996]: 373–89, at 376). And while many started out working in other European nations as well as farther abroad, after the rise of the Nazis, Hollywood was, for most, the most attractive and viable option: "The reality of émigré life was that most exiled filmmakers had to migrate from country to country in order to find employment in Europe's various film industries. Other countries accepting German Jewish refugees—Italy, Switzerland, Spain, Portugal, Egypt and Czechoslovakia—could in fact only offer very temporary employment. . . . Due to these uncertainties, and the proximity to Nazi Germany, most émigré filmmakers remained transients in the capitals of the European film industry, choosing sooner or later to make their way to Hollywood, provided they possessed a sought-after American 'affidavit' and entry visa" (377).
3. Jan-Christopher Horak, "Sauerkraut and Sausages with a Little Goulash: Germans in Hollywood, 1927," *Film History* 17, no. 2–3 (2005): 241–60, at 243.
4. See Horak, "Sauerkraut and Sausages."
5. Richard W. McCormick, *Gender and Sexuality in Weimar Modernity: Film, Literature, and "New Objectivity"* (New York: Palgrave, 2001).
6. Anton Kaes, *Shell Shock Cinema: Weimar Culture and the Wounds of War* (Princeton, NJ: Princeton University Press, 2009).
7. Noah Isenberg, ed., *Weimar Cinema: An Essential Guide to Classic Films of the Era* (New York: Columbia University Press, 2009).
8. Christian Rogowski, ed., *The Many Faces of Weimar Cinema: Rediscovering Germany's Filmic Legacy* (Rochester, NY: Camden House, 2010).
9. Sabine Hake, *The Cinema's Third Machine: Writing on Film in Germany, 1907–1933* (Lincoln: University of Nebraska Press, 1993), 99.
10. Tom Gunning defined this notion of the "cinema of attractions" in "The Cinema of Attraction: Early Film, Its Spectator, and the Avant-Garde," *Wide Angle: A Film Quarterly of Theory, Criticism, and Practice* 8, no. 3–4 (1986): 63–70. A central element of this early cinema is, Gunning notes, "its fascination with the thrill of display rather than the construction of a story." Tom Gunning, "'Primitive' Cinema: A Frame-Up? Or the Trick's on Us," *Cinema Journal* 28, no. 2 (1989): 3–12, at 9. Gunning's concept is an important term in film studies, not only in its application to early film but also in examining the ways in which later films draw on, differentiate themselves from, or reinvent the structures he identified. See, for example, the collection *The Cinema of Attractions Reloaded*, ed. Wanda Strauven (Amsterdam: Amsterdam University Press, 2006).

Chapter 1

1. For a detailed discussion of political changes in Weimar Germany, see, for example, Mary Fulbrook, *A History of Germany, 1918–2009: The Divided Nation*, 3rd ed. (Chichester, UK: Wiley-Blackwell, 2009); Hans Mommsen, *The Rise and Fall of Weimar Democracy*, trans. Elborg Forster and Larry Eugene Jones (Chapel Hill: University of North Carolina Press, 1996); Detlev Peukert, *The Weimar Republic:*

Notes to Chapter 1

The Crisis of Classical Modernity, trans. Richard Deveson (New York: Hill and Wang, 1992); or Eric D. Weitz, *Weimar Germany: Promise and Tragedy* (Princeton, NJ: Princeton University Press, 2007).

2. "Socialist Fury: Last Days of Imperial Rule," *The Times* (London), November 12, 1918.
3. "At Last! Paris on the Great Day," *The Times* (London), November 12, 1918.
4. "The Lights of London: Scenes of Rejoicing at Night," *The Times* (London), November 12, 1918.
5. Fulbrook, *A History of Germany*, 20.
6. Ibid., 21.
7. Ibid., 21–22.
8. "The Berlin Revolution: Eye-Witness's Story; A Saturday Afternoon Affair," *The Times* (London), November 23, 1918.
9. "In Berlin: A City without Joy; Special Dispatch," *The Times* (London), November 30, 1918.
10. Susanne Michl and Jan Plamper, while suggesting the difficulty of accurately estimating the number of soldiers who suffered from war neurosis, note that approximately 200,000 soldiers were diagnosed with the disorder in Germany during the war. Susanne Michl and Jan Plamper, "Soldatische Angst im Ersten Weltkrieg. Die Karriere eines Gefühls in der Kriegspsychiatrie Deutschlands, Frankreichs und Russlands," *Geschichte und Gesellschaft* 35, no. 2 (2009): 209–48, at 213.
11. Sigmund Freud, "Gutachten über die elektrische Behandlung der Kriegsneurotiker" (1920), in *Gesammelte Werke: Nachtragsband, Texte aus den Jahren 1885–1938* (Frankfurt am Main: Fischer, 1999), 707. English translation taken from Sigmund Freud, "Memorandum on the Electrical Treatment of War Neurotics," *The Standard Edition of the Complete Psychological Works of Sigmund Freud*, ed. James Strachey, vol. 17 (London: Hogarth Press), 211–15, at 212.
12. "The conflict is between the soldier's old peaceful ego and his new warlike one, and it becomes acute as soon as the peace-ego realizes what danger it runs of losing its life owing to the rashness of its newly formed, parasitic double." Sigmund Freud, "Introduction to *Psychoanalysis and the War Neuroses*," *The Standard Edition of the Complete Psychological Works of Sigmund Freud*, ed. James Strachey, vol. 17, 205–10, at 209. Original German in: Sigmund Freud, "Einleitung zu *Zur Psychoanalyse der Kriegsneurosen*" (1919), in *Gesammelte Werke 12, Werke aus den Jahren, 1917–1920* (Frankfurt am Main: Fischer, 1999), 323.
13. Unless otherwise noted, translations from German sources are my own. "Der eigentliche Krankheitskeim schlummere daher im Soldaten selbst. Sein Wunsch, nicht mehr an die Front zurückkehren zu müssen, seine Aussicht auf eine Kriegsrente, ja seine 'sittlichen Einstellungen,' sein mangelnder Patriotismus und eine innerliche Ablehnung des Krieges, wurden nun direkt an die Krankheitsentstehung mit einbezogen." Michl and Plamper, "Soldatische Angst im Ersten Weltkrieg," 222.
14. "Die Tendenz ging unmissverständlich zu einer Pathologisierung von Angstzuständen sowie zu einer Stigmatisierung der betroffenen Soldaten nicht nur als nervenschwache, sondern auch als moralisch verwerfliche Individuen. Tapferkeit und Männlichkeit ließen sich mit diesen Angstzuständen nicht vereinbaren." Michl and Plamper, "Soldatische Angst im Ersten Weltkrieg," 224.
15. "An der Kriegsfront, wo Kameradschaft und eine 'gesunde und derbe Konstitution' der Männer vorherrschend seien, bestehe noch keine Ansteckungsgefahr. Sie steige jedoch, je näher man der 'Heimatfront' komme, d. h. dem weiblichen Einflussbereich." Michl and Plamper, "Soldatische Angst im Ersten Weltkrieg," 225.
16. "Heimat und Kriegshysteriker im Narrativ der Dolchstoßlegende gleichermaßen eine revolutionäre Bedrohung darstellten." Michl and Plamper, "Soldatische Angst im Ersten Weltkrieg," 243.
17. Kaes, *Shell Shock Cinema*, 2.
18. Ibid.
19. For more information on employment patterns, see, for example, Günter Berghaus, "Girlkultur: Feminism, Americanism, and Popular Entertainment in Weimar Germany," *Journal of Design History* 1, no. 3/4 (1988): 193–219, at 193–95.
20. Maria Tatar, *Lustmord: Sexual Murder in Weimar Germany* (Princeton, NJ: Princeton University Press, 1995), 12.
21. McCormick, *Gender and Sexuality in Weimar Modernity*, 20.
22. "Wären auf diese Weise die gerissenen Lücken im Arbeitsheer nicht durchweg durch Frauen ausgefüllt worden, Deutschland hätte—das gleiche Tempo der Aushebung vorausgesetzt—wirtschaftlich zusammenbrechen müssen. Ist doch im Laufe des ersten halben Jahres 1915 die

Zahl der weiblichen Industriearbeiter um mehr denn eine halbe Million gestiegen." Luise Zietz, *Zur Frage der Frauenerwerbsarbeit während des Krieges und nachher* (Berlin: Vorwärts, 1916), 6.

23. "Die Frauen jener Familien, in denen der Mann als Verstümmelter heimkehrt, der zu seiner Rente wenig verdienen kann, werden gleichfalls durch Lohnarbeit das fehlende Bargeld herbeischaffen müssen." Zietz, *Zur Frage der Frauenerwerbsarbeit während des Krieges und nachher*, 12.
24. "Nie darf dabei vergessen werden, daß die Frau von heute . . . als unmittelbares Produkt der Kriegszeit und ihrer Folgen angesehen werden muß, die sie in das aktive Leben gestoßen hat." Else Herrmann, *So Ist die Neue Frau* (Berlin: Avalun-Verlag, 1929), 41–42.
25. "Wir sind ein Geschlecht zwischen den Zeiten. Nur von ferne her tönen die Klänge des kulturgläubigen Entwicklungsglaubens des vorigen Jahrhunderts an unser Ohr, hin über das Trümmerfeld des großen Weltenbrandes, den wir erlebt. . . . Diese Erschütterung des Gleichgewichts tritt nirgendwo so kraß hervor als auf dem Sexualgebiet." Luise Scheffen-Döring, *Frauen von heute: Frauengedanken zur Sexualethik und Bevölkerungspolitik* (Leipzig: Quelle und Meyer, 1931), v.
26. She is referring, here, to a book by August Bebel, a leading social democrat in Germany at the turn of the century, whose book *Die Frau und der Sozialismus* (1879) had a wide influence.
27. "Seit [August] Bebel in seinem Buche 'Die Frau' Weib und Umsturz unlöslich zu verbinden gesucht hat, steht es für Millionen irregeleiteter Volksgenossen unumstößlich fest, daß die revolutionäre Gewalt das weibliche Geschlecht befreien, das freie Weib aber mit den letzten Resten der bürgerlichen Ordnung, Gesetzlichkeit, Moral und Religion aufräumen würde." Fanny Imle, *Die Frau in der Politik: Eine Einführung in das Staats- und Wirtschaftsleben für Frauen und Jungfrauen* (Freiburg im Breisgau: Herder, 1920), 1.
28. McCormick, *Gender and Sexuality in Weimar Modernity*, 3.
29. Ibid., 21.
30. Ibid., 21–22.
31. Lynda J. King, "The New Woman in Robert Musil's Comedy *Vinzenz und die Freundin Bedeutender Männer*," *Modern Austrian Literature* 16, no. 1 (1983): 23–36, at 24.
32. King, "The New Woman in Robert Musil's Comedy." 24. For further discussion of the role of the New Woman in Weimar and internationally, see Elizabeth Otto and Vanessa Rocco, eds., *The New Woman International: Representations in Photography and Film from the 1870s through the 1960s* (Ann Arbor: University of Michigan Press, 2011). Of particular interest are the essays by Brett M. Van Hoesen, "Postcolonial Cosmopolitanism: Constructing the Weimar New Woman out of a Colonial Imaginary" (95–114) and by Vanessa Rocco, "Bad Girls: The New Woman in Weimar Film Stills" (213–30).
33. Dorothy Rowe, "Desiring Berlin: Gender and Modernity in Weimar Germany," in *Visions of the "Neue Frau": Women and the Visual Arts in Weimar Germany*, ed. Marsha Meskimmon and Shearer West (Hants, England: Scolar Pres, 1995), 143–64, at 152.
34. McCormick, *Gender and Sexuality in Weimar Modernity*, 21.
35. Ibid.
36. For further discussion of the often-violent fantasies associated with the female body, see Klaus Theweleit, *Männerphantasien: 1. Frauen, Fluten, Körper, Geschichte* and *2. Männerkörper: Zur Psychoanalyse des weißen Terrors* (Frankfurt am Main: Verlag Roter Stern, 1977–78). Theweleit draws on primary sources from the writings and fantasies of a group of Freikorps soldiers in order to trace the ways in which they conceptualized femininity and the connections between these images of women and fascist ideology.
37. Rowe, "Desiring Berlin," 159.
38. Carol Diethe, "Beauty and the Beast: An Investigation into the Role and Function of Women in German Expressionist Film," in Meskimmon and West, eds., *Visions of the "Neue Frau": Women and the Visual Arts in Weimar Germany*, 108–23, at 117.
39. Sabine Hake, *German National Cinema* (London: Routledge, 2002), 30.
40. Kristin Thompson, "Lubitsch, Acting, and the Silent Romantic Comedy," *Film History* 13, no. 4 (2001): 390–408, at 390.
41. Many scholars have interrogated the label of cinematic expressionism, essentially suggesting that it is both insufficient and extremely limited in scope. For further discussion of this issue, see, for

example, Thomas Elsaesser's *Weimar Cinema and After: Germany's Historical Imaginary* (London: Routledge, 2000); Sabine Hake's *German National Cinema*; and Dietrich Scheunemann's "Activating the Differences: Expressionist Film and Early Weimar Cinema," in *Expressionist Film: New Perspectives*, ed. Dietrich Scheunemann (Rochester, NY: Camden House, 2003), 1–31.
42. Hake, *German National Cinema*, 29.
43. Ibid., 29–30.
44. Ibid., 30.
45. Ibid., 36.
46. McCormick, *Gender and Sexuality in Weimar Modernity*, 19.
47. Leonardo Quaresima, "Introduction to the 2004 Edition: Rereading Kracauer," trans. Michael F. Moore, in *From Caligari to Hitler: A Psychological History of the German Film* (Princeton, NJ: Princeton University Press, 2004), xv–xlix, xix–xx.
48. Siegfried Kracauer, *From Caligari to Hitler: A Psychological History of the German Film* (Princeton, NJ: Princeton University Press, 2004), 8.
49. Kracauer, *From Caligari to Hitler*, li.
50. Lotte Eisner, *The Haunted Screen: Expressionism in the German Cinema and the Influence of Max Reinhardt*, trans. Roger Greaves (Berkeley: University of California Press, 1973), 9.
51. "Das Ornament der Masse," first published in the *Frankfurter Zeitung* in 1927.
52. Originally published in the *Frankfurter Zeitung* in 1928 as "Die kleinen Ladenmädchen gehen ins Kino." For an interesting analysis of the essay's implications for notions of spectatorship, see Patrice Petro, *Joyless Streets: Women and Melodramatic Representation in Weimar Germany* (Princeton, NJ: Princeton University Press, 1989), 67–68.
53. Miriam Hansen, "Decentric Perspectives: Kracauer's Early Writings on Film and Mass Culture," *New German Critique* 54 (Autumn 1991): 47–76. 48. See also Hansen, "Mass Culture as Hieroglyphic Writing: Adorno, Derrida, Kracauer," *New German Critique* 56 (Spring/Summer 1992): 43–73; Hansen, "'With Skin and Hair': Kracauer's Theory of Film, Marseille 1940," *Critical Inquiry* 19, no. 3 (1993): 437–69; and Hansen, *Cinema and Experience: Siegfried Kracauer, Walter Benjamin, and Theodor W. Adorno* (Berkeley: University of California Press, 2012).
54. Isenberg, introduction to *Weimar Cinema: An Essential Guide to Classic Films of the Era*, 9.
55. Kracauer, *From Caligari to Hitler*, 8.
56. Kaes, *Shell Shock Cinema*, 2.
57. Thomas Elsaesser, "Weimar Cinema, Mobile Selves, and Anxious Males: Kracauer and Eisner Revisited," in Scheunemann, *Expressionist Film: New Perspectives*, 33–71, at 39.
58. In addition to Elsaesser's "Weimar Cinema, Mobile Selves, and Anxious Males," see, for example, his "Social Mobility and the Fantastic: German Silent Cinema," in *Fantasy and the Cinema*, ed. James Donald (London: British Film Institute, 1989), 23–38, as well as his *Weimar Cinema and After*; Noah Isenberg's introduction to and the essays collected in his *Weimar Cinema: An Essential Guide to Classic Films of the Era*; Johannes von Moltke and Gerd Gemünden's, eds., *Culture in the Anteroom: The Legacies of Siegfried Kracauer* (Ann Arbor: University of Michigan Press, 2012); and Patrice Petro's *Joyless Streets*.
59. As Petro notes, women became important (perhaps *the* most important) consumers of entertainment in the 1920s, "when middle-class patrons, mostly young women, flocked to the movies and theater, eager for racy tales of prostitution and exposure to the world of speakeasies, Harlem nightclubs, and drag balls hosted by an emerging gay subculture. Thus were the 1920s a turning point for women in the cities—for their visibility, mobility, and economic clout within an urban culture not confined to New York or Berlin or Paris or London but interconnected through an entertainment network at once cosmopolitan and international." In "Legacies of Weimar Cinema," in *Cinema and Modernity*, ed. Murray Pomerance (New Brunswick, NJ: Rutgers University Press, 2006), 235–52, at 248.
60. Elsaesser, *Weimar Cinema and After*, 204.
61. Ibid., 206.
62. Petro, *Joyless Streets*, xxii.
63. Ibid., 25.
64. Ibid., 36.

Notes to Chapter 1

65. Ibid., 144.
66. Ibid., 17.
67. Laura Mulvey, "Visual Pleasure and Narrative Cinema," in *Film Theory and Criticism: Introductory Readings*, ed. Leo Braudy and Marshall Cohen, 5th ed. (New York: Oxford University Press, 1999), 833–44, at 835–36.
68. Mulvey, "Visual Pleasure and Narrative Cinema," 838.
69. Ibid., 840.
70. Ibid.
71. Gaylyn Studlar, "Visual Pleasure and the Masochistic Aesthetic," *Journal of Film and Video* 37 (Spring 1985): 5–26, at 5. Studlar develops her argument further in her book *In the Realm of Pleasure: Von Sternberg, Dietrich, and the Masochistic Aesthetic* (New York: Columbia University Press, 1988).
72. Studlar, "Visual Pleasure and the Masochistic Aesthetic," 8.
73. Ibid., 13.
74. Ibid., 14.
75. Ibid., 21.
76. Ibid., 23.
77. Laura Mulvey, "Afterthoughts on 'Visual Pleasure and Narrative Cinema' Inspired by King Vidor's *Duel in the Sun* (1946)," in *Feminist Film Theory: A Reader*, ed. Sue Thornham (1981; rpt. New York: New York University Press, 1999), 122–30, at 123.
78. Elsaesser, *Weimar Cinema and After*, 206.
79. Mary Ann Doane, *The Desire to Desire: The Woman's Film of the 1940s* (Bloomington: Indiana University Press, 1987), 67.
80. Doane, *The Desire to Desire*, 37.
81. Ibid., 41.
82. Ibid., 180–81.
83. Kathleen Rowe, *The Unruly Woman: Gender and the Genres of Laughter* (Austin: University of Texas Press, 1995), 4.
84. Rowe, *The Unruly Woman*, 5.
85. Judith Mayne, *Cinema and Spectatorship* (London: Routledge, 1993), 35.
86. Mayne, *Cinema and Spectatorship*, 77. See also Judith Mayne, "Paradoxes of Spectatorship," in *Viewing Positions: Ways of Seeing Film*, ed. Linda Williams (New Brunswick, NJ: Rutgers UniversityPress, 1995), 155–83, at 155.
87. Mayne, *Cinema and Spectatorship*, 72–73.
88. Ibid., 75.
89. Ibid., 76.
90. Ibid.
91. Ibid.
92. Linda Williams, "When the Woman Looks," in *The Dread of Difference: Gender and the Horror Film*, ed. Barry Keith Grant (Austin: University of Texas Press, 1996), 15–34, at 18.
93. Williams, "When the Woman Looks," 23.
94. Ibid.
95. Ibid., 27.
96. Carol J. Clover, "Her Body, Himself: Gender in the Slasher Film," *Representations* 20 (1987): 187–228, at 212.
97. Clover, "Her Body, Himself," 220.
98. Clover, "The Eye of Horror," in Williams, *Viewing Positions: Ways of Seeing Film*, 204.
99. "So common is the theme of failed gazing in horror that I would venture as a rule of the genre that *whenever* a man imagines himself as a controlling voyeur—imagines, in Lacanian terms, that his 'look' at women constitutes a gaze—some sort of humiliation is soon to follow, typically in the form of his being overwhelmed, in one form or another, by the sexuality of the very female he meant to master." Clover, "The Eye of Horror," 204.
100. Rhona J. Berenstein, "Spectatorship-as-Drag: The Act of Viewing and Classic Horror Film," in Williams, *Viewing Positions: Ways of Seeing Film*, 231–69, at 232.

Notes to Chapter 1

101. Berenstein, "Spectatorship-as-Drag," 250.
102. Ibid., 250–51.
103. Ibid., 251.
104. Ibid., 261–62.
105. Anne Friedberg, "Cinema and the Postmodern Condition," in Williams, *Viewing Positions: Ways of Seeing Film*, 59–83, at 62.
106. Friedberg, "Cinema and the Postmodern Condition," 63.
107. Ibid., 65.
108. Sabine Hake, *The Cinema's Third Machine: Writing on Film in Germany, 1907–1933* (Lincoln: University of Nebraska Press, 1993), 53.
109. Hake, *The Cinema's Third Machine*, 52.
110. Ibid.
111. Ibid., 99.
112. Mulvey, "Visual Pleasure and Narrative Cinema," 837.
113. Ibid., 838.
114. Clover, "The Eye of Horror," 203.
115. Elsaesser, *Weimar Cinema and After*, 207.
116. Noël Carroll, *The Philosophy of Horror; or, Paradoxes of the Heart* (New York: Routledge, 1990), 22.
117. S. S. Prawer, *Caligari's Children: The Film as Tale of Terror* (Oxford: Oxford University Press, 1980).
118. Carroll, *The Philosophy of Horror*, 32.
119. David J. Russell, "Monster Roundup: Reintegrating the Horror Genre," in *Refiguring American Film Genres: History and Theory*, ed. Nick Browne (Berkeley: University of California Press, 1998), 233–54, at 238.
120. Russell, "Monster Roundup," 237.
121. Steven Schneider, "Monsters as (Uncanny) Metaphors: Freud, Lakoff, and the Representation of Monstrosity in Cinematic Horror," in *Horror Film Reader*, ed. Alain Silver and James Ursini (New York: Limelight Editions, 2000), 167–91, at 169.
122. Schneider, "Monsters as (Uncanny) Metaphors," 174.
123. Prawer, *Caligari's Children*, 32.
124. Anton Kaes, "Silent Cinema," *Monatshefte* 82, no. 3 (1990): 246–56, at 250.
125. Prawer, *Caligari's Children*, 83.
126. Ibid., 48.
127. See Mikhail Bakhtin, *Rabelais and His World*, trans. Hélène Iswolsky (Cambridge, MA: MIT Press, 1968).
128. "Jene Art des Schreckhaften, welche auf das Altbekannte, Längstvertraute zurückgeht." English from: Sigmund Freud, "The 'Uncanny,'" *The Standard Edition of the Complete Psychological Works of Sigmund Freud*, ed. James Strachey, vol. 17 (London: Hogarth Press, 1955), 217–52, at 220. Original German in: Freud, "Das Unheimliche," *Gesammelte Werke* 12, 229–68, at 231.
129. English: Freud, "The 'Uncanny,'" 227. German: Freud, "Das Unheimliche," 238.
130. "Die Identifizierung mit einer anderen Person, so daß man an seinem Ich irre wird oder das fremde Ich an die Stelle des eigenen versetzt, also Ich-Verdopplung, Ich-Teilung, Ich-Vertauschung." English: Freud, "The 'Uncanny,'" 234. German: Freud, "Das Unheimliche," 246.
131. "Wenn die psychoanalytische Theorie in der Behauptung recht hat, daß jeder Affekt einer Gefühlsregung, gleichgültig von welcher Art, durch die Verdrängung in Angst verwandelt wird, so muß es unter den Fällen des Ängstlichen eine Gruppe geben, in der sich zeigen läßt, daß dies Ängstliche etwas wiederkehrendes Verdrängtes ist." English: Freud, "The 'Uncanny,'" 241. German: Freud, "Das Unheimliche," 254.
132. "Das Unheimliche des Erlebens kommt zustande, wenn *verdrängte* infantile Komplexe durch einen Eindruck wieder belebt werden oder wenn *überwundene* primitive Überzeugungen wieder bestätigt scheinen." English: Freud, "The 'Uncanny,'" 249. German: Freud, "Das Unheimliche," 263.
133. Cynthia Freeland, "Explaining the Uncanny in *The Double Life of Véronique*," in *Horror Film and Psychoanalysis: Freud's Worst Nightmare*, ed. Steven Jay Schneider (Cambridge: Cambridge University Press, 2004), 87–105, at 89.

134. Freeland, "Explaining the Uncanny," 92.
135. Ibid., 98.
136. "Das von verdrängten infantilen Komplexen ausgeht, vom Kastrationskomplex, der Mutterleibsphantasie usw." English: Freud, "The 'Uncanny,'" 248. German: Freud, "Das Unheimliche," 263.
137. "Selbst ein schlechtes Kinostück, über dessen Kitschigkeit ich mir vollkommen klar bin und über dessen Geschmacklosigkeit ich mich wohl auch ärgere, [wirkt] wie ein Zauber auf meine Stimmung und mein Gefühl. . . . Es ist mir—auch wenn das Stück in unserer gewohnten Wirklichkeit spielt—wie wenn ich eine Reise in ein anderes Land machte, wie wenn ich in eine fremde Stadt käme, in der ich die Menschen hasten und schaffen sehe, ohne daß ich mit ihrem Treiben etwas zu tun habe, weil ich alles rein als Zuschauer erlebe. Trete ich nach der Vorstellung wieder auf die Straße, so erscheint mir auch das gewohnte Leben irgendwie verwandelt und unwirklich. Auf diesem Herausgerissenwerden aus dem Gewohnten, auf diesem plötzlichen übergehen aus einer Realität in die andere . . . beruht, wie mir scheint, zum größten Teil der faszinierende Reiz des Filmtheaters und die ungeheure Anziehungskraft, die es ausübt." Ed. v. Bendemann, "Das Phantastische im Film. Der Kinostil," *Film-Kurier* (August 9, 1919): 1–2, at 1.
138. "Es leuchtet ein, daß das Hauptbedürfnis des Kinobesuchers, jene Sensation des Entrücktwerdens, viel vollkommener befriedigt wird, wenn auch der Gegenstand phantastisch und illusionär ist." Bendemann, "Das Phantastische im Film," 2.
139. "Wir haben eine Film-Phantastik—aber eine von der Literatur geborgte. Wir reproduzieren die Phantastik eines E. Th. A. Hoffmann, eines Eichendorff, eines Chamisso, eines Meyrinck: eine überbewußte, überwache Phantastik—in einer naiven, unterbewußten Kunst-Sphäre, nämlich in der Film-Sphäre. Das ist das Geheimnis des Mißerfolges." Willy Haas, "Der phantastische Film," *Kinematographische Monatshefte* (July 1922): 3–5, at 5.
140. Robert Spadoni, "The Uncanny Body of Early Sound Film," *Velvet Light Trap* 51 (2003): 4–16, at 11.
141. Spadoni, "The Uncanny Body of Early Sound Film," 12.

Chapter 2

1. "Im Unionpalast erscheint ein exotisches, von mystischer Spannung getragenes Filmspiel 'Die Augen der Mumie Ma' (Union), das bei seinen Zuschauern starkes und berechtigtes Interesse findet. . . . Der Film ist in einer gut aufgebauten, glaubhaft eingefädelten Folge lebendiger und spannender Bilder mit auffallendem Geschick für das Bildtechnische von Ernst Lubitsch in Szene gesetzt. Pola Negri spielt die Titelrolle: ihre erste Arbeit in ihrem neuen Engagement bei der Union. Zweifellos hat sie durch die treffliche Spielleitung eine Unterstützung gefunden, welche ihre ausgezeichneten darstellerischen Eigenschaften zu bestem, wirkungsvollem Gelingen zu leiten verstand. Nicht minder gut waren Emil Jannings und Harry Liedtke." Review of "Mumie Mâ," *Der Film* (October 12, 1918): 82.
2. Tom Gunning, "An Aesthetic of Astonishment: Early Film and the (In)Credulous Spectator," in Williams, *Viewing Positions: Ways of Seeing Film*, 114–33, at 123.
3. Thompson, "Lubitsch, Acting, and the Silent Romantic Comedy," 390.
4. "Pola Negri: Biografie," www.filmport.de, n.d.
5. Sabine Hake, *Passions and Deceptions: The Early Films of Ernst Lubitsch* (Princeton, NJ: Princeton University Press, 1992), 25.
6. Hake, *Passions and Deceptions*, 26.
7. Ibid., 28.
8. Ibid., 38.
9. Ibid., 37.
10. "Natürlich lachen wir heute über die Fahrigkeit übertriebener Gesten und über den Stand der 'Ausstattung.' . . . Das Publikum der Kamera, von historischen Reminiszenzen unbeschwert, nahm das ganze als köstlichen Jux." "Wiedersehen mit alten Filmen: 'Erotikon' und 'Die Augen der Mumie Ma' in der Kamera." *Kinematograph* 164 (August 25, 1933). Accessed via filmportal.de.
11. Thompson, "Lubitsch, Acting, and the Silent Romantic Comedy," 391.
12. Richard McCormick notes that "Pola Negri, the famous female actor who starred in a number of Lubitsch's films of this period, explained the success of the first of Lubitsch's costume films, *Die Augen der Mumie Mâ* (The Eyes of the Mummy Ma, 1918), as a product of 'its intensely

Notes to Chapter 2

romantic oriental fatalism,' which was 'precisely the kind of escapism that a war-weary people craved for.'" Richard McCormick, "Desire versus Despotism: The Politics of *Sumurun* (1920), Ernst Lubitsch's 'Oriental' Fantasy," in Rogowski, *The Many Faces of Weimar Cinema*, 67–83, at 67. McCormick is citing Pola Negri, *Memoirs of a Star* (Garden City, NY: Doubleday, 1970), 140.

13. Hake, *Passions and Deceptions*, 21.
14. Paul Lerner, "Hysterical Cures: Hypnosis, Gender, and Performance in World War I and Weimar Germany," *History Workshop Journal* 45 (Spring 1998): 79–101, at 80.
15. Lerner, "Hysterical Cures," 80.
16. Ibid., 89. Lerner is citing a letter from the State Health Office of Dresden to the minister of the interior from August 21, 1924.
17. Kaes, *Shell Shock Cinema*, 62–63.
18. Kristin Thompson, *Herr Lubitsch Goes to Hollywood: German and American Film after World War I* (Amsterdam: Amsterdam University Press, 2005), 21.
19. "Besuchte in Ägypten das Grabmal der Königin Mah [sic], überwältigte den dortigen Hüter Radu und entführte die von ihm gefangen gehaltene Inderin Mah, die er in Europa heiratete"; "seine entflohene Mah." *Paimanns Filmlisten*, July 26, 1918.
20. "Ein exotisches, von mystischer Spannung getragenes Filmspiel," *Der Film* (October 12, 1918): 82.
21. "Sehr interessantes Sujet, das die Grundlage zu dem Film bot und den Hauptdarstellern die Möglichkeit zur Entfaltung ihres höheren künstlerischen Könnens verschaffte"; "ganz im Banne des grandiosen Spiels von Pola Negri." *Lichtbild-Bühne*, October 5, 1918.
22. Rhona J. Berenstein, *Attack of the Leading Ladies: Gender, Sexuality, and Spectatorship in Classic Horror Cinema* (New York: Columbia University Press, 1996), 11.
23. Berenstein, *Attack of the Leading Ladies*, 91.
24. Noël Carroll, *Engaging the Moving Image* (New Haven, CT: Yale University Press, 2003), 91.
25. Like many of these early films, *Eyes of the Mummy* is divided into acts—here five of them—that are introduced in intertitles.
26. I base my analysis on the 35 mm version available at the Berlin Kinemathek. A version with English intertitles is also available (Alpha Home Entertainment, 2006). There are certain differences between the two versions; I will not enumerate these, touching on them only where they are of particular interest. In order to remain as true as possible to the German version, translations of intertitles are my own. Screen shots are taken from the Alpha Home Entertainment version.
27. Diane Negra, "Immigrant Stardom in Imperial America: Pola Negri and the Problem of Typology," in *A Feminist Reader in Early Cinema*, ed. Jennifer M. Bean and Diane Negra (Durham, NC: Duke University Press, 2002), 374–403, at 374.
28. Negra, "Immigrant Stardom in Imperial America," 388.
29. Hake, *Passions and Deceptions*, 46.
30. "Der junge Maler Albert Wendland befindet sich auf einer Studienreise in Aegypten."
31. The print of the film available through the Berlin Kinemathek explains the setting in an interestingly tongue-in-cheek prefatory title screen: "Die echt orientalischen Außenaufnahmen wurden in Kalkberge-Rüdersdorf gedreht" ("The authentic Oriental exterior shots were filmed in Kalkberge-Rüdersdorf").
32. "Der Besuch bei der Königin Mâ ist bisher noch Jedem verhängnisvoll geworden."
33. "Die Augen leben! Die Augen leben!"
34. Quoted in Linda Williams, "When the Woman Looks," in *The Dread of Difference: Gender and the Horror Film*, ed. Barry Keith Grant (Austin: University of Texas Press, 1996), 15–34, at 22.
35. Williams, "When the Woman Looks," 24.
36. Carroll, *Engaging the Moving Image*, 91.
37. Prawer, *Caligari's Children*, 167.
38. Ibid., 180.
39. "Wer bist Du, Mädchen?"
40. "Auf Deine Liebe verzichte ich—aber von nun ab wirst Du tun, was ich Dir befehle!"
41. "Seit diesem Tage befinde ich mich im Banne dieses Mannes."

Notes to Chapter 3

42. "Um Mâ mit der europäischen Bildung vertraut zu machen, lässt sie Wendland von einer Lehrerin unterrichten."
43. This moment in the scene, in which Mâ is distracted by the kitten, is not present in the film version; there, the sequence moves directly from the teacher lecturing Mâ to Wendland entering and the lesson being abandoned.
44. Here, again, the film version is missing a section available on the DVD; it does not show Mâ's initial reaction to the party, instead opening with the shot of Wendland circulating among guests, then, after an intertitle asking, "Wo ist denn Mâ," moving directly to the moment in which the crowd goes in search of her and discovers her in front of the mirror in her room.
45. Studlar, "Visual Pleasure and the Masochistic Aesthetic," 21.
46. "Spiel doch Mâ zu Liebe irgend etwas Orientalisches!"
47. "Das Mädel muss zum Varieté!"
48. "Tanzen! Tanzen! Tanzen!!"
49. While the DVD version highlights this moment in a medium close-up, the film version shows it only in the background of a long shot.
50. "In seinem Banne."
51. "Ich fühle es—mein Leben hängt davon ab!"
52. "Zu spät." This intertitle is shown later in the DVD version, which here inserts the same image of Mâ's body as we saw earlier from Radu's point of view, then inserts the intertitle after Wendland has placed Mâ's body on the chaise.
53. "Auch Fürst Hohenfels ist von seiner Orient-Reise zurückgekehrt."
54. "Ich flehe zu meinem Gott, mir den Weg zu der Treulosen zu weisen!"
55. *Lichtbild-Bühne*, October 5, 1918.
56. Stefan Andriopoulos, *Possessed: Hypnotic Crimes, Corporate Fiction, and the Invention of Cinema* (Chicago: University of Chicago Press, 2008), 103.
57. Andriopoulos, *Possessed*, 107.
58. "Er lebt, um Rache an mir zu nehmen."
59. Hake, *Passions and Deceptions*, 21.
60. Ibid., 46.
61. Ibid.
62. Friedberg, "Cinema and the Postmodern Condition," 65.
63. Ibid., 72.
64. Ibid., 63.

Chapter 3

The film was released in the United States under the title *Eerie Tales*, but here I draw on what I see as a more accurate translation of the original German.

1. "*Berliner Tageblatt*: 'Zum ersten Male ist hier eine Reihe von Filmeinaktern geboten, die auf einen ganz bestimmten Ton gestimmt sind. Diese Art ist neu. Es wird hier gewissermaßen der Beweis erbracht, daß zu einem wirksamen Film nicht Tausende von Statisten und eine Riesenaufmachung gehören, sondern daß sich dies auch auf einem anderen Wege erzielen läßt.' *B. Z. am Mittag*: 'Die Ambition, aus der ewig gleichen Langatmigkeit des Kinodramas wieder herauszufinden, ist sehr anzuerkennen. Und die Idee ist wohl richtig erfaßt, wenngleich sie hier, auf den ersten Anblick, noch lange nicht befriedigend gestaltet ist.'" "De Gustibus: 'Unheimliche Geschichten,'" *Film-Kurier*, November 11, 1919, 1.
2. "Diese fünf Einakter zeigen mit verblüffender Deutlichkeit, auf welchem Gebiet der Erfolg des Kinos zu suchen ist. Seit dem 'Student von Prag' ist meines Wissens ein derartig wirksamer Stoff noch nicht wieder verfilmt worden. Hier ist ureigenstes Filmland, und Richard Oswald war der berufene Führer, der mit geschickter Hand hier Wege zu ebnen und Ausblicke zu eröffnen verstand, die unbedingt Bewunderung auslösen müssen. Wie sehr verblassen neben der Phantastik, dem bunten Wirbel dieser wirklich spannenden Begebenheiten, die langatmigen und, leider muß es gesagt werden, oft auch recht langweiligen Salonfilme und literarischen Filme, die der

Notes to Chapter 3

Filmkunst noch immer viele Gegner erhalten." Review of "Unheimliche Geschichten," *Der Kinematograph* 671 (November 12, 1919).

3. "Reizvoller Versuch, die literarische Kleinkunst der Sprechbühne auch auf der Leinwand heimisch zu machen"; "im ganzen und in einzelnen Stücken ein ausgesprochener Erfolg"; "eine einheitliche Grundstimmung ist trotz des Titels nicht festgehalten"; "an sich [überflüssig]." Review of "Unheimliche Geschichten," *Der Film* 45 (November 2, 1919): 32.

4. For more information on Oswald, see Helga Belach and Wolfgang Jacobsen, *Richard Oswald: Regisseur und Produzent* (Munich: Text + Kritik, 1990); and Jürgen Kasten and Armin Loacker, *Richard Oswald: Kino zwischen Spektakel, Aufklärung und Unterhaltung* (Vienna: Filmarchiv Austria, 2005). Sources that examine Oswald in the context of his *Aufklärungsfilme* include Mel Gordon, "Erotica in the Service of Social Hygiene: Sexual Enlightenment Melodramas in Austro-Hungarian and Weimar German Cinema," in *From the Arthouse to the Grindhouse: Highbrow and Lowbrow Transgression in Cinema's First Century*, ed. John Cline and Robert G. Weiner (Lanham, MD: Scarecrow Press, 2010), 3–9; and Jill Suzanne Smith, "Richard Oswald and the Social Hygiene Film: Promoting Public Health or Promiscuity?" in Rogowski, *The Many Faces of Weimar Cinema*, 13–30.

5. Susan Laikin Funkenstein, "Anita Berber: Imaging a Weimar Performance Artist," *Woman's Art Journal* 26, no. 1 (2005): 26–31, at 26.

6. As Funkenstein notes, Weimar law "allowed for full nudity on stage if the performer was immobile, as in a tableau or in the background. . . . For dancing women, some covering over the genital region was legally required, and in accordance with these restrictions, most nude dancers performed only bare-breasted." Funkenstein, "Anita Berber: Imaging a Weimar Performance Artist," 28.

7. Funkenstein, "Anita Berber: Imaging a Weimar Performance Artist," 28.

8. Barbara Hales, "Mediating Worlds: The Occult as Projection of the New Woman in Weimar Culture," *German Quarterly* 83, no. 3 (2010): 317–32, at 327.

9. Sometimes also called anthology films, portmanteau films, or package films; in German, *Omnibusfilm, Anthologiefilm,* or *Episodenfilm*. While there have been few scholarly studies of such films as a genre, one that focuses on the genre (albeit narrowed to include only those by multiple directors) is Andreas Schreitmüller, ed., *Filme aus Filmen: Möglichkeiten des Episodenfilms* (Oberhausen: K. M. Laufen, 1983).

10. Donald Haase, "The *Arabian Nights*, Visual Culture, and Early German Cinema," *Fabula* 45, no. 3/4 (2004): 261–74, at 269.

11. Haase, "The *Arabian Nights*," 270.

12. Although older usage encompasses a more general sense of "girl," "Dirne" generally carries a sense of sexual transgression and would more suitably be translated as "harlot," "strumpet," even "prostitute."

13. Eve Kosofsky Sedgwick, *Between Men: English Literature and Male Homosocial Desire* (New York: Columbia University Press, 1985), 82.

14. All translations from credits and intertitles are my own. I base my analysis on the 35 mm print held at the Berlin Kinemathek.

15. Gunning, "An Aesthetic of Astonishment," 118.

16. "Richard Oswald's direction tied together the one-act pieces within a frame narrative à là Hoffmann's tales, thus making a film drama out of the separate parts." ("Die Regie Richard Oswalds band die Einakter nach Art von Hoffmann's Erzählungen in einem Rahmen zusammen, machte also aus den Einaktern wieder ein Kinodrama.") "De Gustibus: 'Unheimliche Geschichten,'" 1.

17. Thus Eduard von Bendemann laments: "We need an E. T. A. Hoffmann, a Poe, a Paul Scheerbart of cinema, who sets down his serious and grotesque dreams and visions not in words, but in images." ("Es müßte ein E. T. A. Hoffmann, ein Poe, ein Paul Scheerbart des Kinos erstehen, der seine Träume und Visionen, ernster und grotesker Art, nun nicht in Worten, sondern in Bildern niederlegte.") Bendemann, "Das Phantastische im Film," 1. Another critic, Willy Haas, criticizes more directly the tendency to borrow Hoffmann's style of the uncanny and attempt to transpose it onto film: "We have a tradition of the fantastic in film—but one that is borrowed from literature. We reproduce the fantastic of E. Th. A. Hoffmann, of Eichendorff, of Chamisso, of Meyrinck: an overly conscious, overly aware fantastic—in an artistic sphere that is naive and subconscious, that is

in film." ("Wir haben eine Film-Phantastik—aber eine von der Literatur geborgte. Wir reproduzieren die Phantastik eines E. Th. A. Hoffmann, eines Eichendorff, eines Chamisso, eines Meyrinck: eine überbewußte, überwache Phantastik—in einer naiven, unterbewußten Kunst-Sphäre, nämlich in der Film-Sphäre.") "Der Phantastische Film," *Kinematographische Monatshefte*, July 1922, 3–5, at 5.

18. "Daß ein wirklicher Film nur unter Berücksichtigung seiner ureigenen Technik geschrieben werden kann, daß also die sklavische Verwendung von der Literatur entlehnten Stoffen von vornherein seine Wirksamkeit erheblich in Frage stellen muß." G. V. Mendel, "Eigenschöpferische oder entlehnte Stoffe," *Kinematografische Monatshefte* (January/February 1924): 7–10, at 10.

19. Citing a statement by Martha Dix (the wife of Otto Dix, who painted Berber), Funkenstein notes the way in which Berber staged herself as sexually transgressive: "'[Berber] spent an hour putting on her make-up and drank a bottle of cognac at the same time. Yes, and the part about her walking the streets, that was par for the course. We went out for a walk in Wiesbaden . . . and she took advantage of every opportunity. Someone would approach her, and she would say: "200 Marks." I didn't find that very awful. She had to earn money somehow.' As Martha Dix did not explicitly state in her remembrance whether or not Berber completed the transaction, it is possible that Berber may have consciously performed this behavior to keep herself alive in the tabloids. Regardless of her financial need, Berber's public expected certain conduct, and offering herself sexually functioned as part of her cultivated persona." Funkenstein, "Anita Berber: Imaging a Weimar Performance Artist," 29.

20. "Niemand durfte erfahren, daß sie an der Pest gestorben war."

21. "The strong effect of this scene is, however, strongly undermined by the rather dry explanation at the end—the woman has died of the plague, her death is to be hushed up." ("Die starke Wirkung dieser Szene wird aber durch die etwas nüchterne Erklärung am Schluß—die Frau ist an der Pest verstorben, ihr Tod soll verheimlicht werden—sehr beeinträchtigt.") Review of *Unheimliche Geschichten*, *Der Film* 45 (November 2, 1919): 32.

22. "Trotz unserer Scheidung verfolgt er mich auf Schritt und Tritt."

23. "'Die Erscheinung' (nach Anselma Heine) blieb wohl allen . . . ganz unverständlich." Review of *Unheimliche Geschichten* from *B. Z. am Mittag*, cited in *Film-Kurier*, November 11, 1919, 1.

24. "Sie muß sich für einen von uns entscheiden."

25. Susan Laikin Funkenstein, "Fashionable Dancing: Gender, the Charleston, and German Identity in Otto Dix's 'Metropolis,'" *German Studies Review* 28, no. 1 (2005): 20–44, at 22.

26. Mulvey, "Visual Pleasure and Narrative Cinema," 837.

27. Funkenstein, "Anita Berber: Imaging a Weimar Performance Artist," 27.

28. "Bei völliger Ruhe können wir auch den Geist eines Verstorbenen zitieren."

29. Excerpted from a review in *Vossische Zeitung*, in "De Gustibus: 'Unheimliche Geschichten,'" *Film-Kurier*, November 11, 1919, 1.

30. "Hier kann sich die bildliche Darstellung in Phantasien ergehen, wie sie sonst nur den frei schweifenden Gedanken zu erträumen und den Worten auszudrücken möglich war. . . . All die Verwandlungen, Fabelwesen und Zaubereien, von denen wir in Märchen lesen, die auf der Bühne immer nur durch kümmerliche Surrogate ersetzt werden müssen, können jetzt geschaute Wirklichkeit werden." Bendemann, "Das Phantastische im Film," 1.

31. Hales, "Mediating Worlds: The Occult as Projection of the New Woman in Weimar Culture," 322.

32. Ibid., 326.

33. "Sehr fein hat Oswald hier die akustische Wirkung auf die optische umgeschaltet. Es löst im Film die beabsichtigte Wirkung viel stärker aus, wenn bei der Haussuchung plötzlich an der Stelle, wo die Tote eingemauert ist, der Kalk abbröckelt und die Wand sich zu lockern beginnt." Review of *Unheimliche Geschichten*, *Der Film* 45 (November 2, 1919): 32.

34. "Ebenso fein ist die Selbstironisierung, mit der das vierte und fünfte Stück ihre unheimliche Wirkung selbst aufheben." Review of *Unheimliche Geschichten*, *Der Film* 45 (November 2, 1919): 32.

35. "Die Dame ist meine Schwester, Sie befinden sich in einem Klub, den man freiwillig betritt, um ihn freiwillig nie wieder zu verlassen."

36. "Der Schreck hat ihn getötet."

37. "Wenn hier Reinhold Schünzel mit dem Blick auf die große Wanduhr die wenigen Minuten zählt, die ihn noch von seinem Tode trennen, wenn der Zeiger immer weiter vorrückt und die Uhr

schließlich zum zwölften Schlage aushebt, ohne daß sich Rettung zeigt, da hält man tatsächlich den Atem an." Review of *Unheimliche Geschichten, Der Kinematograph* 671 (November 12, 1919).
38. "Ich junge Frau—es ist zum Lachen!— / Ich sitze ganz vereinsamt hier. / Mein Mann beschäftigt sich mit allen Sachen, / Nur nicht—mit mir."
39. "Fremd ist mir Furcht. Mir strafft die Glieder / des Mannesmutes Feuerbrand. / Im Zweikampft stach ich lächelnd nieder / Erst gestern einen Leutenant."
40. "Der Mann hat Mut! In seiner Nähe / Fühlt jede Frau sich neu gestählt. / Ganz anders ist's, wenn ich Dich sehe, / Dich, dem zum Manne alles fehlt."
41. "Man ruft in eiligem Alarme / Mich fort in wichtiger Mission. / Ich leg' in Ihre starken Arme / Mein Weib zum Schutze, Herr Baron."
42. "Ein mut'ger Mann! Bei seinem Handeln / Bewies er Mut, der mir gebricht. / Mit meiner Frau mal anzubandeln, / Den Mut, den hab' ich nämlich nicht."
43. "Zu mir fühlst Liebe Du entbrennen? / Wenn eine Frau den Gatten küßt, / Muß das man 'ne Geschichte nennen, / die wirklich ganz unheimlich ist."
44. "Mit geschickter Anpassung an die Bedürfnisse des Kinopublikums, sind nur die ersten drei Stücke auf das Grausige gestellt." Review of *Unheimliche Geschichten, Der Film* 45 (November 2, 1919): 32.
45. Although the official title of the film when released in the United States was, inexplicably, *The Living Dead*, I will refer to it as *Uncanny Tales*, thus drawing on a more literal translation of the German title.
46. "Richard Oswald hat seine 'Unheimlichen Geschichten,' mit denen er sich dereinst den Erfolg in der Stummfilmzeit holten, für den Tonfilm, umgeformt, mit Glück wieder aufgenommen." Review of *Unheimliche Geschichten, Film-Kurier*, September 8, 1932.
47. "In unserer Zeit, die sich trotz der Neusachlichkeit immer wieder mit transzendentalen Dingen befaßt, hat der Film des Unheimlichen seine Auferstehung gefunden." Review of *Unheimliche Geschichten, Film-Kurier*, September 8, 1932.
48. Hans Wollenberg, review of *Unheimliche Geschichten, Lichtbild-Bühne*, September 8, 1932.
49. "Was aber in diesem Film grausig und unheimlich ist, beruht auf menschlicher Einbildung und Phantasie. . . . Das Unheimliche weicht endgültig der Sphäre krankhaften Verbrechens, das durch einen sehr diesseitigen jungen Mann aufgeklärt wird." Review of *Unheimliche Geschichten, Der Film* (September 10, 1932).
50. Robert Spadoni, *Uncanny Bodies: The Coming of Sound Film and the Origins of the Horror Genre* (Berkeley: University of California Press, 2007), 32.
51. The German specifically implies a masculine subject in the adjectival noun. The 35 mm version of the film with which I worked at the Berlin Kinemathek retains this working title.

Chapter 4

This chapter is a revised and extended version of my article "Schatten: Eine nächtliche Halluzination: Staging the Punishment for Women's Emancipation," *New German Critique* 120, no. 3 (2013): 41–64.

1. Although the title under which the film has been released in the United States is *Warning Shadows*, a literal translation would be *Shadows: A Nocturnal Hallucination*. Of the films I examine in this study, *Warning Shadows* is one of the few that has a well-done restoration widely available; given the quality of that version, I base my analysis here on it: Artur Robison, *Warning Shadows* (New York: Kino International, 2006).
2. Bernd Widdig, *Culture and Inflation in Weimar Germany* (Berkeley: University of California Press, 2001), 37.
3. Artur Robison biography (in English), www.filmportal.de, n.d., accessed December 12, 2011.
4. Ibid.
5. "Eine Kunstleistung, die dem deutschen Film neue Wege weisen, seinen Ruf über alle Länder der Erde verbreiten helfen wird." Review of *Schatten, Kinematographische Monatshefte* 7 (1923): 8.
6. "Der zum erstenmal auch dem schärfsten Kinogegner beweist: hier gibt es eine neue Kunstgattung mit eigenen Gesetzen, in denen ebensogut Höchstes geleistet werden kann, wie in der Malerei, der Bildhauerei, der Musik usw." Paul Hildebrandt, "Schatten: Eine Analyse," *Kinematographische Monatshefte* 10/11 (1923): 1–4, at 1.

Notes to Chapter 4

7. "Wir haben inzwischen die Wegner-Filme [sic] gesehen . . . und wir konnten auf die einzigartige Bedeutung dieses Reformators des Spielfilms hinweisen; wir sahen gute historische Filme wie die "Dubarry" und "Anna Boleyn," wir lernten an den Filmen der Svenska, daß in der einheitlichen Geschlossenheit der schwedischen Bauernkultur ein Element läge, das den dortigen Film sozusagen a priori dem deutschen überlegen mache; wir fanden im "Caligari" und "Nosferatu" die Note des Phantastisch-Unheimlichen aufs stärkste angeschlagen—und doch ist allen diesen Filmen weitaus der Schatten überlegen, weil er alle ihre Vorzüge in eins zusammenrafft und schlechterdings das Höchste gibt, das bis jetzt geleistet ist, vielleicht das überhaupt Höchsterreichbare." Hildebrandt, "Schatten: Eine Analyse," 1.
8. "Es ist etwas durchaus Ungewöhnliches in diesen Heften, daß einem einzigen Film zwei Aufsätze gewidmet werden. Indessen—die alles, was wir bis jetzt von deutschen und ausländischen Erzeugnissen sahen, überragende Bedeutung der 'Schatten' rechtfertigt die Abweichung von der Regel." ("It is truly unusual in this magazine to dedicate two essays to a single film. Still, the significance of "Schatten," which far exceeds everything which we have thus far seen from German and foreign productions, justifies breaking this rule.") Hildebrandt, "Schatten: Eine Analyse," 1.
9. Hildebrandt is referring to a meeting in Stettin in April 1917, where various potential reforms for film were discussed. For more information on the meeting, see Tilman Welther, *Medienrevolutionen und Redereflexe—die Etablierung neuer Medien im Spiegel ihrer Diskurse* (Germany: GRIN Verlag, 2008), 14–15.
10. "Fast in allen Kritiken fand ich rühmend hervorgehoben, daß der Film keine Titel hat, also die Erfüllung einer Forderung, die 1917 auf der Stettiner Tagung erhoben wurde. Daß die 'Schatten' auch so verständlich bleiben, ja, daß Titel hier nur störend wirken würden, liegt nach dem Gesagten daran, daß primitive Triebe sich mimisch ohne weiteres ausdrücken, mithin unmittelbar durch das Bild zum Zuschauer sprechen; daß die Titel hier nur stören würden, liegt an der Sphäre, in der sich der Film abspielt: im Phantastischen, mit dem sich Rationales nicht verträgt." Hildebrandt, "Schatten: Eine Analyse," 4.
11. "Aber zugleich erspart uns der Autor das Letzte: die furchtbare Spannung, die dieses Filmwerk gewiß auch als Kunstwerk, aber doch nicht als *das* Kunstwerk, das letztmögliche empfinden ließe. Wir *wissen* ja durch die Rahmenhandlung bereits, daß alle diese Furchtbarkeiten, dieses Hinmorden der Frau, dieses Wahnsinnigwerden des Mannes, diese Gewalttat der Kavaliere nichts Wirkliches mehr ist. Es ist 'die andere Seite ihres Wesens,' die sich ans Licht drängt—symbolisch ausgedrückt dadurch, daß sie plötzlich unter der Beschwörung des Gauklers an der anderen Seite des Tisches erscheinen. Dadurch ist der Raum für das Ungeheuerlichste geschaffen, für eine Traumwelt, eine Welt der blinden Triebe, der letzten Möglichkeiten, in der sich die Leidenschaften ohne Hemmungen austoben, ohne doch uns in dem Allerletzten unserer Seele als *Wirklichkeiten*, wohl aber als *Wahrheiten* zu berühren." Hildebrandt, "Schatten: Eine Analyse," 2.
12. "Der gute Film . . . der einzig wahre Film, das ist der titellose Film." Walter Jonas, "Warum keine Titel," *Film-Kurier*, January 14, 1924, n.p.
13. "Ich höre schon die Antwort: zunächst allgemeine Phrasen wie "optisches Erlebnis". . . "bildhaft gesehen". . . "visuell" und was dergleichen Wörtchen mehr sind, die sich ja immer zur rechten Zeit einstellen, wenn die Begriffe fehlen. Dann aber kommt das eigentliche Argument (das einzige): Texte seien eine Entlehnung aus der Literatur und der Film, der sei ja etwas ganz Selbstverständiges, sei optisch, habe nichts mit anderen Kunstgattungen zu tun, nichts mit der Epik, der Bühne, der Musik, der Malerei." Jonas, "Warum keine Titel."
14. "Es ist bezeichnend, daß die Manie des titellosen Films in Deutschland entstand, denn bei uns ist es von jeher üblich, organisches Wachstum durch starre Theorien einzuengen, durch müßige Spekulationen allzu witziger Köpfe, ohne jede Beziehung zum Leben; erst die (halb durchdachte) ästhetische Doktrin, dann die Kunst (siehe Expressionismus)!" Jonas, "Warum keine Titel."
15. "Weniger dem Verfasser, der es mit der überlegen lächelnden Geste des Beneidenswerten mit der soliden Hirnschale abprallen lassen wird—und dem heimlichen Kitzel, so ernst genommen worden zu sein—als für den mit andern Dingen beschäftigten Leser, der zum titellosen Film noch keine Einstellung hat." Artur Robison, "Warum kein titelloser Film? Eine Erwiderung," *Beiblatt zum Film-Kurier* 17, January 19, 1924.

16. "Dem Durchschnittsgeschmack entsprechend Unterhaltungsfilme geben müssen und zweitens, weil sich nur wenige Themen zur reinen, wortlosen Filmgestaltung eignen." Robison, "Warum kein titelloser Film? Eine Erwiderung."
17. "Den Film ein Kompositum zu nennen, ist eine alte und oberflächliche Definition, ihn ein Kompositum aus Bild und Wort zu nennen, ist ein Nonsens. Und selbst wenn man die Analyse 'der Film ist eine Mischkunst' als exakt hinnehmen wollte, so wäre damit doch noch nicht bewiesen, daß er auch das Wort als Komponente enthalten muß." Robison, "Warum kein titelloser Film? Eine Erwiderung."
18. "auf diesem allzu-persönlichen Boden nur noch wenige, sachlich fruchtbare Perspektiven." Editorial note to Walter Jonas, "Nochmals der titellose Film," *Film-Kurier*, January 23, 1924.
19. "zwei wirklich gelungene Versuche, titellose Filme zu schaffen." The other of the two films Jonas cites is Lupu Pick's *Scherben* (1921). Jonas, "Nochmals der titellose Film."
20. "Die Monopolbestrebungen der Propagatoren des titellosen Films." Jonas, "Nochmals der titellose Film."
21. "Film mit Titeln = Unterhaltungssache, Film ohne Titel = Kunstwerk." Jonas, "Nochmals der titellose Film."
22. Kracauer, *From Caligari to Hitler*, 114.
23. Ibid., 112.
24. Ibid., 114.
25. Frances Guerin, *A Culture of Light: Cinema and Technology in 1920s Germany* (Minneapolis: University of Minnesota Press, 2005), 106.
26. James C. Franklin, "Metamorphosis of a Metaphor: The Shadow in Early German Cinema," *German Quarterly* 53, no. 2 (1980): 176–88, at 182.
27. Franklin, "Metamorphosis of a Metaphor," 182.
28. Heide Schlüpmann, *The Uncanny Gaze: The Drama of Early German Cinema* (Urbana: University of Illinois Press, 2010), 9–10.
29. Schlüpmann, *The Uncanny Gaze*, 15.
30. Joan Riviere, "Womanliness as Masquerade," *International Journal of Psychoanalysis* 10 (1929): 303–13, at 313.
31. Riviere, "Womanliness as Masquerade," 305.
32. In addition to suggesting an allegorical dimension to the narrative, this peculiarity also serves to maintain the ambiguity of the film; for example, it is never certain whether the youth is "only" the wife's most ardent admirer or, in fact, her lover.
33. Sabine Hake, "Self-Referentiality in Early German Cinema," *Cinema Journal* 31, no. 3 (1992): 37–55, at 44.
34. Sigmund Freud, *Die Traumdeutung* (1900), in *Gesammelte Werke* 2 (Frankfurt am Main: Fischer, 1998), 227–78, at 244.
35. Freud, "Das Unheimliche" (1919), *Gesammelte Werke* 12, 247.
36. Studlar, "Visual Pleasure and the Masochistic Aesthetic," 21.
37. Andriopoulos, *Possessed*, 107.
38. Kaes, *Shell Shock Cinema*, 49.
39. Hake, *The Cinema's Third Machine*, 99–100.

Chapter 5

This chapter is an expanded and reworked version of my earlier essay, "'These Hands Are Not My Hands': War Trauma and Masculinity in Crisis in Robert Wiene's *Orlacs Hände* (1924)," in *The Many Faces of Weimar Cinema: Rediscovering Germany's Filmic Legacy*, ed. Christian Rogowski (Rochester, NY: Camden House, 2010), 102–15.

1. L. K. Fredrik, Review of *Genuine*, *Film-Kurier*, September 3, 1920, 1.
2. For more information on Robert Wiene, see Uli Jung and Walter Schatzberg, *Robert Wiene: Der Caligari-Regisseur* (Berlin: Henschel, 1995).
3. Jung and Schatzberg, *Robert Wiene: Der Caligari-Regisseur*, 116.

Notes to Chapter 5

4. See, for example, the discussion of such fears connected to organ transplants in Bruce M. Hood et al., "Moral Contagion Attitudes towards Potential Organ Transplants in British and Japanese Adults," *Journal of Cognition and Culture* 11, no. 3–4 (2011): 269–86.
5. "Die Hoffnung, daβ aus Wien bald ein Film von groβer Klasse kommen möge, hat lange auf sich warten lassen, ehe dieser Pan-Film unter Robert Wienes Regie zu uns kam." Peterhans, review of *Orlacs Hände, Der Film* 6 (February 8, 1925): 38.
6. "Eine Etappe auf dem Wege zum künstlerischen Film." Heinz Michaelis, review of *Orlacs Hände*, *Film-Kurier* 28, February 1, 1925.
7. "Warum muβ sich dieser geheimnisvolle Unbekannte plötzlich als ein trivialer Verbrecher aus der kriminalistischen Chronik der Tageszeitungen entpuppen, nachdem der Zuschauer sich schon darauf eingerichtet hat, in ihm eine Art 'Revenant' zu sehen? Und wiβt [sic] ihr auch, daβ ein solcher Stimmungsumschlag sogar den von euch doch mit so glühender Inbrunst ersehnten Publikumserfolg gefährden kann?" Michaelis, review of *Orlacs Hände*.
8. "Leider ist seine Mimik nicht immer frei von Bewuβtheit, von der berühmten Conrad Veidt-Note, die bei ihm schon mitunter Klischee geworden ist." Michaelis, review of *Orlacs Hände*.
9. Review of *The Hands of Orlac*, *Variety*, June 20, 1928.
10. In this sense, *The Hands of Orlac* functions like so many other films of the era, which Kaes argues in his *Shell Shock Cinema* can and should be read as directly thematizing the experience of war, in spite of not being "war films" per se. Similarly, Jay Winter writes that "the Great War was the biggest industrial accident in history, but not only did it create more injuries than any that came before, it also transformed the framework of compensation and treatment for such industries" (29). This notion parallels that of the train accident standing in for the war; war itself becomes representable in other guises, with its effect mirrored by other "accidents" tied to modernity. Winter's essay presents an interesting overview of the ways in which shell shock was treated and made into a "metaphor about the war" (39) in culturally specific ways. Jay Winter, "Shell Shock and the Lives of the Lost Generation," in *War Wounds: Medicine and the Trauma of Conflict*, ed. Ashley Ekins and Elizabeth Stewart (Wollombi, Australia: Exisle, 2011), 28–40.
11. "Liebste! In 24 Stunden werde ich bei Dir sein und Dich in meine Arme schlieβen. Meine Hände werden Dein Haar streicheln, und Dein heiβer Körper wird in meiner Umarmung erbeben." All translations of intertitles are my own.
12. One of the difficulties that arises in the analysis of early films in general and that seems particularly acute in connection with *Orlacs Hände* is that there exist so many versions with fairly significant differences. The first—and apparently most complete—version I have been able to see was the 35 mm version available for rental through the Friedrich-Wilhelm-Murnau Stiftung in Wiesbaden, Germany, and presented at the German Film Institute symposium at the University of Michigan, Ann Arbor, August 6–12, 2006. This version, importantly, includes the actual depiction of the initial train collision, while all other version with which I have worked omit this. The Kinemathek Berlin holds a 35 mm and an identical VHS version; in these, the collision is not shown, nor is the sequence showing Paul's final concert included. Finally, a restored DVD version that is fairly complete, omitting only the initial train accident, is available for purchase through Kino Video. Although the bulk of my analysis and, in particular, the cited intertitles are based on the version held at the Kinemathek Berlin, I include analysis of the initial crash scene, as depicted in the version I viewed at Ann Arbor, as well as examinations of a number of other moments omitted in the Kinemathek version, in particular the shot of Orlac performing in the concert and his strangely erotic interaction with Regine, their maid. When including analysis of a sequence omitted in the Kinemathek version, I have noted this.
13. As noted, the initial accident is omitted from all but the print I was able to screen at Ann Arbor; however, the aftermath is shown in all versions I have screened.
14. Freud, "Gutachten über die elektrische Behandlung der Kriegsneurotiker," *Gesammelte Werke: Nachtragsband*, 706.
15. As John D. Barlow notes in his discussion of this scene: "The train wreck, although staged entirely with a naturalistic set, is shot to highlight its disorder. As in the set of *Raskolnikow*, there are no parallel lines. We find instead an emphasis on crisscrossings and oblique angles, all shot in a

Notes to Chapter 5

shadowy atmosphere, with steam from the rescue train floating through the transecting searchlight beams." John D. Barlow, *German Expressionist Film* (Boston: Twayne Publishers, 1982), 59.

16. "Retten Sie seine Hände! Sie bedeuten ihm das Leben! . . . Retten Sie seine Hände! Sie sind für ihn mehr als das Leben."
17. "Hier haben Sie Ihren Mann zurück. Nun unterliegt er Ihrer Obhut."
18. See also Ursula von Keitz's discussion of this in "Prothese und Transplantat: *Orlacs Hände* und die Körperfragment-Topik nach dem Ersten Weltkrieg," in *Unheimlich anders: Doppelgänger, Monster, Schattenwesen im Kino*, ed. Christine Rüffert et al. (Berlin: Bertz + Fischer, 2005), 62.
19. "Du hast so schöne, leuchtende Augen, . . . ich kann mich nicht genug daran satt sehen, . . . und solch weiches Haar." The statement is slightly jarring: it seems to be a more "fitting" utterance for a man, yet the placement of the intertitle and the fact that Orlac is depicted as being largely silent while interacting with his wife suggests that it is, indeed, Yvonne whose statement we witness.
20. "Deine Hände, deine lieben Hände werden für mich sorgen."
21. "Dort, . . . dort hinten ist ein Kopf, . . . er schaut auf mich, . . . auf meine Hände."
22. "Er lacht über mich! Der Tod lacht über mich!"
23. "Sagt mir, was ist mit meinen Händen los? Was versteckt ihr unter diesen Hüllen?"
24. "Werden diese Hände wieder so spielen können wie einst?"
25. "In einem gesunden Körper wohnt ein gesunder Geist. Wenn Ihre Hände heilen, wird Ihr Geist sich durch die Fertigkeit Ihrer Hände der Menschheit offenbaren."
26. "Seine Hände waren nicht mehr zu retten. Dr. Seral hat sie durch die Hände eines Toten ersetzt, die Hände des Mörders Vasseur."
27. "Es stimmt also? Ich habe die Hände eines Mörders?"
28. "Diese Hände dürfen kein Lebewesen berühren."
29. Von Keitz, "Prothese und Transplantat," 63.
30. "Der Mörder Vasseur vor Gericht . . . Vasseur leugnet immer noch, ist aber durch Fingerabdrücke, die man am Tatort fand, überführt. . . . Das Stilett trug am Griff das Zeichen X, und darauf fand man die Fingerabdrücke Vasseurs. Somit war bewiesen, daß Vasseur der Mörder war."
31. "Ich spüre, wie er von mir Besitz ergreift, von meinen Schultern, . . . meinem Gehirn . . . kalt, . . . furchterregend und grauenvoll."
32. "Verfluchte Hände!"
33. "Komm mir nicht nahe . . . geh!" This or an intertitle to a similar effect is present in all versions of the film I viewed excepting the print held at the Kinemathek Berlin.
34. "Aber ich, kann ich denn anders! Habe ich denn nicht dieses Verfluchte in mir? Das Feuer, die Stimme, die Qual? . . . immer spür ich, da ist einer hinter mir her, das bin ich selber, das verfolgt mich."
35. The scene with the creditors is omitted from the print held at the Kinemathek.
36. "Ich darf niemanden zu ihm lassen, schon gar nicht von euch."
37. "Paul kann nicht mehr spielen. Armut droht uns. Er ahnt noch nichts. Helfen Sie uns!"
38. "Es ist doch Ihr Sohn, Ihr eigen Fleisch und Blut. Sie können ihn doch nicht im Stich lassen."
39. "Ich kenne meinen Sohn und dessen Frau nicht mehr. Ich habe keine Verwandten!"
40. "Ich kann es nicht mehr hören, kann es nicht mehr ertragen, . . . ich traue Dir nicht mehr, . . . auch wenn Du mich töten wolltest, . . . ich kann Dir nicht mehr zu Willen sein."
41. "Verzeih' mir! Ich verspreche Dir, nie mehr ungehorsam zu sein."
42. "Morgen gehe ich selbst zu seinem Vater, wenn du ihn nicht dazu bewegen kannst."
43. "Mich hat er abgewiesen, trotzdem ich ihn händeringend darum bat."
44. "Verführe seine Hände." This scene is not included in the print of the film held at the Berlin Kinemathek; however, since it was present in all other versions I was able to view and given its significance in elucidating further the specifics of the hostility Orlac exhibits toward his wife, it bears examination here.
45. "Wie Mörderhände."
46. The Kinemathek print omits Yvonne's role in pushing her husband to go to the police.
47. "Wenn Vasseur kein Mörder war, dann sind ja meine Hände unschuldig."
48. Von Keitz reads this element of the film in a similar manner in her analysis of *Orlacs Hände*, though she focuses on Orlac's psychosis not as a representation of a response to the trauma of

Notes to Chapter 6

the First World War and to postwar social change, but rather as a result of a problematic relationship to his fragmented body. "Prothese und Transplantat," 61.

49. The first ending discussed is that to the print held at the Berlin Kinemathek; this second one is the ending present in all other versions viewed.
50. Klaus Kreimeier, "Notorisch anders: Conrad Veidt: Zur schauspielerischen Repräsentation der Devianz," in *Unheimlich anders: Doppelgänger, Monster, Schattenwesen im Kino*, ed. Christine Rüffert et al. (Berlin: Bertz + Fischer, 2005), 69–76, at 74. My translation.
51. Freud, "Introduction to *Psychoanalysis and the War Neuroses*," *The Standard Edition of the Complete Psychological Works of Sigmund Freud*, ed. James Strachey, vol. 17 (London: Hogarth Press), 205–10, at 209. Original German in: Freud, "Einleitung zu Zur Psychoanalyse der Kriegsneurosen" (1919), *Gesammelte Werke* 12, 323.
52. Freud, "Gutachten über die elektrische Behandlung der Kriegsneurotiker" (1920), *Gesammelte Werke: Nachtragsband*, 707. English translation taken from Freud, "Memorandum on the Electrical Treatment of War Neurotics," *The Standard Edition*, vol. 17, 212.
53. McCormick, *Gender and Sexuality in Weimar Modernity*, 20.
54. See also von Keitz, "Prothese und Transplantat," 61–62.
55. Mulvey, "Visual Pleasure and Narrative Cinema," 838.
56. Ibid., 837.
57. Ibid., 838.
58. Doane, *The Desire to Desire*, 40.
59. Ibid., 41.
60. Ibid., 39.
61. This is, as discussed, the closing sequence present in all versions except that held at the Kinemathek.

Chapter 6

1. For more information on Ewers, see Reinhold Keiner, *Hanns Heinz Ewers und der phantastische Film* (Hildesheim: Olms, 1988); Marion Knobloch, *Hanns Heinz Ewers: Bestseller-Autor in Kaiserreich und Weimarer Republik* (Marburg: Tectum, 2002); Hans Krüger-Welf, *Hanns Heinz Ewers: Die Geschichte seiner Entwicklung* (Leipzig: Rainer Wunderlich, 1922); Michael Sennewald, *Hanns Heinz Ewers: Phantastik und Jugendstil* (Meisenheim am Glan: A. Hain, 1973).
2. "Luna erklärte, daß ihre 'Alraune' nach dem Roman von Hanns Heinz Ewers verfaßt sei, also der richtige erste 'Alraune'-Film wäre, während Neutral geltend machte, daß sie im April 1918 von dem Autor F. das Manuskript zu einem Film 'Alraune' erworben habe, dessen Stoff an die Sage von der Alraunwurzel anschließe." "'Alraune' vor Gericht," *Der Film* (April 5, 1919): 38.
3. There was also another 1919 film, titled *Alraune and the Golem* (*Alraune und der Golem*) and directed by Nils Chrisander for Bioscop, which likely did not draw on elements of the novel.
4. "Jenseits von gut und böse." Review of *Alraune*, *Film-Kurier*, January 26, 1928.
5. The main character in Frank Wedekind's Lulu play. Originally published as two parts: "Earth Spirit" ("Erdgeist," 1895) and "Pandora's Box" ("Die Büchse der Pandora," 1902).
6. *Metropolis*, 1927.
7. *Der blaue Engel* (*The Blue Angel*, 1930).
8. David Davidson, "From Virgin to Dynamo: The 'Amoral Woman' in European Cinema," *Cinema Journal* 21, no. 1 (1981): 31–58, at 48.
9. Davidson, "From Virgin to Dynamo," 48.
10. "Langweilig-braven Mädchenfiguren." Daniel Semler, *Brigitte Helm: Der Vamp des deutschen Films* (Munich: Belleville, 2008), 44.
11. Semler, *Brigitte Helm*, 45.
12. Andreas Huyssen, "The Vamp and the Machine: Technology and Sexuality in Fritz Lang's *Metropolis*," *New German Critique* 24–25 (1981/82): 221–37, at 227.
13. Huyssen, "The Vamp and the Machine," 227.
14. Ibid., 228.
15. Ibid., 231.

Notes to Chapter 6

16. The biography of Henrik Galeen at filmportal.de notes that neither the details of Galeen's early life nor his credit as coauthor of the screenplay of Wegener's 1920 film can be verified. "Henrik Galeen: Biografie," www.filmportal.de, n.d., accessed January 27, 2013.
17. "Zwei Möglichkeiten standen ihm offen: Den Weg einer Dirne zu schildern, die rotes Blut trinkt und kindlich bleibt bei allem Elend, das sie anrichtet. Dazu brauchte es nicht unbedingt der konstruktiven Mischung von Gehenkten-Samen und Dirnenschoß. Oder aber, es wurde eine Spukgeschichte daraus, eine Filmfabel, mit unheimlichen Licht- und Schattenwirkungen. . . . Henrik Galeen, zu gründlich, sucht zwei Stilarten zusammenzukoppeln. Eine Alraune entsteht aus dieser Retorte indessen nicht." Review of *Alraune*, *Film-Kurier*, January 26, 1928.
18. Valerie Weinstein, "Henrik Galeen's *Alraune* (1927): The Vamp and the Root of Horror," in Rogowski, *The Many Faces of Weimar Cinema*, 198–210, at 199.
19. "Lulu, die Erbschlange." Review of *Alraune*, *Film-Kurier*, January 26, 1928.
20. "Geistige Anverwandte von Wedekinds Lulu." Dr. R. P., review of *Alraune*, *Deutsche Filmzeitung*, March 9, 1928, 7.
21. Intertitles for Galeen's version of *Alraune* are taken from a DVD copy located on eBay; there is no identifying company/publisher information.
22. Weinstein, "Henrik Galeen's *Alraune* (1927)," 204.
23. Studlar, "Visual Pleasure and the Masochistic Aesthetic," 8.
24. Ibid., 23.
25. Ibid.
26. Weinstein, "Henrik Galeen's *Alraune* (1927)," 202–3.
27. Ibid., 203.
28. Ibid., 205.
29. "'Alraune' als Tonfilm—die Ufa hat sich um des sicheren Theatergeschäfts willen und wegen der Bombenrolle für Brigitte Helm zu diesem Programmfilm entschlossen." "'Alraune' als Tonfilm," *Film-Kurier*, December 3, 1930, 1.
30. "Daß dies der einzige Fall ist, in dem in beiden Fassungen die Hauptrolle von derselben Person gespielt wurde, was nach dem ersten großen Erfolg Brigitte Helms eigentlich selbstverständlich schien." L. v. Seuffert, "On revient toujours: Doppelverfilmungen," *Deutsche Filmzeitung* (February 6, 1931): 1–3, at 3.
31. "[Er] schuf eine neue Alraune, eine völlig verschiedene ihres alten Vorbildes: statt des bösen, triebhaften Pensionsmädchens ein junges Geschöpf, ahnungslos gegenüber dem Schicksal, das über ihr liegt, Unheil um sich verbreitend; statt des sich durch dämonische Gemeinheit rächendes Weibes die liebende, wissende Frau, die aus dem Leben geht, weil sie den Fluch, der auf ihr liegt, nicht mit dem Mann, den sie liebt, teilen will." Brigitte Helm, "Alraune und ich," *Filmwelt*, December 7, 1930. Reproduced in Semler, *Brigitte Helm*, 101.
32. Semler notes the contrast between the mobility of her body and the immobility of her face: "That sinuous, supple body contrasts tantalizingly with her classical profile that appears as though sculpted in stone and her minimal facial expressions." ("Dieser geschmeidige, biegsame Körper steht in aufreizendem Widerspruch zu ihrem wie aus Stein gehauen wirkenden klassischen Profil und ihrem reduzierten Mienenspiel.") Semler, *Brigitte Helm*, 11.
33. See Spadoni, "The Uncanny Body of Early Sound Film." He expands on this in Spadoni, *Uncanny Bodies*.
34. Spadoni, *Uncanny Bodies*, 2.
35. Ibid., 6.
36. Ibid., 7.
37. Mihaela Petrescu, "Unmasking Brigitte Helm and Marlene Dietrich: The Vamp in German Romantic Comedies (1930–33)," in Rogowski, *The Many Faces of Weimar Cinema*, 299–316, at 300.
38. Petrescu, "Unmasking Brigitte Helm and Marlene Dietrich," 300.
39. "Meine wissenschaftlichen Experimente erfordern ungeheure Mittel . . . sonst wären wir beide wohl nie zusammengekommen." My analysis of Oswald's version of Alraune is based on the 35 mm print available at the Berlin Kinemathek; all translations of the dialogue are my own.
40. "Das Ding hier ist heruntergefallen, hat eine deiner alten, kostbaren Vasen zerschlagen."

Notes to Conclusion

41. "Das ist eine Alraune. Man nennt sie auch Mandragora. Eine Wunderwurzel, nach dem Aberglaube bringt sie ihrem Besitzer Glück und Reichtum, aber Unglück und Tod, wenn er sich von ihr trennt. . . . Merkwürdig ist die Sage von der Entstehung dieser Wurzel. In dem Augenblick, da ein Gehenkter sein Leben aushaucht, empfängt die Erde seine letzte Kraft. Durch die Paarung von Mensch und Erde sind diese Wurzeln entstanden. . . . Gerade diese unscheinbare Wurzel war für mich der Ausgangspunkt für meine Experimente zur künstliche Befruchtung."
42. Weinstein, "Henrik Galeen's *Alraune* (1927)," 205.
43. "Wenn mich Männer betrügen / Ist es mir ein Vergnügen / ich such mir einen andern / Es gibt so viel. / Wenn mich Männer verlassen / Kann ich niemals sie hassen / Ich bin's nicht anders gewöhnt / Es lässt mich kühl. / Ja ich bedanke mich noch / Dass es so lange gewährt / Und fühl mich aus diesem Grund / Direkt geehrt. / . . . Du kannst mich haben / Du kannst mich haben / Wer du auch immer bist / Mich interessiert nur, ob du bei Kasse bist. / Lieb ich mal einen / Dem ich gehör / Als wär's zum ersten Mal / Will ich ihn halten/ lässt er mich stehen / Egal!"
44. "Nanu? Was is'n los? Hab dich nur nicht so!"
45. "Komm, mein Kind!"
46. "Aber ich habe dich nicht lieb."
47. "Fragen Sie doch nicht, als ob Sie nicht wissen, was in diesem Hause los ist! Wer führt denn hier das Regiment, seitdem das Fräulein aus der Pension zurück ist? Es ist ja nicht mehr zum Aushalten, was die aus den Mannsbildern macht. . . . Hampelmänner!"
48. "Wir gehen rechtzeitig. Ehe es zu spät ist."
49. Anton Kaes, "Silent Cinema," *Monatshefte* 82, no. 3 (1990): 246–56, at 248.
50. See, for example, Matt Biro, "The New Man as Cyborg: Figures of Technology in Weimar Visual Culture," *New German Critique* 62 (Spring/Summer 1994): 71–110.
51. "Dir ist—nichts—geschehen?"
52. "Sag, dass du mich lieb hast."
53. "Alraune, ich hab dich lieb."
54. "Warum wollen Sie so schnell fortgehen? Ich bin Ihnen doch nachgelaufen."
55. "[W]ir sind doch verwandt und müssen zu einander 'Du' sagen."
56. "Hier hat sich viel verändert."
57. "Du bist ein—"
58. "Vater Jakob, das Haus hier ist ja der reinste Gesangsverein."
59. "Ach, mein liebes Kind, das war nicht immer so. Noch vor sechs Monaten hat es hier wenig Gesang gegeben."
60. "Du wirst dort sehr glücklich sein, Alraune. Du wirst alles, alles vergessen."
61. "Du weißt wohl auch nicht, was du bist? Du bist ein Kuckuck. Ich war ja dabei. Dein lieber Frank hatte die lustige Idee, statt Ratten einmal Menschen künstlich zu produzieren. . . . Du bist ja nur das Ergebnis eines Experiments ten Brinkens. Du Tochter einer Dirne und eines Gehenktens."
62. "Dann wissen Sie alles."
63. "Aber ich, ich bin draußen ein neuer Mensch geworden."
64. The first time is the moment in which she sits in front of her mirror after the ball and ten Brinken's attempt to kiss her, a moment that is discussed below. To some degree, the presence of the mirror might be read as representing an objectifying viewer, taking the place of the desiring viewer in other scenes.
65. Petro, *Joyless Streets*, 76.
66. Ibid., 71.
67. Sabine Hake, *Popular Cinema of the Third Reich* (Austin: University of Texas Press, 2001), 113.
68. Hake, *Popular Cinema of the Third Reich*, 122.
69. Ibid.

Conclusion

1. "Children, kitchen, church." This phrase came to represent the female sphere of influence in the Third Reich.

Notes to Conclusion

2. See, for example, Antje Ascheid, *Hitler's Heroines: Stardom and Womanhood in Nazi Cinema* (Philadelphia: Temple University Press, 2003).
3. See, for example, Sabine Hake's chapter on the film in *Popular Cinema of the Third Reich*, 107–27.
4. See, for example, Eric Rentschler's chapter on the film in *The Ministry of Illusion: Nazi Cinema and Its Afterlife* (Cambridge, MA: Harvard University Press, 1996), 125–45.
5. Janet McCabe, "Regulating Hidden Pleasures and 'Modern' Identities: Imagined Female Spectators, Early German Popular Cinema, and *The Oyster Princess* (1919)," in *Light Motives: German Popular Film in Perspective*, ed. Randall Halle and Margaret McCarthy (Detroit: Wayne State University Press, 2003), 24–40, at 32.
6. McCabe, "Regulating Hidden Pleasures and 'Modern' Identities," 36.
7. Petro, *Joyless Streets*, xxii.

INDEX

Alraune (1928). See *Daughter of Destiny, A*
Alraune (1930). See *Daughter of Evil*
Alraune (1952). See *Mandragore*
Alraune lawsuit, 218
Am Rande der Welt. See *At the Edge of the World*
Anders als die Andern. See *Different from the Others*
Andriopoulos, Stefan, 90, 174
artificial life in *Alraune*, 13, 216–18, 222, 234, 238, 242–43, 246, 258; compared to *Metropolis*, 221
Askenas, Paul, 211
At the Edge of the World (*Am Rande der Welt*), 220
Aufklärungsfilme (social/sex education films), 98, 99
automaton, 53, 76, 220

Bakhtin, Mikhail, 53
Bassermann, Albert, 236
Berber, Anita, 16, 99–100, 268, 275, 287n19. See also *Uncanny Tales* (1919)
Berenstein, Rhona J., 43, 44, 68
blaue Engel, Der. See *Blue Angel, The*
Blue Angel, The (*blaue Engel, Der*), 5

Cabinet des Dr. Caligari, Das. See *Cabinet of Dr. Caligari, The*
Cabinet of Dr. Caligari, The (*Cabinet des Dr. Caligari, Das*), 10, 26, 28, 76–77, 150
carnivalesque, 39, 53
Carroll, Noël, 51, 73, 227, 234, 242; category violations, 239; horrific metonymy, 227, 242
Cartelieri, Carmen, 181
castration complex: female body as representing, 25, 32, 36, 55, 234; female gaze as representing, 72; film as representing, 47, 53–54; swords as representing, 166
category violations (Carroll), 239
cinema of attractions, 11, 61, 65, 227n10
Clover, Carol, 42, 43, 49; concept of the "Final Girl," 42, 102, 213
cross-identification, 44

Dagover, Lil, 2, 264
Daughter of Destiny, A (*Alraune*, 1928), 12–13, 26, 38, 216–36, 261–63; compared to Oswald's 1930 version, 237, 239–42, 253, 265–66
Daughter of Evil (*Alraune*, 1930), 1, 12–13, 27, 216–22, 236–66, 267
Davidson, David, 219
Deleuze, Gilles, 37
Destiny (*Der müde Tod*), 2, 100, 103
Diary of a Lost Girl (*Tagebuch einer Verlorenen*), 27
Die Büchse der Pandora. See *Pandora's Box*
Die Todesschleife. See *Looping the Loop*
Diethe, Carol, 26
Dietrich, Marlene, 5, 37, 38, 171
Different from the Others (*Anders als die Andern*), 99, 102
Dix, Otto, 26, 287n19
Doane, Mary Ann, 38, 39, 175, 214
Döblin, Alfred: *Berlin Alexanderplatz*, 15
Dolchstoβlegende, 21, 202, 210
Dr. Mabuse, der Spieler. See *Dr. Mabuse, the Gambler*
Dr. Mabuse, the Gambler (*Dr. Mabuse, der Spieler*), 52, 65, 90, 174

Eisner, Lotte, *The Haunted Screen*, 5, 30–32, 52

Index

Elsaesser, Thomas, 32, 33, 38, 49–50
Es werde Licht! See *Let There Be Light!*
Ewers, Hanns Heinz, 12, 217, 222
excess, 9, 39, 41, 55, 271; and Anita Berber, 100, 119; and association with visual culture, 175; sexual, 156
exile during Nazi period, 4, 277n2; Eisner and Kracauer as writing from viewpoint of, 31, 32
expressionism, 12, 28, 29; and poetry, 15
Eyes of the Mummy, The (*Augen der Mumie Mâ, Die*), 1, 11, 27, 59–96, 203, 204, 235, 268

female body: as object of the gaze, 39, 173, 175; as symbol of broader emancipation, 25, 275; as symbol of castration, 25; as symbol of cinema, 272; as symbol of other anxieties, 9, 46, 263; as uncanny, 3, 56, 224, 263, 269, 272; empowered, 2, 214, 269; fetishized, 173, 250; objectified, 246; subjugated or violated, 2, 26, 42, 275. See also woman
film: as composite art, 153; development of, 27–28, 147, 149–50, 182, 218–19, 267; development of cinematic tropes in, 55, 157, 218–19, 261; horror genre in, 239; impact of WWI on, 28, 62; international qualities of, 4, 5, 28, 62, 180, 270; without intertitles, 12, 150, 152–54
Final Chord (*Schlußakkord*), 264–65, 272
final girl (Clover), 42, 102, 213
Foreign Correspondent, 236
Frankenstein, 12, 225
Franklin, James C., 155–56
Freeland, Cynthia, 34, 55
Friedberg, Anne, 94; concept of spectator-as-shopper, 44–45
Fulbrook, Mary, 17

Galeen, Henrik, 217, 220, 222–23, 294n16. See also *Daughter of Destiny, A*; *Student of Prague, The* (1926)

Geheimnisse einer Seele. See *Secrets of a Soul*
gender as masquerade, 159–60
generational conflict, 29, 185, 202, 210–11
genre, 3, 10, 13, 68, 98; and the *Straßenfilm*, 180; and the two version of *Alraune*, 218, 264, 265; and *Uncanny Tales*, 100, 108, 140; and *Warning Shadows*, 149, 152; of Hollywood horror, 41, 239
Genuine, 180
Goetzke, Bernhard, 237
Golden Twenties, 27
Golem, The (*Golem, Der*), 57, 150, 217, 222, 223
Gordon, Linda, 41
Granach, Alexander, 148, 154
Grosz, George, 16, 26
Guerin, Frances, 155
Gunning, Tom, 61, 106, 277n10

Hake, Sabine, 29, 47, 65, 93, 94, 161, 175, 264
Hales, Barbara, 121–22
Hands of Orlac, The (*Orlacs Hände*), 12, 26, 148, 179–215, 216, 268
Hangmen Also Die!, 149
Hansen, Miriam, 31
Heath, Stephen, 72–73
Heimat (concept), 6, 20, 25, 210
Helm, Brigitte, 220, 222–23, 236, 239, 246, 275. See also *Daughter of Destiny, A*; *Daughter of Evil*
Hollywood: cinematic conventions of, 40, 62, 171, 177, 212; development of classic cinema in, 4, 28, 35, 36; German influence on, 4–5, 63, 99, 148–49, 236, 270, 277n2; horror genre in, 239; Weimar cinema as challenge to, 4, 28
home front, 6, 17, 19, 25, 210; as source of war neurosis, 20
Homunculus, 217
horrific metonymy (Carroll), 227, 242
horror film, 3, 6, 41, 50–51, 99, 270; and *Alraune*, 224; and *Eyes of the Mummy*, 65, 68, 72–73; and films of terror,

51–53; and identification, 44; and sound film, 239; and the theme of severed limbs, 182; as expression of sociocultural anxieties, 53; gender in, 42, 43; punishment of powerful male gaze in, 49; structures of seeing in, 42

Huyssen, Andreas, 220–21

hypnosis, 65–66; association of film and, 66, 90, 91, 174; as treatment for war neurosis, 65–66, 175; in *Eyes of the Mummy*, 91, 95; in *Warning Shadows*, 155; symptoms of, 66

hypnosis films, 68

Imle, Fanny, 24

inflation, 19, 27, 147

intertitles, film without, 12, 150, 152–54

isolation of German film industry during and after WWI, 4, 28, 62

Jannings, Emil, 28, 63. See also *Eyes of the Mummy, The*

Jonas, Walter, 152–54

Jules and Jim (Jules et Jim), 219

Kaes, Anton: 5, 21, 52, 66, 175, 291n10

Keitz, Ursula von, 196, 292–93n48

Kirchner, Ernst Ludwig, 16

Knef, Hildegard, 218

Kortner, Fritz, 148. See also *Hands of Orlac, The*; *Warning Shadows*

Kracauer, Siegfried, 5, 30–33; on *Warning Shadows*, 155

Kreimeier, Klaus, 209

laboratory of modernity, Weimar as, 4

Lang, Fritz, 149. See also *Destiny*; *Dr. Mabuse, the Gambler*; *Hangmen Also Die!*; *M*; *Metropolis*;

Last Command, The, 28

Laurence, Max, 67

Lerner, Paul, 65–66

Let There Be Light! (Es werde Licht!), 99

Liebe der Jeanne Ney, Die. See *Love of Jeanne Ney, The*

Liebknecht, Karl, 16

Liedtke, Harry, 63. See also *Eyes of the Mummy, The*

Loder, John, 222

Lola-Lola, 219

Looping the Loop (Die Todesschleife), 148

Love of Jeanne Ney, The (Liebe der Jeanne Ney, Die), 220

Lubitsch, Ernst, 62–63, 93, 98, 99, 148. See also *Eyes of the Mummy, The*; *Oyster Princess, The*; *Ninotchka*

mad scientist, 13, 217–18, 225–26, 241. See also Rotwang

male creation, fantasy of, 13, 217–21, 222, 224–25, 231, 241, 257

Mandragore (Alraune, 1952), 218

mandrake, 234; legend of the, 217, 218, 225–26, 238, 241–42

masochism and spectatorship (Studlar), 37–38, 123, 229, 231, 269

Mayne, Judith, 40–41

McCabe, Janet, 273

McCormick, Richard W., 5, 6, 24; "discourse of castration," 26; historical specificity of Weimar sexual politics, 29, 30; on Pola Negri, 283–84n12

medical discourse films (Doane), 38, 39; applied to *Hands of Orlac, The*, 214

Medusa, 72

melodrama, 4, 13, 33, 38–39; *Alraune* (Oswald) as, 218, 237, 240, 247, 262, 265; *Eyes of the Mummy* as, 94; *Hands of Orlac* as, 184, 215; indeterminacy in, 264

Metropolis, 2, 9, 10, 26, 217; figure of Maria in, 219, 220, 221

müde Tod, Der. See *Destiny*

Mulvey, Laura, 5, 35–36, 38, 48, 119; and *Alraune*, 234; and *Hands of Orlac*, 213; strong male on-screen double, 49, 212; woman as object of male gaze, 157, 171, 175, 177

Murnau, F. W. See *Nosferatu*

Negri, Pola, 62; as dancer, 275. See also *Eyes of the Mummy, The*

Index

Neue Frau. See New Woman
Neue Sachlichkeit. See New Objectivity
New Objectivity (*Neue Sachlichkeit*), 5, 12, 28, 29, 143; and *Alraune*, 224; and *Hands of Orlac*, 179, 180, 182–84, 198, 211
New Woman (*Neue Frau*), 3, 12, 22–24, 27, 270, 271; Alraune as, 233; as embodiment of changing gender norms, 25; as performance, 159; as sexually liberated, 122, 204; in *Uncanny Tales*, 114, 116, 118, 125, 140; linkage to dance, 119; Mâ as, 92; Yvonne in *Hands of Orlac* as, 203, 208
Ninotchka, 149
Nosferatu, 2, 10, 26, 149, 150, 179, 222; external vs. internal urges, 199; James C. Franklin on, 155

occult, 121–22, 141
omnibus film, 11, 100–101, 140, 286n9
on-screen double for director, 162
on-screen male double as flawed, 49, 89, 119, 232, 275
Orlacs Hände. See *Hands of Orlac, The*
Oswald, Richard, 98–99, 148. See also *Daughter of Evil*; *Different from the Others*; *Let There Be Light!*; *Prostitution*; *Uncanny Tales* (1919); *Uncanny Tales* (1932)
Oswalda, Ossi, 63
Oyster Princess, The (*Austernprinzessin, Die*), 273

Pabst, G. W. See *Diary of a Lost Girl*; *Love of Jeanne Ney, The*; *Pandora's Box*; *Secrets of a Soul*
Pandora's Box (*Die Büchse der Pandora*), 2, 27, 148, 219
Pandora's Box (Wedekind), 225
pantomime acting, 64, 101, 211
Paulsen, Harald, 142, 143, 145, 236
Petrescu, Mihaela, 240
Petro, Patrice, 33, 34, 35, 36, 262–63, 274; on women as film consumers, 280n59
Petrovich, Ivan, 223

Prawer, S. S., 51–53, 76
Prostitution, 99
psychoanalysis, film as representation of, 155

Rabenalt, Arthur Marie. See *Mandragore*
Riviere, Joan, 159
Robison, Artur, 148–49; and films without intertitles, 150, 152–54. See also *Looping the Loop*; *Warning Shadows*
Rotwang, 217, 220, 221, 225
Rowe, Dorothy, 26
Rowe, Kathleen, 39
Russell, David J., 51

Schatten: eine nächtliche Halluzination. See *Warning Shadows*
Scheffen-Döring, Luise, 23
Schiele, Egon, 16
Schlüpmann, Heide, 158–59
Schlußakkord. See *Final Chord*
Schneider, Steven, 51
Schünzel, Reinhold, 99, 102. See also *Uncanny Tales* (1919)
Secrets of a Soul (*Geheimnisse einer Seele*), 155
self-reflexive elements of film, 7, 12, 29; and *Eyes of the Mummy*, 66; and the omnibus film, 101; and the uncanny, 52; and *Uncanny Tales*, 100, 103, 108, 109; and *Warning Shadows*, 157, 162; Freeland on the sublime and, 54; shadow play, 154, 160, 162, 164, 166, 169, 174, 176
Sierck, Detlev, 264
Sorina, Alexandra, 181, 211
sound film, 13, 28, 148; and *Alraune*, 218, 236, 239; and *Uncanny Tales*, 142; Spadoni on the medium, 57–58, 144, 239
Spadoni, Robert, 57–58, 144, 239
spectatorship, 268, 273–74; and expressionist film, 29; and spectator-as-shopper, 44–45; and the uncanny, 53–54, 56–59; as drag, 43–44; assumed masculine, 33, 43, 49–50; female, 8, 33–35, 38–39, 46; feminized masculine spectator, 37–38; in *Alraune*, 226,

300

229, 232–33, 250, 262–63, 265; in *Eyes of the Mummy*, 65, 70, 82–83, 85, 92, 94–96; in *Hands of Orlac*, 190, 214–15; in *Uncanny Tales*, 101, 108, 111, 119, 123; in *Warning Shadows*, 156–59, 171, 173–76; Weimar conceptualization of, 46–49; woman as object of, 7, 36, 65
stage curtain as cinematic metaphor, 161
Sternberg, Josef von, 5, 171. See also *Blue Angel, The*; *Last Command, The*
Strassny, Fritz, 211
Straub, Agnes, 237
Student of Prague, The (*Student von Prag, Der*, Galeen, 1926), 9, 222
Student of Prague, The (*Student von Prag, Der*, Robison, 1935), 9, 148
Student of Prague, The (*Student von Prag, Der*, Rye, 1913), 9, 217, 223
Student von Prague, Der. See *Student of Prague, The*
Studlar, Gaylyn, 37–38, 44, 123, 171, 213; on masochistic spectator, 229, 231; on maternal, 228, 269; on performance and staging, 81, 235
suffering body as erotic object, 168–69

Tagebuch einer Verlorenen. See *Diary of a Lost Girl*
Thompson, Kristin, 28, 64, 67
train accident as representative of war, 184, 186–88, 209
trauma: and war neurosis, 19; as fundamental to Weimar culture, 21, 268; at basis of castration anxiety, 36; connection to hypnotism and cinema, 174–75; expressed in film, 7; expressed in hostility toward women, 6, 198–99, 209; in *Alraune*, 217; in *Hands of Orlac, The*, 12, 180, 183–85, 192, 195, 209–10, 215; in *Uncanny Tales* (1919), 141; in *Warning Shadows*, 156, 174, 192; masculine subject as experiencing multiple, 21, 176, 209, 215; of war tied to that resulting from railroad accidents, 187–88; resulting from changed social norms, 6, 22, 217, 265; resulting from women's emancipation, 22, 35, 176, 210, 217, 265, 274; resulting from World War I, 2, 5, 27, 32, 209; uncanny films as response to, 269
trick photography, 7, 101, 121, 122, 123, 124, 161, 194

Ultimatum, 181
Uncanny Tales (*Unheimliche Geschichten*, 1919), 11–12, 97–146, 183, 268
Uncanny Tales (*Unheimliche Geschichten*, 1932), 12, 141–45
uncanny, the: and frame narrative, 107–8; and sound film, 57–58, 144–45; and trick photography, 121, 194; as quality of film, 9, 55–57, 272; association with body in *Uncanny Tales* (1919), 117–18, 120; emancipated woman as, 55–56, 122, 124, 223–24, 234, 269, 271–72; Freud's definition of, 53–54, 128, 139–40; in *Alraune* (Galeen), 218, 222–24, 236, 265; in *Alraune* (Oswald), 13, 237, 238–40, 247, 262–63, 265; in *Eyes of the Mummy, The*, 11, 65, 75, 87; in films examined, 3, 7, 9, 45, 268, 270; in *Hands of Orlac*, 182–83, 189–91, 193, 211–12, 215; in *Uncanny Tales* (1919), 11–12, 98, 100, 106–8, 110, 112, 115, 140–41; in *Uncanny Tales* (1932), 142–43, 144; in *Warning Shadows*, 12, 150; New Objectivity's shift away from, 29, 180, 269; relationship to horror, 41, 50, 51–53; revealed as illusion or trickery in *Uncanny Tales* (1919), 129, 134, 137–39; tie to changing gender norms, 6, 271; tie to the sublime (Freeland), 54–55; Wegener and, 223
Unheimliche Geschichten (1919). See *Uncanny Tales*
Unheimliche Geschichten (1932). See *Uncanny Tales*
Unheimliche, Das. See uncanny, the

Veidt, Conrad, 99, 102, 183, 222. See also *Hands of Orlac, The*; *Uncanny Tales* (1919)

Index

Wangenheim, Gustav von, 149, 154
war neurosis, 278n10; and tie to railroad accidents, 187; as feminine, 19–21; hypnosis as tool against, 65–66, 175
Warning Shadows (*Schatten: eine nächtliche Halluzination*), 12, 29, 42, 43, 52, 66, 128, 141, 147–78, 179, 183, 203, 211, 219, 274, 275
Wax Works (*Wachsfigurenkabinett, Das*), 100, 222
Way of All Flesh, The, 28
Wedekind, Frank, 224–25
Wegener, Paul, 37, 142, 150, 217, 222, 223. See also *Golem, The*
Weinstein, Valerie, 224, 227, 234, 242
Weyher, Ruth, 148, 154
Wiene, Robert, 149, 179–81. See also *Cabinet of Dr. Caligari, The*; *Genuine*; *Hands of Orlac, The*; *Ultimatum*
Williams, Linda, 41–42, 72
woman: and hypnosis, 65; as catalyst for action, 43, 102, 129–31, 133; as challenge to masculine subjectivity, 25, 42, 46, 56, 92, 115, 159, 173, 204, 205, 210; as commodity, 245–46; as disruptive, 116–17, 120, 175; as exotic other, 61–62, 64, 70, 93, 121; as image/cinematic object, 2, 4, 12, 34, 41–42, 49, 62, 71–72, 80, 84, 86, 89, 105, 154, 162, 171–72, 226, 247, 261, 272; as object of the gaze, 85, 87, 89–90; as (passive) object of desire, 12, 13, 36, 39, 50, 59, 65, 76, 123, 157, 260; as performer staging self, 159–60, 231, 235, 260; as projection of (masculine) fears and desires, 34, 90, 270–71; as spectator, 34–35, 38–39, 41–42, 44–46, 94–95, 214–15, 262, 273–74; as symbol of changing social norms, 22–24, 25, 124, 145–46, 203, 271–73; as symbol of cinema, 272; as symbol of lack, 36; as threat, 13, 102, 161, 184, 217, 247, 265, 271; as unnatural, 221, 234, 261, 272; as victim, 245, 261; blamed for defeat in war, 20, 25; connected to uncanny, 3, 55–56, 139–40, 223, 224, 269; emancipated, 3, 9, 11, 13, 23, 25, 46, 109, 119, 122, 156, 202, 205, 224; employment patterns, 23; fear of, 2, 8, 46; linked to moral decline, 24, 48, 115, 225, 251, 258; linked to nature, 220, 251; linked to occult, 121–22; linked to technology, 220, 251; transgressive, 3, 12, 25, 51, 159, 177, 218–19, 263–65; violent subjugation of, 2, 25–26, 154, 167–69. *See also* female body; New Woman; spectatorship
Wood, Robin, 51
World War I, 5; and German film production, 28, 62; compared to industrial accident, 291n10

Zietz, Luise, 22
Zilzer, Wolfgang, 222

www.ingramcontent.com/pod-product-compliance
Lightning Source LLC
Chambersburg PA
CBHW051536230426
43669CB00015B/2620